nil me poenitet

ex libris
Jan Broadway Ph. D

IN DEFIANCE OF TIME

In Defiance of Time

Antiquarian Writing in Early Modern England

ANGUS VINE

OXFORD
UNIVERSITY PRESS

OXFORD
UNIVERSITY PRESS

Great Clarendon Street, Oxford OX2 6DP

Oxford University Press is a department of the University of Oxford.
It furthers the University's objective of excellence in research, scholarship,
and education by publishing worldwide in

Oxford New York

Auckland Cape Town Dar es Salaam Hong Kong Karachi
Kuala Lumpur Madrid Melbourne Mexico City Nairobi
New Delhi Shanghai Taipei Toronto

With offices in

Argentina Austria Brazil Chile Czech Republic France Greece
Guatemala Hungary Italy Japan Poland Portugal Singapore
South Korea Switzerland Thailand Turkey Ukraine Vietnam

Oxford is a registered trade mark of Oxford University Press
in the UK and in certain other countries

Published in the United States
by Oxford University Press Inc., New York

© Angus Vine 2010

The moral rights of the author have been asserted
Database right Oxford University Press (maker)

First published 2010

All rights reserved. No part of this publication may be reproduced,
stored in a retrieval system, or transmitted, in any form or by any means,
without the prior permission in writing of Oxford University Press,
or as expressly permitted by law, or under terms agreed with the appropriate
reprographics rights organization. Enquiries concerning reproduction
outside the scope of the above should be sent to the Rights Department,
Oxford University Press, at the address above

You must not circulate this book in any other binding or cover
and you must impose the same condition on any acquirer

British Library Cataloguing in Publication Data
Data available

Library of Congress Cataloging in Publication Data
Data available

Typeset by SPI Publisher Services, Pondicherry, India
Printed in Great Britain
on acid-free paper by
MPG Books Group, Bodmin and King's Lynn

ISBN 978–0–19–956619–8

1 3 5 7 9 10 8 6 4 2

For Angus and Annette Vine

One tries to imagine what it must have been like when they were all in position: from the distance they must have looked like shining multi-coloured cypresses surrounding the temple of the Pythia. One tries to visualize them; and there comes into the mind that dawn when Ion saw Delphi.

George Seferis, *Delphi*

Preface

This book has been proverbially long in the making; the debts which I have accrued, intellectual, financial, and personal, are correspondingly large. It is therefore with great pleasure that I now have the chance to acknowledge all the help and support that I have received over the years. *In Defiance of Time* began life as a doctoral thesis at the University of Cambridge, where I was funded by the Arts and Humanities Research Board. A Junior Rouse Ball Scholarship generously awarded by the Master and Fellows of Trinity College, Cambridge, in 2004–5 enabled me to complete the thesis and also start to revise it for publication as a book. Throughout my doctorate Raphael Lyne provided expert supervision (and also a great deal of encouragement). He thought that he was going to be supervising a project on Ovid: it is to his enormous credit as a scholar, but also personally, that he has retained such a keen interest in a book where Ovid is barely mentioned at all. I have also benefitted considerably from the comments and suggestions of my doctoral advisers, Colin Burrow and John Kerrigan. A wise comment from the former—made in passing, as he was introducing a paper of mine on a completely different subject at a conference in Cambridge in 2008—deserves particular mention, as it led me to rethink the scope of this project, whilst the latter has continued to show enthusiasm for the project, and has also been an invaluable source of references and further reading. My examiners, Claire Preston and Daniel Woolf, offered valuable advice at a crucial time. Without their comments and suggestions this would have been an immeasurably worse book; indeed, it is doubtful whether it would have been a book at all. The debt that I owe to both will be apparent to anyone who has read their work.

Most of the work on this book was done at the Centre for Research in the Arts, Social Sciences, and Humanities (CRASSH) in Cambridge, where I spent three happy years from 2005 to 2008 as a Research Associate funded by the Newton Trust. CRASSH is a unique place, and this book is the beneficiary of the spirit of collaboration and scholarly exchange that it so keenly promotes. Whilst at CRASSH I had the great fortune to work with Richard Serjeantson on Volume 3 of the Oxford Francis Bacon project. Richard is an exemplary scholar and a model colleague; I am delighted that our collaboration on the Bacon edition continues. In 2008 I moved to the Faculty of English at Cambridge to join the *Scriptorium: Medieval and Early Modern Manuscripts Online* project, where my colleagues have been unfailingly generous and supportive. Richard Beadle has been a witty and receptive boss, whilst Andrew Zurcher, Raphael Lyne, Colin Burrow, and Christopher Burlinson have all been excellent colleagues and collaborators. Sebastiaan Verweij has also been an excellent colleague, and I must thank him in particular for sharing an office with me with such good humour. His day-to-day encouragement of this project has not gone unnoticed. He also made a crucial intervention late in the day, checking an ownership inscription in the Bodleian Library, which I would not otherwise have had the opportunity to see. All have been unstinting in their encouragement, and my successful completion of this book owes a considerable amount to them. Whilst finishing the book, I have also had the good fortune to work closely with Sarah Cain: a great colleague and a great friend. Our conversations after work—and also the occasional dinner—gave me much of the impetus to finish the last bits.

Debts for this kind of project, however, are often more diffuse, and *In Defiance of Time* has also benefitted from numerous conversations and friendships over the years. Those that have made suggestions, advised, commented, and helped in various ways include David Colclough, Katrin Ettenhuber, Katie Halsey, Jonathan Harrison, Felicity Henderson, Thirza Hope, Catherine Hurley, Robert Jones, Ludmilla Jordanova, Mihail Raev, Geoffrey Roper, Ian Rowley, Fred Schurink, Harvey Shoolman, Tony Trowles, the late Brodie Vine, Daniel Wakelin, and Melanie Wood. I am indebted to Hester Lees-Jeffries and Jonathan Sanders, both of whom took time out from their busy schedules to read the manuscript in its entirety. Both are astute and intelligent readers; both also have a keen eye for a comma. Their criticisms have undoubtedly made this a better book; so too their friendships. I am similarly grateful to the three anonymous readers at Oxford University Press, who also made many useful suggestions. It goes without saying that any errors that remain are my own. Maartje Scheltens advised on matters Dutch and helped with translations, as well as keeping my spirits up on many an occasion. Alastair Craft, Andrew Rudd, and Jane Slinn have been a constant support; none is an early modern scholar, let alone a scholar of antiquarianism, but each has endured endless conversations about antiquaries with remarkable forbearance. I also owe a considerable debt to the late Jeremy Maule, who introduced me to antiquarianism in my first week as an undergraduate at Cambridge. It is safe to say that if he had not persuaded me to read Thomas Browne thirteen years ago, this book would never have been written.

I have had the opportunity to present much of this material at conferences and seminars, and I am grateful to audiences in Cambridge and Norwich for their feedback and questions. Part of Chapter 2 appeared in an earlier form in 'Etymology, Names and the Search for Origins: Deriving the Past in Early Modern England', *Seventeenth Century*, 21 (2006), 1–21. I am very grateful to the editor, Richard Maber, and to Manchester University Press for giving me permission to include some of that material here.

My debts to librarians are equally numerous, and in writing this book I have had the very great pleasure of working in many libraries and archives. The staff of the following libraries have answered my queries and fetched and found volumes with good humour and remarkable efficiency: Cambridge University Library, the English Faculty Library, the Seeley Historical Library, the Whipple Library, and the libraries of St John's College and Trinity College, Cambridge; the British

Library, and the libraries of the College of Arms, Lambeth Palace, and Westminster Abbey; the Bodleian Library, Oxford; the Robinson Library, Newcastle University Library, Newcastle-upon-Tyne; the National Library of Scotland, Edinburgh; the National Library of Wales, Aberystwyth; and the Bibliothèque nationale de France, Paris. I should also like to thank the owner of the Arcadian Library, London, for permitting me to use and cite from his collections. Particular thanks are owed to the staff of the Munby Rare Books Room in Cambridge University Library, where I did most of my research for this book. They provide a wonderful service and a highly conducive environment. Thanks are also due to all the regulars, who have shared the Rare Books Room with me over the past eight years.

This book was commissioned by Andrew McNeillie, and I am extremely grateful to him for his enthusiasm, generosity, and support. He has now moved on to other things, but Jacqueline Baker, Lindsey Hall, and Ariane Petit at Oxford University Press have all answered my questions with great efficiency, haste, and tact. My copy-editor Bonnie Blackburn saved me from the occasional enormity and helped me clarify my argument in various places. I am particularly grateful that she checked my translations so attentively.

As luck would have it, the completion of this book coincided with the arrival of the newest member of my family. I hope that this book is one way of repaying them all, for as always my greatest debts are familial. Aidan and Sally Vine have provided a warm and welcoming home in Oxford, whilst Ailsa and Mark Chick have done the same in London. They and their children have also reminded me that there is life after the seventeenth century. I am eternally grateful. My largest debt, however, is to my parents, Angus and Annette Vine. They believed in this long before I did. For that, and for much else besides, I cannot thank them enough.

Contents

List of Illustrations — xii
Note on Text and Conventions — xiii
List of Abbreviations — xiv

Introduction — 1

1. Material Beginnings: John Leland, John Twyne, John Stow — 22
2. Origins and Names: Etymology and the Elizabethan Society of Antiquaries — 51
3. Restoring Britain: Courtesy and Collaboration in Camden's *Britannia* — 80
4. Monuments and Megaliths: From Stonehenge to 'Stonage' — 109
5. A Peripatetic Education: Antiquarian Travellers and the Apodemic Arts — 139
6. Antiquarian Readers: The Case of Drayton and Selden — 169

Conclusion — 200

Appendix: List of Contents of Westminster Abbey Library and Muniment Room, CB 7 (14) — 208
Bibliography — 210
Index — 233

List of Illustrations

Intro. 1. The frontispiece to *Note overo memorie del museo di Lodovico Moscardo* (Padua, 1656)	8
3.1. 'VRBES BRITANNIAE IOH. IONSTONO Scriptore'	102
4.1. Title page of William Camden, *Britannia sive florentissimorum regnorum, Angliæ, Scotiæ, Hiberniæ, et insularum adiacentium ex intima antiquitate chorographica descriptio* (London, 1600)	116
4.2. Stonehenge, in William Camden, *Britannia sive florentissimorum regnorum, Angliæ, Scotiæ, Hiberniæ, et insularum adiacentium ex intima antiquitate chorographica descriptio* (London, 1600)	117
4.3. Stonehenge, in Inigo Jones, *The most notable Antiquity of Great Britain, vulgarly called Stone-Heng on Salisbury Plain* (London, 1655)	121
5.1. Map of the Troad, in Pierre Belon, *Les Observations de plusieurs singularitez et choses memorables, trouées en Grece, Asie, Iudée, Egypte, Arabie, & autres pays estranges, redigées en trois liures* (Paris, 1553)	154
5.2. Map of the Troad, in George Sandys, *A Relation of a Iourney begun An: Dom: 1610* (London, 1615)	155
5.3. 'A Delineation of the Amphitheater of Verona', in Thomas Coryate, *Coryats Crudities* (London, 1611)	165
5.4. The theatre at Verona, in *T. Saraynæ... de origine et amplitudine ciuitatis Veronæ* (Verona, 1540)	166
6.1. The frontispiece to Michael Drayton, *Poly-Olbion* (London, 1612)	185
6.2. Map to Song XVI (Hertfordshire), in Michael Drayton, *Poly-Olbion* (London, 1612)	195
6.3. 'The title of the house of yorke in Edwarde the fowrth'. John Bladen's annotations to Song XXVIII in his copy of Michael Drayton's *Poly-Olbion* (London, 1622)	197

Note on Text and Conventions

All translations are my own except where otherwise indicated. Original spelling has been preserved, including u/v and i/j; long s, however, has been modernized. Original punctuation and capitalization have also been preserved, except in book titles where I have followed standard conventions. Accents and diacritics in quotations from French, Greek, Latin, and Spanish follow the original. Abbreviations and contractions have been expanded with italics where appropriate. Superscript letters have mostly been lowered. On a few occasions—most obviously when I am quoting from prefaces—I have silently emended quotations from early modern texts from italic to roman type. In manuscript transcriptions I have used the following conventions:

<xxx> deleted text

ˇxxxˇ text lost through damage or cropping

`xxx´ supralinear text

[xxx] supplied text

Where possible I have supplied text, but where this has proved impossible points have been used to represent the missing letters.

List of Abbreviations

AV   Authorized Version
BL   British Library, London
BNF   Bibliothèque nationale de France, Paris
CUL   Cambridge University Library, Cambridge
HMC   Historical Manuscripts Commission
LPL   Lambeth Palace Library, London
ODNB   *Oxford Dictionary of National Biography*, <http://www.oxforddnb.com>
OED   *The Oxford English Dictionary*, 2nd edn., prepared by J. A. Simpson and E. S. C. Weiner, 20 vols. (Oxford: Clarendon Press, 1989)
STC   *A Short-Title Catalogue of Books Printed in England, Scotland, & Ireland and of English Books Printed Abroad 1475–1640*, compiled by A. W. Pollard and G. R. Redgrave, revised by W. A. Jackson, F. S. Ferguson, and Katharine F. Pantzer, 3 vols. (London: The Bibliographical Society, 1976–91)
WAL   Westminster Abbey Library and Muniment Room

Introduction

In July 1836 an astonishing discovery, 'the envy of every antiquarian in this or any other country', was reported in London. A traveller had unearthed an extraordinary old stone in the village of Cobham in Kent, which he had found 'partially buried in the ground, in front of a cottage-door'. After much washing and scraping, and ably assisted by others, a greater treasure still was revealed:

The stone was uneven and broken, and the letters were straggling and irregular, but the following fragment of an inscription was clearly to be deciphered:

$$+$$
$$\text{B I L S T}$$
$$\text{U M}$$
$$\text{P S H I}$$
$$\text{S. M.}$$
$$\text{A R K}$$[1]

The traveller's pride in this 'strange and curious inscription of unquestionable antiquity' was boundless, and on his return to London it became a source of feverish speculation and celebrity. Only a Mr Blotton doubted its veracity, and this villain travelled to Cobham to investigate. Having examined the stone, Blotton returned to London and 'sarcastically observed' that 'he had seen the man from whom the stone was purchased; that the man presumed the stone to be ancient, but solemnly denied the antiquity of the inscription—inasmuch as he represented it to have been rudely carved by himself in an idle mood, and to display letters intended to bear neither more nor less than the simple construction of—"Bill Stumps, his mark:"'. Blotton then attributed the irregular orthography to Mr Stumps's low level of literacy. But his pettifogging received short shrift. The reporter of the discovery announced that 'to this day the stone remains an illegible monument' of the traveller's greatness, and 'a lasting trophy of the littleness of his enemies'.[2]

This traveller was of course none other than Charles Dickens's amateur scientist and inveterate discoverer of ancient manuscripts, Samuel Pickwick

---

[1] Charles Dickens, *The Pickwick Papers*, ed. James Kinsley (Oxford: Clarendon Press, 1986), 157.
[2] Ibid. 168–9.

Dickens's satire in the episode of the Cobham stone is gentle. His sympathies—as throughout *The Pickwick Papers* (1836–7)—lie firmly with his antiquary, Pickwick. And that magnificent, portly figure is himself an example of an old type. Antiquaries have long been the butt of intellectual jokes, portrayed as the unacceptable, undiscriminating, other face of history. Satire of antiquarianism has a long tradition, reaching as far back as the third-century Roman poet Ausonius, who characterized the antiquary in his *Commemoratio professorum Burdingalensium* as a scholar obsessed with antiquity, reading mouldy and dog-eared documents at the expense of more palatable and rewarding fare.[3] This satire had its early modern examples too.[4] In his *Micro-cosmographie* (1628), a popular series of character sketches, John Earle defined the antiquary as 'one that hath that unnaturall disease to bee enamour'd of old age, and wrinkles, and loves all things (as Dutchmen doe Cheese) the better for being mouldy and worme-eaten'; as one who admires 'the rust of old Monuments' and reads only 'those Characters, where time hath eaten out the letters'.[5] John Donne satirized the same trait in an eponymous epigram, undated, but probably written in the 1590s: 'If in his study he hath so much care / To hang all old strange things, let his wife beware'.[6] Shackerley Marmion distilled this veneration of antiquity into the superannuated Veterano, the central character of *The Antiquary*, his comedy performed by the Queen's Men at the Cockpit Theatre in 1636. In this case, the veneration is such that Veterano himself is presented as an antique, as the first description of him by his nephew Lionell illustrates:

> Now I must travel, on a new exploit,
> To an old Antiquary; he is my uncle
> And I his heir. Would I could raise a fortune
> Out of his ruins! He is grown obsolete,
> And 'tis time he were out of date.[7]

Blinded by his absurd veneration for the past, Veterano is vain and selfish, as he 'doats on the decays / With greater love than the self-lov'd Narcissus / Did on his beauty'. He is also foolish. His nephew, disguised as a scholar, tricks him into buying two mouldy, half-eaten manuscripts, identified by Veterano as an

---

[3] Ausonius, *Commemoratio professorum Burdingalensium*, in *The Works of Ausonius*, ed. R. P. H. Green (Oxford: Clarendon Press, 1991), XI. 22. 1–4: 'Victori, studiose, memor, celer, ignoratis / assidue in libris nec nisi operta legens, / exesas tineis opicasque evolvere chartas / maior quam promptis cura tibi in studiis.'

[4] For satire of antiquarianism, see Daniel Woolf, 'Images of the Antiquary in Seventeenth-Century England', in Susan M. Pearce (ed.), *Visions of Antiquity: The Society of Antiquaries of London 1707–2007* (London: Society of Antiquaries of London, 2007), 11–43.

[5] John Earle, *Micro-cosmographie. Or, A Peece of the World Discovered; in Essayes and Characters* (London, 1628), sigs. C1^v–C2^r.

[6] John Donne, 'The Antiquary', in *The Complete English Poems*, ed. A. J. Smith (Harmondsworth: Penguin, 1971), ll. 1–2.

[7] Shackerley Marmion, *The Antiquary*, in *The Dramatic Works*, ed. James Maidment and W. H. Logan (New York: Benjamin Blom, 1967; first published 1874), 210 (Act I, Scene i).

autograph copy of Cicero's *De republica*, that holy grail of antiquarian scholarship, and a treatise on mathematics restored by the hand of Ptolemy. Needless to say, they are nothing of the sort.

Such sketches emphasize the acquisitiveness, credulity, and historical reaction of the antiquaries. But the early modern antiquary was not the dusty dullard of popular satire. Antiquarianism in its early modern manifestation was not the intellectually conservative pursuit that the satirists portray. Instead, it was a dynamic, recuperative, resurrective response to the past. And for this reason it was also an essentially imaginative response to the past. As Peter Miller observes, 'No attempt to reconstruct the past...was possible without the capacity to envision the broken and fragmentary made whole again', and he rightly points out that it is 'this act of the imagination that lies at the heart of the antiquary's reconstructive ambition'.[8] When Meric Casaubon commented that 'Antiquaries are so taken with the sight of old things...because those visible superviving evidences of antiquitie represent unto their minds former times, with as strong an impression, as if they were actually present, and in sight as it were', he was not speaking pejoratively.[9] Instead, his comment was meant to illustrate how the best scholars were able to discern the truth about the past. Casaubon also noted that the scholar who knows

what hath beene the particular estate, if not of all (since there are not bookes extant of all:) yet of most ages of the World, wherein they differed from one another and wherein they agreed; what peculiar, and what common to every one; he doth as it were enjoy the memorie, of so many yeares, and so many ages past, even as if hee himselfe had lived all those yeares, and outlasted all those ages.

The antiquary, in other words, is so familiar with past customs and traditions that he sees the past as if it were the present.

The origins of this kind of imaginative antiquarianism are humanist and Italian.[10] Petrarch was one of the first to give voice to it in an oft-cited letter to his friend Giovanni Colonna. In this letter (*Familiares*, 6. 2), written shortly after his visit to Rome in 1341, Petrarch recalled the walks that he and Colonna had taken together, the places that they had visited, and the subjects that they had discussed.[11] As they walked around the city, they remembered. The city, its traces

---

[8] Peter N. Miller, *Peiresc's Europe: Learning and Virtue in the Seventeenth Century* (New Haven and London: Yale University Press, 2000), 31.

[9] Meric Casaubon, *A Treatise of Vse and Custome* (London, 1638), 97–8. '[S]uperviving' here is simply a synonym for 'surviving'.

[10] For the humanist origins of early modern historiography more generally, see Joseph Levine, *Humanism and History: Origins of Modern English Historiography* (Ithaca and London: Cornell University Press, 1987), and F. J. Levy, *Tudor Historical Thought* (Toronto, Buffalo, and London: University of Toronto Press, 2004; first published 1967), 33–78.

[11] Discussions of this letter include Thomas Mommsen, 'Petrarch's Conception of the "Dark Ages"', *Speculum*, 17 (1942), 226–42; Ernest H. Wilkins, 'On Petrarch's *Ep. Fam.* VI 2', *Speculum*, 38 (1963), 620–2; Roberto Weiss, *The Renaissance Discovery of Classical Antiquity* (Oxford: Basil

4 *Introduction*

and ruins, even its emptiness, conjured memories of its former glories. The splendours of ancient Rome were (for a moment at least) restored:

> Here was the palace of Evander, there the shrine of Carmentis, here the cave of Cacus, there the famous she-wolf and the fig tree of Rumina with the more apt surname of Romulus, there the overpass of Remus, here the circus games and the rape of the Sabines, there the marsh of Capri and the place where Romulus vanished, here the conversations of Numa and Egeria, there the battle line of the *trigemini*. Here the conqueror of enemies who was in turn conquered by a thunderbolt, and the builder of militia; there the architect king Ancus Martius; here the organizer of social classes, Priscus Tarquinius, lived; there the head of Servius glowed; there sitting in her carriage cruel Tullia crossed and made the street infamous because of her crime.[12]

Petrarch's letter presents here a series of visions taken from the pages of Livy and Virgil, literary and historical memories stimulated by the topography of the places that he and Colonna had visited. Everywhere there were spurs to the memory and the imagination. Indeed, topography is presented as so powerful a stimulus that Petrarch not only remembered the Roman past, but at places saw it re-enacted in front of his eyes. He still saw, for example, the wretched Lucretia lying upon her sword and the foul rapist, Sextus Tarquinius, fleeing his crime.[13] With this curious temporal displacement a past memory becomes a present vision. Ancient Rome may be in ruins, but Petrarch's letter entertains the hope that these might nevertheless be restored and rebuilt. But his letter also contains a lament for the neglect of the ancient city, a despairing jeremiad at the ignorance of the citizens of the present-day city. Petrarch excepted Colonna from his criticism, praising him as *curiosissimus*, and recognizing that he had long been attentive to Roman remains and history, but he had less faith in other Romans. As he observed in the letter, nowhere is Rome less known than in Rome.[14]

For Petrarch, antiquarianism was about resurrection; it was concerned primarily with restoring fragments of antiquity to bring the past and its virtues back to

---

Blackwell, 1969), 32–3; Leonard Barkan, *Unearthing the Past: Archaeology and Aesthetics in the Making of Renaissance Culture* (New Haven and London: Yale University Press, 1999), 24–5; and, in a very different argument from mine, Jennifer Summit, 'Topography as Historiography: Petrarch, Chaucer, and the Making of Medieval Rome', *Journal of Medieval and Early Modern Studies*, 30 (2000), 211–46.

[12] Francesco Petrarca, *Rerum familiarum libri I–VIII*, trans. Aldo S. Bernardo (Baltimore and London: The Johns Hopkins University Press, 1975–85), VI. 2; Francesco Petrarca, *Le Familiari*, ed. Vittorio Rossi, 4 vols. (Florence: G. C. Sansoni, 1933–42), VI. 2, 47–56: 'hic Evandri regia, hic Carmentis edes, hic Caci spelunca, hic lupa nutrix et ruminalis ficus, veriori cognomine romularis, hic Remi transitus, hic ludi circenses et Sabinarum raptus, hic Capree palus et Romulus evanescens, hic Nume cum Egeria colloquium, hic tergeminorum acies. Hic fulmine victus victor hostium artifexque militie Tullus Hostilius, hic rex architector Ancus Martius, hic discretor ordinum Priscus Tarquinius habitavit; hic Servio caput arsit, hic carpento insidens atrox Tullia transivit et scelere suo vicum fecit infamem.'

[13] Petrarca, *Le Familiari*, VI. 2, 59–61: 'Hic miserabilis Lucretia ferro incumbens, et in mortem fugiens adulter.'

[14] Ibid., l. 117: 'invitus dico: nusquam minus Roma cognoscitur quam Rome'.

life. If only Rome paid sufficient attention to herself, he wrote in the letter to Colonna, she would doubtless rise again.[15] Petrarch's successors too recognized this resurrective impulse. Leonardo Bruni, for example, commenting on his style, praised Petrarch as the first man to have sufficient wit to recognize the gracefulness of ancient style and bring it back to life.[16] The same could be said of his antiquarianism. The letter to Colonna sets out a model, where material traces of antiquity have mostly been lost, but where that antiquity itself can still be restored through recourse to literary texts. It was on literary memories that Petrarch drew to envisage ancient Rome, to restore and bring it back to life.

This idea of imaginative antiquarianism found a receptive audience in early modern England. *In Defiance of Time* traces its emergence, showing how English scholars and writers adopted these humanist methods and approaches, and sought not only to collect the scattered traces of the past, textual, material, and so on, but also to restore that past through the process of writing. Richard Bauman and Charles Briggs have recently demonstrated how influential this recuperative impulse was.[17] In general terms, the antiquary conceived of himself as bridging the gap between past and present, affording 'olden time' presence so that it might speak to or inform the current time. For this reason John Aubrey likened antiquarianism to 'the Art of a Conjuror who makes those walke and appear that have layen in their graves many hundreds of yeares: and represents as it were to the eie, the places, customs and Fashions, that were of old Time'.[18] He himself illustrated this in an early draft of the *Monumenta Britannica*, when he described the barrow cemeteries near Stonehenge. 'The greatnesse and numerousnes of the Tumuli (the Beds of Honour where now so many Heroes lye buried in Oblivion),' Aubrey wrote, 'speake plainely to us, that death and slaughter ragd there; & that these were the scenes where those terrible Battles were fought; wherin fell so many thousands mentioned by the Historians'. By the sight of them 'one may well enough guesse whereabout the Engagement began, and which way the Victor made the pursuit: and by the Imperiall Generalls Camps one may trace out which way the Roman Eagle tooke her course'.[19] The anonymous, but clearly antiquarian, author of the preface to William Burton's

---

[15] Ibid., l. 21: 'Quis enim dubitare potest quin illico surrectura sit, si ceperit se Roma cognoscere?'
[16] Leonardo Bruni, *Le Vite di Dante e del Petrarca*, ed. Antonio Lanza (Rome: Archivio Guido Izzi, 1987), 57: 'Francesco Petrarca fu il primo il quale ebbe tanta grazia d'ingegno che riconobbe e rivocò in luce l'antica leggiadria dello stile perduto e spento.'
[17] Richard Bauman and Charles L. Briggs, *Voices of Modernity: Language Ideologies and the Politics of Inequality* (Cambridge: Cambridge University Press, 2003), 72–8.
[18] John Aubrey, 'An Essay Towards the Description of the North Division of Wiltshire', in *Wiltshire: The Topographical Collections of John Aubrey*, ed. John Edward Jackson (Devizes: The Wiltshire Archaeological and Natural History Society, 1862), 4. See also the discussion in Michael Hunter, *John Aubrey and the Realm of Learning* (London: Duckworth, 1975), esp. 172–9.
[19] John Aubrey, *Monumenta Britannica: or A Miscellany of British Antiquities*, ed. John Fowles and Rodney Legg, 2 vols. (Sherborne: Dorset Publishing Company, 1980), i. 259 (fo. 149ʳ).

A Commentary on Antoninus his Itinerary (1658) made a similar point when he argued that 'the Learned by judicious view and diligent inquiry restore in great measure the past to the present, and future Ages'.[20] Quite simply, as my title asserts, the antiquaries sought to defy the passage of time.

An excellent illustration of this comes from seventeenth-century France. A doctor and chemist from Castres, Pierre Borel was an antiquary and collector of some repute, whose fame reached across the Channel.[21] In 1649 he published a study of the antiquities of Castres, to which he appended a catalogue of his own cabinet or collection, 'Catalogue des choses rares qui sont dans le Cabinet de Maistre Pierre Borel Medecin de Castres au haut Languedoc'. The inscription written over the door to the room where his collection was housed is exemplary:

Siste gradum (curiose) hic enim orbem in domo, imo in Musao, id est microcosmum seu rerum omnium rariorum Compendium cernes, in eo stans regiones omnes momento lustrare poteris, cæmeterium forsan vocabis, cum multa cadauera contineat, sed dic potius campos Elisæos, vbi mortua felici tranquillitate fruentia reuiuiscunt vel licita necromantia resurgunt, vel dic Herculis trophæa hic iacere, cum serpentum exuuias, ossaque gigantum videas.

Hold your step, curious one, for you will see here in this house, in this museum, the world—that is, a microcosm or compendium of all the rarest things; standing in it you will be able to pass through all the regions of the world in a single moment. You will perhaps call it a cemetery, since it contains many cadavers; but rather call it the Elysian Fields, where the dead enjoy a happy tranquillity, where they come to life and rise up again through a licit necromancy. Or say that here lie the trophies of Hercules, since you see the skins of snakes and the bones of giants.[22]

The inscription perfectly illustrates the resurrective impulse behind antiquarianism. Borel presents the dead bodies (giants' bones, snakes' skins, and so on) as coming back to life in his cabinet. The act of collecting becomes a form of legitimate necromancy. The inscription likens the cabinet to the Elysian Fields, the abode of those who, in Virgil's words, 'have won remembrance amongst men'.[23] As a metaphor, this suggests that the objects in Borel's collection will also be preserved and remembered. But the inscription implies another kind of resurrection as well. Not only are the objects brought back to life by Borel himself, the collector, but they are also revived each time that a viewer (and by

---

[20] William Burton, *A Commentary on Antoninus his Itinerary, or Journies Of the Romane Empire, so far as it concerneth Britain* (London, 1658), sig. a1ʳ.
[21] See Pierre Chabbert, 'Pierre Borel', *Revue d'histoire des sciences*, 21 (1968), 303–43.
[22] Pierre Borel, *Les Antiquitez, raretez, plantes, mineraux, & autres choses considerables de la ville, & comté de Castres d'Albigeois, & des lieux qui sont à ses enuirons, auec l'Histoire de ses Comtes, Euesques, &c. Et un recueil des inscriptions Romaines, & autres antiquitez du Languedoc et Provence. Avec le roolle des principaux cabinets, & autres raretez de l'Europe* (Castres, 1649), 132.
[23] Virgil, *Aeneid*, trans. H. Rushton Fairclough, rev. G. P. Goold (Loeb Classical Library; Cambridge, Mass.: Harvard University Press, 1999), vi. 664: 'quique sui memores aliquos fecere merendo'.

extension also a reader, since the catalogue was printed) beholds the cabinet. Borel's collection was made up predominantly of natural curiosities, which might lend themselves more obviously to the Elysian analogy, but it did also contain artificial rarities, including antiquities. It contained, for example, 'Des couuercles & autres pieces de petites vrnes de terre sigillée auec des inscriptio[n]s & des os qui estoient dans les vrnes', a funerary urn 'de marbre grisastre fait en forme d'hydre', and a splendid sounding urn 'de bronse, ou metal de Corinthe, (resonnant comme vne cloche si on le frappe) auec des inscriptions inconnuës à l'entour incrustées d'argent'. More numerous still were his bronze, silver, and gold medals of Greek, Roman, Hebraic, and Gothic origin, and his ancient coins. His collection also contained books and manuscripts, with the catalogue lavishing particular attention on a fine parchment Bible.[24]

Not every antiquary was quite so sanguine about the act of conjuration. The resurrective impulse was frequently undercut by a sense of loss, the awareness that time could never be fully defied. Antiquaries encountered ruined buildings, dispersed libraries, and obscured genealogies, a past that was, and alas would often remain, fragmentary. For all the positivity of their project, antiquarian voices were often tinged with disappointment. This struggle between the antiquaries and time is neatly illustrated by the frontispiece to the catalogue of Lodovico Moscardo's museum in Verona, *Note overo memorie del museo di Lodovico Moscardo* (1656). This frontispiece was engraved by Alberto Pasi, and it represents a tripartite struggle between art, nature, and time (Fig. Intro. 1). Three personified figures sit on a plinth at its centre. In the middle is the superfecund NATURA ('Nature'); to her right sits ARS ('Art'), and to her left VETUSTAS ('Old Age'). ARS is writing the legend *Museo Moscardo* on a banner, but, as fast as she writes, VETUSTAS snatches that banner away. In the background is the Verona amphitheatre. The frontispiece as a whole is an iconic representation of the paradox of the early modern antiquarian project: the faith on the one hand that time might be defied through collections, reconstructions, and texts, and the belief on the other that all sublunary things were subject to mutability. The frontispiece both celebrates the endurance of ancient monuments and acknowledges the inexorable march of time. The Verona amphitheatre still stands, but it is falling into ruin. Time has begun its destructive work.

For English antiquaries of the sixteenth and seventeenth centuries this paradox may have had a particular resonance. Henry VIII's dissolution of the monasteries was but a recent memory, and, as Margaret Aston has shown, the consequent sense of literary, historical, and cultural loss was profound.[25] Kenneth Clark even suggested that English antiquarianism might owe its origin to the Dissolution, for scholars 'saw monasteries destroyed and libraries dispersed, and were moved

---

[24] Borel, *Antiquitez*, 145–6.
[25] Margaret Aston, 'English Ruins and English History: The Dissolution and the Sense of the Past', *Journal of the Warburg and Courtauld Institutes*, 36 (1973), 231–55.

FIG. Intro. 1. The frontispiece to *Note overo memorie del museo di Lodovico Moscardo* (Padua, 1656). Cambridge University Library, M. 14. 28. Reproduced by kind permission of the Syndics of Cambridge University Library

to perpetuate their vanishing glories'.[26] Whilst this argument neglects other factors, such as the philological and classical studies of Continental scholars, and ignores medieval predecessors such as William of Worcester and John Rous, Clark was surely right to detect a new urgency following the Dissolution.[27] For early modern English antiquaries there was an added human dimension: the neglect and sometimes even wanton destructiveness of mankind.

Even Aubrey recognized that there were some things which could not be saved from the ravages of time or man. When he visited Gorhambury, Francis Bacon's estate near St Albans, for example, he was moved to lament its fate. He noted that the gardens, 'rarely planted and kept in his lordship's time', were now abandoned. The east side of the estate, 'heretofore, in his lordship's prosperitie, a paradise', was now just 'a large ploughed field'. The famed summer-houses, built after the Roman fashion, were 'yet standing, but defaced, so that one would have thought that the Barbarians had made a Conquest here'. Verulam House, Bacon's seat just a few miles away, fared little better. Although it was still standing in 1656, when Aubrey visited, just a few years later it was 'pulled downe for the sale of the materialls'.[28]

The antiquarian imagination has received little attention from scholars. Only one aspect has been widely appreciated: archaeology. Philip Schwyzer, for example, has recently explored archaeological themes and motifs in early modern poetry, prose, and drama in his *Archaeologies of English Renaissance Literature* (2007). More provocatively, he also explores the connections between the modern academic disciplines of archaeology and literary criticism, drawing upon the work of post-processual archaeologists such as Christopher Tilley. 'Nothing is more common in each field,' Schwyzer argues, 'than to invoke the other as a metaphor for its own practice.'[29] But studies of the archaeological imagination have mostly focused on later historical periods, when antiquarianism came to be associated more explicitly with archaeology. In *Digging the Dirt*

---

[26] Kenneth Clark, *The Gothic Revival: An Essay in the History of Taste* (London: John Murray, 1962; first published 1928), 23.
[27] For the medieval tradition, see Antonia Gransden, *Historical Writing in England II: c.1307 to the Early Sixteenth Century* (Routledge: London and New York, 1996; first published 1982), 308–41.
[28] '*Brief Lives*', *Chiefly of Contemporaries, Set Down by John Aubrey, Between the Years 1669 & 1696*, ed. Andrew Clark, 2 vols. (Oxford: Clarendon Press, 1898), i. 78–83.
[29] Philip Schwyzer, *Archaeologies of English Renaissance Literature* (Oxford: Oxford University Press, 2007), 6. Tilley argues that archaeology has witnessed 'a move away from attempts to establish what basically amounted to the search for a methodology for assigning meaning to artefact patterning to a more fully self-reflexive position involving consideration of what is involved in the act of *writing the past*'; see 'Interpreting Material Culture', in *The Meaning of Things: Material Culture and Symbolic Expression*, ed. Ian Hodder (London and New York: Routledge, 2004; first published 1989), 185–94 at 185. For similar arguments, see Julian Thomas, *Time, Culture and Identity: An Interpretive Archaeology* (London and New York: Routledge, 1996), 55–82; and Clive Gamble, *Archaeology: The Basics* (London: Routledge, 2001), 1–2.

(2004), for example, Jennifer Wallace explores what she calls the power to 'turn stones into words and the barest bones of our existence into something meaningful and lasting', tracing the fascination from the eighteenth century to the present day with bringing past worlds back to life.[30] Looming over all these studies is Rose Macaulay's magisterial *Pleasure of Ruins* (1953), an encyclopedic, if unhistorical, attempt 'to explore the various kinds of pleasure given to various people at various epochs by the spectacle of ruined buildings'.[31] But it is important to remember here—and many scholars have not—that antiquarianism and archaeology were not the same thing as each other in the early modern period. As Stuart Piggott has reminded us, 'archaeology' was used in the seventeenth century to denote the study of the past and antiquities in general rather than in the narrower sense current today of the study of the material culture of early man.[32] Archaeology, as *In Defiance of Time* shows, was only one aspect of early modern antiquarianism, no more or less important than many other fields, from etymology and epigraphy to numismatics and numerology.

Scholars, especially literary scholars, have often been reluctant to engage with this broad scheme. Antiquarianism has typically been seen as unfit matter for literary study, and critics have long turned up their noses at antiquarian writing. When in the 1940s Mario Praz relegated the poetry of Michael Drayton 'to the backrow of our bookcase, only to be consulted by the curious antiquary', he articulated the prejudices of more than one generation of scholars.[33] And historians have had a comparable attitude. Until recently, they have been similarly restrictive in their approach to antiquarianism, reserving their interest only for when antiquarian methods betray the beginnings of modern disciplinarity. By taking a broader approach here, I hope to bring a clearer understanding of antiquarianism, to further our knowledge of the early modern obsession with the resurrection of the past, and most importantly to refocus literary and historical attention on the antiquarian interventions in early modern literary and intellectual culture.

---

[30] Jennifer Wallace, *Digging the Dirt: The Archaeological Imagination* (London: Duckworth, 2004), 12. See also Andreas Wetzel, 'Reconstructing Carthage: Archaeology and the Historical Novel', *Mosaic*, 21 (1988), 13–23; and Christine Finn, *Past Poetic: Archaeology in the Poetry of W. B. Yeats and Seamus Heaney* (London: Duckworth, 2004).
[31] Rose Macaulay, *Pleasure of Ruins* (London: Weidenfeld and Nicolson, 1953), p. xv.
[32] Stuart Piggott, *Ancient Britons and the Antiquarian Imagination: Ideas from the Renaissance to the Regency* (London: Thames & Hudson, 1989), 7. This broader sense still seems to have been current in the 19th c., when John Britton described John Aubrey as the first Englishman to devote 'his studies and abilities to archaeology, in its various ramifications of architecture, genealogy, palaeography, numismatics, heraldry, &c'; see his *Memoir of John Aubrey, F. R. S., Embracing his Auto-biographical Sketches, a Brief Review of his Personal and Literary Merits, and an Account of his Works; with Extracts from his Correspondence, Anecdotes of Some of his Contemporaries, and of the Times in Which he Lived* (London: Wiltshire Topographical Society, 1845), 3. Britton's laudatory description unfortunately ignores the greater part of 16th- and 17th-c. antiquarian activity—as subsequent chapters of this book amply attest.
[33] Mario Praz, 'Michael Drayton', *English Studies*, 28 (1947), 97–107 at 107.

Recent scholars have begun to make tentative steps in this direction. In *The Trophies of Time* (1995), for example, his survey of seventeenth-century antiquarianism, Graham Parry comments that much 'could be said about the literary exploitation of antiquarian studies', describing this as 'a rich topic that has been little explored'.[34] Parry himself takes a biographical approach to the subject, and so the writing of the antiquaries plays second fiddle in his book to their lives. But subsequent scholars have started to take up his suggestion. In 'Identity and Ownership: Narratives of Land in the English Renaissance' Melanie Hansen delineates antiquarian narrative as a distinct genre of the sixteenth and seventeenth centuries, and explores the diverse narrative strategies and disciplines employed by antiquaries to construct pictures of the land, whilst Marjorie Swann's *Curiosities and Texts* (2001) examines how literary texts participated in the craze for collecting in the early modern period.[35] Nevertheless, we still await a full-length study of early modern antiquarian writing that focuses on antiquarianism not merely as a context for the emerging literary culture, but as an integral part of that culture, a study that explores the notes and narratives of the antiquaries as texts, and considers their circulation and readership amongst fellow antiquaries and the wider public. This book is an attempt to fill that gap, bringing together material as diverse as play texts, catalogues of collections, and architectural surveys, as it demonstrates the permeation of antiquarian methodology and thought in the literary and intellectual culture of early modern England. Moreover, whilst previous studies of antiquarianism have tended to focus on the later seventeenth century, when antiquarianism, natural history, and scientific inquiry came to be directly connected, with the antiquaries often Royal Society men, this book considers its earlier incarnation. Institutions such as the Elizabethan Society of Antiquaries, which met on and off from 1586 through to the early years of James I's reign, and writers such as William Camden and John Stow are its focus.

In making the case for antiquarian writing—and even more so, as I do in Chapter 6, for antiquarian poetry—this book might seem to muddy the prevailing contemporary distinction between history as narrative and antiquarianism as description or survey. Arnaldo Momigliano provided the classic exposition of this in his essay 'Ancient History and the Antiquarian' (1950). Momigliano established the popular conception of the antiquary as 'a student of the past who is not quite a historian', who eschews linear, chronological narrative in favour of

---

[34] Graham Parry, *The Trophies of Time: English Antiquarians of the Seventeenth Century* (Oxford: Oxford University Press, 1999; first published 1995), 20.
[35] Melanie Hansen, 'Identity and Ownership: Narratives of Land in the English Renaissance', in William Zunder and Suzanne Trill (eds.), *Writing and the English Renaissance* (London and New York: Longman, 1996), 87–105; Marjorie Swann, *Curiosities and Texts: The Culture of Curiosity in Early Modern England* (Philadelphia: University of Pennsylvania Press, 2001); see also Hansen's 'Writing the Land: Antiquarianism in the English Renaissance' (Ph.D. thesis, University of Liverpool, 1993).

systematic description and collection.[36] Historians follow the literary models of Livy and Tacitus, whereas antiquaries follow in the footsteps of Marcus Terentius Varro. For Momigliano, history was a recognizably literary genre, even if its predominant forms such as the chronicle were highly derivative: antiquarian surveys and catalogues of collections, by contrast, were mere accumulations of records and objects, compiled with scant regard for narrative. Momigliano also believed that, despite the often identical aims of antiquaries and historians, this distinction held good until the nineteenth century, when there emerged a new method which synthesized the chronological narrative of the historian with the archival research of the antiquary. This book does not dispute the usefulness of Momigliano's distinction, but it does argue for a broader, and generically and intellectually more diverse, conception of the different forms of history writing.[37] Antiquarian writing, it suggests, should take its place alongside more familiar forms such as the chronicle and history play. Too often modern scholars have considered antiquarianism only for its technical and critical innovations, ignoring other aspects which fit less easily into teleological accounts of historiographic progress.

Furthermore, antiquarianism needs to be assessed on its own terms, not as some approximation of modern historical method. Stephen Bann has argued, in relation to the eighteenth and nineteenth centuries, that antiquarian attitudes towards the past should not be seen as a somehow disreputable 'other face' of scientific history, but as a specific, lived relationship to the past, which deserves to be treated on its own terms.[38] Rosemary Sweet makes the same case, arguing that modern scholarship has tended 'to cherrypick the most outstanding scholars ... in order to accommodate them into a grand narrative of the rise of history or of the emergence of archaeology, whilst ignoring the works of other antiquaries whose researches fit less neatly with the requirements of our teleological frameworks'.[39] The eschewal of a teleological approach is surely correct: we need to

---

[36] Arnaldo Momigliano, 'Ancient History and the Antiquarian', in *Studies in Historiography* (London: Weidenfeld and Nicolson, 1966), 1–39 at 3. His distinction is repeated by Denys Hay in 'Historians and Antiquaries in the Eighteenth Century: The Emergence of the Modern Method', in *Annalists and Historians: Western Historiography from the Eighth to the Eighteenth Centuries* (London: Methuen, 1977), 169–85.

[37] For a re-evaluation of Momigliano's thesis, see Mark Salber Phillips, 'Reconsiderations on History and Antiquarianism: Arnaldo Momigliano and the Historiography of Eighteenth-Century Britain', *Journal of the History of Ideas*, 57 (1996), 297–316; for a more critical study, see Ingo Herklotz, 'Arnaldo Momigliano's "Ancient History and the Antiquarian": A Critical Review', in Peter N. Miller (ed.), *Momigliano and Antiquarianism: Foundations of the Modern Cultural Sciences* (Toronto, Buffalo, and London: University of Toronto Press, 2007), 127–53.

[38] Stephen Bann, 'Clio in Part: On Antiquarianism and the Historical Fragment', in *The Inventions of History: Essays on the Representation of the Past* (Manchester and New York: Manchester University Press, 1990), 100–21.

[39] Rosemary Sweet, *Antiquaries: The Discovery of the Past in Eighteenth-Century Britain* (London and New York: Hambledon, 2004), p. xv.

understand the broader cultural and intellectual context in which antiquarian works, pioneering or not, were produced and consumed. The history of antiquarianism should not just be an account of historiographic progress or failure.[40]

This book might also therefore appear to muddy the older, more fundamental distinction between poetry and history. Aristotle's summation of the distinction in the *Poetics* is something of a literary commonplace, but it is worth restating here, first because it became such a central tenet of Renaissance literary criticism, and second because it demonstrates by means of contrast what was innovative about much early modern antiquarian writing. For Aristotle the underlying difference between history and poetry is that the former relates only actual events (*ta genomena*), whereas the latter relates the kind of things that might occur (*ta dynata*). For this reason, 'poetry is more philosophical and more elevated than history, since poetry relates more of the universal, while history relates particulars'.[41] Aristotle's distinction was echoed by Philip Sidney in *The Defence of Poesy*, his laudatory oration in justification of the primacy of poetry over philosophy and history. The terms of Sidney's discussion are recognizably Aristotelian. Drawing on Aristotle's concept of *mimesis*, Sidney defines poetry as the art of imitation: 'it is that feigning notable images of virtues, vices, or what else, with that delightful teaching, which must be the right describing note to know a poet by'.[42] Poetry is the superior art precisely because it is the best teacher, presenting the clearest and most universal images of virtue, and so establishing general precepts and reasons most convincingly. 'Poetry ever setteth virtue so out in her best colours', whereas history 'being captived to the truth of a foolish world, is many times a terror from well-doing, and an encouragement to unbridled wickedness'.[43] Tied to the particulars of a vicious world, history more often than not fails to move man to virtue. Furthermore, history also fails to draw the necessary consequences and doctrine from its examples, ignoring 'the general reason of things'.[44] With this distinction in mind, antiquarian matter (undoubtedly tied to the particular and the actual) might seem a troubling or unattractive subject for poetry.

As a number of scholars have pointed out, however, the distinction between poetry and history was not so fast in the sixteenth century as it might initially

---

[40] For a critique of the Whiggish nature of much of the history of early modern historiography, see Joseph H. Preston, 'Was There an Historical Revolution?', *Journal of the History of Ideas*, 38 (1977), 353–64.
[41] Aristotle, *Poetics*, ed. and trans. Stephen Halliwell (Loeb Classical Library; Cambridge, Mass., and London: Harvard University Press, 1995), 1451^{a}35–1451^{b}10.
[42] Philip Sidney, *An Apology for Poetry, or The Defence of Poesy*, ed. Geoffrey Shepherd (London: Nelson, 1965), 103.
[43] Ibid. 111.
[44] Ibid. 107.

appear.[45] Sidney himself recognized the permeable boundary between the two, remarking that historians 'have been glad to borrow both fashion and perchance weight of poets'. To illustrate his point, Sidney recalls Herodotus and his followers, who 'either stole or usurped of Poetry their passionate describing of passions, the many particularities of battles, which no man could affirm, or, if that be denied me, long orations put in the mouths of great kings and captains, which it is certain they never pronounced'.[46] In a letter to his brother Robert, Sidney repeated the point, emphasizing the rhetoric of history, and adducing its profit and ornament:

> Besides this the Historian makes himself a discourser for profite and an Orator, yea a Poet sometimes for ornament. An Orator in making excellent orations *e re nata* which are to be marked, but marked with the note of rhetoricall remembrances; a Poet in painting forth the effects, the motions, the whisperings of the people, which though in disputation one might say were true, yet who will marke them well shall finde them taste of a poeticall vaine, and in that kinde are gallantly to be marked, for though perchance they were not so, yet it is enough they might be so.[47]

The historian borrows from the orator, as he writes rhetorical set-pieces, speeches which are to be read and imitated for the excellence of their style. But the historian also borrows from the poet, as he invokes passions and emotions for historical figures, explaining events by recourse to causes that might be true, but for which there is no certain record or evidence. In *The Defence* Sidney presents the very fact that poetry and history are admixed in this way as a key argument for the superiority of poetry as an art.

Continental theorists were more relaxed about the blurred distinction between the two. In his influential commentary on the *Poetics*, first published at Vienna in 1570, the Italian scholar Lodovico Castelvetro consistently treated poetry and history not as opposed, but as sister arts. Castelvetro argues that we cannot properly understand poetry until we understand history, and we cannot properly understand history because as yet there has not been written an adequate *ars historica*. Since history is an account of memorable human actions that have happened, and poetry is a recital of memorable human actions that may have happened, whose distinguishing mark is verisimilitude; and, moreover, since

---

[45] For the blurring of this distinction, see Patrick Collinson, 'Truth, Lies and Fiction in Sixteenth-Century Protestant Historiography', in Donald R. Kelley and David Harris Sacks (eds.), *The Historical Imagination in Early Modern Britain: History, Rhetoric, and Fiction, 1500–1800* (Cambridge: Cambridge University Press, 1997), 37–68. For more theoretical discussions, see Hayden White, 'The Historical Text as Literary Artifact', in *Tropics of Discourse: Essays in Cultural Criticism* (Baltimore and London: The Johns Hopkins University Press, 1978), 81–100; and Lionel Gossman, *Between History and Literature* (Cambridge, Mass., and London: Harvard University Press, 1990).
[46] Sidney, *Defence of Poesy*, 97.
[47] Sir Philip Sidney to Robert Sidney, 18 Oct. 1580, in *The Complete Works of Sir Philip Sidney*, ed. Albert Feuillerat, 4 vols. (Cambridge: Cambridge University Press, 1912–26), iii. 131.

history is a thing represented and poetry a representation, no *ars poetica* can offer a complete and accurate knowledge of poetry because our knowledge of history remains deficient.[48] One of the questions that an *ars historica* should consider is whether a historian might properly, without offence to his own art, treat some matters in the manner of the poets, that is, by narrative or representation, or whether that is the exclusive privilege of the art of poetry.[49] Reinforcing the connections of the two, Castelvetro proposes that if such an *ars historica* had been written it might well have been considered sufficient to teach the writing of both history and poetry.[50] There was, though, a limit to how far he was prepared to blur the boundary. He might have recognized that the styles of the two arts frequently coincide, but he was not prepared to elide their subject matter. Like Aristotle, he believed that the history of things that have happened could not furnish fit matter for poetry. For Castelvetro, when a poet treats of historical material, he fails to use his *ingegno*, the faculty (synonymous with the imagination) by which the poet invents plots, metaphors, and figures, and so also fails to imitate things similar to the truth.[51]

Other Renaissance critics were prepared to do even more to relax the boundary between poetry and history. Castelvetro himself admitted that many famous men of letters have found it distasteful that the name of poet should not be afforded to those authors who have written metrical compositions on apparently unpoetic matter, including historical subjects.[52] One example was the Italian poet and physician Girolamo Fracastoro. In his *Navgerius*, a dialogue on poetics, Fracastoro raised the possibility that a poet may turn himself to whatever subject he likes and may still be termed a poet, so long as he seeks to express himself eloquently.[53] For Fracastoro, it really was a question of style over substance. This is reflected in his own poetry: his best-known work, for example, is *Syphilis, sive morbus Gallicus* (1530), which gives an account in verse of the titular disease. In

---

[48] Lodovico Castelvetro, *Poetica d'Aristotele vulgarizzata e sposta*, ed. Werther Romani, 2 vols. (Rome and Bari: Gius. Laterza, 1978–9), i. 14: 'Adunque, poiché istoria è narrazione secondo la verità d'azzioni umane memorevoli avenute e poesia è narrazione secondo la verisimilitudine d'azzioni umane memorevoli possibili ad avenire, e, appresso, l'istoria è cosa rappresentata e la poesia cosa rappresentante, come si mostrerà procedendo avanti, non si dee potere avere perfetta e convenevole notizia della poesia per arte poetica che sia stata scritta infino a qui o sia per iscriversi per l'avenire, se prima non s'ha notizia compiuta e distinta dell'arte istorica.'
[49] Ibid. 15: 'e parimente si sarebbe determinato se si convenga e se si possa per l'istorico far palese alcuna materia per via di racconto e di rappresentamento, come si fa per lo poeta, o se pur ciò sia privilegio della poesia sola'.
[50] Ibid.: 'che altri non si sarebbe indotto a scrivere l'arte della poesia, giudicando che sufficientemente quella dell'istoria ben compilata bastasse per iscrivere istoria e poema'.
[51] Ibid. 44: 'Perché adunque, prendendo il poeta materia d'istoria, cioè di cose già avenute, non dura fatica niuna, né quindi appare se sia buono o reo poeta, cioè se sappia o non sappia ben trovare cose simili al vero e rassomigliarle, non può essere lodato.'
[52] Ibid. 45–6.
[53] Girolamo Fracastoro, *Navgerius, sive de poetica dialogus*, in *Opera omnia* (Venice, 1555), sig. 2R2ᵛ: 'poeta vero per se nullo alio mouetur fine nisi simpliciter bene dicendi circa vnumquodque propositum sibi'.

this light, antiquarian matter—traces, ruins, and origins—seems a less controversial or problematic subject for poetry. Antiquarian matter may have been historical but, as *In Defiance of Time* shows, antiquarian writing was nevertheless inventive and in its own terms imaginative.

What exactly did the early modern period understand by antiquarianism?[54] This is not a straightforward question: the stereotype of a bumbling, but essentially genial, amateur indiscriminately and obsessively peering at *objets*, valuable or otherwise, does not really fit the early modern model. Part of the difficulty arises from the very diversity of interests of those who were styled or considered to be 'antiquaries'. Subjects that attracted their attention included monuments, names, precedents, coins, families, and traditions—in short, everything described by Francis Bacon as 'Historie defaced, or some remnants of history which have casually escaped the shipwreck of time'.[55] The antiquary Thomas Westcote reflected on this diversity in *A View of Devonshire*, the survey of his home county which he compiled in the late 1620s. In his introduction he enumerates the contents of the survey, asserting that he has intermixed 'a pleasant tale with a serious discourse, and an unwritten tradition with a chronicled history, old ancient armories and epitaphs, well near buried in oblivion'; he has also added 'ancient families now extinct, or rather transanimated into others' and 'some etymologies seeming and perchance strange and far fetched'. Readers, he notes, take delight in such variety. Genealogy, etymology, epigraphy, chronicle history, and oral tradition are all fit matter for the antiquary. The 'severe critic' might be troubled by *A View of Devonshire*, bristling at its 'simplicity, vulgarity, or doubt of verity', but Westcote is confident that other readers will appreciate its copiousness, its fantastic encyclopedism.[56]

For all his emphasis on diversity, the subjects of Westcote's survey are still related. They can all be categorized under what were the two predominant strands of early modern antiquarian thought. As Daniel Woolf has shown, at the heart of Tudor and Stuart antiquarianism lay two activities or impulses. On the one hand, there was the humanist philological tradition, inherited from the great Continental philologists of the sixteenth century, from Guillaume Budé to Joseph Scaliger, and their Italian predecessors, Lorenzo Valla and Angelo

---

[54] In addition to the works already cited, studies of early modern antiquarianism include H. B. Walters, *The English Antiquaries of the Sixteenth, Seventeenth, and Eighteenth Centuries* (London: Edward Waters, 1934); Joan Evans, *A History of the Society of Antiquaries* (Oxford: Oxford University Press, 1956); Stan A. E. Mendyk, *'Speculum Britanniae': Regional Study, Antiquarianism, and Science in Britain to 1700* (Toronto, Buffalo, and London: University of Toronto Press, 1989); and D. R. Woolf, 'The Dawn of the Artifact: The Antiquarian Impulse in England, 1500–1730', *Studies in Medievalism*, 4 (1992), 5–35.

[55] Francis Bacon, *The Advancement of Learning*, ed. Michael Kiernan (The Oxford Francis Bacon, 4; Oxford: Clarendon Press, 2000), 65.

[56] Thomas Westcote, *A View of Devonshire in MDCXXX, with a Pedigree of Most of its Gentry*, ed. George Oliver and Pitman Jones (Exeter: William Roberts, 1845), p. xvi.

Poliziano. Antiquaries in this tradition sought verbal or linguistic remains, primarily manuscripts and inscriptions, but also names and words themselves, to fill in the gaps in the chronicle tradition and historical record. On the other, there were the peripatetic antiquaries, who sought ancient objects and buried artefacts, who studied contours of the landscape rather than changes in language.[57] By the end of the seventeenth century the second tradition, the precursor of archaeology, predominated, and it is certainly the more familiar today. In the sixteenth and early seventeenth centuries, however, the traditions often overlapped: Camden and Leland, to name but the two most prominent figures, belonged to both.[58] Together these two traditions delimited the early modern antiquarian field of inquiry.

What unifies the two strands of antiquarianism was an unswerving belief in the importance of antiquity and antiquities, a recognition of the value of ancient remains and traces. The antiquaries studied these remains not because they offered lessons, moral or otherwise, for the present, in the way that the narrative historians responded to the past, but simply because they were old. The antiquaries valued the old over the new and, more often than not, the very old over the old. But this veneration of antiquity is itself in need of clarification. Antiquity was a fluid and uncertain term in the early modern period, lacking temporal specificity. Like today, antiquity could refer uniquely to the time of the ancient Greeks and Romans, but it could also refer to 'olden time' generally.[59] As a result, the Roman past might be considered antiquity, but so might a generation ago. There existed what Lucien Febvre called a *passé imprécis*, where the historical and the mythological sat together, and where different historical epochs vied and merged with one another.[60] There was, to use the phrase of a more recent scholar, 'an amorphous spatio-temporal context, where some parts of the past appeared close, whilst others seemed irretrievably distant'.[61] Chronology was by no means the most important factor in gauging this distance. As Erwin Panofsky commented, reflecting on a Venetian forgery of the 1520s: 'The works of a great Cinquecento sculptor appeared to his contemporaries as no less classical, if not more classical than Greek and Roman originals . . . or, put it the other way, Greek

---

[57] Daniel Woolf, *The Social Circulation of the Past: English Historical Culture 1500–1730* (Oxford: Oxford University Press, 2003), 141–50.

[58] *Pace* Evans, who considered the two approaches as distinct strands, and focused overwhelmingly on the peripatetic and archaeological tradition; see *A History of the Society of Antiquaries*, 1–15.

[59] *OED*, s.v. 'antiquity', *n.* 4(a) and 4(b). For a useful discussion of the meanings of antiquity and its cognates, see Judith H. Anderson, 'The Antiquities of Fairyland and Ireland', *Journal of English and Germanic Philology*, 86 (1987), 199–214.

[60] Lucien Febvre, *Le Problème de l'incroyance au XVIe siècle: La religion de Rabelais* (Paris: Albin Michel, 1947), 432–3.

[61] Elizabeth L. Eisenstein, *The Printing Press as an Agent of Change: Communications and Cultural Transformations in Early Modern Europe*, 2 vols. (Cambridge: Cambridge University Press, 1979), i. 187.

18   *Introduction*

and Roman originals appeared to them as no less modern, if not more modern, than the works of a great Cinquecento sculptor.'[62] Panofsky's comment is equally applicable to early modern England. For English scholars and antiquaries, also brought up on a diet of classical authors, the island's Roman heritage seemed as familiar, if not more so, than much of its more recent past.

One effect of this 'amorphous spatio-temporal context' was that the antiquaries conceived antiquity extremely broadly. One moment an antiquary might be describing the tessellated fragments of an unearthed Roman pavement, whilst the next he might report an oral tradition or rumour associated with the same place. He might then switch his attention to the ancestors of the local gentry. The point is to note how easily and readily the antiquaries moved from one context to another. The Roman past was often their focus, but invariably their notes and narratives exceeded this subject to reveal a wider fascination with the past. Encyclopedism, as the example of Thomas Westcote shows, was the name of the antiquarian game. Furthermore, if antiquity understood as a period or portion of the past was a broad and fluid term, so too was antiquity understood as an antique, a remnant or relic preserved from that past. Frequently (as today) an antiquity referred to an object—a scratched coin, a broken urn, even a gigantic bone—but its referents did not have to be material, since it could also connote a custom, law, or precedent.[63] In the 'Comentarius Solutus', the audit of his business and books that he undertook in July 1608, Bacon used the word in precisely this sense: 'For p^{r}sid^{ts} and antiquities to acquaint my self and take collections from Sr Rob. Cotton; Bowyear'.[64] Six months later Bacon wrote to Robert Bowyer, the clerk and keeper of the Rolls of Chancery, requesting the loan of certain records, grants, and ordinances, 'antiquities', in preparation for his work on the union of English and Scottish law.[65] Antiquarian territory, delimited as it was, turns out to have been a remarkably large field.

Antiquarianism, then, is perhaps best understood as a form of curiosity about the past. Indeed, for the sixteenth-century French lexicographer Jean Nicot, it was synonymous with curiosity, as one of his entries under the word *curieux* attests: '*Vn homme curieux d'auoir, ou sçauoir choses antiques*, Antiquarius'.[66] Nicot's definition links curiosity with the search for knowledge, a connection which, as modern scholars have shown, had great importance in the early modern period. Lorraine Daston and Katharine Park, for example, have explored the connection between curiosity and wonder, and also the importance of this

---

[62] Erwin Panofsky, *Renaissance and Renascences in Western Art* (London: Paladin, 1970; first published 1965), 41.
[63] *OED*, s.v. 'antiquity', *n.* 7 and 6.
[64] Francis Bacon, 'Comentarius Solutus', in James Spedding, *The Letters and the Life of Francis Bacon*, 7 vols. (London: Longman, 1861–74), iv. 49.
[65] Spedding, *Letters and the Life*, iv. 128–9.
[66] Jean Nicot, *Dictionaire francois-latin, augmenté outre les precedentes impressions d'infinies dictions françoises, specialement des mots de marine, venerie & faulconnerie* (Paris, 1573), sig. m6^v.

Introduction 19

connection for stimulating intellectual inquiry and for the advancement of a new learning based on particulars.[67] As Bacon puts it in Book 2 of his *Novum organum* (1620), 'rare and strange works of nature stir and raise the intellect to investigate and discover forms capable of encompassing them, so too do the splendid and wonderful works of art'.[68] Curious wonder properly conceived was reasoned and articulate, concerned with detailed description and explanation of what was rare and strange about an object, natural or artificial. Antiquarianism, therefore, as much as natural philosophy, can be explained as a form of curiosity.

In the chapters that follow I explore the ideas propounded in this introduction. Together the chapters trace the historical progression of antiquarianism from the sixteenth to the mid-seventeenth century, whilst individually they focus on different antiquarian methodologies, interests, or approaches. The first two chapters consider the interest in traces, the very heart of the antiquarian project to restore the fragmentary remnants of the past and the attempt thereby to defy the passage of time. Chapter 1 focuses on material remains, discussing the antiquarian interest in unearthed objects and antiquities from John Leland to John Stow. The archaeological aspect of antiquarianism has often been considered a seventeenth-century development, related to the increasing dominance of the peripatetic tradition, but this chapter demonstrates that the interest was present from the outset. The problem for the early antiquaries was that they often failed to integrate this in their writing. Allusions to antiquities were made in passing: rather than being subjects of study or discussion in their own right, they tended to form part of larger historical and topographical narratives. As much as anything this reflects the struggle of the first antiquaries to organize their material and develop a distinctively antiquarian voice and style. Tudor antiquarian texts often appear uncontrolled, sprawling collections of fragments and remains that lack the singularity of purpose or focus properly to bridge the gap between past and present. Whilst this chapter acts as a survey, it focuses most heavily on the humanist and schoolmaster John Twyne and the historian and topographer John Stow. Both made significant contributions to the emergence of antiquarianism in the early modern period, and both had a vital role in the establishment of an antiquarian form of writing. Chapter 2 considers the related interest in linguistic traces, examining how writers of an antiquarian bent turned to etymology and

---

[67] Lorraine Daston and Katharine Park, *Wonders and the Order of Nature 1150–1750* (New York: Zone, 2001), 311–6. Other studies of early modern curiosity include Neil Kenny, *Curiosity in Early Modern Europe: Word Histories* (Wiesbaden: Harrassowitz, 1998); id., *The Uses of Curiosity in Early Modern France and Germany* (Oxford: Oxford University Press, 2004); and R. J. E. Evans and Alexander Marr (eds.), *Curiosity and Wonder from the Renaissance to the Enlightenment* (Aldershot: Ashgate, 2006).

[68] Francis Bacon, *The Instauratio magna Part II: Novum organum and Associated Texts*, ed. Graham Rees with Maria Wakely (The Oxford Francis Bacon, 11; Oxford: Clarendon Press, 2004), 300 (II. §31): 'quemadmodùm ab Operibus Naturæ Raris & inconsuetis erigitur Intellectus & eleuatur ad inquirendas & inueniendas Formas, quæ etiam illorum sunt capaces, ita etiam in Operibus Artis egregijs & admirandis hoc vsu-uenit'.

names to access the past and unearth historical origins, and sometimes also to establish narratives of genealogical descent. The belief was widespread that the name of a people or place was a form of record, memorializing ancestors or founders. As such, etymology was a highly effective means to know the past, and so the etymological approach united writers and scholars from various backgrounds and in different genres.

Chapter 3 focuses on what was perhaps the pre-eminent early modern antiquarian book, William Camden's *Britannia* (1586). This work may be the first antiquarian text to find a means of organization adequate for its encyclopedic scope. Revisiting Camden's networks of correspondents and friends, and drawing on extensive archival research, this chapter argues that the key to Camden's success as an antiquary was collaboration. The *Britannia* should be seen not as the product of one brilliant mind (although Camden was undoubtedly that), but as a public collaborative project, which united scholars and schoolmasters, both Continental and provincial, with Camden himself at the heart of this nexus, collating the great mass of antiquarian material. Collaboration, the chapter argues, therefore needs to be understood as an important antiquarian method.

Chapters 4 and 5 turn towards the peripatetic strand of antiquarianism. Chapter 4 considers the antiquarian response to ancient monuments through a detailed account of early modern discussions of Stonehenge. The Wiltshire stone circle enthralled the antiquaries, but it also taxed their imaginations. Enigmatic and inadequately explained in historical sources, it was perhaps the archetypal antiquarian curiosity. The chapter proposes that a new, practical methodology emerged to enable viewers to make sense of such monuments: measurement, or, as it was known at the time, mensuration. This became an important way of describing ancient remains, conveying both their size and their wonder, but it was also increasingly a strategy to interpret or make sense of them. Chapter 5 builds on this discussion of the peripatetic tradition, examining more closely the links between antiquarianism and travel narratives. Drawing on both guides to travel, which frequently contained injunctions to travellers to collect objects and excerpts and instructions in how to interpret and respond to antique remains, and accounts and reports themselves, the chapter demonstrates that curiosity for natural rarities was matched by a similar curiosity for antiquities. The chapter also discusses the way in which many travellers sought to 'complete' the fragmentary ruins that they encountered on their travels through recourse to literary or textual memories. As with Petrarch, a material encounter often evoked a literary remembrance.

In Chapter 6 I move from antiquarian writers to antiquarian readers by exploring how early modern poets took up the antiquarian baton. The chapter focuses on Michael Drayton, Camden's close friend and the most antiquarian of all English poets, and in particular on *Poly-Olbion* (1612 and 1622), his massive antiquarian and chorographic epic. With its elaborate paratext and its scholarly apparatus, courtesy of John Selden, *Poly-Olbion* offers an exemplary study in both antiquarian reading and in the production, publication, and reception of early modern antiquarian books. As well as the familiar context of Camden and his *confrères*, the chapter also locates Drayton's work in a less known, but long established, tradition of antiquarian poetry. Through the example of Drayton, therefore, I also explore how poets more generally responded to and shaped the forms of antiquarian writing that emerged at the time. I end with a short conclusion which returns explicitly to the idea of the defiance of time, as I look forward to the next generation of more scientifically inclined antiquaries. For them, despite Aubrey's best efforts, restitution of the past was an altogether harder matter. Defiance of time gradually faded from the scholarly purview, and the antiquarian imagination was thus all the more pressed.

1

Material Beginnings: John Leland, John Twyne, John Stow

In 1607 the diarist Sir John Oglander returned to his family seat at Nunwell on the Isle of Wight. One of the first things that he did was to investigate the surrounding countryside. His attention was soon drawn to Quarr Abbey, the great Cistercian house in the north of the island, which had been almost entirely destroyed at the dissolution of the monasteries in 1539. Oglander enquired of various old men who lived in the vicinity, where the abbey's church had formerly stood. Only one man knew, an elderly priest named Father Penny, and he told Oglander 'what a goodly church itt wase; and furthor sayd that itt stoode to ye sowthward of all ye ruins, corne then growinge where it stoode'. Oglander then hired workmen to dig to see whether he 'myght finde ye fowndation butt cowld not'. Father Penny also told him about the common cellar and buttery, which, as Oglander later recorded in his journal, 'wase then livinge, altho' mutch demolished'. Unfortunately this elderly priest was unable to supply any further information, and he did not know 'whoe pulled downe ye sayd church'. Oglander himself suggested that it might have been George Mills, the Southampton merchant who was the first purchaser of the abbey after it had been dissolved. But he also regretted—Father Penny had presumably died in the interim—that 'sutch are ye ruins of time, that there now liveth not anye yt that can tell where ye Church of Quarr stood'.[1]

Oglander's journals and notebooks contain other such passages, detailing both his interest in the material remains of the past and his readiness to excavate in search of them. Modern scholars have often therefore seen him as an archaeological pioneer, as one of the first Englishmen to recognize the potential of material evidence to confirm or deny oral testimony and to undertake the kind of deliberate excavation associated with the modern discipline of archaeology.[2]

---

[1] *The Oglander Memoirs: Extracts from the MSS. of Sir J. Oglander, Kt., of Nunwell, Isle of Wight, Deputy-Governor of Portsmouth, and the Deputy-Lieutenant of the Isle of Wight, 1595–1648*, ed. W. H. Long (London: Reeves and Turner, 1888), 198–9.

[2] M. C. W. Hunter, 'The Royal Society and the Origins of British Archaeology: I', *Antiquity*, 45 (1971), 113–21 at 118–19; and Alain Schnapp, *The Discovery of the Past: The Origins of Archaeology*, trans. Ian Kinnes and Gillian Varndell (London: British Museum Press, 1999; first published 1996), 141–2.

Most Renaissance discoveries, after all, as Zachary Schiffman has pointed out, were accidental, the result of ploughing and sowing rather than deliberate digging.[3] When Petrarch described archaeological finds—a gold funerary urn, an ancient jewel, or a cache of coins—as 'the gifts of fortune, not the laudable merits of men', he could have been speaking about sixteenth-century England.[4] For there too objects and remains were typically turned up by builders, ploughmen, and, in the case of one remarkable discovery reported by William Harrison, rabbits; the likes of Oglander are hard to find.[5] Moreover, modern scholarship has tended to downplay the material, archaeological aspect of antiquarianism in its sixteenth-century manifestation. Joan Evans, for example, argued that the study of antiquity at that time was not, and could not be, a 'vision of ancient things newly dug from the reluctant earth'.[6] Reflecting her own position as an archaeologist concerned with the emergence and history of her discipline, and the Whiggish tendency that such an endeavour often entails, Evans described sixteenth-century antiquarianism as an essentially documentary enterprise, which was concerned first and foremost with literary texts and written records. Since scholars did not usually undertake the kinds of excavation which we now associate with archaeology, her argument goes, material remains must have been of minor importance.

But a lack of intention does not necessarily equate to a lack of interest. In his deliberateness Oglander was indeed a pioneer, anticipating some of the archaeological developments which the rise of the Royal Society in 1660 heralded. In his interest in material remains, however, he was less innovative. Collections of unearthed antiquities, especially coins, had been put together from the beginning of the sixteenth century. Initially, at least, this interest may well have been documentary; early accounts of antiquities tend to be descriptive and brief. But by the end of the sixteenth century the historical and imaginative potential of those remains had been more fully realized. A writer such as John Stow, for example, recognized their importance for the resurrective project upon which he and the other antiquaries had embarked. In Stow's hands material remains become tokens of the potential of antiquarianism to defy time, the goal which the early modern antiquaries sought, but also, in their fragmentations and imperfections, illustrations of the chimerical nature of that project. Evans's argument begins to look anachronistic, corresponding more with modern

---

[3] Zachary Sayre Schiffman, 'Jean Bodin, Roman Law and the Renaissance Conception of the Past', in Penny Schine Gold and Benjamin C. Sax (eds.), *Cultural Visions: Essays in the History of Culture* (Amsterdam: Rodopi, 2000), 271–87 at 273.
[4] Francesco Petrarca to Francesco Nelli, *Rerum familiarum libri I–VIII*, trans. Bernardo, xviii. 8.
[5] In all seriousness, Harrison emphasized the importance of these cunicular excavators for the discovery of a hoard of ancient coins at Richborough on the Kent coast; see 'Of the Antiquities, or auncient Coines found in England', in his 'The Description of Britaine', in Raphael Holinshed, *Chronicles*, 2 vols. (London, 1577), sigs. M4ʳ–M5ʳ.
[6] Evans, *A History of the Society of Antiquaries*, 2.

conceptions of disciplinarity than with the sixteenth-century intellectual context which she sought to describe. We may not be able to use the word archaeology in its modern sense, but we should not deny its use altogether.

In the chapter which follows, I trace the emergence of this interest in material remains from its Tudor beginnings through to its flourishing in late Elizabethan England. My account begins with John Leland, the Tudor bibliophile and antiquary, whose interests, according to Evans, were 'entirely and narrowly documentary'. Contrary to his own styling, she also argued that he 'was, indeed, rather geographer than antiquary'.[7] To a certain extent, this characterization is true—but it also ignores the important role which material remains had in his historical, polemical, and political projects. Alongside Leland, the chapter also considers other sixteenth-century antiquaries, in whose collections, surveys, and works we may similarly glimpse the beginnings of this interest in the material traces of the past. In the second half of the chapter, I then turn in more detail to two figures, John Twyne and John Stow, for whom unearthed remains were patently more than just objects to be documented and described. Employing remains more profitably and integrally in their literary and historical evocations of the past, both writers became important influences on the form of antiquarianism which was emerging at the time. These material beginnings, as the examples of Twyne and Stow attest, were significant indeed.

MATERIAL TRACES

Most accounts of early modern antiquarianism rightly begin with Leland. By his own account Leland was the first (and, to date, only) *antiquarius*, or king's antiquary. Henry VIII had commissioned Leland in 1533 'to peruse and diligently to serche al the Libraries of Monasteries and Colleges of this [his] noble reaulme to the intente that the Monumentes of auncient Writers as welle of other nations, as of this [his] owne province mighte be brought owte of deadely darkenes to lyvely lighte'.[8] Leland took his commission seriously. Nearly ten years of travel followed, during which he visited libraries up and down the country, compiling vast quantities of notes, on British and English authors, as Henry's commission dictated, but also on antiquities and ancient monuments. Like so many antiquarian projects, Leland's did not end happily. Weighed down by the size of his commission, and apparently exhausted by the punishing nature of his researches, Leland went mad in 1547 and he was incapacitated for the remaining five years of his life. His notes and collections were not published until

---

[7] Evans, *A History of the Society of Antiquaries*, 3.
[8] John Leland, 'New Year's Gift', in *The Itinerary*, ed. Thomas Hearne, 9 vols. (Oxford, 1744–5), i, p. xviii.

after his death, when they were printed, first through the editorial labours of John Bale, and then, more extensively, in the eighteenth century by the Oxford antiquary Thomas Hearne.

Aside from his fate, Leland is best known today for his bibliophily, for his vital role in the preservation of books and manuscripts following the dispersal of the monastic libraries.[9] But, as Cathy Shrank has shown, his antiquarian interests also stretched to the kinds of numismatic and material evidence found in artefacts and landscapes, which Continental humanist scholars such as Guillaume Budé, whom Leland had met in Paris, had begun to popularize.[10] In those writings which he did complete, and which were published in his lifetime, Leland demonstrates that he understood how these kinds of evidence might be used, how they might inform and complement literary and textual remains. For Shrank, Leland is therefore 'a bridging figure', as he also sought to fuse this new Continental antiquarianism with British medieval traditions about King Arthur and the Brut. By connecting these different models, he attempted to forge a new and authoritative history, which bulwarked English traditions, asserted English autonomy, and defended both from Continental attacks. For Leland, the defence of a figure such as King Arthur was a matter of national honour. As the supposed ancestor of the Tudor monarchs, Arthur carried dynastic significance, and his heroic deeds contributed to a vision of a glorious and unbroken national history. Given the Reformation context in which Leland travelled and wrote, his motivation for defending Arthur is not hard to surmise.

Indeed, the historicity of Arthur had been under threat for some time from Continental scholars. The account given by the twelfth-century monk and chronicler Geoffrey of Monmouth in his *Historia regum Britanniae*, in particular, had been called into question.[11] In his *Anglica historia* (1534), for example, the Italian humanist and historian Polydore Vergil had cast doubt on the whole of Geoffrey's history on the reasonable grounds of its anachronisms and lack of contemporary sources. A noted textual critic, who had already published well-received editions of Niccolò Perotti's *Cornucopiae* (1496), Gildas's *De calamitate excidio & conquestu Britanniae* (1525), and John Chrysostom's *De perfecto monacho* (1530), Vergil sought to apply a similar editorial method to the sources

---

[9] See e.g. Ronald Harold Fritze, '"Truth hath lacked witnesse, tyme wanted light": The Dispersal of the English Monastic Libraries and Protestant Efforts at Preservation, ca. 1535–1625', *Journal of Library History*, 18 (1983), 274–91; and Nigel Ramsay, '"The Manuscripts flew about like Butterflies": The Break-Up of English Libraries in the Sixteenth Century', in James Raven (ed.), *Lost Libraries: The Destruction of Great Book Collections since Antiquity* (Basingstoke: Palgrave Macmillan, 2004), 125–44.

[10] Cathy Shrank, *Writing the Nation in Reformation England, 1530–1580* (Oxford: Oxford University Press, 2004), 66.

[11] For a recent account of the 16th-c. controversy over Geoffrey, see Arthur B. Ferguson, *Utter Antiquity: Perceptions of Pre-History in Renaissance England* (Durham, NC, and London: Duke University Press, 1993), 84–105.

for his history.[12] In the dedicatory epistle to his *Anglica historia* Vergil explained the origins of this historical method: 'I, who had long ago devoted myself to investigating things from the past, began carefully to read, study, exhaust, and transcribe those very annals of the English and of other peoples who might be relevant to the composition of a new history.'[13] In this light, Geoffrey's *Historia*, which lacked not only contemporaneousness, but also corroboration from any other authority or source, had to be discarded. And Vergil did not shirk from the task, berating the impudent vanity of an author, who is unnamed, but clearly Geoffrey, for extolling the Britons above even the Romans and Macedonians.[14] On the subject of King Arthur, he was no less critical, bemoaning at length the myriad exaggerations and lies which had been told about this wondrous prince.[15]

Leland's response was swift and robust. Demonstrating his own familiarity with the humanist scholarship that Vergil in a different way represented, Leland rebuffed the Italian historian with humanist and antiquarian arguments of his own. In the unpublished 'Antiquarii Codrus, sive laus & defensio Gallofridi Arturii Monumetensis contra Polydorum Vergilium' he first attacks Vergil for his prose, for what he presents as the Italian's hubristic assumption that he was the true inheritor of Ciceronian style.[16] Leland then turns to the historical matter at hand, and he marshals three principal arguments in defence of the historicity of King Arthur. The first is textual; the other two depend on material remains. First, he mentions the 'permulti libelli, qui Britannica lingua scripti a Cambris' (the very many books, which were written in the British language by the Welsh), presumably a reference to Welsh chronicles which detail Arthur's life and deeds. Then, he mentions 'antiquissimis tabulis', ancient tablets which he had seen attached to columns in churches in Wales, and which, although he does not specify this, presumably also detailed Arthur's life and deeds. Finally, he presents his most compelling evidence, a wax seal of Arthur preserved in Westminster Abbey.[17]

---

[12] For more on Vergil's textual criticism, see Denys Hay, *Polydore Vergil: Renaissance Historian and Man of Letters* (Oxford: Clarendon Press, 1952), 106–13.

[13] Polydore Vergil, *Anglicae historiae libri XXVI* (Basle, 1534), sig. a2^v: 'ego, qui me iampridem ad inuestigandas ueterum res dederam, coepi illos ipsos Anglorum ac aliarum gentium annales accuratius euolere, legere, haurire, & excribere [*sic*], quae ad confectionem nouae historiae pertinerent'.

[14] Ibid., sig. b3^v: 'At contra quidam nostris temporibus, pro expiandis istis Britonum maculis, scriptor emersit, ridicula de eisdem figmenta contexens, eosque longe supra uirtutem Macedonum, & Romanorum, impudenti uanitate attollens.'

[15] Ibid., sig. e6^{r-v}.

[16] John Leland, 'Antiquarii Codrus, sive laus & defensio Gallofridi Arturii Monumetensis contra Polydorum Vergilium', in *De rebus Britannicis collectanea*, ed. Thomas Hearne, 6 vols. (Oxford, 1715), Appendix, i. 3. What Leland thought of Vergil is apparent from his title: 'Codrus' is an allusion to the carping and jealous shepherd of Virgil's fifth and seventh *Eclogues* (see *Eclogues*, v. 11, and vii. 25–8).

[17] Leland, 'Codrus', *De rebus*, i. 5–6: 'Illud recte adfirmare possum, sigillum Arturii Patricii, cera impressum, inter nobiles vetustatis reliquias ab Westmonasteriensibus religiose servari.'

The 'Codrus', which, until Hearne's edition of 1715, survived only in a single autograph manuscript, is a preliminary version of the defence of King Arthur which Leland later published under the title *Assertio inclytissimi Arturij Regis Britanniae* (1544). This work was enduring enough—or at least the controversy over Geoffrey was—and sufficiently well regarded to warrant the publication of an English translation almost forty years later by Richard Robinson. Leland is markedly more guarded here, as we might expect for a printed text, and in the prefatory epistle he takes care to emphasize his admiration for Vergil as a writer. Whereas the 'Codrus' implies that Vergil's imitation of Cicero is slavish, the *Assertio* praises the Italian for his erudition, eloquence, and imagination. The matter at hand is a strictly historical one; it is here alone that Leland considers Vergil deficient.[18] Early in the work Leland acknowledges that much of what has been written about Arthur is false, but he argues that this is no reason to dismiss the whole matter:

> I will declare nothing rashly: For so much as it appeareth most euidently, that both obscure and absurde reportes haue crept into the historie of Arthure: which thing is of the curious sorte easily found faulte with. But this in deede is not a cause sufficient iust, why any man should neglect, abiect, or deface the Historie otherwise of it selfe, lightsome and true. Howe much better is it (casting awaye trifles, cutting off olde wiues tales, and superfluous fables, in deede of stately porte in outwarde shew, but nothing auayleable vnto credite, beeing taken away) to reade, scanne vpon, and preserue in memorie those things which are consonant by Authorytie.[19]

His defence of Arthur, which then follows, repeats many of the arguments that he had collected in the earlier manuscript. As there, pride of place is given to his sigillographic evidence; a whole chapter is devoted to the Westminster Abbey seal.[20] First, Leland recounts how he had been shown this seal, and he then describes it, recording its damage and also transcribing its inscription: 'PATRICIVS ARTVRIVS BRITANNIÆ, GALLIÆ, GERMANIÆ, DACIÆ IMPERATOR' (Noble Arthur, Emperor of Britain, Gaul, Germany, and Denmark). He also reports that his guide in Westminster Abbey told him that King Edward the Simple had ordered that the seal be placed alongside Arthur's tomb 'to the perpetuall memorie of the most high and mighty prince'. For Leland, there is no better rebuff to Vergil. 'Neither surely is there any thing apparant, (that I doe knowe of),' he concludes, 'which more euidently approueth that Arthure was liuing, then the same Seale

---

[18] John Leland, *Assertio inclytissimi Arturij Regis Britanniae* (London, 1544), sig. A3^r.
[19] John Leland, *A Learned and True Assertion of the original, Life, Actes, and death of the most Noble, Valiant, and Renowned Prince Arthure, King of great Brittaine*, trans. Richard Robinson (London, 1582), sig. D2$^{r\ v}$; cf. Leland, *Assertio*, sig. C2^v: 'Ego vero temere nihil pronunciabo: quandoquidem manifestissime constat, obscura, & absurda irrepsisse in Arturij historiam: id quod a curiosis facile deprehenditur. At haec non satis quidem iusta causa est, ut quis historiam alias luculentam, & veram negligat, abijciat, proterat. Quanto rectius, abiectis nugis, reiectis anilibus fabulis, & auctarijs in speciem vero magnificis, at nihil ad fidem pertinentibus, demptis, quae ex autoritate consonantia sunt legere, discutere, conseruare.'
[20] Leland, *Learned and True Assertion*, sigs. E4^v–F3^r; cf. Leland, *Assertio*, sigs. D4^r–E2^v.

doth.'[21] To set his own seal on the matter, he also cites the Plautine maxim 'Pluris valet oculatus testis vnus, quàm auriti decem'.[22] Visual witnesses outrank aural ones; material remains, Leland seems to be suggesting, are more reliable records than literary texts or other written histories. Further material evidence follows later in the work, including the oft-repeated tale of the discovery of Arthur's tomb by King Henry II.[23] According to this tale, Henry had been entertained during a banquet at St Davids by a bard, who sang of Arthur's burial and tomb. Shortly afterwards, following the directions given in this song, that tomb was discovered at Glastonbury, and greater treasures still were found inside: the preternaturally well-preserved bodies of Arthur and Guinevere. On exposure, though, their bodies immediately crumbled to dust.

Leland's examples hardly stand the test of time. The wax seal and the tomb with its disappearing bodies are not the most convincing pieces of evidence. But then Leland had set himself a difficult task. To uphold the Galfridian matter was much harder than to upbraid it. Keen to show his own awareness of antiquarian developments, but also eager to celebrate Arthur as a national hero, Leland toils to give him a physical, as well as a textual, form. By adducing the seal and tomb, he endeavours to reclaim Arthur from the realm of legend, to which Vergil's *Anglica historia* had threatened to relegate him, and present him once again as a historical figure. As an example, therefore, his *Assertio* underlines the importance of material remains to the antiquaries, even from the outset, and, in his citation from Plautus's *Truculentus*, Leland demonstrates that he had also conceived how these remains might stand in comparison to other forms of historical evidence. The problem for Leland was that to build an authoritative history on material remains, to give the past a physical form, required a large number of remains to have survived. For King Arthur, that was simply not the case. The *Assertio* is thus trapped in a scholarly paradox of its own making. To defend Arthur, Leland turns to new and authoritative forms of evidence; but in adopting that approach, he only succeeds in drawing attention to their relative lack.

This problem of survival is emphasized when we consider some of the other material remains which attracted antiquarian attention in the sixteenth century. Roman remains, for instance, were much safer and more extensive territory, and it is not surprising therefore that, when it came to material traces, subsequent antiquaries tended to focus on the Roman rather than the British past. Leland himself devoted considerable attention to Roman remains. Throughout his *Itinerary*, as T. D. Kendrick has shown, there are glimpses of Roman sites and sculptures, and there is also ample evidence of the pleasure that he took in their

---

[21] Leland, *Learned and True Assertion*, sig. F1^v; cf. Leland, *Assertio*, sig. E1^r: 'Nec certe, quod ego sciam, extat quicquam quod luculentius ipso sigillo comprobet Arturium fuisse.'

[22] Plautus, *Truculentus*, trans. Paul Nixon (Loeb Classical Library; Cambridge, Mass.: Harvard University Press, 1960; first published in this edition 1938), l. 489: 'one sharp-eyed witness outranks ten keen-eared'.

[23] Leland, *Learned and True Assertion*, sigs. I3^r–I4^r; cf. Leland, *Assertio*, sigs. H2^r–H3^v.

discovery.[24] By dint of surviving in larger quantities, Roman remains made the antiquary's task considerably easier. Thus when Sampson Erdeswicke, for example, came to describe the Roman remains in the north of England a few years later, he was able to write copiously and convincingly about them. After touring Cumberland and Northumberland in September 1574 in the company of Edward Threkeld, rector of Great Salkeld and archdeacon of Carlisle, Erdeswicke wrote his observations up. In characteristically antiquarian fashion, his account records material as diverse as antiquities, inscriptions, etymologies, coats of arms, topographical curiosities, and other features of the landscape. Antiquities noted include 'a pece of one octogonall pyramy stone', unearthed in the town of Bampton c.1564, and, two miles from Penrith, 'the ruynes of an old town of a myle compas about, of the countrey called Old Penrith, and digging up ther, they fownde stones fayr of every sorte'.[25] The longest description, though, is reserved for another, better-preserved material remain, Hadrian's Wall:

As towching Hadrians wall, begyning abowt a town called Bonus standing vppon the river Sulway now called Eden. And the sandes notwithstanding are this day called Sullway sands—of the name of the river in old tyme called Solvius, was Ptolemy—Solucas. The sea ebbeth and floweth there. The forsaid wall begynning there, and there yet standing of the heyth of 16 fote, for almost a quarter of a myle together, and so along the river syde estwards, they space of an eight myle by the shew of the trench as certayne ruynes of castills in that wall, tyll a qwarter of a myle of Carlyole and there passeth ower the river of Eden; and then goeth straight estwards hard by a late abbey called Lanvercost, and so crossing ower the mowntaynes toward Newcastell.[26]

Erdeswicke plots the course of the Roman Wall, tracing it from the Solway Firth in the west of the country across to Newcastle in the east. As he follows its geography, he also records its physical remains, noting 'the certayne ruynes of castills' which run its length, and also that, at its western extremity, it stands to 'the heyth of 16 fote'. Erdeswicke's material eased his task, but so did the fact that, unlike Leland, he did not then seek to marshal this evidence in a polemical historical argument. Instead, he seems to have conceived his task as an antiquary solely in terms of collection and documentation.

A similar interest in material remains, especially Roman, may be discerned in the collections put together at that time by the poet Daniel Rogers. Through his Flemish mother Adriana van der Weyden, Rogers was connected with a number of scholars in the Low Countries, including her cousin Abraham Ortelius, and he seems to have served as a conduit for the dissemination of the antiquarian and

---

[24] T. D. Kendrick, *British Antiquity* (London: Methuen, 1950), 55.
[25] 'Certaine verie rare observations of Cumberland, Northumberland, etc., with divers epitaphes, coat armours, and other monuments, verie orderlie and laboriouslie gathered together, on a journey taken mdlxxiv, by Sampson Erdeswicke', in *Reprints of Rare Tracts & Imprints of Antient Manuscripts, &c.*, ed. M. A. Richardson, 7 vols. (Newcastle, 1847–9), vii. 7–16 at 8–9.
[26] Ibid. 11–12.

topographical studies which Ortelius and his circle had begun to explore.[27] He is an important figure, therefore, for the development of English antiquarianism after Leland, providing another bridge with Continental scholarship. But unlike his predecessor, and also Erdeswicke, he does not seem to have undertaken antiquarian journeys. His was not a peripatetic antiquarianism. He relied instead on his reading and on the good grace of friends and correspondents, as he successfully amassed an enormous amount of material on the histories of Britain and Ireland.

Rogers's collections and correspondence suggest that he was particularly keen to acquire coins and inscriptions. In a letter of October 1572, for example, he wrote to Ortelius to ask if he could supply either. From this letter it is apparent that Rogers had begun work on an antiquarian survey of Britain, picking up Leland's mantle. In the letter he complains of the difficulty of the task because of the many fabulous and unreliable sources. Roman Britain poses particular problems in this regard, and Rogers emphasizes that much of his account will, therefore, have to come from material remains, from coins and inscriptions.[28] For this reason he seeks Ortelius's help, asking his kinsman if he might intercede on his behalf with the Flemish antiquary, numismatist, and printer Hubert Goltzius. Under the patronage of Marcus Laurinus, the lord of Watervliet, Goltzius had established a private press at Bruges in the 1560s, known as the Officina Goltziana, and had published a series of richly illustrated folios on Greek and Roman history.[29] These volumes were built on the large collection of coins and medals which Laurinus had acquired, and they became the most notable numismatic works of the sixteenth century. Rogers asks whether Goltzius might be willing to transcribe and send him any Roman inscriptions, either from coins or from ancient monuments, which mention the name of Britain. Aware of the need to keep his correspondents happy, he also takes the opportunity to flatter Goltzius, praising him for his dutiful and meticulous attention to so many ancient coins and inscriptions.[30]

---

[27] F. J. Levy, 'Daniel Rogers as Antiquary', *Bibliothèque d'humanisme et renaissance*, 27 (1965), 444–62 at 460.

[28] Daniel Rogers to Abraham Ortelius, 20 Oct. 1572, in *Abrahami Ortelii (geographi Antuerpiensis) et virorum eruditorum ad eundem et ad Jacobum Colium Ortelianum (Abrahami Ortelii sororis filium) epistulae*, ed. Joannes Henricus Hessels (Cambridge: Cambridge University Press, 1887), 101–2: 'Alia cogitatio maiores mihj difficultates obtulit, scripsj enim de Romanorum in Britanijs imperio, quæ scriptio quam laboriosa mihi fuerit, ipse facile conijcies, cum nullus ante me, id argumentj attigerit, omniaque ex graecis et latinis, ijsque antiquissimis authoribus haurienda sint, veritate nugis et mendacijs recentiorum, ferè obruta et deleta, ad quam eruendam, dicj non potest, quantum lucis et numismata et aliæ marmoreæ inscriptionis [sic] attulerint'.

[29] Herman de la Fontaine Verwey, 'The First Private Press in the Low Countries: Marcus Laurinus and the Officina Goltziana', *Quaerendo*, 2 (1972), 294–310.

[30] Daniel Rogers to Abraham Ortelius, 20 Oct. 1572, in *Abrahami Ortelii... epistulae*, 102: 'Peto autem maiorem in modum a te, agas cum Goltzio nostro, ut sj quas obseruarit inscriptiones, in numismatibus, quorum habet et uidit innumera, uel in marmoribus aliisque monumentis antiquis, qualia multa diligenter inspexit, quæ uel ipsius nominis Britanniæ meminerint, uelit transcriptas ad me transmittere.'

Given his publications, Goltzius was an obvious source of information, and Ortelius was the obvious choice of intermediary. For not only was he a friend of Goltzius, but he also had well-known numismatic interests of his own. In 1573, for example, the year after Rogers's letter, he published *Deorum Dearumque capita ex vetustatis numismatibus in gratiam antiquitatis studiosorum effigiata et edita*, a collection of fifty-four engravings of classical gods and goddesses by Philippe Galle, based almost entirely on the coins and medals in his own collection.[31] In the dedicatory epistle to Joannes Sambucus, the Hungarian antiquary, bibliophile, and numismatist, Ortelius speaks of his deep-seated interest in ancient coins and acknowledges his long-standing desire to collect them.[32] In the epistle to the reader which follows, he also expresses surprise that, despite the proliferation of works on the classical gods, no scholar, to the best of his knowledge, has tried to collect, exhibit, and publish their images.[33] He thus positions his own book as an attempt to fill that numismatic gap.

The book's engravings all take the same form. In a central alcove is a medallion portrait of the god or goddess; on a tablet above, the name of that god or goddess is written in majuscule letters; and on a tablet below is a brief note on the coin from which the engraving has been taken. The seventeenth engraving, for example, is of Flora, the Roman goddess of flowers and nature. The portrait is identified above as 'FLORAE', and described below as 'Ex nummo argentes C. Seruilij C. F. P. N.', thus establishing that it was taken from a silver coin minted by Gaius Servilius.[34] Galle's engravings therefore illustrate the gods and goddesses, but they also advertise Ortelius's collection of coins, serving as a form of a catalogue to his numismatic museum. The book was clearly popular, with subsequent editions appearing in 1582, 1602, 1612, 1680, 1683, and 1699, and it was known by scholars and antiquaries across Europe, including William Camden in England.[35] Rogers, whose letter pre-dates the first edition, must have

---

[31] The only engraving not taken from a coin in Ortelius's collection is that of the Egyptian god Canopus, which was engraved instead 'Ex tabula hieroglyphica Petri Bembi', a reference to the *Mensa Isiaca*, or Bembine Tablet of Isis. This tablet—in fact, a piece of Roman origin, probably from the time of the emperor Claudius—was brought to Cardinal Bembo for his collection of antiquities at Padua, and it became known after Enea Vico published his *Vetustissimæ tabulæ Æneæ hieroglyphicis... literis cælatæ* in 1559. On the *Mensa Isiaca*, see James Stevens Curl, *Egyptomania. The Egyptian Revival: A Recurring Theme in the History of Taste* (Manchester and New York: Manchester University Press, 1994), 58–9.
[32] Abraham Ortelius, *Deorum Dearumque capita ex vetustis numismatibus in gratiam antiquitatis studiosorum effigiata et edita* (Antwerp, 1573), sig. A2^r: 'Quum ego ab ineunte ætate, naturæ quodam, an cuius Genij nescio ductu, citra mea studia & occupationes, etsi mihi fortuna satis tenuis, & ingenium exile fuerit, semper mihi tamen solebam huiusmodi antiqua numismata comparare.'
[33] Ibid., sig. A3^r: 'Plurimi fuerunt & olim, & nostra ætate, qui Deorum scripserunt Historias; at qui ipsas iconicas imagines exhiberet, hactenus (quod sciam) inuentus est nemo.'
[34] Ibid., sig. F2^r.
[35] C. E. Dekesel, 'Abraham Ortelius: Numismate', in Robert W. Karrow, Jr (ed.), *Abraham Ortelius (1527–1598): Cartographe et humaniste* (Turnhout: Brepols, 1998), 181–92 at 182–4.

known about Ortelius's collection through private channels; as the Fleming's correspondent and kinsman, this is easily explained.

Rogers's letter is important for what it tells us about his historical method, about how he conceived different forms of historical evidence and proof. Speaking of the gaps in ancient texts, he acknowledges in the letter how many Roman histories of Britain have been lost. He describes part of Livy, for instance, as having fallen victim to the antiquary's perennial enemies, time and man, whilst he regrets that the description of Britain by Ammianus Marcellinus is missing altogether.[36] But in one of the clearest signals of his antiquarianism he asserts that these textual gaps can nevertheless be filled by coins, marbles, and monuments. Where authors are silent, he writes, coins often speak.[37] Just as Leland tried to connect medieval literary traditions with the material evidence for them, so Rogers, with a more explicitly classical bent, recognizes how Roman authors and remains might inform and complement one another.

Rogers's notebooks also betray his antiquarian interests. Two of these survive in the British Library, both of which, like the letter to Ortelius, seem to have been preliminary to a major antiquarian study. The first notebook (BL, Additional MS 21088), which is signed and dated on one of its flyleaves 'Danielis Rogersij. 1569', consists mostly of reading notes. The greater part of the manuscript is a copy of Henry of Huntingdon's *Historia Anglorum*, although the book also contains a genealogy of the Norman dukes, the beginning of the 'Historia Hierosolimitana', a passage from Nicetas Choniates' *Historia* ('Nicetas Choniata, in analib: fa. 207'), and an epitaph on William the Conqueror. Most of the manuscript is in the fine italic hand of a scribe. Since Rogers was living in Paris in 1569 as part of the household of the English ambassador Sir Henry Norris, that scribe was probably a Frenchman.[38] Samuel Pegge, the eighteenth-century antiquary, who acquired the manuscript in 1755, suggested the same thing on the basis of the hand itself and also certain marginal annotations: ''tis a French Hand, & the Lemmata in the margin are in that Language; from whence I judge the scribe was a Frenchman, being probably employ'd to make this Transcript for Daniel Rogers'.[39]

This collection of medieval texts did not go unread. Throughout the volume there are extensive notes in Rogers's own, more cursive italic hand. At fo. 3ʳ, for example, he added a précis and table of contents for Henry's *Historia*, which he

---

[36] Daniel Rogers to Abraham Ortelius, 20 Oct. 1572, in *Abrahami Ortelii...epistulae*, 102: 'Scio etiam eam partem Liuij, quæ Julij in Britanniam expeditionem continet, iniuriâ temporum et hominum, amissam: Ammianus Marcellinus, ait se Britanniam descripsisse, ea pars desideratur.'

[37] Ibid.: 'Fit igitur sæpenumero, ut numismata eorum mentionem faciant, de quibus apud probatos authores, silentium.'

[38] For Rogers's Parisian sojourn, see James E. Phillips, 'Daniel Rogers: A Neo-Latin Link between the Pléiade and Sidney's "Areopagus"', in *Neo-Latin Poetry of the Sixteenth and Seventeenth Centuries* (Los Angeles: William Andrews Clark Memorial Library, 1965), 5–28 at 13.

[39] Pegge wrote his note on one of the manuscript's flyleaves (BL, Additional MS 21088, fo. 2ʳ).

titled 'In hoc uolumine continetur historia Anglorum, nouiter edita, ab Henrico Huntedunensj Archidiacono'. Detailed notes on the text then follow at various places, although Rogers's enthusiasm clearly wavered after Book 1. By far the largest number of glosses appear early in the manuscript. Most of these annotations concern the text itself. At fo. 6ᵛ, for example, alongside four lines of Latin verse, Rogers identified another source, adding a cross-reference to Ranulf Higden's *Polychronicon*: 'Vide Ranul: Higd. <fa>. cap. 41'. Evidently Rogers also began to collate his manuscript with other copies of the *Historia Anglorum*, for, at fo. 84ʳ, he queried the internal organization of his own text. Here, alongside the beginning of Book 8, he wrote in the margin that some manuscripts give this as the tenth book ('Hic in quibusdam codicibus scriptis est, decimus liber'). By the same token, at the beginning of the tenth book (fo. 104ᵛ), as we would expect, he wrote the converse ('Hic in quibusdam codicibus est ordine octauus'). Other annotations are illustrative, as, at fo. 7ʳ, where Rogers expanded on Henry's list of the Four Wonders of England. Rogers identified the first of these, the caverns of the Peak District, as 'The Diuels arse of Peke', and he also rendered Henry's name for Stonehenge, 'Stanenges', more recognizably as 'Stoninges'. His annotations also include corrections: at fo. 8ʳ, for example, Rogers emended the name of a Roman consul 'Lucio Bubulo' to 'Bibulo', underlining the incorrect form which his scribe had given in the process.

Rogers's second notebook (BL, MS Cotton Titus F. X) illustrates his antiquarianism even better. This volume is a small quarto of 153 leaves, entirely in Rogers's autograph. He titled the volume 'Antiquæ Britannæ obseruationes', and it contains his notes on ancient Britain gleaned from a wide range of literary and material sources. The manuscript begins with exhortations to study history from classical authors, including Polybius, Sallust, and Cicero. Then follows 'Authorum Elenchus', an exhaustive index of the sources, mostly, but not exclusively, classical, which pertain to the study of ancient Britain.[40] The remainder of the manuscript appears to be a form of antiquarian commonplace book. Rogers seems to have taken a blank notebook and, as humanist pedagogues advocated, marked out his categories in advance.[41] Instead of the rhetorical and moral categories, however, which they typically recommended, his divisions are strictly antiquarian. His heads are chronological, geographical, etymological, and ethnographical, and they include the names of Roman emperors from Augustus

---

[40] BL, MS Cotton Titus F. X, fos. 4ʳ–10ʳ.

[41] See e.g. Juan Luís Vives's instructions for commonplace books in his *Introductio ad sapientiam. Satellitium siue symbola. Epistolæ duæ de ratione studii puerilis* (Bruges, 1526), sigs. S3ᵛ–S4ʳ: 'Compones tibi librum chartæ puræ iustæ magnitudinis. quem in certos locos ac velut nidos partieris. in vno eorum annotabis vocabula vsus quotidiani... in altero vocabula rara, exquisita. in alio idiomata & formulas loquendi, vel quas pauci intelligunt, uel quibus crebro est vtendum. in alio sententias. in alio festiue, in alio argute dicta. in alio prouerbia. in alio scriptorum difficiles, locos, & quæ alia tibi aut institutori tuo videbuntur.' For Vives's place in the commonplace tradition more generally, see Ann Moss, *Printed Common-Place Books and the Structuring of Renaissance Thought* (Oxford: Clarendon Press, 1996), 115–19.

to Valentianus, 'De nomine Britanniæ', 'Vestitus Britannorum', 'De linguâ veterum Britannorum', 'Milita Britannorum', 'Gentes, quae migravint in Britanniam', 'Matrimonia Britannorum', and 'Artes Britannorum'.[42] The fact that some of the categories are then blank—the 'Cocceius Nerua', 'Opilius Macrinus', and 'Moneta Britannorum' sections, for example—demonstrates that he must have drawn up his heads in advance, leaving the pages to be filled with pertinent quotations, as and when he came across them in the course of his reading.[43] Under his heads he included quotations and excerpts, but also, in a departure from the strict commonplace tradition, his own notes on the subjects and any comments on relevant sources.

Interspersed in these notes and commonplaces, there are also several occasions where Rogers recorded material remains. In the section devoted to the third-century emperor Publius Septimius Geta, for example, Rogers copied the following numismatic inscription: 'P. Septimius GETA. PIVS AVG. <..> BRIT'.[44] From a comment alongside, we discover that he took the inscription from the *Discorsi... sopra le medaglie* (1555), an important study of classical coins and medals by the Italian engraver Enea Vico.[45] Elsewhere in the commonplace book Rogers recorded an inscription from the time of Claudius, which he copied from Justus Lipsius, an inscription found on a bridge over the river Volturno at Capua, which attested that the emperor Antoninus Pius was known as Britannicus, and which he copied from Aldus Manutius, and an inscription which was in the possession of Lord Burghley, displayed in the garden at Burghley House in London, and which he had probably seen in person.[46] Burghley was one of the great collectors of antiquities in sixteenth-century England, and his antiquarian interests ran the whole gamut from pedigrees and genealogies—'what nobleman or gentleman and their dwellings, matches, and pedigrees did he not know', a flattering biographer asked—to coins and stones.[47] Another Roman inscription copied

---

[42] BL, MS Cotton Titus F. X, fos. 18^r–71^v, 14^r, 86^{r-v}, 88^r, 102^r, 104^r–105^r, 116^r, and 122^v respectively.

[43] Ibid., fos. 34^r, 43^r, and 89^r respectively.

[44] Ibid., fo. 42^v.

[45] Rogers evidently had access to the second edition of 1558, as his note makes clear: 'In commentario inscripto: (Discorsi dj. M. Ænea. Vico Parmigiano sopra le medeglie) impresso Venetijs anno 1558. hæc inscriptio numismati insculpta legitur'; cf. Enea Vico, *Discorsi... sopra le medaglie* (Venice, 1558), sig. K4^v. Rogers was not the only Tudor antiquary to show an interest in Vico's book. The British Library copy of the 1558 edition (class-mark 602.e.8) was once owned by the antiquary Humphrey Lhwyd, as the ownership inscription on its title page attests: 'Io sono Del humfredo lloyd. 1564'. Like Rogers, Lhwyd also attempted to compile an antiquarian survey of Britain. Later this book was owned by the great collector John, Lord Lumley, whose inscription is also on the title page, and with whom Lhwyd was closely associated, as he was married to Lumley's sister Barbara.

[46] BL, MS Cotton Titus F. X, fos. 25^v, 37^r, and 81^v.

[47] *The Anonymous Life of William Cecil, Lord Burghley*, ed. Alan G. R. Smith (Lampeter: Edwin Mellen Press, 1990), 126–7. This biography was written within five years of Burghley's death in 1598, and was probably the work of one of his secretaries.

Material Beginnings 35

by Rogers came from the town of Chester.[48] From the manuscript, we learn that this inscription was only discovered in August 1589. Since Rogers died shortly afterwards in February 1591, we may surmise from the note that he continued to copy and collect material for his antiquarian survey of Britain until the end of his life.

One of Rogers's poetic manuscripts also reveals the depth of his antiquarian interests. This volume came into the hands of Pierre Dupuy, the librarian of King Louis XIII, some time after Rogers's death, and it is now preserved among the Dupuy manuscripts (Dupuy 951) in the Bibliothèque nationale de France in Paris.[49] The volume is a large quarto of 334 leaves, and its contents, which are mostly in Rogers's hand, are highly miscellaneous.[50] Dupuy titled the volume 'Poemata variorum', and the manuscript contains a broad corpus of neo-Latin poetry, including works by Jean Dorat, George Buchanan, Hadrianus Junius, Jean Passerat, Michel de l'Hôpital, and Rogers himself. Most are familiar pieces, written in praise of Rogers's network of friends, or political verses relating to current affairs, especially in the Low Countries and France. As such, the volume speaks of the literary milieu in which Rogers found himself during his time in Paris, where many of the poets whose works he copied also resided. But scattered throughout the volume are entries which are less easily classified as 'Poemata'. Some of these, at least, are antiquarian in subject. Early in the volume, for example, there are entries that attest to Rogers's antiquarian reading. On one of the first leaves he copied a couple of maxims from Marcus Terentius Varro, the father of antiquarian studies, whilst shortly afterwards he copied a poem explaining the frontispiece to one of the Goltzius volumes, the *Fastos magistratuum et triumphorum romanorum ab urbe condita ad Augusti obitum* (1566).[51] Some of the poems which he copied were also antiquarian in subject, such as de l'Hôpital's verses on the great Provençal aqueduct, the Pont du Gard.[52] De l'Hôpital's short poem shares the frustration which the antiquaries so often expressed at the sight of ancient monuments. He berates iniquitous time ('iniqua dies') for concealing the author ('authorem') of so splendid a monument. This kind of rebuke of concealed histories and forgotten origins is something which we shall encounter again in this book; ancient monuments, to the antiquaries' great frustration, often lay just beyond their reach.

As always with Rogers, inscriptions seem to have caught his attention, and at various points in the manuscript he duly copied them down. His inscriptions

---

[48] BL, MS Cotton Titus F. X, fo. 112ʳ.
[49] On an early leaf Dupuy recorded the Rogers provenance in Greek: 'Κτῆμα Δανιῆλος Ῥωγηρίου Βρετάννου', BNF, Dupuy 951, fo. 5ʳ.
[50] For an item-by-item description, see Léon Dorez, *Catalogue de la collection Dupuy*, 2 vols. (Paris: E. Leroux, 1899), ii. 678–85.
[51] BNF, Dupuy 951, fos. 6ʳ, 14ʳ–15ʳ.
[52] Ibid., fo. 93ʳ: 'Admirandj operis monimenta superba inator / Aspicis, authorem pressit iniqua dies. / At tu dignus eras meliorj niuere, fato, / Dignus eras operj uel superesse tuo.'

include a pair of Roman epitaphs from the towns of Arles and Saint-Gilles in Provence, copied on consecutive leaves of the manuscript.[53] Since de l'Hôpital's poem is copied on the next leaf, and also concerns Roman remains from Provence, it is tempting to suppose a common origin for the three entries. At the very least, their grouping together implies some kind of internal coherence to the ostensibly miscellaneous contents of the manuscript. In the case of the inscription from Saint-Gilles, 'Epitaphium antiquum inuentum in parua ciuitate in Prouincia dicta Sainct Gilles', Rogers added an annotation, somewhat akin to the notes which he made on his copy of Henry of Huntingdon. This inscription came from the tomb of a man who had held the office of *administrator rationum*. Rogers underlined this phrase in the epitaph, added a note in explanation of the Roman title and office, and also gave its Greek equivalent. Other, more recent inscriptions copied by Rogers include a memorial at Fontainebleau, recording the recapture of Havre-de-Grâce by the French army in 1563, and a Latin inscription marking the capture of Gotha by the elector of Saxony in 1567.[54] Again, given their proximity in the manuscript, these inscriptions may have come from a common source.

What Rogers intended to do with his notes and collections is a matter of conjecture. His letters suggest that he had grand, if abortive, publication plans. As early as 1570 he had written to Ortelius about a work on the customs and laws of the ancient Britons, 'de Veterum Britannorum moribus et legibus', which, from the tone of his letter, he had evidently finished.[55] By its subject matter alone, this work must have had some relation to his 'Antiquæ Britannæ obseruationes', although by the time of his death the scope of his commonplace book was considerably larger. Shortly afterwards, he also began to voice his plans for the publication of a work on the history of Ireland. In a letter of February 1575 he claimed that friends had long solicited him to commit this work to the press, whilst two years later he wrote to Janus Dousa, asking him to contribute prefatory epigrams and odes.[56] The following year he even had a printer lined up, the famous Wechel press at Frankfurt-am-Main, as another letter to Dousa attests.[57] But this work never appeared; all that survives today is a poem, 'Elegia, quae Hiberniae descriptionem...continet', written during his visit to Ireland in 1572, which serves as a prospectus for what the longer work might have

---

[53] BNF, Dupuy 951, fos. 90^r–91^r.

[54] Ibid., fos. 192^v, 193^v.

[55] Daniel Rogers to Abraham Ortelius, 15 Feb. 1570, BL, MS Harley 6990, fo. 96^r: 'Scripsi tamen de Veterum Britannorum moribus et legibus, commentarium, qui me egregie exercuit, uideorque mihj elaborasse aliquid quod doctis etiam placere possit.'

[56] Daniel Rogers to Hadrianus Junius, 4 Feb. 1575, in *Hadr. Junii epistolæ, quibus accedit ejusdem vita & oratio de artium liberalium dignitate* (Dordrecht, 1652), sigs. 2D2^v–2D3^r; Daniel Rogers to Janus Dousa, 3 May 1577, BL, MS Burney 370, fo. 11^r.

[57] Daniel Rogers to Janus Dousa, 16 Jan. 1578, BL, MS Burney 370, fo. 12^{r–v}. On the Wechel press, see R. J. W. Evans, *The Wechel Presses: Humanism and Calvinism in Central Europe, 1572–1627* (Oxford: Past and Present Society, 1975).

resembled.[58] And his work on Britain did not even get that far. Despite amassing a vast quantity of germane material, and apparently completing one part of it, he seems to have been unable to transform the whole into a coherent narrative. For all his good intentions and sincerity of purpose, Rogers was crippled by the scale of his task. His antiquarian survey of Britain never went beyond the first stage of collection.

ANTIQUARIAN DIALOGUE

The examples of Leland, Erdeswicke, and Rogers all, in their different ways, illustrate the importance of material remains to antiquaries of the age. Leland found in them a means of buttressing newly threatened historical and national traditions, whilst Rogers and Erdeswicke both had their attention arrested by these physical traces of the past. But none of them fully realized the historical potential of these remains, nor were they entirely successful in their use of this kind of evidence. Leland, in his defence of King Arthur, was hampered by the matter at hand and compromised by his larger vision of national history. Rogers, for his part, seems to have been overwhelmed by the evidence itself, leaving it to later scholars, such as Camden, to make use of it, whilst Erdeswicke only ever sought to report what he had found.[59] In the next part of this chapter, I turn to an antiquarian writer who was more successful in his use of material remains, who both offered a more sophisticated rationale for their usefulness as evidence and, through the formal, dialogic qualities of his writing, contributed to the development of a broader antiquarian methodology. That writer was the Canterbury schoolmaster John Twyne.

Today, Twyne is a little-known figure and is barely mentioned in modern scholarship at all. Yet in his own day he was an individual of some importance. In Canterbury, for example, where he lived from 1526, after graduating from Oxford, until his death in 1581, he held a number of prominent positions. He was the first headmaster of the King's School; he sat as an MP for the city in 1553–4; and he was mayor of the city in the same year.[60] He was also a scholar of some repute, especially in historical studies, and the scion of an important antiquarian dynasty. His son Thomas was a collector and bibliophile, whilst

---

[58] See J. A. van Dorsten, *Poets, Patrons, and Professors: Sir Philip Sidney, Daniel Rogers, and the Leiden Humanists* (Leiden: Leiden University Press, 1962), 22–3.

[59] After Rogers's death, Camden inherited his notebooks and made ample use of them in his own antiquarian researches. See Levy, 'Daniel Rogers as Antiquary', 461; and van Dorsten, *Poets, Patrons, and Professors*, 20.

[60] Twyne's fortunes took a turn for the worse after the accession of Elizabeth I in 1558, as he faced allegations of drunkenness, a charge of harbouring a familiar spirit, 'a black thing, like a great rugged dog, which would dance about the house and hurl fire about the house', and constant suspicion of recusancy. For a biography of Twyne, see G. H. Martin, 'Twyne, John (*c.*1505–1581)', *ODNB*, accessed 3 Feb. 2006.

his grandson Brian was a well-known antiquary in early seventeenth-century Oxford.[61] Brian Twyne wrote the first printed history of the university; he was the first keeper of the university archives; and, like his father, he was a collector and bibliophile, whose library contained a number of important antiquarian titles.[62]

John Twyne too was a collector, and, like many of his contemporaries, his antiquarianism appears to have stemmed, at least in part, from this interest. He was, for instance, a significant figure in the preservation of medieval manuscripts after the dispersal of the monastic libraries. His own collection included at least ten manuscripts from the Cathedral Priory in Canterbury and a similar number from St Augustine's Abbey in the city.[63] He also acted as an agent for Matthew Parker, Elizabeth's first archbishop of Canterbury, and perhaps the pre-eminent collector of the day. Twyne sent Parker various manuscripts from Canterbury, including a copy of the 'Itinerarium Regis Ricardi', a Latin prose narrative of the Third Crusade, which has the following note on its flyleaf: 'Sent from Mr. Twyne'.[64] But Twyne's antiquarian interests were not just limited to collecting. He was also the author of a well-regarded study of the early history of Britain, published after his death by his son Thomas: *De rebus Albionicis, Britannicis atque Anglicis, Commentariorum libri duo* (1590).[65] This work takes the form of a dialogue, set in the summer residence of the last abbot of St Augustine's, John Foche, in the village of Sturry. It purportedly records a conversation between Foche, Twyne, John Dygon, the last prior of St Augustine's, and Nicholas Wotton, who would later become dean of Canterbury in 1541.

The dialogue is divided into two books. Book 1 is primarily a rebuttal of the Trojan origins of the Britons, another historical tradition which derived from

---

[61] For Twyne's family, see Walter H. Godfrey, 'Thomas and Brian Twyne', *Sussex Notes and Queries*, 2 (1929), 197–201, and 3 (1930), 40–2, 82–4; and Strickland Gibson, 'Brian Twyne', *Oxoniensia*, 5 (1940), 94–114.

[62] Books in Twyne's library included Aelfric's *A Saxon treatise concerning the Old and New Testament* (1623), the third edition of Camden's *Reges, reginæ, nobiles, et alij in ecclesia collegiata B. Petri Westmonasterij sepulti* (1606), his father's translation of Dionysius Periegetes' *The surueye of the world* (1572), Leland's *Assertio inclytissimi Arturij Regis Britanniae* (1544), Lhwyd's translation of Caradoc of Llancarfan's *The historie of Cambria* (1584), Richard Verstegan's *A Restitution of Decayed Intelligence* (1605), and Ausonius Popma's Franeker edition of Varro's *Fragmenta* (1589); see R. F. Ovenell, 'Brian Twyne's Library', *Oxford Bibliographical Society Publications*, 4 (1950), 3–42.

[63] See Andrew G. Watson, 'John Twyne of Canterbury (d. 1581) as a Collector of Medieval Manuscripts: A Preliminary Investigation', *The Library*, NS 8 (1986), 133–51; and Nigel Ramsay, 'The Cathedral Archives and Library', in Patrick Collinson, Nigel Ramsay, and Margaret Sparks (eds.), *A History of Canterbury Cathedral* (Oxford: Oxford University Press, 1995), 341–407 at 372–5.

[64] Now Corpus Christi College, Cambridge, MS 129; see May McKisack, *Medieval History in the Tudor Age* (Oxford: Clarendon Press, 1971), 28–9.

[65] On his death, a number of Twyne's manuscripts passed to his son, including a copy of *De rebus Albionicis*. In the dedicatory epistle to Robert Sackville, which he added to the work, Thomas Twyne explains the circumstances surrounding its publication; see John Twyne, *De rebus Albionicis, Britannicis atque Anglicis, Commentariorum libri duo* (London, 1590), sig. $A3^{r-v}$.

Geoffrey of Monmouth.[66] Twyne's approach, as befits the good humanist that he was, is essentially philological. He compares the Galfridian history with what he considers to be authoritative—that is to say, classical—sources, and in this way attempts to show the anachronisms of the former. Occasionally, though, he has recourse to other forms of evidence. His principal speaker, Foche, for example, notes that the Britons' ancestors left material footprints (*vestigia*) in the landscape, an idea which, as we shall see in Chapter 2, became increasingly important for antiquarian attempts to read topography and reconstruct the past. These footprints include ramparts, castles, subterranean hollows, stone monuments, and even giants' rings.[67] Book 1 also includes Twyne's most significant and innovative argument: his suggestion that the island of Britain once formed part of the European mainland.[68] 'At first, this land, which is now an island, was joined to the continent,' Foche asserts, 'and it was a dry or terrestrial journey from here to there across an isthmus, in the same way as it is now from the rest of Greece into the Peloponnese.'[69] In keeping with the philological approach of the book as a whole, Foche's evidence is primarily textual. First, he cites '*Aristotelis rationes*', probably a reference to Aristotle's discussion in the *Meteorologica* of shifts in the seabed.[70] Then, he cites more specific textual evidence in the form of the gloss of Servius Grammaticus on Virgil's *Eclogues*, i. 66: 'DIVISOS quia olim iuncta fuit orbi terrarum Britannia: est enim insula reposita in Oceano septentrionali.'[71] But he also offers a more obviously antiquarian defence, directing his listeners to similar topography, to the examples of other places (*aliorum locorum exempla*). He likens Britain to a range of Mediterranean islands, whose rupture from the European landmass is explicitly documented in classical sources. For Twyne, therefore, comparative geography helps to solve a historical enigma, the question of the origins of the first inhabitants of Britain, complementing his literary evidence from Aristotle and Servius Grammaticus.

---

[66] According to Geoffrey, Aeneas's great-grandson Brutus brought a party of Trojans to Britain after the fall of Troy and colonized the island; see *The History of the Kings of Britain*, trans. Lewis Thorpe (Harmondsworth: Penguin, 1966), i. 3–i. 15.

[67] Twyne, *De rebus Albionicis*, sig. E6ᵛ.

[68] This idea gained further currency at the beginning of the 17th c., when Richard Verstegan expounded it at greater length; see his *A Restitution of Decayed Intelligence: In antiquities. Concerning the most noble and renovvmed English nation* (London, 1605), 96–100.

[69] Twyne, *De rebus Albionicis*, sig. B5ʳ: 'Principiò, hæc quæ modò insula est, terra continenti iuncta, pars *Galliæ* fuit, siccusque transitus hinc indè per isthmum, quomodò nùnc ex reliqua *Græcia* in *Peloponesum* seu *Moream*, & contrà, erat.'

[70] Ibid., sig. C8ᵛ; cf. Aristotle, *Meteorologica*, trans. H. D. P. Lee (Loeb Classical Library; Cambridge, Mass.: Harvard University Press, 1962; first published in this edition 1952), 353ª19–353ª24.

[71] Servius Grammaticus, *In Vergilii carmina commentarii*, ed. Georg Thilo and Hermann Hagen, 3 vols. (Leipzig: Teubner, 1881–7), iii. 15: 'DIVIDED because Britain was once joined to the rest of the world: it is now an island lying in the northern Ocean'; see also Virgil, *Eclogues*, trans. H. Rushton Fairclough (Loeb Classical Library; Cambridge, Mass.: Harvard University Press, 1999; first published in this edition 1916), i. 66: 'et penitus toto divisos orbe Britannos'.

In Book 2 Twyne turns more explicitly to antiquarian arguments. Here, he supplements, and occasionally replaces, his philological approach with material remains, with unearthed artefacts and objects. Thus, when his speakers discuss giants' bones, a subject of considerable interest in early modern England, Wotton recalls a find in the Kentish village of Barham.[72] A funerary urn was unearthed there, filled with prodigious bones and massive armour:

> At the time of our Henry, just a few years ago, . . . I remember that a certain mound at Barham was excavated. . . . A huge urn, full of ash and the fragments of enormous bones, along with bronze and iron helmets and shields of unusual size, almost consumed by rust, was unearthed. But there was no inscription to explain its name, no record of its date or its fortune.[73]

Twyne's reason for citing the story is to demonstrate that there were indeed once giants in Britain. The urn is presented as material and archaeological evidence, a physical trace of these monstrous ancestors. But Twyne's description of the find is not just documentary. It also reflects his sense of the evanescence of historical memory and awareness of the destructiveness of time. It is hard not to hear a note of antiquarian regret in his description of gigantic bones reduced to splinters and dust, and of bronze and iron helmets consumed with rust. His words echo the antiquaries' unequal struggle with time, and help to explain the persistence of their urge to conserve any traces that have survived. His regret is then channelled through the urn itself. Despite surviving the passage of time, the urn remains silent. Uninscribed and bare, it fails to communicate its own history, and so resists the antiquary's scrutiny. The promise of the defiance of time is disappointed; the gigantic history of the urn is forgotten, as its name, date, and fortune remain hidden.

When Twyne turned to Roman remains, the situation was rather different. Later in Book 2 Foche is asked to comment on the extent of the Roman occupation of the island. He answers in two ways. First, he surveys the literary evidence, primarily Caesar's *Commentaries*, but also later authorities such as Eutropius and Aelius Spartianus' *Life of Hadrian*, summarizing their arguments and collating their narratives. But then he turns to material remains, to traces of the Roman occupation which can still be seen the length and breadth of Britain. These traces include roads, bridges, and ramparts, remains which, in Foche's words, are incontrovertible proof of the Roman preference for public magnificence over private luxury.[74] For Foche, there is no better answer to the question.

---

[72] On giants and their bones, see Daniel Woolf, 'Of Danes and Giants: Popular Beliefs about the Past in Early Modern England', *Dalhousie Review*, 71 (1991), 166–209.

[73] Twyne, *De rebus Albionicis*, sigs. F5ᵛ–F6ʳ: '*Henrici* verò huius nostri temporibus, paucis elapsis annis, . . . recordor, vt agger quidam *Baramdunæ* effoderetur . . . . ingens vrna cinere ossiumque maximorum fragmentis plena, cùm galeis ac clypeis æreis & ferreis rubigine penè consumptis inusitatæ magnitudinis, eruta est.'

[74] Ibid., sig. L4ʳ: 'Hinc *Romanis* monumentis adornata *Britannia*, non tàm priuatis ædificiis Equestris virorum ordine, quàm etiàm ídque imprimis omnis generis ad defensionem propugnaculis,

Moreover, there is no clearer evidence that the Romans held sway over the whole island, he goes on, than that provided by their coins, inscriptions, and sepulchres.[75] In a moment of archaeological candour he speaks here not only of past discoveries, but also of future unearthings ('hodiéque effosis, atque posthàc effodiendis'). The strength of archaeological evidence is unquestioned; Twyne evidently believed that material remains held the key to the Roman history of Britain. He evidently also believed in excavation, in searching the soil for buried evidence.

Roman remains, as we have seen, were especially attractive to the antiquaries. As the example of Twyne shows, the corroborative power of material evidence in general also tended to excite them. Roman Britain consequently excited them very much because it yielded such rich pickings. In contrast to the Barham urn, which resisted interpretation, and became a vehicle for Twyne to lament the limits of historical knowledge, Roman traces (the bridges, roads, and ramparts) were easily interpreted. Here, material evidence could take its place easily and comfortably alongside other forms of record and testimony. For Twyne, whose purpose was essentially recuperative, this resulted in an overwhelming focus on the Roman origins of Britain. Despite the broad promise of its title, *De rebus Albionicis*, like so many antiquarian books of the day, is first and foremost a Roman history.

One of the curious aspects of Twyne's work is the attention given to its date and setting. In its published form at least, the work probably dates from the 1560s, as it opens with an apostrophe to Thomas Twyne, and refers to him as a current student at Oxford.[76] Since Thomas became a scholar of Corpus Christi College on 6 July 1560, graduated BA on 18 April 1564, was elected a fellow of Corpus Christi on 9 November 1564, and proceeded MA on 10 July 1568, the work was presumably written in that decade. But as the identities of its speakers illustrate, and its allusions to recorded events attest, Twyne set the work considerably earlier. The best clue to this is given at the beginning of the dialogue, where we learn that Dygon and Wotton have just returned from accompanying the Spanish humanist Juan Luís Vives on a journey from Louvain to Oxford.[77] This refers to an actual journey that Vives had made in 1523, when he travelled to Oxford to teach at the newly founded Corpus Christi College.[78] Given the exigencies of early modern travel, and the fact that the dialogue takes place in the

---

pontibus ac vijs etiàm Prætorijs & Militaribus, mira industria ac immensis sumptibus positis. Populus enim *Romanus* non priuatim luxuriam, sed publicam magnificentiam amabat.'

[75] Ibid., sig. L4ᵛ: '*Romani* imperij per vniuersam hanc insulam eiúsque locos numero penè infinitos diffusi, nullum est argumentum manifestius, quàm quòd à *Romanorum* publicis ac priuatis ædificiis conspectis, numismatibus inuentis, inscriptionis perlectis, sepulturis multis iam retroactis sæculis, hodiéque effosis, atque posthàc effodiendis, peti solet.'

[76] Ibid., sigs B1ʳ–B2ᵛ.

[77] Ibid., sig. B3ʳ.

[78] Brian P. Copenhaver and Charles B. Schmitt, *Renaissance Philosophy* (Oxford and New York: Oxford University Press, 1992), 201.

garden of Foche's summer residence, we may infer the summer of 1524 as the likeliest date.

There are at least two explanations why Twyne might have wanted to evoke such a specific historical setting for his dialogue. First, as Arthur Ferguson has argued, there is every reason to believe that there was a vibrant antiquarian circle in 1520s Canterbury, and that Twyne's dialogue does accurately reflect the activities and concerns of these men.[79] In the introduction Twyne himself recollects that he had often heard Foche, Dygon, and Wotton dispute antiquity in this way.[80] By the same token, when Foche meticulously catalogues his collection of Roman artefacts near the end of the dialogue, there is no reason to question the accuracy of what he lists.[81] Although Twyne is unlikely to be documenting an actual conversation, as Foche would surely not have catalogued his collection in such a laborious fashion for scholars who would already have been familiar with it, the level of detail and precision suggests that Twyne does accurately describe its objects. A second reason for Twyne to insist on the chronological setting of his dialogue may have been to emphasize that the events described in the work took place before the dissolution of the monasteries. In this light, *De rebus Albionicis* becomes intellectually, as well as chronologically, retrospective, the work of an older scholar looking back on the halcyon days of his youth, when a particular mode of historical exchange, centred on the chapter of Canterbury Cathedral, and specific historical repositories, in the shape of the monastic houses and their libraries, flourished.

Moreover, there is one place in the dialogue where Twyne does seem to comment more particularly upon the historical and cultural loss following the Dissolution, albeit speaking there in a coded way. This point occurs in Book 2, when Foche recounts a destructive fire which had broken out in the prior's library at St Augustine's and destroyed most of its contents.[82] The one book whose loss he laments by name is that antiquarian grail, that prize for all Renaissance collectors and bibliophiles: a manuscript of Cicero's *De republica*. Since the *De republica* was essentially lost, surviving only as minor fragments until the nineteenth century, when Cardinal Angelo Mai, prefect of the Vatican Library,

---

[79] Arthur B. Ferguson, 'John Twyne: A Tudor Humanist and the Problem of a Legend', *Journal of British Studies*, 9 (1969), 24–44 at 26.

[80] Twyne, *De rebus Albionicis*, sig. B3^r: 'sæpiùs de omni antiquitate disputantes audiuerim'.

[81] Ibid., sigs. L4^v–L5^r: 'Quorum generum non pauca sunt mihi in manibus, videlicèt, lateres *Romani*: numismata aurea, argentea, ærea: lapides ac cera cùm incisis epigraphis, ac idolis: vrnæ maiores ac minores: lampades combustili materia plenæ: vitrea aquata substantia, redolente, lustrali, lachrimosa, vèl ichorosa repleta: diuersarúmque itèm formarum fictilia, quæ in antiquitatis studiosorum gratiam conserus omnia.'

[82] Ibid., sig. I1^{r-v}: 'Quorum tamèn, meo iudicio, nullum fuit luctuosius, quàm quod proximè, atque annos non ità ante multos quidèm, in ædibus Christo sacris exortum est, quo prætèr alia ædificia, ipsa celeberrima bibliotheca à Theodoro Archiepiscopo instituta, à multis benemerentibus amplificata, ac posteà ab *Henrico Chichleo* successore consummata, exarsit, ibíque intèr multa librorum millia, alterum, pròh dolor, exemplar diuini illius operis *Marci Ciceronis* de Republica, flammis exusta est.'

discovered a much more substantial text as a palimpsest under a copy of Augustine's commentary on the Psalms, Foche's comment is striking.[83] It is also uncorroborated, and it is therefore hard to escape the suspicion that Twyne is not speaking directly here. In bemoaning the loss of a mythical Ciceronian manuscript, he seems also to be commenting on the dreadful consequences of the Dissolution. To readers in the know—that is to say, those of an antiquarian bent, familiar with both the transmission of classical texts and the bibliographical treasures formerly preserved in the houses—Foche's comment becomes less fanciful. An elusive classical manuscript stands as a microcosm for the lost libraries of medieval England, whilst an incendiary accident stands for the altogether more culpable actions that caused their dispersal.

In choosing to write his work as a dialogue, Twyne invokes a literary form well suited to the multifariousness of the antiquarian project. Foche may be his best-informed and principal speaker, but the dialogic form ensures that other voices are also heard. This seems particularly appropriate for a scholarly endeavour that sought to place all kinds of things side by side with different things from different eras. Twyne's form lends itself to that strand of antiquarian thought which led ineluctably to the diversity of antiquarian books, that strand which, historiographically speaking, sought to bring a range of approaches, palaeographical, philological, and archaeological, rather than a single preferred method, to bear on historical problems. Moreover, the form also lends itself to the idea of discovery, which was equally important to the antiquarian project. Foche's interlocutors speak with him to discover the origins and early history of the Britons. In the context of this chapter, therefore, material remains take their place alongside other forms of proof and evidence, and all have a role to play in the antiquary's unearthing of the past.

LAYERS OF HISTORY

Thus far, this chapter has focused on argument, on the ways in which sixteenth-century antiquaries interpreted and made use of material remains as testimony. In the last part of the chapter, I turn from evidence to excavation, for although archaeological discoveries continued in the main to be 'the gifts of fortune', the process of their discovery did not go unremarked. For John Stow, for example, whose *A Survey of London* (1598) looks into the soil as well as across it, the possibility of what was buried beneath was a powerful stimulus. Stow seems to have realized that traces of the past might exist beneath the surface as well as in books and objects open to view. Excavation raised the possibility that these traces could be brought before an onlooker's eyes. On a number of occasions, therefore,

---

[83] For an account of Mai's discovery, see the introduction to Cicero, *De re publica librorum sex quae supersunt*, ed. Carlo Pascal (Turin: I. B. Paravia, 1916), pp. x–xii.

he seeks to emulate the excavatory process in the *Survey*, to conjure memories of the city's past by bringing to his readers' attention bodies and objects previously buried in the London soil. In documenting actual excavations, he re-enacts those events, repeating the initial thrill of each archaeological discovery, and thereby allows the past to commune directly and repeatedly with the present. For Stow, the antiquary really could unearth the past, and antiquarian writing really could afford it presence. Layers of history were easily discovered; it was the task of the antiquary and topographer to peel them back.

Throughout the *Survey* Stow records objects unearthed in the London soil. In the Lime Street Ward, for example, he notes the discovery of an hearth decorated with tiles, found by workmen as they attempted to erect a water pump:

In the yeare 1576. partly at the charges of the parish of saint *Andrew*, and partly at the charges of the chamber of London, a water pompe was raised in the high street of Limestreete warde, neare vnto Limestreet corner: for the placing of the which pumpe, hauing broken vp the ground they were forced to digge more then two fadome deepe before they came to any maine ground, where they found a harth made of Britain, or rather Roman Tile, euery Tile halfe yarde square, and about two inches thick.[84]

As well as locating the find geographically, 'neare vnto Limestreet corner', Stow's description also locates it within the soil, 'two fadome deepe', thus establishing a vertical, historical axis in addition to the more familiar horizontal, geographical one. The find is significant enough for Stow also to detail the tiles themselves; in giving their measurements he can satisfy any reader's curiosity and also establish his own documentary credentials. Another, less easily verifiable find reported in the *Survey* is the cache of oxen's skulls discovered when foundations were dug for a new chapel at St Paul's in the fourteenth century. With the disadvantage of greater historical distance, Stow's description is less precise than that of the Lime Street find: 'Some haue noted that in digging the foundation of this new worke, namely of a chappell on the south side of Powles church, there were found more then an hundred scalpes of Oxen or Kine, in the yeare one thousand three hundred and sixeteene.' He adds that this find has been used to defend a particular historical belief, as he notes that it 'confirmed greatly the opinion of those which haue reported that of olde time there had beene a Temple of *Iupiter*, and that there was dayly sacrifice of beastes'.[85] From the second edition of the *Survey* (1603), we learn that Stow's source for this bovine discovery is one William Paston.[86]

---

[84] John Stow, *A Survey of London*, ed. Charles Lethbridge Kingsford, 2 vols. (Oxford: Clarendon Press, 1908), i. 160.
[85] Ibid. 333.
[86] John Stow, *A Survay of London. Conteyning the Originall, Antiquity, Increase, Moderne estate, and description of that City, Written in the yeare 1598* (London, 1603), sig. Y8ʳ.

In places Stow imagines a parallel city buried beneath the streets of London, with the same water-channels, the same pavements, and so on. One such place is Cheapside:

Thomas Tomlinson causing in the high streete of Cheape a Vaulte to be digged, and made, there was found at fifteene foote deepe, a fayre pauement like vnto that aboue ground, and at the further end at the chanell, was founde a tree sawed into fiue steppes, which was to steppe ouer some brooke running out of the west towardes Walbrooke, and vpon the edge of the saide Brooke, as it seemeth, there were found lying along the bodies of two great trees, the endes whereof were then sawed off.[87]

Taken on its own, the description is merely documentary, recording what Thomas Tomlinson found beneath the street. But in the larger context of the *Survey* it takes on a greater significance, since it also illustrates the imaginary potential of the history buried in the soil and raises the possibility that the past may be restored by digging in that soil. Stow thus presents the ground as a form of muddy palimpsest on which the city's histories have been inscribed and thereby introduces the idea of the stratigraphic nature of the earth.

Stow returns to this idea later in the *Survey*, when he describes a similar multilayered discovery at the end of Chancery Lane. 'On this north side of Fleet-streete, in the yeare of Christ 1595,' he writes, 'I obserued, that when the laborers had broken vp the pauement, from agaynst Chancerie lanes end, vp towards Saint *Dunstons* Church, and had digged foure foote deepe, they found one other pauement of hard stone, more sufficient then the first, and therefore harder to bee broken.' In turn, below this pavement 'they found in the made ground, pyles of Tymber, driuen verie thicke, and almost close togither, the same being blacke as pitch or coale, and many of them rotten as earth, which prooueth that the ground there (as sundrie other places of the Citie) haue beene a Marish or full of springs'.[88] The earlier layers of history may have disappeared from the surface, but they can be restored to view when pavements are broken or (in the case of the St Paul's cache) foundations dug. As an antiquary and topographer, Stow also uses the buried timber as evidence for the city's former landscape. If he admits an element of doubt about his historical explanation for the skulls buried beneath St Paul's, the rotten timber under Fleet Street and Chancery Lane 'prooueth' that there were once marshes or springs beneath this part of the city.

---

[87] Stow, *Survey*, ed. Kingsford, i. 345. Stow's description is copied almost word for word from a note sent to him by a friend: 'The Vaute beinge digged fifteene foote deepe there was found a faire pauement like vnto that of cheapside now, and at the farther end of the vaute in Cheapside at a channell there was found a tree sawed into fiue steppes w*h*ich was (as it should seeme) to steppe over somme brooke and vppon the edge, of the said brooke, (as it seemeth), there were found lying along the bodies of two greate trees the ends whereof were then sawed of' ('A Description of a Vaute made for Thomas Tomlinson at the Corner of Bredstreete in Cheapside', BL, MS Harley 367, fo. 47ʳ).

[88] Ibid. ii. 43.

Stow's closest attention to material remains, however, comes in his report of the great Spitalfields find of 1576. Labourers quarrying for clay in Spitalfields had discovered a Roman cemetery that year; Stow's report is the only extant record, although other accounts were apparently published at the time.[89] Evidently the haul was a rich one, for he lists burial urns filled with ashes and coins, jugs, dishes and statues, stone coffins, skulls and bones, and a number of extremely large nails. He pays particular attention to the funerary urns:

> Many earthen pots called *Vrnæ*, were found full of Ashes, and burnt bones of men, to wit, of the Romanes that inhabited here: for it was the custome of the Romanes to burne their dead, to put their Ashes in an *Vrna*, and then burie the same with certaine ceremonies, in some field appoynted for that purpose, neare vnto their Citie: euerie of these pots had in them with the Ashes of the dead, one peece of Copper mony, with the inscription of the Emperour then raigning: some of them were of *Claudius*, some of *Vespasian*, some of *Nero*, of *Anthonius Pius*, of *Traianus*, and others.[90]

Stow's account of the urns moves from the straightforwardly descriptive, as he recalls their appearance and contents, to the interpretative, as he seeks to restore them to their proper historical context. First, he identifies the urns as Roman by drawing on his knowledge of Roman funerary custom and cemetery practice. Then, he confirms his identification by numismatic evidence. The coins found in the urns allow Stow to date them, since each coin bears the inscription of whichever emperor was reigning at the time. Other objects found at the site and described by Stow include pots 'made of a white earth with long necks, and handels, like to our stone Iugges', 'diuerse dishes and cups of a fine red coloured earth, which shewed outwardly such a shining smoothenesse, as if they had beene of Currall', 'lampes of white earth and red, artificially wrought with diuerse antiques about them', 'three or foure Images made of white earth, about a span long each of them', and a curious-sounding vessel that Stow reserved for himself, 'made in the shape of a Hare, squatted vpon her legs, and betweene her eares is the mouth'.[91] Stow does not miss the irony that 'many of those pots and glasses were broken in cutting of the clay, so that few were taken vp whole'. The very act of excavation, which brought the hidden layers to the surface and into the present, is in its own way destructive.

Having described the urns, jugs, dishes, and lamps, Stow switches his attention to a more recent layer of history:

> There hath also beene found in the same field diuers coffins of stone, containing the bones of men: these I suppose to bee the burials of some especiall persons, in time of the

---

[89] According to the 18th-c. shoemaker and antiquary John Bagford, the discovery was also reported in a small quarto; see 'A Letter to the Publisher, Written by the Ingenious Mr. John Bagford, in which are many Curious Remarks Relating to the City of London, and some Things about Leland', in Leland, *De rebus Britannicis collectanea*, i, p. lxii.
[90] Stow, *Survey*, ed. Kingsford, i. 168.
[91] Ibid. 168–9.

Brytons, or Saxons, after that the Romanes had left to gouerne here. Moreover there were also found the sculs and bones of men without coffins, or rather whose coffins (being of great timber) were consumed.[92]

Stow's description of the skulls and bones is curiously matter of fact. Despite being confronted with such visible signs of mortality, he is unreflective; he offers none of the familiar comments on time, preservation, or loss that we associate with the antiquaries. In this instance, his purpose is strictly documentary. But this should not be seen as a failure on his part. Contemporaries could be similarly matter of fact when confronted with bodies and bones. Oglander, for example, with whom this chapter began, was equally unreflective when he recorded the tale of a mysterious petrified body from Crete. 'One Captain Stevens of London, one that had been in the straits 34 times,' he writes in one of his notebooks, 'told me that one time being on the Isle of Candy in digging of a fountain for fresh water there were found the bones and head of a man that was, with time and the coldness of the water, converted to marble.' At first it was unclear 'whether it was natural or artificial but, at last, it did appear to be natural, the teeth, the temples and parts plainly appearing'. Having reported the story, Oglander adds comments of his own. For him, the mystery is not the petrified body itself, 'Of things converted to stones we have had divers examples', but 'how the body of a man should come to lie so deep under the earth'. His interest is stratigraphic, in the layers buried in the soil. He offers none of the reflections on preservation or loss that a find such as a petrified body might lead us to expect. His curiosity is directed towards explanation, as he seeks a natural cause for a strange phenomenon. He is, however, defeated in this search, admitting that 'many strange things happeneth and are found in the bowels of the earth, far beyond any human understanding'.[93]

Stow's interest in urns and bones reflects the focus of a considerable body, so to speak, of early modern scholarship. Ancient funerary practice was a subject of great interest at the time, and pots and urns attracted widespread attention.[94] In 1621, for example, the French antiquary Jean Guénebauld published an extended dissertation on the subject in his *Le Réveil de Chyndonax*. This book reports the discovery in November 1598 of a splendid vase, unearthed in a vineyard belonging to Guénebauld in the district of Poussot half a league from Dijon.[95]

---

[92] Ibid. 169.
[93] Oglander, *A Royalist's Notebook: The Commonplace Book of Sir John Oglander Kt. of Nunwell*, ed. Francis Bamford (London: Constable, 1936), 76–7.
[94] See the discussion in Schnapp, *The Discovery of the Past*, 145–8.
[95] News of Guénebauld's discovery had earlier spread through its inclusion in Jan Gruter's *Inscriptiones antiquae totius orbi Romani* (Heidelberg, 1602–3), 1159. Gruter attracted Guénebauld's ire, as he mistook the location of the discovery as Autun rather than Dijon; see Guénebauld's sharp riposte in *Le Réveil de Chyndonax Prince des Vacies Druydes Celtiques Diionois, auec la saincteté, religion, & diuersité des ceremonies obseruees aux anciennes sepultures* (Dijon, 1621), 12.

On the base of the vase there was an inscription in Greek, carved in two concentric circles. From this inscription Guénebauld deduced that the vase was the funerary urn of Chyndonax, archpriest of the Celtic druids. As well as reporting the find, Guénebauld's book also surveys the funerary practices of various ancient peoples, including the Hebrews, Egyptians, Ethiopians, Persians, Scythians, Indians, Greeks, Romans, Germans, and Gauls. A few years earlier Johannes Kirchmann had also published a study of this subject, offering a comprehensive account of Roman funerary practice in his *De funeribus Romanorum libri quattuor* (1605). Kirchmann relies primarily on the evidence of classical authors, although he does occasionally record inscriptions and also indulges in the odd etymological speculation. His four books address respectively: the origins of Roman funerary rites and observances, and the preparation of bodies prior to the funeral; the *elatio*, or the bearing of a body to a grave; the *sepultura*, the burial itself; and the forms of memorial and remembrance of the dead current amongst the Romans. His account is compendious, but for impatient readers he also includes an appendix, 'BREVIARIUM OPERIS', consisting of four synoptic tables which anatomize and summarize the contents of the books.[96] Both works, incidentally, were known in seventeenth-century England. Thomas Browne, for example, refers to Guénebauld's discovery in his 'Brampton Urnes' and quotes from Kirchmann in one of his commonplace books.[97]

If Stow's description of the Spitalfields find is an offshoot of this scholarly tradition, it is also a rebuttal of popular misconceptions about the discovery. Stow also reports that enormous iron nails were found at Spitalfields, 'being each of them as bigge as a mans finger, and a quarter of a yard long, the heads two inches ouer'. These, he adds, 'were more wondred at then the reste of thinges there found', and they seem to have generated a great deal of lurid interest amongst the London public. Rumour had it that 'the men there buried were murdered by driuing those nayles into their heads'. Stow himself doubts this, pointing out that 'a smaller naile would more aptly serue to so bad a purpose, and a more secret place would lightly be imployed for their buriall'. His own explanation is more sober and convincing, based as it is on careful observation:

But to set downe what I haue obserued concerning this matter, I there behelde the bones of a man lying (as I noted) the heade North, the feete South, and round about him, as thwart his head, along both his sides, and thwart his feete, such nailes were found, wherefore I coniectured them to be the nailes of his coffin, which had beene a trough

---

[96] Johannes Kirchmann, *De funeribus Romanorum libri quattuor* (Hamburg, 1605), sigs. 2V3ᵛ–2V5ᵛ.
[97] Thomas Browne, 'Brampton Urns', in *The Works of Sir Thomas Browne*, ed. Geoffrey Keynes, 4 vols. (London: Faber & Faber, 1964; first published 1928), i. 236; Graham Parry, 'In the Land of Moles and Pismires: Thomas Browne's Antiquarian Writings', in Neil Rhodes (ed.), *English Renaissance Prose: History, Language, and Politics* (Tempe, Ariz.: Medieval & Renaissance Texts & Studies, 1997), 247–58 at 250.

cut out of some great tree, and the same couered with a planke, of a great thicknesse, fastned with such nayles.[98]

With his three verbs of observation Stow's description of the nails has an authority that the 'many opinions of men' can never have. His interpretation is based on what he has seen and what he can deduce from that: the rumours, on the other hand, merely reflect a popular fascination with gruesome murder. To investigate the matter further, Stow also ordered that some of the nails be sent to him. In due course he 'found vnder the broad heades of them, the olde wood, skant turned into earth, but still retaining both the graine, and proper colour', thus confirming his suspicion that they were the nails of a wooden coffin that had rotted.[99] The popular tradition is dispensed with: the evidence itself disproves the lurid speculation.

For all the carefulness of his descriptions, and his awareness of the traces of the past buried in the soil, Stow was still not immune from criticism by later commentators. John Bagford, for instance, characterized him as 'little acquainted with the Coyns and other Antiquities of the Romans', and took great pleasure in drawing attention to the mistakes in his work.[100] Bagford notes, for example, with considerable relish, that in his description of Goodman's Fields (in what is now Whitechapel) Stow 'takes no notice that they were a Roman Burying Place'. This egregious oversight was brought to light, when later 'there were found many Urns, together with the Ashes and Bones of the Dead, and several other Antiquities, as Brass and Silver Money, with an unusual Urn in Copper, curiously enamelled in Colours, red, blew and yellow'.[101] To emphasize Stow's inadequacy further, Bagford then asserts that he has also seen 'many other Antiquities' found in Goodman's Fields, and that he has even had some in his 'Possession'. The implication is that, unlike Stow, he is a careful scholar, who does recognize the significance of Roman antiquities, and so is capable of making a proper assessment of the extent of Roman settlement in and around London.

Bagford's criticism is harsh. Since the cemetery at Goodman's Fields was only discovered in 1678–9, Stow did not really have a chance. Bagford was also a far from impartial commentator. He believed that Stow had shamelessly plagiarized the *Antiquities of London*, a lost, and in fact probably apocryphal, work by Leland. 'I must be free in my Thoughts to tell you,' he writes in his letter to Hearne, 'that (to say nothing of what Camden borrowed from him) 'tis my Opinion, that Stow had in his Possession Leland's Antiquities of London, and for want of Learning most grievously mangled the Work on purpose to make it his own.'[102] For this reason he takes every opportunity to denigrate Stow's work,

---

[98] Stow, *Survey*, ed. Kingsford, i. 169–70.
[99] Ibid. 170.　[100] Bagford, 'Letter', i, p. lxix.
[101] Ibid., p. lxi.　[102] Ibid., pp. lxviii–lxix.

to draw attention to the errors in his observations and conjectures about Roman antiquities.

In one way, though, Bagford's criticism is not unjustified. Whilst sixteenth-century scholars and antiquaries were manifestly interested in the material traces of the past, responding to them historically and imaginatively, few devoted their attention entirely to them. Stow was no different, plotting the geographical spread of antiquities across London, as the chorographic form of the *Survey* demanded, but never offering the kind of comprehensive discussion that Bagford sought. And the same goes for Twyne, Rogers, and Oglander. For most early modern antiquaries, other traces of the past were equally, if not more, important. Linguistic traces, for example, the subject of the next chapter, were followed with greater alacrity, as they held out the promise of unveiling reliable historical origins. In etymology there was an approach that united antiquarian writing, a subject not just of passing interest, like material remains, but which defined the whole antiquarian enterprise.

2

Origins and Names: Etymology and the Elizabethan Society of Antiquaries

In his preface to the *Britannia* (1586) William Camden confesses that his first task when researching the work had been to 'search after the Etymologie of Britaine and the first inhabitants'. He describes this as a 'doubtfull' subject, since 'the first originalls of nations are obscure by reason of their profound antiquitie, as things which are seene very deepe and farre remote', and acknowledges that some readers will therefore censure him for adventuring 'to hunt after the originals of names by conjectures'. Nevertheless, he defends his approach on two grounds. First, great swathes of knowledge depend on conjecture anyway. Second, and perhaps more convincing, his etymologies are always guided by the Platonic injunction that 'the name be consonant to the nature of the thing'. Whenever they are 'dissonant', he rejects them. As a final reassurance, he also tells his readers that he has vouchsafed no place in the work for etymologies that are 'obscure', 'far fetched', and 'hardly wrested', nor for any 'which may be drawne diversly'.[1]

Camden's terms here are striking. To 'search after the Etymologie of Britaine' is clear enough; we are in the familiar territory of the origins of words and names. To search after the etymology of 'the first inhabitants' is less familiar. Etymology here seems to be understood not in a linguistic sense, but as a synonym for genealogy.[2] Camden's concern seems to be with peoples as well as names, with ancestral bloodlines as well as linguistic derivations. By identifying etymology with genealogy in this way, Camden makes it a powerful historical tool. By following linguistic traces, he can unearth previously hidden historical and genealogical origins. As he asserts later in the *Britannia*, 'if all the histories that ever were had miscarried and perished; if no writer had recorded, that we

---

[1] William Camden, *Britain, or A Chorographicall Description of the Most flourishing Kingdomes, England, Scotland, and Ireland, and the Ilands adioyning, out of the depth of Antiquitie*, trans. Philemon Holland (London, 1610), sig. π4^{r-v}.

[2] For a different account of the relationship between etymology and genealogy in the early modern period, see Marvin Spevack, 'Beyond Individualism: Names and Namelessness in Shakespeare', *Huntington Library Quarterly*, 56 (1993), 383–98; and for a suggestive discussion of their relationship more generally, see R. Howard Bloch, *Etymologies and Genealogies: A Literary Anthropology of the French Middle Ages* (Chicago and London: University of Chicago Press, 1983).

Englishmen are descended from Germanes, the true and naturall Scots from the Irish, the Britons of Armorica in France from our Britans; the society of their tongues would easily confirme the same'.[3] Language, he seems to be saying, allows us to restore knowledge of the past, even where conventional historical evidence no longer survives.

Camden was not alone in championing etymology in this way. Many of his contemporaries, especially other antiquaries, also placed etymology at the heart of their historical inquiry and research. On one level, this privileging of etymology simply reflected the larger philological basis of English antiquarianism. The antiquaries, after all, considered language to be as secure a record of historical change, and therefore also continuity, as any other form of evidence. As Richard Verstegan put it in his *A Restitution of Decayed Intelligence* (1605), 'as all things vnder heauen do in length of tyme enclyne vnto alteration and varietie, so do the languages also, yea such as are not mixed with others that vnto them are strange and extrauagant, but euen within themselues do these differences grow and encrease'.[4] But etymology may also have held a more particular appeal to the antiquaries. The sixteenth century had witnessed a revival of interest in etymology as a validation or proof of origins, an interest which, as a number of scholars have shown, was increasingly orientated towards the historical.[5] And this search for origins, as Graham Parry has argued, also lay at the heart of the antiquarian project.[6] It is not surprising, therefore, that etymology came to be associated with antiquarianism. For the antiquaries, names were a rich historical source, and etymologies could provide authoritative historical arguments. By tracing the origins of names, they could explain the origins of peoples, explore the development of customs and institutions, and establish the histories of towns, countries, and other locations. Etymology, in short, offered the antiquaries another way to defy the march of time.

In the chapter which follows, I explore this emergence of etymology as a historical method, and demonstrate how this sometimes abstruse, and often mocked, branch of linguistic scholarship came to be an authoritative form of argument. My discussion begins with the papers—or discourses, as their eighteenth-century editor styled them—presented at the meetings of the Elizabethan Society of Antiquaries. These papers are often little more than short etymological discussions of topics of legal, historical, or archaeological interest. Typically, they address the history and origin of a custom, office, or practice, and, more often than not, they do this by tracing the etymology of its name. The chapter then

---

[3] Camden, *Britain*, 16.
[4] Verstegan, *A Restitution of Decayed Intelligence*, 194.
[5] Frank R. Borchardt, 'Etymology in Tradition and in the Northern Renaissance', *Journal of the History of Ideas*, 29 (1968), 415–29 at 424; Paul Zumthor, *Langue, texte, énigme* (Paris: Éditions du Seuil, 1975), 154; and Umberto Eco, *The Search for the Perfect Language*, trans. James Fentress (London: FontanaPress, 1997; first published 1995), 80.
[6] Parry, *The Trophies of Time*, 9.

considers the various influences which explain why etymology came to such prominence amongst the antiquaries: a philosophical tradition of etymology, which originates with Plato's *Cratylus*; the topic of etymology, or, more properly, *notatio*, in sixteenth-century logic; and, most importantly, the defence of arguments from etymology in historical methods (the *artes historicae*) published at the time. In the last part of the chapter, I return to Camden's identification of etymology with genealogy, showing the growing importance of etymology for discussions of national origins. Etymologies provided historically sanctioned narratives of descent, enabling writers to bring particular genealogies to the fore. In some hands, therefore, etymology could become politicized as well as historicized. The antiquaries might have considered etymology one of the keys to the past, but sometimes this was as much for its political force and rhetorical effect as for any impartial origins that they might adduce by it.

ETYMOLOGICAL METHOD

The Elizabethan Society of Antiquaries was the principal institution in late sixteenth- and early seventeenth-century England for historical debate. Scholars disagree on when it was founded, but it was certainly in existence by the late 1580s. Linda Van Norden, in what remains the most authoritative modern history of the Society, concluded on the basis of Sir Henry Spelman's posthumously published 'The Occasion of this Discourse' that it was founded in, or within a year of, 1586.[7] The Society met every Friday during the law terms to discuss two questions of interest that had been raised at the end of the previous week's meeting. According to Spelman, who was himself a member, all who were present were expected to contribute. The most impressive submissions were then entered in the Society's register-book for the sake of posterity. Like its chronology, the membership is also uncertain, since the documentary evidence is somewhat contradictory. From surviving manuscripts, some forty-three names emerge, although we cannot say with any confidence that these were all members of the Society. What can be said is that the membership numbered heralds, common lawyers, and men of letters, and that members included the likes of Camden, Sir Robert Cotton, Sir John Doderidge, and John Stow.[8]

Much of what we know today about the Society is thanks to the editorial work of Thomas Hearne. In the early eighteenth century, assisted by other antiquaries,

---

[7] Linda Van Norden, 'The Elizabethan College of Antiquaries' (Ph.D. diss., University of California at Los Angeles, 1946), 71–118; 'The Occasion of this Discourse', in Henry Spelman, *Reliquiæ Spelmannianæ: The Posthumous Works of Sir Henry Spelman Kt. Relating to the Laws and Antiquities of England* (Oxford, 1698), sig. I3^{r-v}.

[8] For lists of the membership, see Van Norden, 'The Elizabethan College of Antiquaries', 560–73; and R. J. Schoeck, 'The Elizabethan Society of Antiquaries and Men of Law', *Notes & Queries*, 190 (1954), 417–21.

such as the Nonjuror and former fellow of Magdalen College, Oxford, Dr Thomas Smith, Hearne began to collect and transcribe manuscripts of the papers submitted at the Society's meetings. In 1720 he published an edition of these under the title *A Collection of Curious Discourses, Written by Eminent Antiquaries Upon several Heads in our English Antiquities*. A revised and augmented edition by Sir Joseph Ayloffe followed in 1771. The importance of etymology to the antiquaries is apparent from the titles of these pieces alone. Of the papers published by Hearne, eleven have the word 'etymology' in their titles. These include Francis Thynne's 'Of the Antiquity and Etymology of Terms and Times for Administration of Justice in England', delivered on 2 November 1601; Cotton's 'The Etymology, Antiquity, and Privilege of Castles' and the 'Antiquity, Etymology, and Privilege of Towns', submitted on 9 February 1598 and 23 June 1599 respectively; and the papers of Thomas Doyley and Arthur Agarde, both entitled 'Of the Etymology, Dignity, and Antiquity of Dukes', presented at a meeting of uncertain date. Like Cotton, Agarde also wrote a paper on the 'Etymology, Antiquity, and Privileges of Castles in England'; a third, anonymous paper on this topic was also published by Hearne. Other etymological papers include Joseph Holland's 'Of the Antiquity, Etymology, and Privilege of Towns'; a pair of anonymous submissions on measurement, 'Of the Antiquitye, Etimologie, and Varietye of Dimentions of Land in England' and 'Of the Antiquity, Variety, and Etimology of Measuring Land in Cornwayl'; and Camden's paper 'The Etymology and Original of Barons'.[9]

Although we cannot discount the possibility that Hearne himself may have added some of these titles, the papers clearly still reflect the importance of etymology to antiquarian method. They also illustrate the breadth of linguistic material with which the antiquaries were prepared to engage. The paper on Cornwall, for example, is primarily concerned with a series of Cornish measurements, 'parck', 'tre', 'misne', 'trouz', 'lorgh', 'Luce teere', 'errow', and 'ferthen teere', but the author also gives the English equivalents of these terms and the etymologies for the English words (Latin, French, and Dutch). This paper also neatly illustrates the historical dimension to antiquarian etymologizing. Its central argument is that, because the measurements used in Cornwall are different from those used elsewhere in the island, the manner of measuring land in the county is likely to be very ancient, perhaps even dating back to the original colonization of Britain. 'The measuring of Land in Cornwayl should seem to be auncient,' the author argues, 'because the manner and termes thereof do differ from those in other parts of the realme, for seeing we find not whence it hath

---

[9] According to its headnote, Camden's paper was 'Transcribed from his *Adversaria*, in the possession of Christopher Hatton'; see *A Collection of Curious Discourses Written by Eminent Antiquaries upon Several Heads in our English Antiquities*, ed. Thomas Hearne, rev. Sir Joseph Ayloffe, 2 vols. (London, 1771; first published 1720), i. 124. The manuscript from which it was printed is now in the Bodleian Library (MS Smith 17); see Peter Beal, *Index of English Literary Manuscripts*, i: *1450–1625* (London: Mansell, 1980), item CmW 53.

been borrowed, wee may the more probably conjecture, that the same was brought in by the Britons at their first inhabitance, and so ever since retayned.'[10] The key to the argument is the uniqueness of the Cornish measurements; the answer lies in the unfathomable origins of the Cornish terms.

In addition to the eleven papers printed by Hearne in 1720, there is also the short note 'Of the Etymology, Dignity, and Antiquity of Duke or Dux', first published by Ayloffe, and Spelman's piece on the origins of the law terms, 'Of the Antiquity and Etymology of Terms and Times for Administration of Justice in England'. Spelman's paper was written for the proposed revival of the Society of Antiquaries in 1614. After seven years' discontinuance for reasons that remain uncertain, four of the founding members (Camden, Cotton, Sir James Ley, and Spelman himself) resolved to re-establish the Society. They drew up a new series of rules, 'whereof this was one, That for avoiding offence, we should neither meddle with matters of State nor of Religion', and decided that one of the questions which they should discuss at the first meeting of the revived Society 'was, touching the Original of the Terms'.[11] That meeting famously never took place: James I took a dislike to the Society's proceedings, apparently doubting the members' resolution not to meddle in matters of state or religion, and banned any further meetings.[12] Encouraged by several of his friends, Spelman decided to circulate his paper in manuscript instead. As he writes in 'The Occasion of this Discourse', he 'thought good upon a review and augmentation to let it creep abroad in the form you see it, wishing it might be rectify'd by some better judgement'.[13] After his death the paper was printed, first as a small octavo, *Of the Law-Terms: A Discourse* (1684), and then in Edmund Gibson's edition in *Reliquiæ Spelmannianæ* (1698).[14] Spelman's piece begins with a discussion of the etymology of 'term'. Having defined 'term' as that portion of the year when cases are heard in court, he offers the following derivation: 'the Greek $Τέρμα$, which signifieth the Bound, End, or Limit of a thing, here particularly of the Time for law-matters'.[15] In the remainder of the piece Spelman gives several other etymologies, providing a glossary for the antiquity and derivation of various legal practices and terminology.

---

[10] *Curious Discourses*, ed. Hearne, i. 195–7.
[11] Spelman explains the plan to revive the Society in the preface to his piece on the law terms; see 'The Occasion of this Discourse', in *Reliquiæ Spelmannianæ*, sig. I3^v.
[12] Van Norden, 'The Elizabethan College of Antiquaries', 74, 414.
[13] Spelman, 'The Occasion of this Discourse', sig. I3^v.
[14] In his preface Gibson makes clear that his text is printed from a different (and superior) manuscript from that of *Of the Law-Terms, Reliquiæ Spelmannianæ*, sig. a3^v: 'That, concerning the *Original of the four Terms*, was publisht in the Year *1684*. from a very uncorrect and imperfect Copy, which probably had been taken, when the Author first wrote the Discourse. The Original Manuscript (with very many Additions and Corrections, that Sir *Henry* afterwards made in it) is preserv'd in the *Bodleian* Library; from whence the Work is now printed entire.'
[15] *Curious Discourses*, ed. Hearne, ii. 332.

Despite not having the word in their titles, many of the other discourses also focus on the etymologies of the topics under discussion. One example is Ley's 'Of the Antiquity of the Office of the Chancellor of England', a paper which typifies the etymological method of the majority of the *Curious Discourses*. Ley begins his paper by discussing the etymology of 'chancellor', reporting the derivations of others, before proceeding to give his own: 'I rather conjecture, that other courts being publick for the access of all men, and being *quasi in foro* for hearing and ending of civil and criminal causes, the chancery was a more private and sequestered place, and inclosed from the press of people, where the chancellor might sit and observe the sealing of writs.' In other words, the word derives from the court, chancery, where the chancellor would sit. Ley defines the office by recourse to its linguistic origin. After establishing this origin, he turns to its antiquity: 'The first chancellor that I find was *Dunstanus*, who is said to be *Cancellarius Regius*, who lived in the Saxons time, both in and before the time of K. Edgar.' His paper then ends with an account of the authority of the office, delimiting the chancellor's ministerial and judicial powers.[16] The structure of the paper characterizes the antiquaries' method. The argument begins with the word's etymology, defining it by establishing its origin. Once this is established, its antiquity is also thereby proved. Not only therefore is etymology put to a lexicographical end, it also serves a recognizably historiographic purpose.

The same etymological impulse is apparent in the commonplace book of Francis Tate, another of the Society's members. This manuscript is a quarto of 164 folios, and is now preserved in the British Library (MS Stowe 1045). On its second leaf the eighteenth-century scholar John Anstis described the manuscript as 'the Collections of Fran. Tate of whom see Seldens preface to Hengham upon subjects treated upon (as I take it) in the Society of Antiquaries'.[17] Anstis's supposition seems to be correct. The manuscript appears to be a commonplace book, in which Tate gathered specifically antiquarian quotations. His titles or heads include 'Of thantiquity of marquesses in England. the manner of their Creation. & signification of their name' and, strikingly, 'Of the Ætimology, Original, erection & Iurisdiction of County Palentines in Englande', dated 11 February 1590 and 27 November 1594 respectively.[18] The majority of entries under these heads come from Camden, although the first also includes quotations from Robert Fabyan's chronicle and the lawyer and antiquary William Fleetwood, whilst the second includes various statutes and a quotation from

---

[16] *Curious Discourses*, ed. Hearne, i. 119–20.
[17] BL, MS Stowe 1045, fo. 2^r; see also 'Introduction: Containing An Historical Account of the Origin and Establishment of the Society of Antiquaries', *Archaeologia*, 1 (1770), pp. i–xxxix at p. vi, where the manuscript is described as 'common-place notes or excerpts from all the several authors who have treated on the subject, or the records illustrating them'.
[18] BL, MS Stowe 1045, fos. 9^r–10^r, and 37^r–38^v.

Bracton.[19] Tate's collections have no order other than the rudimentary structure imposed by his heads. But, as Hearne suggested in his preface to the *Curious Discourses*, no doubt he later 'methodized some, if not all of them, and afterwards offered accurate discourses to the society at their meetings'.[20] MS Stowe 1045 illustrates the first step in early modern antiquarian research: the gathering together of pertinent sources and quotations. It also illustrates that from the outset etymology was one of the antiquaries' primary concerns.

In putting etymology at the service of history in this way, the antiquaries drew upon a number of sources. First, there was Plato's *Cratylus*, the dialogue of naming which stands at the head of the Western etymological tradition.[21] The *Cratylus* is concerned with the relationship between words and things, exploring whether names derive from nature or convention. The two positions are summarized at the beginning of the dialogue by Hermogenes, whose own conclusion is that there is no 'correctness of names other than convention and agreement'. The eponymous Cratylus, by contrast, believes that 'everything has a right name of its own, which comes by nature, and that a name is not whatever people call a thing by agreement, just a piece of their own voice applied to the thing, but that there is a kind of inherent correctness in names, which is the same for all men, both Greeks and barbarians'.[22] These two views are then modified by Socrates. Initially, he defends Cratylus' position, asserting that he 'is right in saying that names belong to things by nature'.[23] But by the end of the dialogue he has forged a middle way: 'I myself prefer the theory that names are, so far as possible, like the things named; but really this attractive force of likeness, is, as Hermogenes says, a poor thing, and we are compelled to employ in addition this commonplace expedient, convention, to establish the correctness of names'.[24] He concludes on this basis that 'surely no man of sense can put himself and his soul under the control of names, and trust in names and their makers to the point of affirming that he knows anything'.[25]

Plato's dialogue was immensely influential, spawning what Gérard Genette has called 'a sort of etymological hermeneutics', which persisted into the Middle Ages and beyond via the works of Christian exegetes such as Isidore of Seville.[26]

---

[19] *Bracton*, or to give it its full title, *De legibus et consuetudinibus Angliae*, is a treatise on the common law, usually attributed to the 13th-c. justice Henry of Bratton. The treatise survives in about fifty different manuscripts, most of which are contemporary with it; the first printed edition appeared in 1569 (*STC* 3475).
[20] *Curious Discourses*, ed. Hearne, i, p. lviii.
[21] For a useful introduction to this dialogue, see Timothy M. S. Baxter, *The Cratylus: Plato's Critique of Naming* (Leiden: E. J. Brill, 1992).
[22] Plato, *Cratylus*, trans. H. N. Fowler (Cambridge, Mass.: Harvard University Press, 1996; first published in this edition 1926), 384 C–D, 383 A–B.
[23] Ibid. 390 C–D.
[24] Ibid. 435 B–C.
[25] Ibid. 440 C.
[26] Gérard Genette, *Mimologics*, trans. Thaïs E. Morgan (Lincoln, Nebr., and London: University of Nebraska Press, 1995), 29. On the influence of the *Cratylus*, see also Ernst Robert Curtius,

For Isidore, etymology was the basis of all knowledge, and he argued in the first book of his voluminous *Etymologiae* that the true meaning of a word or name could always be inferred by tracing it back to its origin.[27] English interest in this Platonic tradition can be found as early as Chaucer. Twice in *The Canterbury Tales* Chaucer repeats the cratylic argument that names should correspond with the nature of their referents, although neither instance necessarily refers directly to the *Cratylus*. In *The General Prologue* the narrator remembers the argument, perhaps satirically, as an accompanying aside on the difficulties of reading Plato suggests: 'Eek Plato seith, whoso kan hym rede, / The wordes moote be cosyn to the dede.' His words are later echoed admiringly by the Manciple in his second tale: 'The wise Plato seith, as ye may rede, / The word moot nede accorde with the dede.'[28] Chaucer probably knew the argument as a commonplace from Boethius' *Consolation of Philosophy*; he is unlikely to have been familiar with the *Cratylus* itself.[29]

By the sixteenth century, though, knowledge of Plato's dialogue would have been more direct, and there is good reason to believe that Camden at least had read it. His argument in the preface to the *Britannia* that 'the name be consonant to the nature of the thing', for example, seems to be a direct invocation of Cratylus. Camden too seems to have believed that there was a natural correctness to names and that their origins are therefore perpetually present, investing them with a series of potentials, which the linguistically adept can make manifest at any time.[30] Furthermore, elsewhere in his preface, he also mentions Plato's dialogue by name:

Plato in his *Cratilus* commandeth that we recall the originalls of names to the barbarous tongues (for so he called all but Greek) as being most ancient. I thereupon in Etymologies and my coniectures have made recourse to the British, or Welsh tongue (so they now call it) as being the same which the primitive and most ancient inhabitants of this land vsed, and to the English-Saxons tongue which our Progenitours the English spake.[31]

'Etymology as a Category of Thought', in *European Literature and the Latin Middle Ages*, trans. Willard R. Trask (London: Routledge & Kegan Paul, 1953), 495–500; Anne Barton, *The Names of Comedy* (Oxford: Oxford University Press, 1990); and Vivian Salmon, 'Views on Meaning in 16th-Century England', in *Language and Society in Early Modern England: Selected Essays, 1981–1994*, ed. Konrad Koerner (Amsterdam: John Benjamins, 1996), 55–75.

[27] Isidore of Seville, *Etymologiarum sive originum libri XX*, ed. W. M. Lindsay, 2 vols. (Oxford: Clarendon Press, 1985; first published in this edition 1911), I. xxix. ii: 'Nam dum videris unde ortum est nomen, citius vim eius intellegis.'

[28] *The General Prologue* and *The Manciple's Tale*, in *The Riverside Chaucer*, ed. Larry D. Benson et al. (Oxford: Oxford University Press, 1988; first published 1987), ll. 741–2, and 207–8.

[29] Sears Jayne, *Plato in Renaissance England* (Dordrecht: Kluwer, 1995), 47–9.

[30] For the Renaissance belief in the perpetual presence of origins, see Marian Rothstein, 'Etymology, Genealogy, and the Immutability of Origins', *Renaissance Quarterly*, 43 (1990), 332–47 at 344.

[31] Camden, *Britain*, sig. π4ᵛ.

He thereby links his own method, his own etymologizing, directly to the Platonic model. Later in the preface he again recollects the dialogue: 'In things, saith he, there is *ΦΩNH, ΣXHMA, XPΩMA*: that is, but I cannot aptly expresse them, *A sound, a forme, and colour*.'[32] And he again also links his method to the dialogue, noting afterwards that 'if these discover not themselves in the name I reiect the coniecture'.

Another, perhaps less familiar, influence on the antiquaries may have been the importance of etymology in Ramist logic. Petrus Ramus (Pierre de la Ramée) published the first edition of his handbook on logic, the *Dialecticæ institutiones*, in 1543. Discarding the medieval form of the dialectic manual, this work divides logic into just two parts: invention and judgement.[33] Invention describes the selection of topics which generate propositions; judgement corresponds to the motives for organizing those propositions. In its first part, the work also lists various topics of invention, and these include *notatio*, or an argument taken from etymology. Ramus defines this topic as the interpretation of a name and, citing Plato's *Cratylus*, he points out that, so long as a name is properly imposed, it will also be a declaration of the nature of what is named.[34] As an example, he cites that old chestnut, the derivation of *homo* (man) from *humus* (earth). In the French version of his handbook which followed in 1555, he discourses on the topic at greater length, and gives further examples of it, such as 'courageux, plain de courage' and 'homicide, qui a occis quelque homme'. But he also points out the difficulties in etymology, stressing that 'quand les noms sont faulx, la notation est perilleuse'.[35] His point is that an argument drawn from etymology is strong only if the names were correctly given in the first place.

Ramus's discussion of *notatio* was enthusiastically taken up by English readers and translators. The standard English translation appeared in 1574 under the title *The Logike of the Moste Excellent Philosopher P. Ramus Martyr*; the translator was Roland MacIlmaine, a Scot who taught logic at St Andrews. His translation expands upon the original at various places, including Ramus's discussion of *notatio*. First, as Ramus had done, MacIlmaine defines *notatio* as 'the interpretation of a worde: For wordes are nothing els but notes of matters signified'. He then provides a long list of examples, which are not taken from Ramus, beginning with names from the Old Testament, as he pronounces that 'The Hebrewes vse to geue their sonnes and their daughters names which myght euer put them in

---

[32] Ibid.
[33] For useful introductions to Ramist logic, see Lisa Jardine, *Francis Bacon: Discovery and the Art of Discourse* (Cambridge: Cambridge University Press, 1974), 41–7; and Peter Mack, 'Humanist Rhetoric and Dialectic', in Jill Kraye (ed.), *The Cambridge Companion to Renaissance Humanism* (Cambridge: Cambridge University Press, 1996), 82–99.
[34] *Petri Rami Veromandui dialecticæ institutiones* (Paris, 1543), sig. B6^v: 'Notatio est nominis interpretatio: quæ à Græcis symbolum, & etymologia nominatur. Si autem nomen (ut in Cratylo sapienter Plato disputat) rectè, prudenterque sit impositum: declaratio quædam naturæ est, sed intexta, atque implicata: quæ notatione retexetur, atque explicabitur.'
[35] *Dialectique de Pierre de La Ramee* (Paris, 1555), sigs. f3^v–f4^r.

remembraunce of some poynte of religion, and knowe when they come to perfection, that they were of the chosen people'. More surprisingly, he notes that the same practice adheres amongst the Scots: 'So do we in the Scottyshe tongue (to sturre the youthe to the imitation of them whose name they beare) call some Abraham, others Isaac or Iacob, and some Susanna after the Hebrewes: And agayne other some Timothie, and Christofor after the Grecians.'[36] He then ends his discussion by explaining how the topic should be used: 'The vse then of this place is, to proue or disproue, prayse or dispraise any thing by the Etimologie of it.'[37] It is not hard, then, to see why an argument from etymology might also have appealed to the antiquaries, since they too sought to prove arguments—in their case, about the origins of customs, laws, or peoples.

A few years later the historical dimension to *notatio* was made explicit by Abraham Fraunce in *The Lawiers Logike* (1588). This work was the first formal attempt to connect Ramist logic to common law learning, and it is filled with historical illustrations or examples of *notatio*. The first of these is just the kind of etymology found in early modern antiquarian books: 'Billinsgate, a gate in London builded by king Belus'.[38] It is an etymology of a place name, an historical explanation of its origin. Fraunce also gives a series of legal etymologies, no doubt because of his intended readership for the book:

Court baron, of Barones, quasi virones, magnates, among the Saxons called Thani. Court Leete, of the Saxon woord Lant, which is law, so Lant-day by corruption of speech is come to be called Law-day. Barrettor, of the French Barat, deceipt: or of the Latine, Baratro, or Balatro, a vyle knaue. Apprentice of Apprendre to learne. Sessions à sedendo. Acquittance, quasi acquietantia, &c.[39]

The five examples here are again the kind of material which might be found in early modern antiquarian books, and they are strikingly similar to the etymologies in the *Curious Discourses*: legal terms given their proper meanings by recourse to their origins. Later in the work Fraunce defends his inclusion of so many examples on the grounds that he wanted to 'make it plain, how the notion of the thing is oftentimes expressed by the notation of the woord, contrary to the preiudicate opinion of some seely penmen, and illogicall lawyers, who thinke it a fruiteles poynt of superfluous curiositie'.[40] He, on the other hand, has no doubts about the value of such arguments.

But Fraunce does doubt whether these arguments belong properly to logic. 'Notation, the interpretation of the name,' he argues elsewhere in *The Lawiers*

---

[36] *The Logike of the Moste Excellent Philosopher P. Ramus Martyr*, trans. Roland MacIlmaine (London, 1574), sig. D2^v.
[37] Ibid., sig. D3^v.
[38] Abraham Fraunce, *The Lawiers Logike, exemplifying the præcepts of Logike by the practise of the common Lawe* (London, 1588), sig. P1^r.
[39] Ibid.   [40] Ibid., sig. P4^v.

Logike, 'seemeth rather the dutie of a dictionary, then of any Logicall institution.'[41] It is worth noting here that the first recorded use of notation in English, from John Dee's preface to Henry Billingsley's translation of Euclid, is also in a lexicographical sense: 'Perspectiue, is an Art Mathematicall, which demonstrateth the maner, and properties, of all Radiations Direct, Broken, and Reflected. This Description, or Notation, is brief.'[42] Elsewhere in *The Lawiers Logike* Fraunce also wonders whether *notatio* might be considered a form of rhetoric, describing it as 'a Rhetoricall agnomination'. By 'agnomination' he means the trope known to rhetoricians as paronomasia, the playful or punning allusion of one word to another.[43] He may well have been thinking here of the venerable tradition of etymological puns, which stretches back as far as the *Cratylus*. He was also almost certainly echoing an argument made four years earlier by the Calvinist theologian Dudley Fenner. Preacher to the English merchants at Middelburg in the Netherlands, Fenner was the author of a popular Ramist textbook, *The Artes of Logike and Rethorike* (1584), printed at Middelburg by Richard Schilders.[44] Fenner too believed that *notatio* had more to do with lexicography and rhetoric than logic, and, unlike Fraunce, he excised it from his textbook altogether. In his prefatory epistle he explains why. Notation 'apperteineth not to Logike but to Dictionaries'; it is 'neyther reason, nor new force of reason; but only an elega*n*cie of the Trope called *Paranomasia*, or chaunge of the name'.[45] Fenner and Fraunce both refer to a specific trope, paronomasia, but in their suggestion that etymology might in fact be understood as a form of rhetoric they touched upon something of larger importance, and something to which we shall return later in the chapter.

There were those, antiquaries included, who did not share this enthusiasm for Ramus and his methods. Camden, for example, distanced himself from the Ramist vogue for reducing all knowledge by methods and systems.[46] In his *Remains Concerning Britain* (1605) he expressed his unease at the proliferation of overly ingenious etymological methods. 'To reduce surnames to a Methode is,' he asserts in his chapter on names, 'matter for a *Ramist*, who should happily finde

---

[41] Ibid., sig. O2ᵛ.
[42] 'Iohn Dee his Mathematicall Præface', in *The Elements of Geometrie of the most auncient Philosopher Euclide of Megara*, trans. H. Billingsley (London, 1570), sig. b1ʳ; see *OED*, s.v. 'notation', *n*. 1.
[43] *OED*, s.v. 'agnomination', *n*. 2.
[44] For Schilders's relationship with Fenner, see J. Dover Wilson, 'Richard Schilders and the English Puritans', *Transactions of the Bibliographical Society*, 11 (1910–11), 65–134 at 82; see also J. G. C. A. Briels, *Zuidnederlandse boekdrukkers en boekverkopers in de Republiek der Vereingde Nederlanden omstreeks 1570–1630* (Nieuwkoop: B. de Graaf, 1974), 435–8.
[45] Dudley Fenner, *The Artes of Logike and Rethorike, plainelie set foorth in the Englishe tounge, easie to be learned and practised* (Middelburg, 1584), sig. A4ʳ.
[46] Mordechai Feingold, 'English Ramism: A Reinterpretation', in Mordechai Feingold, Joseph S. Freedman, and Wolfgang Rother (eds.), *The Influence of Petrus Ramus* (Basle: Schwabe, 2001), 127–76 at 171–2.

it to be a *Typocosme*.'[47] He was presumably thinking here of *La tipocosmia di Alessandro Citolini* (1561), a short-cut to learning influenced by Ramus. Citolini was an Italian Protestant, who for a time lived in exile in London, and his scheme proposed a knowledge system arranged under six 'days'. Eschewing this kind of ingenious, but reductive, method, Camden himself endeavours simply to set down the origins of English surnames as he finds them: 'I will plainely set downe from whence the most have beene deduced, as farre as I can conceive.'[48] Camden's criticism is measured and light, and lacks the corrosiveness of Francis Bacon's blast at typocosmy in *The Advancement of Learning* (1605). Bacon dismisses all such methods as 'nothing but a Masse of words of all Arts; to giue men countenance, that those words which vse the tearmes; might bee thought to vnderstand the Art; which Collections are much like a Frippers or Brokers shoppe; that hath ends of euerie thing, but nothing of worth'.[49] But Camden's point is clear enough. He is suggesting that Ramist knowledge systems, despite their claims to total classification, are unable to cope with as varied and complex a body of knowledge as the derivations and origins of English surnames. Too prescriptive a system cannot work.

The extent of Ramus's influence more broadly in England is, in fact, hard to gauge. Walter Ong, the pre-eminent modern scholar of Ramus, characterized his influence as pervasive, but also 'juvenile' and in some ways superficial. He noted the widespread 'circulation of Ramist terms', but pointed out that at the same time there was 'practically no serious and mature scholarship oriented by Ramism in the British Isles'.[50] The antiquaries' interest in etymology or notation might fit this pattern. The term was associated with Ramus and his imitators, presented in their reformed logic as one of the topics which generated discourse, but in the antiquaries' hands it was taken out of dialectic altogether. Moreover, it is easy to explain why some of the antiquaries looked to this Ramist topic in their works and tracts. One area of English intellectual life where Ramus does seem to have been influential was the law. Legal writers of the early modern period, especially common lawyers, increasingly used Ramist terms and methodology in their treatises.[51] Some of these lawyers, men such as Doderidge, for example, were also members of the Society of Antiquaries. This legal background might, therefore, be another explanation why etymology, or *notatio*, came to such prominence in antiquarian research and writing.

---

[47] William Camden, *Remains Concerning Britain*, ed. R. D. Dunn (Toronto, Buffalo, and London: University of Toronto Press, 1984), 94.
[48] Ibid. 94.
[49] Bacon, *The Advancement of Learning*, 127.
[50] Walter J. Ong, *Ramus, Method and the Decay of Dialogue: From the Art of Discourse to the Art of Reason* (Cambridge, Mass.: Harvard University Press, 1958), 303–4.
[51] Louis A. Knafla, 'Ramism and the English Renaissance', in Louis A. Knafla, Martin S. Staum, and T. H. E. Travers (eds.), *Science, Technology and Culture in Historical Perspective* (Calgary: The University of Calgary Studies in History, 1976), 26–50 at 40.

The most important influence on the antiquaries, though, may have been a large quarto published at Paris in 1566: the *Methodus ad facilem historiarum cognitionem*. This work by the French jurist and political theorist Jean Bodin was perhaps the most influential of all the *artes historicae* published in the sixteenth century. These works were scholarly guides about how to write, read, and evaluate history.[52] English readers took warmly to Bodin and his works. Speaking of his *De republica libri sex* (1576), Gabriel Harvey commented: 'You can not stepp into a schollars studye but (ten to one) you shall litely finde open ether Bodin de Republica or Le Royes Exposition uppon Aristotles Politiques or sum other like Frenche or Italian Politique Discourses.'[53] The *Methodus* itself probably became known in England slightly later, after Bodin's visits in 1579–81 as part of the Duke of Anjou's entourage.[54] English champions of the work included Harvey, Edmund Spenser, Philip Sidney, William Harrison, Edmund Bolton, and Thomas Nashe. The first English translation appeared in 1608–9, when Thomas Heywood prefaced his version of Sallust's *Catiline* and *Jugurtha* of that year with the fourth chapter of Bodin's work. Heywood titled this preface 'Of the choise of History, by way of Preface, dedicated to the Courteous Reader, vpon occasion of the frequent Translations of these latter times'.[55] A few years later Degory Wheare, first holder of the Camden chair of civil history at Oxford, used the *Methodus* as one of the bases for his own *ars historica*, *De ratione et methodo legendi historias dissertatio* (1623).[56] Precisely what these English writers took from Bodin is hard to categorize, since they tended to mine the *Methodus*, as Fritz Levy has pointed out, essentially for whatever they wanted.[57]

One section of the *Methodus* which does seem to have struck a common chord was the ninth chapter, Bodin's discussion of the origins of peoples. 'No question,' Bodin writes, 'has exercised the writers of histories more.'[58] He then stipulates his own criteria by which these origins may be established and proved: 'the reliability of the writer', the 'situation and character of the region', and

---

[52] For this genre, see Anthony Grafton, *What Was History? The Art of History in Early Modern Europe* (Cambridge: Cambridge University Press, 2007).
[53] *Letter-Book of Gabriel Harvey, A.D. 1573–1580*, ed. Edward John Long Scott (London: Camden Society, 1884), p. 79 (fo. 42ʳ).
[54] Leonard F. Dean, 'Bodin's *Methodus* in England Before 1625', *Studies in Philology*, 39 (1942), 160–6.
[55] Sallust, *The Two most worthy and Notable Histories which remaine vnmained to Posterity: (viz:) The Conspiracie of Cateline, vndertaken against the gouernment of the Senate of Rome, and The Warre which Iugurth for many yeares maintained against the same State*, trans. Thomas Heywood (London, 1608), sig. π4ʳ.
[56] On the history of the Camden chair, see H. Stuart Jones, 'The Foundation and History of the Camden Chair', *Oxoniensia*, 8–9 (1943–4), 169–92, and Hugh Trevor-Roper, *Queen Elizabeth's First Historian: William Camden and the Beginnings of English 'Civil History'*, Neale Lecture in English History (London: Jonathan Cape, 1971), 34.
[57] Levy, *Tudor Historical Thought*, 247.
[58] Jean Bodin, *Method for the Easy Comprehension of History*, ed. Beatrice Reynolds (New York: Columbia University Press, 1945), 334.

'linguistic traces, in which the proof of origins chiefly lies'.[59] He then turns to the importance of names as historical evidence, calling them 'clearly marked footprints for the everlasting record of posterity'.[60] They are records which are not subject to the destructive ravages of time, proofs of genealogical descent which future generations will be able to trace, as Bodin's own discussion of the Celtic peoples indicates:

> The Celts... extended the frontiers of their empire and gave racial names to the subject peoples, like clearly marked footprints for the everlasting record of posterity, as almost all peoples have done. Then, from the Celts come the Celto-Scythians. The Celtiberians, whom Livy called the strength of Spain, are also from the ancient race of Gauls, by combining the name Celt with the Spanish.[61]

From names alone he is able to trace the extent of the Celtic conquests across Europe. He propounds a method which will enable his readers to gloss the geography of the world, to read place names historically, to fix historical knowledge by tracing the origins of the names of peoples and places. In short, he lays out an etymological method for history.[62] But he does more than that, for his method also sanctions that identification of etymology with genealogy which we saw at the beginning of this chapter. In deriving these Celtic 'racial names', he is also deriving the Celtic 'peoples'. He also therefore lays out an invaluable method for deriving the nations, and it may have been this which particularly appealed to his English antiquarian readers.

THE POLITICS OF ETYMOLOGY

As so often, Camden was in the vanguard here. The first part of his *Britannia* builds on the research outlined in his preface, as he considers the origins of the successive colonizers of Britain. In turn, he comments on the origins of the Britons, Romans, Picts, Irish, Saxons, Danes, and Normans, and he follows exactly the method proposed by Bodin. His approach is etymological, as he establishes national origins by tracing names back to their linguistic roots. His discussion of the Britons is an illustrative example. Many early modern accounts still followed Geoffrey of Monmouth, proposing a Trojan origin for the Britons, and deriving them from the eponymous Trojan prince Brutus.[63] This is neatly

---

[59] Jean Bodin, *Method for the Easy Comprehension of History*, ed. Beatrice Reynolds (New York: Columbia University Press, 1945), 336–8. In an apparent echo of this, Camden describes language as 'the surest proofe of peoples originall'; see *Britain*, 16.
[60] Bodin, *Method*, 336.
[61] Ibid. 347.
[62] For a discussion of the place of etymology in Bodin's work more generally, see Henri Sée, 'La Philosophie de l'histoire de Jean Bodin', *La Revue historique*, 175 (1935), 497–505.
[63] According to Geoffrey, Brutus 'called the island Britain from his own name, and his companions he called Britons'; see *The History of the Kings of Britain*, trans. Thorpe, i. 16.

illustrated by one of the heraldic notebooks of Sir William Segar, Garter King of Arms in the early seventeenth century, in which he tricked coats of arms and wrote biographical notes for successive British, Welsh, Saxon, Norman, and English kings, beginning with Brutus.[64] Camden offers a very different account, tracing a biblical genealogy instead. Through a complex etymology, informed by his reading of ancient historians and Christian exegetes, he proposes that the Britons were, in fact, the descendants of Gomer, eldest son of Japheth and grandson of Noah:

> Gomer his eldest sonne, in these farthest and remotest borders of Europe, gave both beginning and name to the Gomerians, which were after called Cimbrians and Cimerians. For, the name of Cimbrians or Cimerians filled in some sort this part of the world: and not onely in Germanie, but also in Gaule spred exceeding much. They which now are the Gaules, were, as Josephus and Zonaras write, called of Gomer, Gomari, Gomeræi and Gomeritæ. From these Gomarians or Gomeræans of Gaule, I have alwaies thought that our Britans drew their beginning, and from thence, for a proofe of the said beginning, brought their name: the very proper and peculiar name also of the Britains, hath perswaded me thereunto. For even they call themselves ordinarily Kumero, Cymro and Kumeri: like as a British woman Kumeraes, and the tongue it selfe, Kumeraeg.[65]

Camden's evidence is both linguistic and genealogical: the Britons' name in their own tongue. This name, 'Kumeri', derives from the former names of their ancestors, the Gauls. These names, 'Gomari, Gomeræi and Gomeritæ', in turn derive from the biblical Gomer. This etymology owes its substance to the account of the Noachian descent in Genesis 10, the biblical passage which describes the colonization of the postdiluvian world. This chapter was invariably cited by early modern historians who wanted to trace national origins back to Noah.[66] As a further proof of the Britons' biblical origin, Camden then turns to the name Gomer itself. 'Gomer in the Hebrew tongue,' he argues, 'betokeneth *vtmost Bordering*', which corresponds exactly with Gomer's descendants colonizing 'the utmost borders of Europe', Germany, France, and especially Britain.[67] Here, Camden was probably drawing on St Jerome's interpretation of Genesis 10: 2. Jerome argued that the sons of Japheth colonized Europe as far west as Cádiz in Spain, bestowing their names upon peoples and places as they went.[68]

---

[64] College of Arms, MS L. 14, fos. 362–84. In heraldry to trick is to draw a coat of arms in outline, the tinctures being denoted by letters or signs.
[65] Camden, *Britain*, 10.
[66] See the discussion in Colin Kidd, *British Identities before Nationalism: Ethnicity and Nationhood in the Atlantic World, 1600–1800* (Cambridge: Cambridge University Press, 1999), 9–33.
[67] Camden, *Britain*, 10.
[68] St Jerome, *Hebraicae quaestiones in libro Geneseos*, in *S. Hieronymi presbyteri opera*, Pars 1: Opera exegetica, 1, ed. Paul de Lagarde, Germain Morin, and Marcus Adriaen (Turnholt: Brepols, 1959), 14. 5–14. 9: 'Iafeth filio Noe nati sunt septem filii, qui possederunt terram in Asia ab Amano et Tauro Syriae Coeles et Ciliciae montibus usque ad fluuium Tanain. In Europa uero usque ad Gadira, nomina locis et gentibus relinquentes: e quibus postea immutata sunt plurima.'

Camden's etymology depends on the widespread assumption at the time that Hebrew names are prefigurative, that they correspond with and also determine the nature of what or whom they name. William L'Isle, best known today for his Anglo-Saxon scholarship, but in his own day reputed as a poet and translator, puts this belief forcefully in his *Babilon* (1595).[69] This work is a translation of the second day of Guillaume de Salluste du Bartas's *La Seconde Semaine*. In 1625 L'Isle reissued the work as part of a longer translation of du Bartas's poem, which also included his translation of Simon Goulart de Senlis's notes on the epic. In the poem L'Isle celebrates Hebrew for the very reason that even its simplest element, its most basic morpheme, has its own significance:

> Thou hast no word but wai'th; thy simplest elements
> Are full of hidden sense; thy points have Sacraments.
> O holy dialect, in thee the proper names
> Of men, tounes, countries, are th'abridgements of their fames
> And memorable deeds.[70]

Every Hebrew name is akin to a historical record, documenting the fame, deeds, or actions of the named. The Old Testament patriarchs, for example, were given their names as 'reasonable markes', which show 'with mightie consequent / What was of all their time the rarest accident'. Eve is 'consterd life', Cain 'first of all begot', Adam 'made of Clay', and Abel 'profit not'.[71] The most compelling illustration, however, that L'Isle considered Hebrew names to be significant, corresponding properly with what they name, is his explanatory gloss on Babylon itself. This is taken from one of Goulart de Senlis's notes, and it repeats an etymology that would have been familiar to all L'Isle's readers: '*Babylon* commeth of the word בבל *Babel*, which is derived of the Verbe בלל *Balal*, to confound, mingle, or trouble, as water when it is muddied.' L'Isle then expands on the linguistic root to reveal why Babylon and Babel were fittingly named: 'For so indeed the earthy *Babel*, that was in *Chadæa*, hath made a hotchpotch of the world.'[72] The Hebrew name is a record of the original confusion, the division of the nations into different tongues after the building of the Tower of Babel.

A more scholarly account of this belief about Hebrew was provided by Claude Duret in his *Thrésor de l'histoire des langues de cest univers* (1613). This monumental work, a compendium of linguistic scholarship, moves from an examination of the origins of language, through an account of all the known tongues of

---

[69] On L'Isle's Anglo-Saxon studies, see Phillip Pulsiano, 'William L'Isle and the Editing of Old English', in Timothy Graham (ed.), *The Recovery of Old English: Anglo-Saxon Studies in the Sixteenth and Seventeenth Centuries* (Kalamazoo: Medieval Institute Publications, 2000), 173–206.
[70] William L'Isle, *Part of Du Bartas, English and French, and in his Owne Kinde of Verse, so neare the French Englished, as may teach an English-Man French, or a French-man English* (London, 1625), sig. N1ʳ. '[W]ai'th' in the first line is simply a variant spelling of *weigheth*.
[71] Ibid., sigs. M4ʳ–N1ʳ.
[72] Ibid., sig. N4ᵛ.

the world, to a discussion of the language of animals. At its centre is the premiss that Hebrew was the original and perfect language, the tongue where names corresponded exactly with nature. Duret demonstrates this by reference to the Genesis story of Adam's naming of the animals.[73] These names, inherently correct because they were given in the language of Paradise, convey the natural histories of the animals. For Duret, there is little doubt that the language of Paradise was Hebrew because in that tongue the names of animals always correspond with their natures. Hebrew names contain their *histoire naturelle*; in illustration of this, he cites the stork, eagle, lion, whale, and crocodile. The stork, for example, is called *chasida* in Hebrew, a word which also means meek, charitable, or pious. In all seriousness Duret seals his argument by noting that the stork is also renowned for its acts of charity.[74] Its name—like all Hebrew names—is correct and properly significant. Having established this, Duret then argues that anyone versed in the Kabbalah, anyone instructed in the secrets of the Hebraic alphabet, will understand 'l'essence, vertu, action, & ressort de toutes les choses de cest univers'. For this reason also, he argues that Hebrew etymologies are more reliable and strong than those in any other language.[75]

Camden's derivation of the Britons from Gomer suggests that he shared Duret's belief about Hebrew etymologies. For Camden, this origin also had the authority of the Bible itself. He seems to have been less certain, though, about the genealogy which followed. His uncertainty is illustrated by a series of autograph notes on the subject, taken from Stow's *The Chronicles of England* (1580). These notes begin confidently enough: 'Wheras it is recorded by the sacred and most auncient hystorie, that after the Vniuersal Floude the ysles of the Gentiles were diuided by the posteritie of Iapheth the sonne of Noah, we doubte not but this ysle of Britanne was also then peopled by his progenie.'[76] But the succession—by which Camden and Stow mean the royal genealogies—that followed is 'irrecoverable, not onely vnto vs, but also to other nations'. The gaps can be filled only 'by the credite and authoritye of a new and small pamphlett falsely forged, and thrust into the world vnder the tytle of the auncient historian Berosus'.[77] That 'pamphlett' is the *Antiquitates* (1498) of Annius of Viterbo, one of the most audacious publications of the Renaissance. Annius's volume purports to contain rediscovered ancient texts, including works by real authors such as Archilochus, Berosus, and Manetho, and imaginary authors like

---

[73] See Genesis 2:19: 'And out of the ground the LORD God formed every beast of the field, and every fowl of the air; and brought them unto Adam to see what he would call them: and whatsoever Adam called every living creature, that was the name thereof' (AV).

[74] Claude Duret, *Thrésor de l'histoire des langues de cest univers* (Yverdon, 1619), 39–40.

[75] Ibid. 41: 'l'Etimologie en langue Hebraıque est sur toutes autres langues si forte & si pregnante'.

[76] BL, MS Harley 530, fo. 82ʳ.

[77] Ibid. On the historical Berosus, see Gerald P. Verbrugghe and John M. Wickersham, *Berossos and Manetho, Introduced and Translated: Native Traditions in Ancient Mesopotamia and Egypt* (Ann Arbor: University of Michigan Press, 1996), 13–34.

Metasthenes. These texts are accompanied by scholarly and apparently scrupulous commentaries.[78] Annius's edition of Berosus, the longest and most important of his texts, appears as Book 15. He claims there that he was given the manuscript of Berosus by two Armenian provincials, Matthias and Giorgio, who had stayed at the priory of San Domenico in Genoa when he was prior. Like the rest of the *Antiquitates*, this text was, in fact, a forgery, and it was quickly revealed as such. Camden (and evidently also Stow) shared this view, as the notes cite the denunciation of Juan Luís Vives and also refer to Gaspar Barreiros's similarly denunciatory tract, *Censura in quendam auctorem, qui sub falsa inscriptione Berosi Chaldæi circumfertur* (1565).

Later in the *Britannia* Camden supplements his biblical etymology with an explanation as to why the descendants of Gomer came to be known as Britons. Once again, his argument follows the method of Bodin. Reflecting on all the cognates of Britain, Camden concludes that 'the word BRIT is doubtlesse the primitive'. This, in turn, he derives from the Welsh word *brith*, meaning painted or coloured:

For, whatsoever is thus painted and coloured, in their ancient countrey speech, they call *Brith*. Neither is there any cause why any man should think this *Etymologie* of Britans to be harsh and absurd; seeing the very words sound alike, and the very name also as an expresse image, representeth the thing, which in *Etymologies* are chiefly required. For *Brith* and *Brit*, doe passing well accord: and that word *Brith* among the Britans, implieth that which the Britans were indeed, to wit, *painted, depainted, died*, and *coloured*.[79]

The etymology has credence on two different grounds. First, the words 'Brit' and 'brith' sound alike. Second, the derivation accords with the Britons' well-known habit of painting or tattooing their bodies with woad. Camden cites Caesar, Pliny, and Pomponius Mela as his authorities for this.[80] The name Briton therefore corresponds with their nature. Camden concludes his etymology by remarking that the Britons 'had no marke whereby they might be distinguished and knowen from the borderers, better than by that maner of theirs to paint their bodies'.[81] The implication is that 'Kumeri', by contrast, with its derivation from Gomer, might be a name common to them and their fellow 'borderers', the

---

[78] On Annius of Viterbo, see Anthony Grafton, 'Invention of Traditions and Traditions of Invention in Renaissance Europe: The Strange Case of Annius of Viterbo', in Anthony Grafton and Ann Blair (eds.), *The Transmission of Culture in Early Modern Europe* (Philadelphia: University of Pennsylvania Press, 1990), 8–38, and Richard Thomas John, 'Fictive Ancient History and National Consciousness in Early Modern Europe: The Influence of Annius of Viterbo's *Antiquitates*' (Ph.D. thesis, Warburg Institute, University of London, 1994).

[79] Camden, *Britain*, 26.

[80] See Julius Caesar, *The Gallic War*, trans. H. J. Edwards (Loeb Classical Library; Cambridge, Mass.: Harvard University Press, 1997; first published in this edition 1917), v. 14; Pliny, *Natural History*, trans H. Rackham et al., 10 vols. (Loeb Classical Library; Cambridge, Mass.: Harvard University Press, 1938–63), xxii. 2; and Pomponius Mela, *De chorographia libri tres*, ed. Carolus Frick (Stuttgart: Teubner, 1968), iii. 51.

[81] Camden, *Britain*, 26.

Gauls and the Germans. The name Briton was therefore coined as a marker of difference between the Britons and their neighbours, the origin of which lay in the Britons' most striking and original characteristic.

Strange as it may sound, by tracing the Britons back to Gomer in this way, Camden was contributing to the articulation of a specifically English national identity. He was advancing an idea of English national and linguistic priority, which depended on this derivation from Noah. Such appropriations of British, and later Welsh, history were, as Philip Schwyzer has shown, not unusual in the sixteenth century.[82] Through his etymology Camden sought to establish a British ancestry for the English. In his possessive phrase 'our Britans'—*nostri Britanni* in the original Latin—he sought to create a community, incorporating his mostly English readers into this vision of English national history.[83] These ancestors are not just the Britons; they are *our* Britons.

However, by the time of the definitive sixth edition of the *Britannia*, published in 1607, the significance of this etymology must have changed.[84] What had previously contributed to the articulation of an English identity, became, following the accession of James I, a contribution to that corporate British identity which he sought to promote in the early years of his reign, and perhaps even a genealogical defence of his policy of the union of the two kingdoms of England and Scotland.[85] That Camden himself intended his etymology to be read in this new way is suggested by another etymology, a derivation which does not appear in the *Britannia* until 1607. Camden notes in this edition, for the first time, that the Lowland Scots descend from 'one and the same originall' as the English.[86] Whether he believed this, or whether this was just a sop to the Scottish James, is immaterial. The addition immediately legitimizes James's right by bloodline to the throne of England. The English and the Scots share a common heritage, and that heritage can be traced by etymology back to the original inhabitants of the island. The addition also therefore offers tacit support for the union, and suggests that the earlier etymology of the Britons also came to be associated with the debates on that policy. In Camden's hands, therefore, etymology was not just historicized, but also politicized.

In this way, the etymologies in the *Britannia* reflect what was a growing trend at the time. Whilst it may be anachronistic to speak of conscious language

---

[82] Philip Schwyzer, *Literature, Nationalism, and Memory in Early Modern England and Wales* (Cambridge: Cambridge University Press, 2004).
[83] William Camden, *Britannia, sive florentissimorum regnorum, Angliæ, Scotiæ, Hiberniæ, et insularum adiacentium ex intima antiquitate chorographica descriptio* (London, 1586), sig. B5ʳ.
[84] For more on the different editions of the *Britannia*, see Ch. 3 below.
[85] For useful introductions to the union, see Bruce R. Galloway, *The Union of England and Scotland, 1603–1608* (Edinburgh: John Donald, 1986), and Jenny Wormald, 'James VI, James I and the Identity of Britain', in Brendan Bradshaw and John Morrill (eds.), *The British Problem, c.1534–1707: State Formation in the Atlantic Archipelago* (Basingstoke: Macmillan, 1996), 148–71.
[86] Camden, *Britain*, 119; and *Britannia, sive florentissimorum regnorum Angliæ, Scotiæ, Hiberniæ, et insularum adiacentium ex intima antiquitate chorographica descriptio* (London, 1607), 85.

politics in the early modern period, the connections between language and politics were, as Peter Burke has pointed out, still present.[87] The notion that the study of languages might contribute to the articulation of national identities, for example, was increasingly popular. In England, this was especially apparent in the interest in tongues other than English. Cornish and Manx, for instance, both started to attract scholarly attention. In the case of Manx, this seems to have been primarily for religious reasons. In 1604 John Phillips, bishop of Sodor and Man, began work on his Manx translations of the Bible and Book of Common Prayer. By 1610 he had completed the latter, and in the convocation of that year he proposed that it should be perused by his clergy, 'so with one uniform consent to have it ready for printing'. According to the antiquary and Governor of the Isle of Man, James Chaloner, Phillips undertook his work 'out of zeal, to the propagation of the Gospel'.[88] With Cornish the motivation seems to have been more explicitly patriotic and also more preservationist. The sixteenth century had witnessed a rapid decline in the number of Cornish speakers, a fact normally attributed to the Reformation.[89] Accordingly, some scholars set about defending and even promoting the language. Richard Carew, for example, in *The Survey of Cornwall* (1602), commented on the origins of Cornish, reporting the theory of Master Thomas Williams that it 'was deriued from, or at least had some acquayntance with the Greeke'. He then prints a table of ten examples of 'wordes of one sence in both':

Greeke.	Cornish.	English.
Teino	*Tedua*	Draw
Mamma	*Mamm*	Mother
Episcopos	*Escoppe*	Bishop
Klyo	*Klowo*	Heere
Didaskein	*Dathisky*	To teach
Kyon	*Kye*	Dogge
Kentron	*Kentron*	Spurre
Methyo	*Methow*	Drinke
Scaphe	*Schapth*	Boat
Ronchos	*Ronchie*	Snorting, &c.[90]

---

[87] Peter Burke, *Languages and Communities in Early Modern Europe* (Cambridge: Cambridge University Press, 2004), 75.
[88] Cited in *The Book of Common Prayer in Manx Gaelic*, ed. A. W. Moore and John Rhys, 2 vols. (Oxford: The Manx Society, 1895), p. xxii.
[89] Burke, *Languages and Communities*, 71; Brian Murdoch, *Cornish Literature* (Cambridge: D. S. Brewer, 1993), 15.
[90] Richard Carew, *The Survey of Cornwall* (London, 1602), sig. P3^{r-v}.

Origins and Names 71

The point here is to claim a kinship for Cornish with an ancient, scholarly, and venerable tongue. On this basis, Cornish can stand as a literary language in its own right. As Carew himself adds, Cornish 'is stored with sufficient plenty to express the conceits of a good wit, both in prose and rime'.[91]

But it was Welsh scholars and linguists who particularly emphasized the links between national consciousness and the triumph of their own tongue. In 1592, for example, Siôn Dafydd Rhys published the *Cambrobrytannicæ Cymraecæve Linguae Institutiones*, a Welsh grammar, which boasted prefatory material from Camden, Humphrey Prichard, and Sir John Stradling. Rhys, who had previously written a work on the Italian language, *De Italicae linguae pronunciatione* (1569), was suffused with a sense of the literary worth of his native tongue.[92] As Carew would do for Cornish, he promotes the *copia*, and therefore also the literariness, of the language. But he also goes further than Carew, for his preface compares Welsh not only with Greek, but also with Arabic and Latin.[93] A year later Henry Salesbury made a similar point in his *Grammatica Britannica* (1593), promoting the kinship between Welsh and Hebrew.[94] Later scholars, such as the seventeenth-century lexicographer and translator John Davies of Mallwyd, shared this perspective, and projected their own studies of the Welsh language in similarly national terms. Camden himself was aware of this, and in his dedicatory poem to the *Institutiones* he predicts the glory that Rhys's grammar will bring, not only to the grammarian himself, but also to his country, Wales.[95] For Camden, then, the history of a language was always more than just scholarly or antiquarian curiosity.

Camden was far from the only scholar to politicize etymology. Other writers too recognized the potential of this antiquarian methodology for advancing particular lines of national descent, and it is to another example, Edmund Spenser, that I turn in the remainder of this chapter. Some time in the mid-1590s Spenser began work on his long prose tract *A View of the Present State of*

---

[91] For a survey of Cornish literature in the early modern period, see Graham Sandercock, *A Very Brief History of the Cornish Language* (Hayle: Kesva an Taves Kernewek, 1996), 7–15.

[92] Rhys's claim to expertise in the Italian language came from the fact that he lived in Italy for a number of years. After studying at Oxford in the 1550s, he first travelled there. By Sept. 1563 he was engaged as tutor to the sons of Vincenzo Gheri at Pistoia. He subsequently studied at the University of Siena, receiving his doctor of medicine in July 1567, and was also public moderator of the school of Pistoia. See R. Brinley Jones, *The Old British Tongue: The Vernacular in Wales 1540–1640* (Cardiff: Avalon, 1970), 12.

[93] Siôn Dafydd Rhys, *Cambrobrytannicæ Cymraecæve Linguae Institutiones et Rudimenta* (London, 1592), sig. *3ᵛ: 'In quo clarissimè liquebit, quàm prægnans, quàm fœcunda sit lingua Cambrobrytannica, quàm apposititijs vocabulis simplicibus, compositis, deductitijs, quamlibet artem & scientiam explicet, quàm non cedat Arabicæ, Græcæ, & Romanæ copiæ'.

[94] Henry Salesbury, *Grammatica Britannica in usum ejus linguæ studiosorum succinctâ methodo & perspicuitate facili conscripta* (London, 1593), sig. 2*3ᵛ: 'ita & Britannica ut est linguis barbaris asperior, sic antiquior & Linguæ Sanctæ consimilior, verborum etymis instructior, prolatione integrior, vocum synonymia locupletior, argumento præstantior & carminum generibus copiosior'.

[95] 'In laudem Ioannis Davidis medicinæ doctoris, ob linguam Britannicam correctam, poesimque fœlicissime restitutam', in Rhys, *Institutiones*, sig. *4ᵛ, ll. 3–4: 'Sed laus (docte Dauid) tibi cedat, namque labore, / Quæ parta est patriæ gloria, parta tuo.'

Ireland, a treatise intended to help restore order to the country which had become his home. On 14 April 1598 this work was entered in the Stationers' Register to the printer Matthew Lownes, but, for reasons which remain unclear, it was not printed until 1633, when it appeared in an edition by the Dublin antiquary Sir James Ware.[96] Today, Spenser's work has gained a certain notoriety for the brutality of some of the measures which it proposes. Irish laws and customs are repeatedly shown up as barbarous and in need of urgent reform. Their etymologies hold the key here, as Spenser explores the dangerousness of these customs by drawing attention to their barbaric origins.[97] Spenser, therefore, speaks in the *View* as an archetypal antiquary, even if his own perspective is highly partial. In its interest in laws, customs, and practices, Spenser's text, as Bart Van Es has shown, has much in common with those papers presented at the meetings of the Elizabethan Society of Antiquaries.[98]

Ware edited his text from a manuscript in the library of James Ussher, Bishop of Armagh. He printed Spenser's work alongside two other Elizabethan accounts of Ireland by Edmund Campion and Meredith Hanmer. Ware's volume is titled *The Historie of Ireland* (1633), and it is notable for the emphasis which it places on the historical and antiquarian dimensions of Spenser's text.[99] In the preface, for example, Ware commends Spenser's many derivations. 'His proofes (although most of them conjecturall) concerning the originall of the language, customes of the Nations, and the first peopling of the severall parts of the Iland,' he tells his readers, 'are full of good reading; and doe shew a sound judgement.'[100] An early manuscript of the *View*, incidentally, also emphasizes Spenser's etymologies in this way. This manuscript, which is now preserved in the Bodleian Library (MS Gough Ireland 2), was probably copied in Spenser's lifetime, and its title similarly draws attention to his interest in etymologies

---

[96] Edward Arber, *A Transcript of the Registers of the Company of Stationers of London; 1554–1640 A.D.*, 5 vols. (Birmingham: privately printed, 1894), iii. 111. For a summary of the complexity of the *View*'s textual transmission and a discussion of its possible censorship and suppression, see Jean R. Brink, 'Constructing the *View of the Present State of Ireland*', *Spenser Studies*, 11 (1990), 203–28.

[97] For previous discussions of Spenser's etymologies, see John W. Draper, 'Spenser's Linguistics in *The Present State of Ireland*', *Modern Philology*, 17 (1919–20), 471–86, and Anne Fogarty, 'The Colonization of Language: Narrative Strategy in *A View of the Present State of Ireland* and *The Faerie Queene*, Book VI', in Patricia Coughlan (ed.), *Spenser and Ireland: An Interdisciplinary Perspective* (Cork: Cork University Press, 1989), 75–108.

[98] Bart Van Es, *Spenser's Forms of History* (Oxford: Oxford University Press, 2002), 78–111.

[99] This did not, however, prevent subsequent readers, including John Milton, from reading the work politically; see Willy Maley, 'How Milton and Some Contemporaries Read Spenser's *View*', in Brendan Bradshaw, Andrew Hadfield, and Willy Maley (eds.), *Representing Ireland: Literature and the Origins of Conflict, 1534–1660* (Cambridge: Cambridge University Press, 1993), 191–208 at 193.

[100] *The Historie of Ireland, Collected by Three Learned Authors viz. Meredith Hanmer Doctor in Divinitie: Edmund Campion sometime Fellow of St Johns College in Oxford: and Edmund Spenser Esq.*, ed. James Ware (Dublin, 1633), sig. ¶4ʳ.

and origins: 'Irelands Survey or A Historical Dialogue and View of ancient and modern times *wherein is discoursed the Ancient Originalls of the Irish Nation*'.[101]

Spenser's most extensive etymology is his long passage in the middle of the dialogue on the genealogical origins of the Irish. As Irenæus, one of his two speakers, puts it: 'Before we enter into the treatye of their Customes it is firste nedefull to Consider from whence they firste spronge, ffor from the sundrie manners of the nacions from whence that people which is now Called Irishe weare derived some of the Customes which now remaine amongest them haue bene firste fetched; and sithence theare Continued amongest them.' He then concludes that their most significant ancestors were the Scythians: 'the Chiefest which haue firste possessed and inhabited it I Suppose to be Scithians which at suche time as the Northern nacions ouerflowed all Christendome Came downe to the sea Coste where inquiringe for other Contries abroad and gettinge intelligence of this Countrye of Irelande fyndinge shippinge Conveniente passed over hither and Arived in the Northe parte thereof whiche is now Called Vlster'.[102]

Later in the *View* Irenæus runs through the customs which the Irish have inherited from the Scythians. His first example is 'boolying', the pasturing of cattle in the hills. This, he asserts, 'appearethe plaine to be the manner of the Scithians'. His interlocutor, Eudoxus, asks why the practice is dangerous, pointing out that 'it is very behoofull in this Countrye of Irelande wheare theare are greate mountaines and waste desertes full of grasse that the same shoulde be eaten downe and norishe manye thowsandes of Cattell for the good of the whole realme'. Irenæus's reply is swift and devastating:

But by this Custome of Bolloyinge theare growe in the meane time manye greate enormityes vnto that Comon wealthe for the firste if theare be any outlawes or loose people (as they are never without some) which live vppon stealthes and spoile, they are evermore succored and finde reliefe onelye in those Bollies being vppon the waste places, whereas els they shoulde be driven shortelye to sterve or to Come downe to the townes to steale reliefe where by one meanes or other they they woulde sone be Caughte: besides such stealthes of Cattell as they make they bringe Comonlye to those *Bollyes* wheare they are receaued readilye and the Thiefe Harbored from daunger of Lawe or suche officers as mighte lighte vppon him.[103]

Not only does the practice of boolying provide refuge for miscreants in general, who can hide from the reach of the law in these mountainous outposts, but it also encourages the more particularly Irish practice of cattle raiding. It is therefore detrimental to the common weal, and runs counter to English attempts to

---

[101] The emphasis and italics here are mine.
[102] Edmund Spenser, *A View of the Present State of Ireland*, in *Spenser's Prose Works*, ed. Rudolf Gottfried (Baltimore: The Johns Hopkins Press, 1949), 82–3.
[103] Ibid. 98.

maintain order in Ireland. The ever willing Eudoxus is quickly convinced: 'By your speache *Irenius* I perceaue more evill Come by this vse of Bollies then good by their grazinge and therefore it maye well be reformed.'[104] Having dealt with boolying in this way, Irenæus then runs through a series of other Irish customs, similarly tracing them back to the Scythians, demonstrating their enormities, and arguing for their reform.

The Scythians were the archetypal barbarians at the gate in much of classical historiography. Scythia itself was a broad term, used by Greek and Roman historians and geographers to characterize the lands to their north and east, and was typically presented as a wilderness of savage and uncivilized practices. Herodotus, for example, mentions the Scythians' fondness for human sacrifice, their pledging and drinking of blood out of the skulls of their enemies, and their taste for garments made from the skin of the men that they kill.[105] Strabo mentions the same things, reporting their 'savage dealings with strangers, in that they sacrifice them, eat their flesh, and use their skulls as drinking-cups'.[106] It is not hard, therefore, to see why Irenæus, and of course also Spenser, might have wanted to invoke this uncivilized origin for the Irish. Things are complicated somewhat by the fact that some classical historiography also records a degree of admiration for the Scythians: Strabo, for example, in the same place notes that the Greeks consider them 'the most straightforward of men and the least prone to mischief'. But if this weakens Irenæus's argument, his repeated critique of the Irish customs inherited from the Scythians leaves readers of the dialogue in little doubt about his (and presumably also Spenser's) perception of these practices.

But Spenser goes further than this, for he also finds in the linguistic origins of individual practices arguments for their reform. Here, he engages in what we might call a rhetoric of pejoration, and here also he exemplifies the idea of etymology as paronomasia, mentioned by Fraunce.[107] Doubts over the names of Irish customs allow Spenser to play with their etymologies and thereby invest them with brutish origins. Echoing the old belief that the origins of words are somehow perpetually present, Spenser's point seems to be that by showing the barbaric linguistic origins of Irish customs, he was also showing the barbarism of the customs themselves.

In other works too Spenser recognizes the rhetorical and playful potential of etymology. At various points in *The Faerie Queene* (1590 and 1596), for example, he both explores the possibilities of names as historical records and plays upon the imaginative space opened up by the sometimes uncertain gap

---

[104] Edmund Spenser, *A View of the Present State of Ireland*, in *Spenser's Prose Works*, ed. Rudolf Gottfried (Baltimore: The Johns Hopkins Press, 1949), 99.

[105] For Herodotus' discussion of Scythian customs, see *The History*, trans. A. D. Godley, 4 vols. (Loeb Classical Library; Cambridge, Mass.: Harvard University Press, 1963–9), iv. 59–81.

[106] Strabo, *The Geography*, trans. Horace Leonard Jones, 8 vols. (Loeb Classical Library; Cambridge, Mass.: Harvard University Press, 1917–32), 7. 3. 7.

[107] See p. 61 above.

between a word and its origin.[108] The chronicle read by Prince Arthur in Eumnestes' chamber in Book 2, for instance, is filled with etymologies, with place names which memorialize their founders. Some are familiar, as Spenser repeats the old Galfridian derivations of Corineus-Cornwall, Albanact-Albania, Humber-Humber, and Sabrine-Severn.[109] Others, however, are not, and seem to be Spenserian inventions. Arthur also comes across such figures as the Trojan princes Debon, whose 'shayre was, that is *Deuonshyre*', and Canutus, who 'had his portion from the rest, / The which he cald Canutium, for his hyre; / Now Cantium, which Kent we commenly inquire'.[110] Neither of these names is mentioned in any previous source or account. They are Spenser's embellishments, chosen, it would seem, principally because of their likeness to the two counties' names. It is hard to know how seriously Spenser intended this to be taken. Any reader familiar with the matter of Britain would have recognized the novelty of the two names. In this light, they might therefore be seen as a comment on both the reliability of the etymological tradition and the veracity of the whole Galfridian matter transmitted in Arthur's chronicle. Indeed, it has been argued that the etymologies here are 'taken to what seems like demonstrative excess', enabling Spenser to show up the nonsense of much of the matter contained therein.[111] They might, in short, be etymological jokes or puns.

In the *View*, however, Spenser's purpose is altogether more serious. He plays on etymology in the same way, but his purpose is more political and also polemical. The derivation of 'palatine' is a case in point.[112] This etymology is occasioned by his two speakers reflecting on the inconveniences of certain privileges relating to Ireland, which were formerly granted by English kings. Irenæus mentions counties palatine as one example. As is his wont, Eudoxus then asks his friend for a gloss. Irenæus replies by giving two possible etymologies:

It was as I suppose firste named Palatine of a pale, as it weare a pale and defence to theire inner landes so as now it is Called the Englishe pale, And thereof allso is a Palsgrave named that is an Earle Palcatine/ Others thinke of the Latine Palare that is to forrage or outrunne because those marchers and borderers vse Comonlye so to doe.[113]

It is hard to believe that Spenser, who was a competent Latinist, or indeed many of his readers, would have believed either of these. The correct derivation of

---

[108] See the discussion in K. K. Ruthven, 'The Poet as Etymologist', *Critical Quarterly*, 11 (1969), 9–37.
[109] Edmund Spenser, *The Faerie Queene*, ed. A. C. Hamilton (London and New York: Longman, 1977), II. x. 12. 2–5, II. x. 14. 2–3, II. x. 16. 6–9, and II. x. 19. 7–8; Geoffrey of Monmouth, *History*, i. 16, ii. 1, ii. 2, and ii. 5.
[110] Spenser, *Faerie Queene*, II. x. 12. 6–9.
[111] Van Es, *Spenser's Forms of History*, 41.
[112] My reading here follows the excellent discussion of this etymology in David J. Baker, 'Off the Map: Charting Uncertainty in Renaissance Ireland', in Bradshaw, Hadfield, and Maley (eds.), *Representing Ireland*, 76–92 at 87–90.
[113] Spenser, *View*, 74.

'palatine' from the Latin *palatium* (palace) was well known at the time. John Selden, for example, gives it in his *Titles of Honour* (1614): 'The Palatins hauing their denomination from *Palatium*, the *Palace* or Kings Court'.[114] But lexical accuracy was not Spenser's primary concern here. As Irenæus's next comment makes clear, the etymology is a rhetorical strategy, a warning of the dangers of counties palatine. He notes that 'to haue a Countie Pallatine is in effecte but to haue a priviledge to spoile the enemies borders adioyninge', and he then links this general maxim to specific events in Ireland. 'And surelye so it is vsed at this daie as a priviledged place of spoiles and stealthes,' he observes, 'for the Countye of Tipperarye which is now the onelye Countye Palatine in Irelande is by abuse of some bad ones made a receptacle to robb the reste of the Countries aboute it by meanes of whose priviledges none will followe theire stealthes.' The geographical position of Tipperary, 'being scituate in the verye lappe of all the lande', only makes matters worse.[115] By the time of the *View*, Tipperary was the only surviving palatinate in Ireland, and it was under the sway of Thomas Butler, eleventh earl of Ormond and cousin of the queen. Irenæus's point is that the current abuses of the jurisdiction demonstrate the truth of his earlier etymologies. The unruliness of the county palatine, which permits spoil and stealth, matches its unruly linguistic origins. The etymologies are intended to reinforce, perhaps for the benefit of one reader in particular, Elizabeth I, the problems which the county palatine, Tipperary, causes for the maintenance of order and authority in Ireland. The politics of this particular etymology are clear.

A similar argument might be made about Spenser's discussion of 'tanistry' earlier in the work. Tanistry was the Irish custom of life-tenure, whereby the succession to an estate was conferred by election rather than primogeniture. 'It is a Custome amongest all the Irisherie that presentelye after the deathe of anie theire Chief Lordes or Captaines,' Irenæus observes, 'they doe presentlye asemble themselues to a place generallie appointed and knowne vnto them to Choose another in his steade, wheare they doe nominate and electe for the moste parte not the eldest soonne nor anie of the Children of theire Lorde deceased but the next to him of bloode, that is the eldest and worthiest.'[116] The custom is a problem for the English because the Irish claim on the basis of tanistry that 'their Auncestors had not estate in anye theire Landes, Segniories, or hereditamentes longer then duringe their owne lives', and thus allege that they are not beholden

---

[114] John Selden, *Titles of Honour* (London, 1614), 241.
[115] Spenser, *View*, 74.
[116] Ibid. 50. Incidentally, Camden gave the same definition. In a letter of 17 Apr. 1605 to the French historian Jacques-Auguste de Thou, answering his request for information about Irish and Scottish history, he defined tanistry in the same way, as he explained why, after the death of Matthew O'Neill, Shane O'Neill claimed the lordship of Tyrone, not Matthew's son Hugh: 'Sin autem Matthæus filius fuisset legitimus lege tamen Hibernica (Tanistriam vocant) virum matura ætate & sanguine proximiorem præferendum puero nondum XXI annos nato' (BNF, Dupuy 632, fo. 102ʳ).

to any previous treaties or agreements with English monarchs. For Spenser, therefore, this is another Irish custom which needs to be reformed, and he reinforces his argument by the origin which he then proposes for it. First, he connects tanistry to the suffix 'Tania', which 'shoulde signifye a province or Seigniorye'. Then, he suggests that this suffix 'came auntientlye from those Barbarous nacions that ouerrane the worlde which possessed those dominions whereof they are now so Called', and finally that 'it may well be That from thence the firste originall of this worde *Tanist* and *Tanistry* came'.[117] Thus, as with the customs inherited from the Scythians, the barbarous origins of tanistry are themselves an argument for the barbarism of the practice.

Some of Spenser's etymologies work in a slightly different way. These are customs which are not in themselves barbarous, but which become so when they are translated into Ireland. Later, for instance, Spenser turns his attention to 'raths', the earthen mounds or hill-forts scattered throughout Ireland. His curiosity here may have been piqued by the landscape around his castle and estate at Kilcolman, since this was dotted with ancient memorials and remains, including a number of raths.[118] But in the *View*, as always, the context is a discussion of an Irish custom and an argument for its reform:

Theare is a greate vse amongst the Irishe to make greate assemblies togeather vppon a Rathe or hill theare to parlye (as they saie) aboute matters and wronges betwene Towneshipp and Towneshippe or one private persone and another But well I wote and trewe it hathe bene often times aproued that in these metinges manye mischiefs haue bene bothe practised and wroughte ffor to them doe Comonlye resorte all the scum of lose people wheare they maye frelye mete and Conferr of what they liste which else they Coulde not doe without suspicion or knowledge of others.[119]

These assemblies are dangerous, Irenæus suggests, because they take place away from the eyes of the law. All kinds of mischief can and do, therefore, occur. By way of illustration, Irenæus adds that he has 'diuerse times knowen that manye Englishemen and other good Irishe subiectes haue bene villanouslye murdered by movinge one quarrell or another amongest them'.

Spenser's argument seems straightforward enough: these assemblies are another threat to order in Ireland, and another custom which must therefore be reformed or replaced. However, things are complicated by what Eudoxus says in reply. He points out that these assemblies, or 'Folkmotes', as he calls them, are not inherently dangerous. He notes that they were 'at firste ordeyned for the same purpose that people mighte assemble themselves theareon', and that they were 'a place for people to moote or talke of anie thing that Concerned anie difference betwene parties and Towneshipps which semethe yeat to me verye requisite'.

---

[117] Spenser, *View*, 51.
[118] Pauline Henley, *Spenser in Ireland* (Cork: Cork University Press, 1928), 93–4.
[119] Spenser, *View*, 128–9.

Furthermore, Irenæus himself apparently agrees: 'ye saie verye Trewe *Eudox*. the firste makinge of these hye hills was at firste indede to verye good purposse for people to mete'. The problems began, he argues, only when these assemblies started to take place in Ireland: 'but howe euer the times when they weare firste made mighte well serue to good accacions as perhaps they did then in Englande yeat thinges beinge since alltered and now Irelande much defferinge from that state of Englande the good vse that then was of them is now turned to abuse'.[120] In England, the assemblies were a source of authority and order; it was only when they moved across the Irish Sea that that authority turned to abuse. Irenæus then concludes his argument about the English origin of these assemblies with a pair of etymologies. These hills or mounds, he suggests, were 'builte by two seuerall nacions'. Some, 'those which youe Cale *Folkemotes*', were 'builte by the Saxons as the worde bewraieth for it signifyethe in Saxon metinge of folke or people'. Others 'weare Caste vpp by the danes as the names of them dothe betoken for they are Called *Deanerathes*'.[121] What is implicit is that the Saxons and the Danes were both also ancestors of the English.

In his discussion of raths Spenser seems to be holding out the prospect of an authentic, virtuous alternative to the Irish custom. Raths *per se* are not a problem. The abuses described by Irenæus are not inherent in the assemblies themselves, but arise instead from their misappropriation on Irish soil. This etymology, then, is another argument for the Anglicization of Irish customs, laws, and practices. Furthermore, in this case, the English equivalent has the virtue not only of being English, but also of being older and more authentic. By turning to etymology in this way, Spenser's discussion also carries the weight, correctness, and authority of antiquarian tradition. To Spenser's readers, who would have been more attuned to etymology than readers today, because of historical guides such as Bodin's *Methodus*, but also because of the central place of etymology in history writing at the time, that authority would have been a given. But Spenser has it both ways. For his argument about raths, and indeed about all the other customs surveyed, also depends on an uncertainty in etymology, on him being able to manipulate the origins of words for a particular political or rhetorical end. Etymology, after all, as Camden reminds us, can be a doubtful and obscure subject.

The *View* might, therefore, be said to demonstrate an antiquarian methodology put into literary practice. The work purports to be recuperative, turning to

---

[120] Spenser, *View*, 129.

[121] Ibid. 129–30. In a note to his edition, Ware adds, on the basis of this etymology, that the Danes may have introduced the custom to Ireland: 'The like reason may be given for the making of such *Rathes* in Ireland, by the *Danes* or *Norwegians*' (*Historie of Ireland*, 55). This was later refuted by his great-grandson, the 18th-c. antiquary Walter Harris, who pointed out that 'danerath' in fact derived from two Irish words, *rath* and *dún*, which 'both signifie a *fortified Place*, generally on a Hill, where such Fortifications were usually made'; *The Whole Works of Sir James Ware Concerning Ireland*, ed. Walter Harris, 3 vols. (Dublin, 1739–46), iii. 137.

etymology to restore knowledge of the past. It follows assiduously the argument that in the origin of a word lies its true meaning or nature. On this assumption, numerous antiquarian works, from the *Curious Discourses* to Camden's *Britannia*, depended. It takes for granted the fundamental antiquarian connection between etymology and genealogy. It illustrates how important the search for origins, linguistic and national, had become, and it demonstrates the formative link between the two. But in its polemic, it also shows that the antiquarian search for origins was rarely, if ever, a disinterested one. In short, it confirms the politics of early modern etymology.

3

Restoring Britain: Courtesy and Collaboration in Camden's *Britannia*

In 1577 Abraham Ortelius renewed his search for a reliable English antiquary. His previous choices had not been inspired. Daniel Rogers, as we saw in Chapter 1, lacked the rigour to complete the task. He had been able to collect a vast array of pertinent material—poems, manuscripts, even inscriptions—but he had signally failed to organize this as a coherent narrative. Humphrey Lhwyd, the Welsh scholar and physician who was similarly encouraged by Ortelius, had fared better, but his field of inquiry was circumscribed, and his publications were similarly limited.[1] Lhwyd's interests were firmly in British antiquity, in the history of his native Wales. Roman Britain, therefore, was still to be restored; the task of identifying Roman place names, Ortelius's principal concern, remained. A new candidate, someone more suited to the antiquarian matter at hand, had to be found.

That candidate was William Camden, at the time under-master at Westminster School, but a scholar who would later become the foremost English antiquary of his generation, and the result was the *Britannia* (1586), the pre-eminent antiquarian book of the day.[2] In his preface to a later edition of that work Camden spoke of his debt to Ortelius, and he traced it back to the Flemish geographer's visit to England in 1577, when the two men evidently met: 'Abraham Ortelius, the worthy restorer of Ancient Geographie arriuing heere in England, aboue thirty-four yeares past, dealt earnestly with me that I would illustrate this Ile of BRITAINE, or (as he said) that I would restore antiquity to Britaine, and Britain to his antiquity'.[3] After Ortelius's return to Antwerp in the

---

[1] For Lhywd's relations with Ortelius, see Theodore Max Chotzen, 'Some Sidelights on Cambro-Dutch Relations', *Transactions of the Honourable Society of Cymmrodorion*, Session 1937 (1938), 101–44 at 118–20, 129–44; and Levy, *Tudor Historical Thought*, 132–3.

[2] F. J. Levy, 'The Making of Camden's *Britannia*', *Bibliothèque d'humanisme et renaissance*, 26 (1964), 70–97 at 87–90. On Camden's period as a master at Westminster, see Wyman H. Herendeen, *William Camden: A Life in Context* (Woodbridge: Boydell, 2007), 91–179.

[3] Camden, *Britain*, sig. π4ʳ. All further references will be to this translation, unless otherwise stated. Camden himself—and scholars have not often realized this—had a hand in the translation.

summer of 1577, the two men began to correspond, and their new antiquarian project started to take shape.

From the correspondence, it is clear that Camden, initially at least, shared Ortelius's end of recovering the place names of Roman Britain. On 4 August 1577, for example, he wrote to Ortelius to ask if he had a manuscript of the Antonine Itineraries, and, if so, whether Ortelius could transcribe and send the British sections to him.[4] The Antonine Itineraries were sequential lists of settlements, way-marks, or posting-stations, often with the distances between them, and they numbered in total some 225 routes across the Roman Empire.[5] The Itineraries were believed to hold the key to identifying Roman place names, and, following Geoffroy Tory's edition of 1512, they had been frequently reprinted and studied. The British routes, for example, of which there were fifteen, had been partly identified by the antiquary and collector Robert Talbot, whose work Camden would later consult. 'Lately have I happened vppon Talbots notes in *Antonini Itinerarium*', he remarked in a letter of December 1599.[6] Twenty years earlier, as the doyen of classical geography, Ortelius was another reliable source for this subject.

Later the same month Camden wrote again, this time to thank Ortelius for a gift. Ortelius had sent him a copy of Sextus Rufus' compendium of Roman history, the *Breviarum de victoriis et provinciis populi Romani*, in an edition prepared by Hubert Goltzius in the 1560s.[7] For Camden, the importance of Goltzius's edition, and therefore also Ortelius's gift, was the light that it shed on the names of the provinces of Roman Britain. Previously he had struggled to reconcile the references in Sextus Rufus to eighteen provinces in Gaul and Britain with that text's enumeration of only seventeen. Thanks to Ortelius's gift, he could now fill the gap, as Goltzius's edition named the eighteenth province: Flavia Caesariensis.[8]

A letter of 25 Aug. 1609 survives, in which Philemon Holland thanks Camden for checking the proofs and correcting his work, and also seeks Camden's assistance in eight further places (BL, MS Cotton Julius C. V, fo. 106ʳ). Thomas Fuller also suggested that Camden might have contributed to the translation, calling Holland's *Britain* 'a *Translation* more then a *Translation*, with many excellent Additions, not found in the *Latine*, done *fifty* years since in Master *Camdens* life time, not onely with his knowledge and consent, but also, no doubt by his desire and help'; *The History of the Worthies of England* (London, 1662), iii. 128.

[4] William Camden to Abraham Ortelius, 4 Aug. 1577, in *Abrahami Ortelii . . . epistulae*, 168: 'et si quod manuscriptum Antonini A. Itinerarium habes, vt Britanniar*um* itinera mihi describas, te humillimè rogo'.

[5] For the Antonine Itineraries, see O. A. W. Dilke, *Greek and Roman Maps* (London: Thames and Hudson, 1985), 125–8; for the British *itinera*, see A. L. F. Rivet, 'The British Section of the Antonine Itinerary', *Britannia*, 1 (1970), 34–82.

[6] William Camden to Thomas James and Mr Causton, 6 Dec. 1599, in *Letters Addressed to Thomas James First Keeper of Bodley's Library*, ed. G. W. Wheeler (Oxford: Oxford University Press, 1933), 19.

[7] Goltzius's edition formed the second part of the *Introductio in historiam romanam* by Joannes Otho Brugensis, published at Bruges in 1565.

[8] William Camden to Abraham Ortelius, 24 Sept. 1577, in *Abrahami Ortelii . . . epistulae*, 170–1.

The correspondence between the two men continued in the same vein, right up to the publication of the *Britannia* in 1586, with Camden seeking, and apparently eliciting, specific historical information from his older and more illustrious friend. Thus on 31 January 1586 he wrote to Ortelius again to ask if Chirius Fortunatianus, an obscure fourth-century Roman grammarian, had anything to say about Britain.[9] The Camden-Ortelius correspondence is well known to scholars, and the Fleming has long been recognized as a formative influence on the *Britannia*. But this correspondence is only one example of a much larger phenomenon. Camden's collaborations, his networks of correspondents, stretched much farther and in less familiar directions. If Camden took advantage of the superior classical knowledge of Ortelius, he also depended on a vast array of provincial scholars and antiquaries, figures who, unlike Ortelius, now stand on the margins of intellectual and literary history. Without the aid of these men, without their discoveries, records, and transcriptions, the *Britannia* would almost certainly not have taken its final shape. Without them, the 'dumpy little quarto in Latin', as Stuart Piggott called the first edition, would probably not have been transformed into the magnificent encyclopedic folios of 1607 and 1610.[10]

A number of scholars have noted the importance of Camden's friendships and correspondences. Maurice Powicke, for example, commented in an important essay that a 'great book might be written about Camden, his life and his works, his wide circle of friends and correspondents and his humanity', an argument restated recently by Wyman Herendeen in his new biography of Camden.[11] But it is not enough simply to note this. We also need to take a more active approach—to explore what these correspondents brought to Camden literally and materially, as well as intellectually. As Peter Miller has shown in his splendid study of Camden's French friend Nicolas-Claude Fabri de Peiresc, a history of an antiquary should also be a history of his circle and correspondents.[12] In the case

---

[9] William Camden to Abraham Ortelius, 31 Jan. 1586, ibid. 335: 'Et si quid sit in Chirio Fortunatiano, quod ad Britanniam faciat, doce.' In the same letter Camden also took the opportunity to notify Ortelius of two books recently published in England that might be of interest to him: Ponticus Virunnius's edition of Giraldus Cambrensis, included in his *Britannicae historiae libri sex* (1585), and a new edition of John Chrysostom's *Homilies* (1586), printed by Joseph Barnes at Oxford.

[10] Stuart Piggott, 'William Camden and the *Britannia*', *Proceedings of the British Academy*, 37 (1951), 199–217 at 206.

[11] Maurice Powicke, 'William Camden', *English Studies*, 1 (1948), 67–84 at 81; and Herendeen, *William Camden*, esp. 6–15. See also George C. Boon, 'Camden and the *Britannia*', *Archaeologia Cambrensis*, 136 (1987), 1–19; Christiane Kunst, 'William Camden's *Britannia*: History and Historiography', in M. H. Crawford and C. R. Ligota (eds.), *Ancient History and the Antiquarian: Essays in Memory of Arnaldo Momigliano* (London: The Warburg Institute, 1995), 117–31 at 120; and Leslie Hepple, 'William Camden and Early Collections of Roman Antiquities in Britain', *Journal of the History of Collections*, 15 (2003), 159–73 at 160–1.

[12] Miller, *Peiresc's Europe*. For more on antiquarian networks, see Woolf, *The Social Circulation of the Past*, 154–63.

of Camden, this argument might also be extended to his literary works. We cannot, I suggest, understand the *Britannia* without first understanding the myriad correspondents who commented on the text and sent material to be included in subsequent versions of it. Camden was not a lone crusader, fighting the ravages of time on his own. His project was a public and collaborative one; preservation of antiquity lay as much in the hands of his circle as in his own.

The chapter which follows explores this collaboration by looking first at what Camden expected of his correspondents, and then at the kinds of material with which they supplied him. New and augmented editions of the *Britannia* appeared in 1587, 1590, 1594, 1600, and 1607, and each contained additional material sent to Camden by correspondents up and down the country. Camden emerges as a literary editor *par excellence*, weaving the notes and observations of others, sometimes, as we shall see, barely transformed at all, into his text to create an ever expanding national repository of antiquarian knowledge. Preservation of the past becomes a literary as well as a historical endeavour. A remnant is saved from time at the moment of discovery, and is then preserved all over again by its inclusion in Camden's work. This is not to downplay his importance or achievement. It is simply to emphasize that from the outset, as the Ortelius correspondence makes clear, he conceived the work as a broad and inclusive one. After all, without the help of others he would never have been able to collect the amount and variety of antiquarian material eventually published in the 1607 and 1610 texts, let alone undertake the kind of large-scale restoration that Ortelius had urged.

In fact, it is hard to know what exactly Ortelius had meant by restoring 'antiquity to Britaine, and Britain to his antiquity'. The first part of the statement is straightforward enough. Ortelius's words echo the resurrective impulse of the larger antiquarian project, and they suggest that he wanted Camden to recover and publish traces of antiquity, here undoubtedly understood in classical terms. This was certainly how Camden took it, as his gloss on the gnomic utterance makes clear: 'which was as I vnderstood, that I would renew ancientrie, enlighten obscuritie, cleare doubts, and recall home the Veritie by way of recovery, which the negligence of writers and credulitie of the common sort had in a manner proscribed and vtterly banished from amongst vs'.[13] If time was the first enemy, previous English writers were not far behind. Camden's task as an antiquary was an epistemological one: to restore knowledge of antiquity to an ignorant and negligent populace. Later in the preface he clarifies the task, reasserting his resurrective purpose and also alluding to Ortelius's original interest. 'Truly it was my proiect and purpose,' he wrote, 'to seeke, rake out, and free from darknesse such places as *Cæsar, Tacitus, Ptolomee, Antonine* the Emperour, *Notitia Provinciarum*, & other antique writers have specified and *TIME* hath

---

[13] Camden, *Britain*, sig. π4^r.

overcast with mist & darknesse by extinguishing, altering, and corrupting their old true names.'[14] The second part of Ortelius's utterance is more ambiguous. In one way, the instruction seems to manifest itself in Camden's organization of his material. The *Britannia* presents a county-by-county survey, one organized not alphabetically, or even strictly geographically, but, as Stuart Piggott first pointed out, according to the ancient tribal divisions of Britain, which the Romans encountered and classical geographers recorded.[15] The *Britannia* does therefore seek to restore Britain to its antiquity, to resurrect textually the Roman provinces and the Celtic divisions. In later editions, though, this utterance must also have taken on a new—and, for Ortelius, unanticipated—political significance. Following the accession of James I in 1603, the name Britain could no longer be understood in just historical or antiquarian terms. To restore Britain to its antiquity necessarily became a political gesture, an intervention in the debates on the union of the two kingdoms of England and Scotland—debates of which, as we shall see later in the chapter, Camden was acutely aware.

The rest of Camden's preface explains how he set about responding to Ortelius's challenge. Camden surveys the material which he has gathered, the sources which he has used, and the approach which he has taken. This includes the expected textual evidence, 'our owne countrie writers, old and new', and 'all Greeke and Latine authors which haue once made mention of Britaine'.[16] It includes material and epigraphic evidence, 'memorials of Churches, Cities, and Corporations' and 'many an old Rowle'. But Camden also twice mentions his correspondents and his debt to collaborators at home and abroad. Thus we learn that he has 'conferred with most skillfull observers in each country' and has 'had conference with learned men in other parts of Christendome'.[17] Furthermore, the preface ends with him inviting his readers also to participate in the project, to correct any errors which they perceive, and then to write to him to point these out:

> Others may be more skilfull and more exactly obserue the particularities of the places where they are conversant, If they, or any other whosoever, will advertise me wherein I am mistaken, I will amend it with manifold thankes, if I have unwitting omitted ought, I will supply it, if I have not fully explicated any point, upon their better information I will more cleere it, if it proceed from good meaning, and not from a spirit of contradiction and quareling, which doe not befit such as are well bred, and affect the truth.[18]

---

[14] Camden, *Britain*, sig. π5^r.
[15] Piggott, 'William Camden and the *Britannia*', 208.
[16] Amongst the volumes of his *collectanea* and notes, there survives an autograph list of classical quotations on Britain, which, given his comment, Camden presumably drew up in preparation for one of the editions of the *Britannia* (BL, MS Harley 2202, fos. 11^r–12^r).
[17] Camden, *Britain*, sig. π4^r.
[18] Ibid., sig. π5^v.

The last comment takes on a particular relevance in light of the mean-spirited and quarrelsome attacks of Ralph Brooke, the herald who, after Camden's appointment as Clarenceux King of Arms in 1597, took such exception to his discussions of genealogy and ancestry.[19] With this invitation Camden's preface establishes a particular mode of courteous collaboration, where antiquaries and others participate in his restorative project, not out of contrariety or intellectual one-upmanship, but because of a common interest in sharing knowledge and illuminating antiquity. It is to that model of courteous collaboration which I turn in the next part of this chapter.

COLLECTORS AND COLLABORATORS

The *Britannia* was neither the only nor the first collaborative historical project in early modern England.[20] Its most notable predecessor was Raphael Holinshed's *Chronicles* (1577 and 1587). That work had begun life as a scheme to publish a vast 'Universall History', which originated with the printer Reiner Wolfe, but which quickly evolved a collaborative model of authorship, bringing together a large and highly diverse body of contributors.[21] Camden himself was involved in other collaborative projects. The Elizabethan Society of Antiquaries, for example, was a collaboration, albeit one which produced little in terms of publications, and was, in the words of its first secretary, Arthur Agarde, 'a courte of *Morespeach*' more than anything else.[22] Camden's *Annales* (1615 and 1625) too were a form of collaboration, as they incorporated the work of his former pupil, Sir Robert Cotton, as well as his own.[23] But, as a collaborative text, the *Britannia* does seem to have been in a league of its own. This is partly because of the sheer number of contributors and correspondents involved. But it is also because of the amount of archival material which survives, the memoranda, letters, and notes which attest to the extent of the collaboration. This material enables us both to chart the development of the

---

[19] On Camden's dispute with Brooke and the ructions in the College of Arms which ensued, see Kendrick, *British Antiquity*, 151–5; Sir Anthony Richard Wagner, *Heralds of England: A History of the Office and College of Arms* (London: HMSO, 1967), 225–9; and Herendeen, *William Camden*, 455–79.

[20] For other historical collaborations at the time, see Alexandra Gillespie, 'Introduction', in Ian Gadd and Alexandra Gillespie (eds.), *John Stow (1525–1605) and the Making of the English Past* (London: The British Library, 2004), 1–11. This idea of collaboration is nevertheless much more familiar to scholars of early modern science; see e.g. Michael Hunter, *Establishing the New Science: The Experience of the Early Royal Society* (Woodbridge: Boydell, 1989), esp. 6–11.

[21] On the collaborative agenda of the *Chronicles*, see Annabel Patterson, *Reading Holinshed's Chronicles* (Chicago and London: University of Chicago Press, 1994), 22–31.

[22] Arthur Agarde, 'Of the Etymology, Dignity, and Antiquity of Dukes in England', in *A Collection of Curious Discourses*, i. 184.

[23] See Patrick Collinson, 'One of Us? William Camden and the Making of History', *Transactions of the Royal Historical Society*, Sixth Series, 8 (1998), 139–63.

Britannia as a literary text, from one edition to the next, and to shed light on the nature of the contributions that Camden's correspondents made.

Amongst Camden's papers, for example, there survives a memorandum, which illustrates the kind of information that he sought and the questions that he asked. This document, titled 'Enquires to be made of Mr Claxton, touching the Picts Wall', was a reminder to himself to write to the Durham antiquary William Claxton. Camden wanted to know four things about Hadrian's Wall, or Picts' Wall, as it was known at the time:

> Desyre M[r] Claxton to certifye you What rare matter he knoweth as concerning the Pictes wall.
>
> Whether ther remayne any ruines or signe of any other wall, sauing of that which crosseth the country from Newcastle to Carlile
>
> Where in the Bisshopricke any Romane coynes are founde sauing att Bincester, and whether he hathe seene any Romane inscriptions founde ther or elswher.
>
> What towne he supposeth that to be which Ptolomey calleth Bremenium, and should be in Northumberland nere vnto Alnewicke.[24]

The memorandum is a briefing document, the equivalent of the instructions issued by later scholars to learned travellers at home and abroad. Camden's questions include Ortelius's concern with classical place names, but they also incorporate the broader antiquarian subjects of archaeology, epigraphy, and numismatics. Already he seems to have envisaged a larger project than that urged by his Flemish friend. The memorandum is undated, but it must have been written by 1597, since Claxton died that year. The fact that the next item in the codex, a letter from Claxton to John Stow, is subscribed 10 April 1594 suggests that the memorandum was probably written in the early 1590s.[25] The destined home for Claxton's answers, his information on Picts' Wall, was undoubtedly an edition of the *Britannia*. Alas, what Claxton made of the four questions is unknown. His reply, if he sent one at all, has not survived; how far he influenced Camden's writing about the Roman Wall is therefore impossible to say.

Other correspondents, however, were more loquacious, and their contributions to the *Britannia* are easier to gauge. One such example was Francis Godwin, Bishop of Llandaff. Godwin was himself something of an antiquary. He was the author of a noted *Catalogue of the Bishops of England* (1601), which used archival sources and manuscript chronicles in the antiquarian manner, and he was also a keen collector of antiquities.[26] His friendship with Camden seems to

---

[24] BL, MS Harley 374, fo. 20[r].

[25] Claxton's relations with Stow date back to at least a decade earlier. As early as 1582, Stow owned a 'simple pece of worke' by him, concerning 'the causes of Busshopbryck of Durrham', and that same year Claxton also promised to supply Stow with 'suche worthy and auncyant record*es* and monument*es* muche more fytter for yo*ur* purpose' (BL, MS Harley 374, fo. 10[r]).

[26] On Godwin's historical interests, see W. M. Merchant, 'Bishop Francis Godwin, Historian and Novelist', *Journal of the Historical Society of the Church in Wales*, 5 (1955), 45–51; and D. R. Woolf, 'Erudition and the Idea of History in Renaissance England', *Renaissance Quarterly*, 40 (1987), 11–48 at 30.

have dated back to 1590, when he accompanied the latter on his antiquarian journey around South Wales. He was also a ready correspondent, and a number of letters to Camden survive, in which he details antiquarian discoveries. A lengthy correspondence, for example, from 1602–4 has been preserved in one of the Cotton manuscripts in the British Library (MS Cotton Julius F. VI).[27] These letters concern a series of inscriptions found in and around Caerleon. In June 1602 Godwin wrote to Camden to report a pair of Roman statues unearthed just outside the town. Only part of this letter survives, and that part is damaged at the outer margin, with some loss of text, but the sense can mostly be inferred.[28] The fragment begins with Godwin comparing the dress of one of the statues to 'our ryding bases', the pleated skirt appended to a doublet, and reaching from the waist to the knee, typically worn in the Tudor period.[29] He noted that underneath this statue there was 'a double Paueˇ . . . .ˇ one of brick, and an other (the vppermost) tessellatu*m*'. Fortuitously, part of an inscription had also survived, allowing him to conjecture the identity of the statue to be 'that *Q: Haterius* often mentioned by *Tacitus*'. From the letter we also learn that he planned to add these statues to his burgeoning collection of antiquities: 'These two stones though a wayne loade I intend god willing to bestowe the fetching of to my howse heere x. myle off, and to affoord them a place som*me* where in my garden.' Like many of his contemporaries, Godwin displayed classical antiquities around his house and grounds.[30]

A year later Godwin wrote again. This time, having undertaken his own antiquarian journey, he reported another discovery, a fragmentary inscription found near Margam Abbey, the seat of Sir Thomas Mansell:

Since my last last le*ttr*es, hauyng trauayled through Glamorga*n* shyre I mett w*i*th a monument of right Venerable antiquity w*hi*ch I ca*n* not but impart Vnto yo[u]. It is a 'hard' stone of some 4 foote long (as I remember) about half a foote thick & happily one foote high. Vpon the Vpmost edge 'of it' are writte*n* these Characters

PVMP EIVS
CAR AN TOPIVS.[31]

---

[27] For a transcription of part of this manuscript, see F. Haverfield, 'Cotton Iulius F. VI. Notes on Reginald Bainbrigg of Appleby, on William Camden and on Some Roman Inscriptions', *Transactions of the Cumberland & Westmorland Antiquarian & Archaeological Society*, NS 11 (1911), 343–78.

[28] Francis Godwin to William Camden, June 1602, BL, MS Cotton Julius F. VI, fo. 296[r–v]. Although this leaf has been repaired, the original fold of the letter can be seen. All but four lines of what survives is below the fold, suggesting that just under half the letter has been lost.

[29] *OED*, s.v. 'base', *n.*³ II, 2.

[30] For this phenomenon, see Leslie W. Hepple, '"The Museum in the Garden": Displaying Classical Antiquities in Elizabethan and Jacobean England', *Garden History*, 29 (2001), 109–20.

[31] Francis Godwin to William Camden, 14 July 1603, BL, MS Cotton Julius F. VI, fo. 297[r–v]. For transcription conventions regarding deletions, insertions, and supralinear text, see p. xiii above.

For the antiquary, this letter contained greater riches still. Not only did Godwin record the inscription, but he also went on to note a popular tradition and aetiology associated with it. Thus we learn that the Welsh read the inscription 'Pimp bis an car an topius, so altering the twoo first wordes & adding the 3ᵈ which they assure themselues to be worne out', and then that, 'rather by tradition then that the moderne interpretation beareth it', they 'affirme it to be the monument of Morgan of whose deˣ ...ˣ the whole County is thought to receaue hys name'. Godwin, as his reference to 'tradition' attests, was clearly not convinced.

The letter concludes with Godwin turning to an altogether more unusual discovery: the Christian artefact known today as the Boduoc stone. Godwin himself had not seen the stone, but he had given 'order to haue it copyed', and he promised Camden that, as soon as this was done, he would send the inscription to him. He duly kept his promise. The very next item in the codex is an undated, but clearly later, letter, which concerns exclusively the Boduoc stone. Godwin told Camden that 'Vppon the topp of a mountaigne called Mynydd Margam & at a place there called Rhyd blaen y kwm, viz betweene Morgam & Langonoyd in Glamorgan shyre, some myle & half from Morgam thys inscription Vnderwrytten, is to be seene Vppon a hard popple stone that is in length 4 foote 9 inches, one foote broad & 8 inches thick'.[32] He added that a friend had 'digged Vp the stone & found it one foote Vnder the ground, & Vppon each syde Vnder the ground a greate O', and also that 'Vppon the topp of the stone was a crosse'. He also noted that it was commonly believed that 'whoso did reade the wryting, should dye soone after'.

Godwin's letter is revealing for a couple of reasons. First, it shows a typically antiquarian awareness of geographical specificity, locating a perhaps unfamiliar ancient artefact within the contemporary Welsh landscape. Second, it manifests an understanding of, and an interest in, the process of excavation: not only does the letter report the find, it also comments on the circumstances in which it was found. Godwin seems to have been anxious about its excavation, since he added that he was 'angry it should be digged Vp', and that he had given the 'order to haue hyt placed agayne'. He seems to have understood—and this runs counter to his museum garden—that for the stone to make historical sense it needed to remain where it was found, in its original geographical context. In the case of Godwin, we see both the antiquary's acquisitive instinct, the desire to collect and possess antiquities, and his preservationist impulse, the wish to save and transmit those rarities to future ages.

Godwin continued to correspond with Camden and to report antiquarian discoveries for a number of years. Thus on 27 May 1608 he mentioned 'the copy of an old Charter', which he had 'long since writ out of the *Autographum*

---

[32] Francis Godwin to William Camden, 14 July 1603, BL, MS Cotton Julius F. VI, fo. 298ʳ⁻ᵛ.

remaining in the Archives of the Church of *Wells*'. In the same letter he alluded to other antiquarian matters, including a tomb near Marthern, which he had recently repaired. Here, incidentally, we may observe an early modern antiquary restoring antiquity in the most literal sense of the word:

This name of *Theodoricus* putteth me in mind of S. *Theodoricus Rex & Martyr*, that lieth entombed here in our Church of Marthern, and gave unto the place the name of *Merthir Tendric*, that is, the Martyrdom of *Tendric*. His tomb partly ruinated I have repaired, and added a Memorial or Epitaph, the copy whereof I send you also enclosed. My Author for what I have there set down, is our book of *Landaff*, called *St. Teylo*'s *book*, which I perceive you have not seen.[33]

Godwin's authority for the restoration is the *Liber Landavensis*, a twelfth-century cartulary from Llandaff. In the same letter he also promised Camden that, if he ever came to London again, he would bring the manuscript with him 'that you may peruse it, if you please'. The letter then finishes with him enjoining Camden to visit Exeter Cathedral, where Godwin was subdean, since it 'hath divers Charters of Saxon Kings, which methinks it were good you did see'. In a spirit of courtesy and generosity, he also offered to copy the charters, if Camden so wished. A few years later he offered a material token of their friendship, presenting Camden with a copy of the *De praesulibus Angliae commentarius* (1616), his historical commentary on the bishops of England.[34]

This correspondence is important for what it tells us about Godwin: a provincial scholar, who was not a member of the Elizabethan Society of Antiquaries, and whose contacts with that circle were limited, but whose intellectual interests ran the whole antiquarian gamut. But it is even more important for what it tells us about Camden and his literary method. For Camden incorporated the letters—in the main, very closely—into the *Britannia*. Thus, in the 1610 translation, his survey of Glamorgan includes the following observation:

Neere unto this *Margan*, in the very top of an hill called *Mynyd Margan*, there is erected of exceeding hard grit, a monument or graue-stone, foure foote long, and one foote broad with an Inscription, which whosoever shall happen to read, the ignorant common people dwelling there about, giue it out upon a credulous error, that hee shall be sure to die within a little while after.[35]

---

[33] Francis Godwin to William Camden, 27 May 1608, *V. cl. Gulielmi Camdeni, et illustrium virorum ad G. Camdenum epistolæ*, ed. Thomas Smith (London, 1691), 109. This selection of Camden's letters was based on a manuscript in the Cotton library (BL, MS Cotton Julius C. V), where, thanks to his friendship with Sir John Cotton, grandson of Robert, Smith was the unofficial librarian.

[34] Now Bodleian Library, class-mark Wood D 21 (1). On the title page, below the imprint, there is the following inscription: 'Gulielmi Camdeni ex dono authoris. Martij 23. 15.'. I am extremely grateful to Dr Sebastiaan Verweij for copying this inscription for me.

[35] Camden, *Britain*, 644.

Godwin's description is barely transformed at all. In almost the sole editorial intervention, the unspecific 'popple stone' (a variant spelling of pebblestone) is replaced with the more particular 'exceeding hard grit'. Disposing of the deadly tradition about the Boduoc stone more effectively than his source, Camden also adds a joke: 'Let the reader therefore looke to him selfe, if any dare read it; for, let him assure himselfe that he shall for certaine die after it.' He then mentions another inscription nearby: 'Moreover, betweene *Margan* and *Kinfeage* by the high way side, there lieth a stone foure foote long with this Inscription. PVNP EIVS CAR AN TOPIVS.' His source is again clear. This time Camden offers a more sober reflection, interrogating the popular tradition not by a humorous aside, but through comparative epigraphy:

> Which the Welsh Britans by adding and changing letters, thus read and make this interpretation; as the right reverend Bishop of *Landaff* did write to me, who gave order that the draught of this Inscription should bee taken likewise for my sake. PIM BIS AN CAR ANTOPIVS, that is, *The fiue fingers of friends or neighbours killed us*. It is verily thought to be the Sepulchre of Prince *Morgan*, from whom the Country tooke name, who was slaine, as they would haue it, eight hundred yeeres before Christs nativity. But Antiquaries know full well, that these Characters and formes of letters be of a farre later date.[36]

Etymology might tempt us to give credence to this belief, but the literate and historically informed audience for Camden's book, the wise 'Antiquaries' to whom he speaks above, know better than that. The form of the inscription itself enables them to posit a more precise and recent date. That, at least, is the hope.

This time too Camden acknowledges his source. The inscription is included, we learn, through the good grace of the bishop of Llandaff. Godwin becomes a kind of co-author, a source of material, who must be openly and honestly thanked. For this reason, he is also acknowledged in the description of Caerleon. 'But for the avouching and confirming of the antiquity of this place,' Camden wrote, 'I think it not impertinent to adioin here those antique inscriptions latly digged forth of the ground, which the right reverend father in God *Francis Godwin* Bishop of *Landaffe*, a passing great lover of venerable Antiquity and all good Literature, hath of his courtesie imparted unto me.'[37] The key term here is, of course, courtesy. If we turn to the original Latin, 'pro sua humanitate', we see that by courtesy Camden means something akin to politeness or good manners.[38] In the context of the *Britannia*, this politeness seems to mean a readiness to participate in Camden's collaborative scheme. Camden himself can repay his debt to his correspondents by acknowledging their contributions in this courteous manner. Courtesy works both ways. Just as Camden depended on

---

[36] Camden, *Britain*, 645.   [37] Ibid. 637.
[38] Camden, *Britannia* (1607), 490.

the co-operation of others for the collection of material, so the continued collection of that material depended on his own good grace and courtesy.

From the description of Caerleon, it is also apparent that Camden employed more formal research assistants, a practice that was not unusual at the time.[39] Camden notes that 'a little before the comming in of the English Saxons, *there was a Schoole heere of 200. Philosophers, ... as wrote Alexander Elsebiensis*, a rare Author and hard to be found'.[40] His authority here is Alexander of Ashby (Alexander Essebiensis), a twelfth-century prior, poet, and religious writer.[41] His source was Thomas James, Thomas Bodley's first librarian, who, as he goes on to admit, 'hath copied out very many notes for me' from Alexander's works.[42] In December 1599 Camden had written to James to ask him to undertake a piece of research for him, requesting that he study various medieval authors and manuscripts, including Alexander of Ashby: 'Only I desire you to looke into that Examen Angliæ and notabilia Bristoliæ and Worcester, if there be any especiall observations, as also in the historicall Epitome of Alexander Essebiensis.' In the same letter he specified by name Alexander's *Liber Festiualis*, 'his Poeme of the festival daies'.[43] He asked James to transcribe material on other occasions too. Thus, in a later letter, he entreated him to transcribe 'out of the Manuscript Julius Firmicus which you specifie in your Catalogue to be in Lincolne College Librarie, the few last lines of the last Chapter of the first book', and also asked him 'what age you iudge the Copie to be'.[44] With ready access to the libraries of Oxford colleges, in this case Lincoln, James could lay his hands on medieval manuscripts more easily than Camden, who was at the time still living in London, and he could therefore supply him with important and rare texts and sources.

Other of Camden's correspondents took his invitation to correct any errors to heart. Nicholas Roscarrock, for example, wrote to Camden on 7 August 1607, as the sixth edition of the *Britannia* was in press, to draw attention to various errors that he had detected in the previous edition. Roscarrock was a Cornish antiquary, who, after studying at Oxford in the 1560s, moved to London, where he was admitted as a student of the Inner Temple in November 1572; his friendship

---

[39] In his *Letter of Advice to Fulke Greville on his Studies* (*c.* 1590), written in the name of the earl of Essex, Francis Bacon had advised on precisely this subject, telling Greville 'what instruction' he should 'give' his 'gatherers' or assistants; see *The Major Works*, ed. Brian Vickers (Oxford: Oxford University Press, 1996), 102.

[40] Camden, *Britain*, 693.

[41] 'Elsebiensis', the name given in Camden's text, is probably a compositorial error: it is easy to imagine how a compositor, unfamiliar with the names of medieval Latin authors, might have misread a long *s* in his copy for an *l*.

[42] For Alexander's literary output, see A. G. Rigg, *A History of Anglo-Latin Literature 1066–1422* (Cambridge: Cambridge University Press, 1992), 131–3.

[43] William Camden to Thomas James, 6 Dec. 1599, *Letters Addressed to Thomas James*, 19.

[44] William Camden to Thomas James, 1600, ibid. 20.

with Camden dates back to this time.[45] Roscarrock is best known today for his Catholicism, which resulted in a period of imprisonment in the Tower of London in the 1580s, and again on three further occasions in the 1590s for recusancy. But at the time he also had a considerable reputation as a scholar, especially in the fields of literature, heraldry, and antiquities. Richard Carew, for example, his fellow Cornishman, praised him in 1602 'for his industrious delight in matters of history and antiquity'.[46] Later in life, after the accession of James I, he moved to Naworth Castle in Cumberland to join his friend and patron Lord William Howard, with whom he had been imprisoned in the 1580s. Howard too had antiquarian interests: he collected Roman antiquities, which he displayed in his garden, and owned a substantial library of manuscripts, records, and printed books.

It was from Naworth Castle that Roscarrock wrote in 1607. His letter begins by excusing any possible slight to Camden. He was highlighting the errors, he wrote, not to show up the limitations of Camden's scholarship, but out of his deep affection for him: 'Understanding, good Mr. Clarenceulx, that your *Britayne* is at this present in printing, and ready to come forth, I thought fit, in a small show of our ancient love, to give you notice of two escapes in the last edition.' Roscarrock's corrections are a favour, ensuring that the next edition of Camden's project is as correct and complete as possible. The first error concerned the Cornish saint Columba, whom Camden had taken for a man, confusing her with the Scottish saint of the same name.[47] Roscarrock pointed out that, contrary to what Camden had written, the town of St Columb 'taketh name of *Columba*, a woman-Saint, who was a Virgin and Martyr'. To support his argument, he refers to a life of St Columba, which he had in his hands, 'translated out of Cornish'. He also noted that 'the day of her Feast differeth from the Feast of S. *Columbanus*, or S. *Columba*, the Scotish or Irish'.[48] Roscarrock's correction reflects his long-standing interest in hagiography, and the fact that at the time he was compiling his unpublished 'A Breife Regester: or Alphabeticall Catologue' of the saints of Britain and Ireland. In that work too he alludes to Camden's error. He describes Columba there as a 'virgin, & Marter, who hath a Church dedicated vnto her in Cornwall', and also writes that in the town of St Columb 'there is a Church dedicated to a virgin & Marter; & not to a Man, as som haue mistaken it'.[49] It is clear whom he meant here. The second error concerns an

---

[45] Nicholas Orme, 'Introduction' to *Nicholas Roscarrock's Lives of the Saints: Cornwall and Devon*, ed. Nicholas Orme (Exeter: Devon and Cornwall Record Society, 1992), 6.

[46] Carew, *The Survey of Cornwall*, sig. 2K3ᵛ.

[47] William Camden, *Britannia sive florentissimorum regnorum, Angliæ, Scotiæ, Hiberniæ, et insularum adiacentium ex intima antiquitate chorographica descriptio* (London, 1600), 156: 'Deinde longiùs à littore S. *Columbani* oppidulum mercatorium sedet, Columbani Scoti viri sanctissimi memoriæ consecratum.'

[48] Nicholas Roscarrock to William Camden, 7 Aug. 1607, *V. cl. Gulielmi Camdeni... epistolæ*, 91–2.

[49] Nicholas Roscarrock, 'A Breife Regester: or Alphabeticall Catologue of such saint*es* ' & sainte like p*er*sons' as the Collector hathe taken notice of, to haue graced our Island of great Brittaine

inscription at Thoresby in Cumberland. 'You were misinformed,' Roscarrock wrote, 'both for the fashion and form of stone, being four times as long as broad.' Roscarrock was familiar with this inscription because Lord William Howard 'hath it now, with a great many more, in his garden-wall at *Naward*'.[50] Despite what he said at the beginning of the letter, Roscarrock mentioned other errors as well, and he also supplied Camden with new material and additional inscriptions.

Camden took Roscarrock's comments on board. On the subject of St Columba he openly admits his error: 'Then, farther from the shore is seated *S. Columbs* a little mercate towne, consecrated to the memoriall of Columba right devout woman and a martyr, & not of Columban the Scot, as now I am given to understand for certaine, out of her life.'[51] On the subject of the Thoresby inscription, he also corrects what he had written. Where he had previously described the stone as just crude ('columna è rudi saxo'), he now more precisely calls it 'a long rude stone in manner of columne'.[52] The distinction is a fine one, but the addition reflects what Roscarrock had told him about the shape of the stone. Moreover, he—or, rather his printers, the Eliot's Court Press—also revised the appearance of the inscription on the printed page. In the 1600 edition the Thoresby inscription is surrounded by an almost square border of printer's lace (45 mm × 52 mm). In the 1610 text, by contrast, the border is rectangular (60 mm × 50 mm), thereby corresponding more closely with Roscarrock's information. In this instance, though, Camden did not make the correction straight away. The 1607 edition repeats the text and border of the previous edition (although Camden did make a couple of alterations to the inscription itself).[53] The likely explanation is that, at such short notice, with the book already in press, the border would have been hard to change, as it would have required the type to be reset. But Camden did not forget Roscarrock's correction: three years later, when the English translation was printed, he duly emended the border and text.

Like Roscarrock, many of Camden's correspondents resided in the North. The explanation for this is simple enough. Northern England was the location of the most visible classical antiquities on the island, the site of Britain's most extensive Roman remains. It was therefore a natural focus of antiquarian attention, an obvious attraction for a resurrective scholar who was keen to collect traces of the

---

Ireland, and other British Iselands bordering about it, with there Births deaths, presence Preachings or Relicks', CUL, MS Add. 3041, fo. 131ᵛ.

[50] Nicholas Roscarrock to William Camden, 7 Aug. 1607, *V. cl. Gulielmi Camdeni...epistolæ*, 92.

[51] Camden, *Britain*, 193; and *Britannia* (1607), 140: 'Deinde longiùs à littore *S. Columbæ* opidulum mercatorium sedet, Columbæ pijissimæ mulieris & Martyris, non Columbani Scoti, memoriæ consecratum, vt iam certo ex eius vita sum edoctus.'

[52] Camden, *Britannia* (1600), 699; and *Britain*, 774.

[53] Camden, *Britannia* (1607), 637.

past and restore former civilizations. Camden himself made a tour of the area in 1599, accompanied by the ever eager Cotton. The two men spent much of that year investigating Roman sites in the North, with the Roman Wall the obvious highlight, liaising with local antiquaries and collectors such as John Senhouse of Ellenborough, and, in the case of Cotton, sketching artefacts and other remains.[54] Camden's own interest in the area, however, considerably pre-dated this trip. Even in the first edition of the *Britannia* he breaks off from his county-by-county progress to insert a chapter dedicated to the Roman Wall.[55] This is the only time in the entire work that he deviates from his strict divisional principle.

Yet, in spite of its subject matter, the chapter on the Roman Wall may be the least antiquarian of all the chapters in the *Britannia*. Camden mostly just rehearses what previous historians, ancient and modern, had written about it. His account is distinguished only by its comprehensiveness, as is illustrated by his opening discursion on the name of the Wall:

Through the high part of Cumberland, shooteth that most famous Wall (in no case to bee passed over in silence) the limit of the Roman province, *the Barbarian Rampier*, the *Fore-fence* and *Enclosure*, for so, the ancient writers tearmed it, being called in *Dion*, Διατείχισμα, that is, a Crosse wall, in Herodian, χωμα, that is, A Trench or Fosse, cast up, by *Antonine, Cassiodore* and others VALLVM, that is, the Rampier, by *Bede* MVRVS, that is, the Wall: by the Britans *Gual-Sever, Gal-Sever, Bal, Val* and *Mur-sever*, by the Scottish, *Scottiswaith*, by the English, and those that dwell thereabout, the *Picts Wall* or *Pehits Wall*, the *Keepe wall*, and simply by way of excellency, *The Wall*.[56]

With its comprehensive enumeration of classical sources, but its almost total neglect of the material remains of the Wall, Camden's description resembles more closely the works of contemporary historians such as John Clapham than the rest of his own antiquarian book. Clapham was the author of *The Historie of England* (1602), a work which, despite the broadness of its title, in its first edition focused exclusively on 'the estate of the Ile of Britannie vnder the Roman Empire'. Clapham's approach was to collect 'so much as I thought necessary to be remembred touching this Subiect', out of the likes of Caesar, Tacitus, and Dio Cassius, and to digest 'the same into the forme of an History'.[57] Material remains barely feature at all. Thus, when he turns to the Roman Wall, Clapham writes that Hadrian fortified the northern border of Britain 'by raising a Wall of *Turues*, about 80. miles in length (betweene the mouthes of the riuers *Ituna*, and *Tina*) to defend the inhabitants thereof, from the sodaine assaultes of their ill neighbours', and, slightly later, that Septimius Severus 'hauing rather staied, then ended the

---

[54] David McKitterick, 'From Camden to Cambridge: Sir Robert Cotton's Roman Inscriptions, and their Subsequent Treatment', in C. J. Wright (ed.), *Sir Robert Cotton as Collector: Essays on an Early Stuart Courtier and his Legacy* (London: British Library, 1997), 105–28 at 106–7.
[55] Camden, *Britannia* (1586), sigs. 2G7^r–2G8^v.
[56] Camden, *Britain*, 789.
[57] John Clapham, *The Historie of England* (London, 1602), sig. B1^r.

troubles, spent some time in repairing and enlarging *Adrians* Wall, which he carried th'wart the Iland, from Sea, to Sea, intrenching and fortefying it, with bulwarkes and square towers, in places most conuenient (to giue warning one to another vpon any sodaine assault) for defence of the borders'.[58] There is little evidence that Clapham had any interest in tracing those fortifications, or indeed in what those fragments of the Wall that still remained might actually indicate. He simply describes the Wall as a series of episodes in Roman history, and also, more slyly, presents it as a reminder of how restive the Scottish Borders could be.

Camden's perspective was, of course, very different. But in 1586 he had not visited the Wall, and he did not have the evidence to write in a properly antiquarian manner. Various correspondents in the North helped to change things. They provided material which allowed him to take his account in a more antiquarian direction, material which, along with his own discoveries in 1599, was then included in the Westmorland, Cumberland, and Northumberland chapters of the *Britannia*. (The chapter on the Wall, by contrast, remains essentially the same in all editions.) They sent him coins, described altars and statues, and, most importantly of all, transcribed inscriptions.[59] There was Thomas Braithwaite, who visited the village of Ribchester in Lancashire to examine a newly found Roman inscription, which he then sketched for Camden. 'I went to Ribchester in Crissimas laste,' he wrote in January 1605, 'to see the stone which goodman Roades & others did make report of. which as I learned was founde by a man plowing the 14th daie of August 1604. about 30^{ti} roodes eastwardes From Ribchester buried a fowte deepe.'[60] In the remainder of the letter he described what was engraved on the stone, transcribed its inscription, and appended his sketch. There was Thomas Aglionby of Carlisle, doubtless a relative of the Edward Aglionby who sat as an MP for the city in the 1550s, and whose modest collection contained 'the image of a man of Armes on horsebacke armed at all peeces, with a launce in his hand'.[61] There was also Senhouse himself, whom Camden praised as 'a lover of ancient Literature' and also for preserving 'most diligently... these inscriptions, which by others that are unskilfull and unlettered be streight waies defaced, broken, and converted to other vses to exceeding great prejudice and detriment of antiquity'. Senhouse is also thanked for 'the right courteous and friendly entertainment' that he gave

---

[58] Ibid. 73, 82.
[59] Epigraphy was a subject of great interest to Camden: he wrote a paper on the subject, which he delivered to the Elizabethan Society of Antiquaries on 3 Nov. 1600 (*A Collection of Curious Discourses* (1771), i. 228–32), and he was also the author of a work on the funerary monuments in Westminster Abbey, *Reges, reginæ, nobiles, & alij in Ecclesia Collegiata B. Petri Westmonasterij sepulti* (1600).
[60] Thomas Braithwaite to William Camden, 18 Jan. 1605, BL, MS Cotton Julius F. VI, fo. 302^r; see also B. J. N. Edwards, *William Camden, his Britannia and some Roman Inscriptions*, a lecture delivered at the Senhouse Roman Museum, Maryport, on October 27th, 1998 (Maryport: Senhouse Roman Museum, 1998), 9–12.
[61] Camden, *Britain*, 780.

Camden and Cotton when they visited in 1599, enabling Camden to acknowledge formally his importance to the *Britannia*.[62]

Perhaps the best known of these northern correspondents was Reginald Bainbrigg, master of the grammar-school at Appleby from December 1580 until his death in 1612 or 1613. Like Godwin, Bainbrigg was something of an antiquary in his own right. He made at least two tours of the Roman Wall, the first in 1599, and the second two years later. During these tours he recorded anything of antiquarian interest, made careful copies of inscriptions, and wrote up his observations as a series of notes on Picts' Wall, which he later sent to Camden.[63] He also put together a small collection of inscribed stones, classical and post-classical, which he displayed in the garden at Appleby Grammar School.[64] Moreover, he was a noted bibliophile, and on his death he bequeathed a large collection of books to the school. This library too attests to the range and extent of his antiquarian interests.

Thanks to a manuscript catalogue drawn up in 1656 by Robert Edmundson, another schoolmaster at Appleby, we know a considerable amount about Bainbrigg's library. Edmundson's catalogue lists 295 items, of which 158 survive today.[65] Most of the books reflect the fact that this was the working library of an early modern humanist schoolmaster. Editions of the classics, commentaries, grammars, and textbooks on dialectic and rhetoric all loom large. But Edmundson's catalogue also lists titles which have little to do with Tudor grammar-school curricula, books which seem instead to reflect Bainbrigg's own antiquarian interests. We know, for example, that Bainbrigg owned 'A survey of London, 1603', the revised second edition of Stow's text, and also 'De antiquitate Oxon: Cantabr:', probably a copy of John Caius's *De antiquitate Cantabrigiensis Academiae libri duo* (1568). Neither book was a stalwart of humanist curricula. Most strikingly, his library also contained 'Occo med: de numismatis Romanor: 1561. Antwerp'.[66] Here, Edmundson seems to have got the details wrong, since the book is in fact the 1579 edition of Adolf Occo's popular *Imperatorum romanorum numismata a Pompeio Magno ad Heraclium*, printed by Christopher

---

[62] Camden, *Britain*, 769.

[63] Edgar Hinchcliffe, *Appleby Grammar School—from Chantry to Comprehensive* (Appleby: J. Whitehead, 1974), 30–5.

[64] For a catalogue of these stones, see Ben Edwards, 'Reginald Bainbrigg, *Scholemaister*, and his Stones', in *Archaeology of the Roman Empire: A Tribute to the Life and Works of Professor Barri Jones* (Oxford: Archaeopress, 2001), 25–33.

[65] The Bainbrigg library is now housed in the Robinson Library of Newcastle University. For a history of the library, see Edgar Hinchcliffe, *The Bainbrigg Library of Appleby Grammar School*, Working Paper of the History of the Book Trade in the North, PH 73 (Wylam: Allenholme Press, 1996).

[66] See 'A perfect catalogue of the bookes belonging to the schole of Appulbye entered upon by Robert Edmundson scholemʳ', in Lionel Budden, 'Some Notes on the History of Appleby Grammar School', *Transactions of the Cumberland & Westmorland Antiquarian & Archaeological Society*, 39 (1939), 227–61 at 246–53.

Plantin.[67] This book was a gift from Cotton in March 1606, as a manuscript inscription on an early leaf attests.[68] Cotton had met Bainbrigg, perhaps with Camden in 1599, but more likely when he made a second tour of the North some time between 1601 and 1607.[69] The two men later corresponded on antiquarian and numismatic matters. A letter in Bainbrigg's own hand, for example, survives, in which he tells Cotton that he 'went to mr Thomas Braithwat of Ambleside', and 'told him what charg you had gyven me to send you those coynes w[th] all expedition'. Happily, he was also able to report that Braithwaite 'p[ro]mised that he wold send them with his letter & in the same an exact plott of the decayed plaice'.[70] It is reasonable, then, to suggest that Cotton's gift, the copy of Occo, may have been his part of a numismatic bargain. Bainbrigg had easier access to Roman coins; Cotton had readier access to Continental books.

Camden too owed a considerable debt to the Appleby schoolmaster. In his chapter on Westmorland he salutes him as 'a right learned man who governeth' the school at Appleby 'with great commendation', and 'who of his courtesie hath exemplified for me many antique inscriptions'.[71] In the later editions the chapter is filled out with these and also with other observations lifted from Bainbrigg's notes. Thus Camden records, for example, that 'hard by *Crawdundale*, there are evident remains of ditches, trenches, and mounts cast up', and that among them a 'Roman inscription (the draught whereof Reginald *Bainbrig* before named, head schoolemaster of *Applebey* tooke out for me) was ingraven in a craggy rock: the forepart of which was quite eaten out with continuance of time, or thrust out by the roote of a tree there growing'.[72] The words are taken almost verbatim from Bainbrigg. He had recorded that there was an inscription 'engraven in a hard rock bysides ⟨Crawedundai′le⟩ Crawedundailewaithe, about the wiche place are yet to be sene fortresses, dytches, trenshes, Bulwork*es* and other things necessarie for wars at that tyme'. He had also recorded that 'the former part of this inscription is eaten furth by contynuance of tyme or els thrust out by the rote of a tre that grows in the rock'.[73] Having introduced the inscription in this way, Camden then reproduces the text itself, and again copies what Bainbrigg had

---

[67] Now Robinson Library Special Collections, Newcastle University BAI 1579 OCC.

[68] 'Docto et dilecto Amico Reginaldo Baynbrige Robertus Cottonus Bruceus L.M.D. CIƆ IƆ CVI. VII Kalend: April'. The book is imperfect and lacks the title page and first leaf; this inscription is copied on the second leaf (sig. A2).

[69] Leslie Hepple, 'Sir Robert Cotton, Camden's *Britannia*, and the Early History of Roman Wall Studies', *Archaeologia Aeliana*, 27 (1999) 1–19 at 14.

[70] Reginald Bainbrigg to Sir Robert Cotton, undated; printed in B. J. N. Edwards, 'Reginald Bainbrigg, Westmorland Antiquary', *Transactions of the Cumberland & Westmorland Antiquarian & Archaeological Society*, NS 3 (2003), 119–25 at 122. Braithwaite's collection of Roman coins eventually amounted to 322, and he later bequeathed it to The Queen's College, Oxford.

[71] Camden, *Britain*, 761.

[72] Ibid. 761.

[73] Reginald Bainbrigg to William Camden, 27 Mar. 1600, BL, MS Cotton Julius F. VI, fo. 337[r].

transcribed for him. Further inscriptions follow in the remainder of the chapter, and these too come from Bainbrigg's pen.

Bainbrigg supplied Camden with other kinds of material as well, and his attention was not just fixed on inscriptions. Near Little Salkeld, for example, he described a series of extraordinary stone monuments:

> Besides litle Salkeld, not far frome Crawdundailewith, wher the Romaines have fought some great Battle. ther standes certaine monument*es* or pyramides of stone, placed ther in equal distance one frome an other in modu*m* coronæ, They are commonlie called meg w*i*th hir daughters They are huge great stones, long meg standes above the ground in sight, xv fote long, and thre fathome about, the other stones are ten fote hie, & fower fathome about. they are in nu[m]ber lxxvij. Ther are w*i*thin the compasse of thes stones two great heapes of small stones vnder the wiche, they say, that the dead bodies were buryed ther. Ther is no suche stones in all the country, & therfore, I mervaile how they were set, and frome whence they came.[74]

There is no equivalent passage in the first five editions of the *Britannia*. In the sixth edition, however, there is, and Camden's description of Long Meg and her Daughters follows closely what his friend had observed:

> At the lesse *Salkeld*, there bee erected in manner of a circle seventie seaven stones, every one tenne foote high, and a speciall one by it selfe before them, at the very entrance riseth fifteene foote in height. This stone the common people there by dwelling, name *Long Megge*, like as the rest, her daughters. And within that ring or circle, are heapes of stones, under which they say, lie the bodies of men slaine.[75]

As with Godwin's contributions, there is little doubt about Camden's source. Bainbrigg's notes are reproduced in almost their entirety. The only omission is his breathless wonder at the end. Camden, whose antiquarian journeys had taken him further, and whose knowledge of antiquities was greater, knew better than that; he was more wary about making such bold statements of a monument's uniqueness and marvel.

Camden seems to have made little attempt even to paraphrase what these correspondents had written. His editorial touch here was signally light. His decision not to pull authorial rank, to reproduce their contributions almost word for word, may be his way of acknowledging them. Collaboration, for Camden at least, begins to look like an integral part of antiquarian methodology. In the case of his northern correspondents, collaboration enabled him to incorporate the archaeological strand of antiquarian thought as well as the philological one, which his exhaustive trawl through classical sources and other manuscripts

---

[74] Reginald Bainbrigg to William Camden, 27 Mar. 1600, BL, MS Cotton Julius F. VI, fo. 335ʳ.
[75] Camden, *Britain*, 777; *Britannia* (1607), 640: 'Ad minorem autem in modum coronæ eriguntur septuaginta septem saxa, singula decem pedes alta, & ante ea in ingressu singulare, XV. pedes in altitudinem surgit. Hoc vulgus vicinum *Long Megg* vt reliquias eius filias vocitant, duoque sunt intra circulum lapidum cumuli, sub quibus occisorum cadauera tegi perhibent. Et sanè par est existimemus hoc victoriæ alicuius fuisse monumentum.'

had already brought to the fore. In the case of some of his other correspondents, their contributions not only added to the stock of antiquarian material, but also took the text in previously unheralded directions, influencing its interpretation and reception as well as augmenting its contents. It is to one such example, a contribution which emphasized a new political significance in Camden's text, that I turn in the remainder of this chapter.

REMEMBERING SCOTLAND

Despite the comprehensiveness of Camden's project, one area which stood conspicuously short was Scotland. A number of Scottish voices raised concern about this. The catalogue of William Drummond's library, for instance, mentions a manuscript titled '*Nuntius Scoto-Britannus*, Or, a paire of Spectacles for W. *Camden*, to looke vpon *North-Britain*'.[76] This anonymous work, which no longer survives, evidently took a satirical sideswipe at what it perceived as Camden's Anglocentrism. This might have been an irritant to Scottish readers, but, in the early editions at least, it could be excused. Camden had not had the opportunity to travel north of the border, and he had far fewer correspondents in Scotland than he did in England. However, after the accession of James I in 1603, this brevity might well have taken on a different complexion. Instead of a blunder, it might have started to look more like a deliberate oversight or even a slight. The antiquaries, after all, as John Kerrigan has recently reminded us, did not necessarily turn up material to the advantage of James.[77] But Camden's position was not instinctively hostile to the king or his policies.[78] After the accession, for instance, he added a new dedication to the *Britannia*, whose wording clearly attempts to align the book with James's plans for the union. Not only does the new dedication follow James's change to the royal style, it also pronounces boldly that he was born to the eternization of the British name.[79] Camden also speaks in a new preface to the section on Scotland of the 'divine and heauenly opportunity . . . now fallen into our laps': namely, the fact that Britain,

---

[76] *Auctarium bibliothecæ Edinburgenæ, sive catalogus librorum quos Guilielmus Drummondus ab Hawthornden bibliothecæ D.D.Q. anno. 1627* (Edinburgh, 1627), 27; see R. H. Macdonald, *The Library of Drummond of Hawthornden* (Edinburgh: Edinburgh University Press, 1971), no. 1339.

[77] John Kerrigan, *Archipelagic English: Literature, History, and Politics 1603–1707* (Oxford: Oxford University Press, 2008), 14; see also Huw Griffiths, 'Britain in Ruins: The Picts' Wall and the Union of the Two Crowns', *Rethinking History*, 7 (2003), 89–105, which argues for unforeseen Jacobean consequences of Camden's project.

[78] Indeed, according to Denys Hay, 'Camden did more to unite Britain in the long run than did King James'; see *Annalists and Historians*, 151.

[79] Camden, *Britannia* (1607), sig. π2ʳ: 'SERENISSIMO, POTENTISSIMOQVE PRINCIPI IACOBO, BRITANNIÆ MAGNÆ, FRANCIÆ, ET HIBERNIÆ REGI, FIDEI PROPVGNATORI, AD ÆTERNITATEM BRITANNICI NOMINIS IMPERIIQVE NATO, PERPETVÆ PACIS FVNDATORI, PVBLICÆ SECVRITATIS AVTHORI GVILIELMVS CAMDENVS MAIESTATI EIVS DEVOTISSIMVS D.D. CONSECRATQVE'.

which was formerly 'disioigned in it selfe and unsociable', should now 'by a blessed Vnion bee conjoyned in one entire bodie'.[80] He also gives an additional reason for his brevity here, explaining that he does not want to 'prevent their curious diligence, who are in hand to set out these matters with a fuller pensill, and to polish the same with more liuelie and lasting collours'.[81] Nevertheless, Camden seems to have felt that further additions were needed, material which would help to ensure that readers would not impute the wrong political motives to his antiquarian project.

Thus it was that in the first years of the seventeenth century Camden renewed his correspondence with the Scottish poet and scholar John Johnston. Johnston had first written to Camden in April 1590, when he was a student at Heidelberg. This letter praises Camden for the *Britannia*, which Johnston had managed to read thanks to Sir Henry Wotton, who had arrived in Heidelberg a few months earlier with a copy of the book.[82] This would have been either the first edition of 1586 or the second edition of 1587. A year later Johnston may have met Camden for the first time. Having concluded his Continental travels in spring 1591, Johnston arrived in London, where he was then detained for more than a year by a bout of the ill health that plagued him throughout his life.[83] This seems as likely a time as any for the two men to have met. There is then a hiatus in their correspondence—at least, in the correspondence that survives—until 1606, when Johnston wrote again. This letter, which he entrusted to his friend Andrew Melville, who was travelling from Anstruther to London along with six other Scottish ministers to meet James I, concerned a manuscript. This manuscript was a copy of Johnston's *Urbes Britanniae*, a series of encomiastic Latin verses on cities in England and Scotland, partly based on Ausonius' *Ordo urbium nobilium*. Johnston asked Camden to correct any errors that he might have made, and also offered to send him any further material that might be of use.[84] There seems little

---

[80] Camden, *Britain*, sig. 4A2^r.
[81] Ibid., sig. 4A2^v. These unnamed scholars probably included the cartographer and chorographer Timothy Pont, who was at work at the time on a series of maps and descriptions of Scotland. Camden was certainly known to Pont: his name appears in Pont's hand at the top of Pont's map of South Uist ('Historia*m* Malross: citat Camdenus'); see NLS, MS Pont 36. On Pont, see J. C. Stone, 'Timothy Pont and the Mapping of Sixteenth-Century Scotland: Survey or Chorography?', *Survey Review*, 35, (2000), 418–30; and Ian C. Cunningham (ed.), *The Nation Survey'd: Essays on Late Sixteenth-Century Scotland as Depicted by Timothy Pont* (East Linton: Tuckwell Press, 2001).
[82] John Johnston to William Camden, 10 Apr. 1590, *V. cl. Gulielmi Camdeni... epistolæ*, 42: 'Sed hæc ipsa mihi obscura & ignota fuissent, nisi Henricus Wottonus juvenis nobilissimus, omnique virtute & liberali literatura instructissimus, è Britannia discedens, Britanniam tuam secum huc asportasset: quâ mihi oblatâ & perlectâ, ita sensi, ut scripsi'; L. P. Smith, *The Life and Letters of Sir Henry Wotton*, 2 vols. (Oxford: Clarendon Press, 1907), i. 10.
[83] *Letters of John Johnston c. 1565–1611 and Robert Howie c. 1565–c. 1645*, ed. James Kerr Cameron (St Andrews: University Court of St Andrews, 1963), p. xlix.
[84] John Johnston to William Camden, 10 Aug. 1606, *V. cl. Gulielmi Camdeni... epistolæ*, 76–7: 'Si qua mihi occurrent ex usu tuo, ea per valetudinem conquista, valente Domino, ad te transmittam. Interea mitto ad te *Vrbes Britanniæ* nostræ carmine à me delineatas, ceu tesseram &

doubt that he was referring here to Camden's work on the new edition of the *Britannia* and, more particularly, given native sensitivities, to the section on Scotland.

Happily, Johnston's manuscript still survives, bound as the last item in a collection of pamphlets, now preserved in the library of Westminster Abbey.[85] This volume, bound in limp seventeenth-century vellum, contains thirteen other pieces, which range from Christopher Ockland's *Anglorum prælia* of 1580 to John Hales's *Bodleiomnema* of 1613. Titles of eleven of the fourteen pieces, including 'Vrbes Britanniæ', are written in ink on the spine. Camden's signature, 'Will. Camden', appears on the title page of the penultimate piece, the pseudonymous *De caede et interitu Gallorum regis, Henrici tertii, valesiorum vltimi, epigrammata* (1589). The volume, which formed part of Camden's own library, came to Westminster Abbey, where he had himself been librarian, after his death in 1623. Although he had bequeathed all his books and manuscripts, 'except such as concernes Armes and Heraldry', to Cotton, Dr John Williams, the Dean of Westminster, managed to acquire many of the printed books. Camden's will invited Cotton to 'have the first view of them, that he may take out such as I borrowed of him', and so, as Richard DeMolen has suggested, Williams may simply have picked up what Cotton did not want to keep.[86] This included a collection of pamphlets, all of which, like the *Urbes Britanniae* volume, have the class-mark 'CB', and most of which, also like that volume, are bound in limp vellum. They also almost certainly came to the Abbey, where they are now housed in one cupboard in the library and muniment room, bound in this way.[87]

The 'Vrbes Britanniæ' manuscript, the only piece in the volume that is not printed, is a single quarto paper book of twelve leaves, stitched through six stab-holes (Fig. 3.1). The first and the last leaves serve as the title page and wrappers. The last leaf is dirtier than the others and also torn, presumably because of this. The paper seems to have come from a single stock; it has a pot watermark, with the initials '$\frac{AO}{B}$' and an ornamental crown. The hand, described by Peter Beal as 'calligraphic', is a beautiful copperplate italic.[88] The manuscript contains twenty-nine poems; there is also an 'APPENDIX Urbium Britanniæ' with four further poems.[89] The title of each poem in the manuscript is capitalized, as are the first one or two words and also some proper nouns. The first letter of each line is also capitalized, and majuscule letters are more heavily inked than the

---

pignus observantiæ & amoris erga te mei, quas juris facias tui, ut de iis statuas pro arbitratu tuo: & sicubi à me erratum est, pro humanitate tuâ ignoscas & corrigas.'

[85] WAL, CB 7 (14).
[86] 'M^r. Camden's Will', in *A Collection of Curious Discourses* (1720), 277–80; Richard L. DeMolen, 'The Library of William Camden', *Proceedings of the American Philosophical Society*, 128 (1984), 327–409 at 331–2.
[87] I am extremely grateful to Dr Tony Trowles, the librarian at Westminster Abbey, for information about the Camden pamphlets.
[88] Beal, *Index of English Literary Manuscripts*, i. 161 (CmW 127).
[89] For a list of the contents of the manuscript, see the Appendix at pp. 208–9.

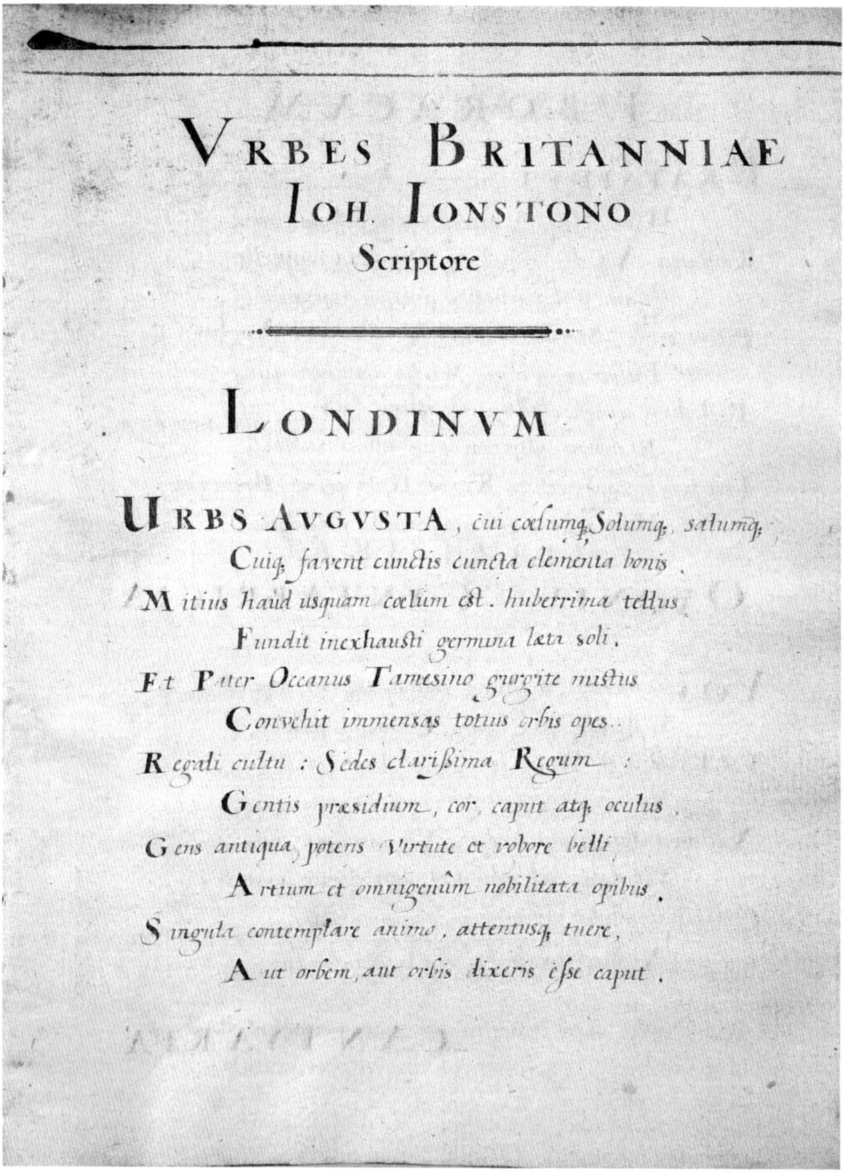

VRBES BRITANNIAE
IOH. IONSTONO
Scriptore

LONDINVM

Urbs Avgvsta, cui coelumq̧ Solumq̧, salumq̧,
 Cuiq̧ favent cunctis cuncta elementa bonis.
Mitius haud usquam coelium est. huberrima tellus
 Fundit inexhausti germina læta soli.
Et Pater Occanus Tamesino gurgite mistus
 Convehit immensas totius orbis opes.
Regali cultu : Sedes clarißima Regum
 Gentis præsidium, cor, caput atq̧ oculus.
Gens antiqua, potens virtute et robore belli,
 Artium et omnigenûm nobilitata opibus.
Singula contemplare animo, attentusq̧ tuere,
 Aut orbem, aut orbis dixeris eße caput.

FIG. 3.1. 'VRBES BRITANNIAE IOH. IONSTONO Scriptore'. Westminster Abbey Library and Muniment Room, CB 7 (14), fo. 2^r. Copyright: Dean and Chapter of Westminster

others. Despite the manuscript being neither ruled nor lined, the lineation and penwork are regular and consistent, both of which suggest that it may have been copied by a professional scribe rather than by Johnston himself. This would fit with the manuscript being a presentation copy, albeit one which Johnston invited Camden to correct.

Camden did as he was asked. A number of the poems bear corrections in his distinctive italic hand. Most of these are grammatical, emending mistakes in the Latin. Thus in the poem on Edinburgh, 'EDINBVRGVM', he corrected the form of one of the verbs. In the manuscript, the eleventh and twelfth lines originally read 'An quisquam Arctoi extremo sub limite mundi / Aut hæc, aut paria his cernere posse putat?'[90] Camden crossed out the *a* of 'putat', inserted a caret, and wrote a superscript *e* above, thus changing the mood of the verb from an indicative to a subjunctive. But a few of his corrections are also to the contents. He emended, for example, the title of the appendix to 'APPENDIX Urbium ANGLIAE' to reflect more accurately its contents; the four poems all take English towns as their subjects (Canterbury, Chester, Dover, and Yarmouth).[91] And at least one correction, and this is perhaps the most significant, is historical. In the title of the twenty-first poem, 'LIMNVCHVS, SIVE LINDVNVM', on Linlithgow, Camden corrected the Latin place name to 'LINDVM' by scoring through its second syllable, and he repeated this correction in the last line of the poem.[92] Camden, it seems, had not forgotten his original purpose; he still had his eye on Roman toponyms.

But Camden did more than he was asked as well, for he also included many of the poems, more or less revised, depending on the poem itself, in the next edition of the *Britannia*. Of Johnston's thirty-three poems, Camden published twenty. Of these twenty, it is surely indicative that more than half were on Scottish subjects: 'HADINA' (Haddington), 'EDINBVRGVM' (Edinburgh), 'ÆRA SIVE AERIA' (Ayr), 'GLASCVA' (Glasgow), 'STERLINVM' (Sterling), 'FANVM REGVLI SIVE ANDREAPOLIS' (St Andrews), 'CVPRUM FIFAE' (Cupar), 'OPPIDA AD FORTHAM' (towns on the Forth), 'PERTHVM' (Perth), 'TAODVNVM SIVE DEIDONVM' (Dundee), 'CELVRCA, SIVE MONS-ROSARVM' (Montrose), 'ABREDONIA' (Aberdeen), and 'ENNERNESSVS, ET ENNERLOTHEA' (Inverness and Inverlochy).[93] Where Camden had emended the manuscript—in the poem on Edinburgh, for example—the

---

[90] WAL, CB 7 (14), fo. [5]ʳ; *Britain*, sig. 4B2ʳ: 'In parts remote of Northren [*sic*] clime would any person ween, / That euer these or such like things might possibly be seene.'

[91] WAL, CB 7 (14), fo. [10]ᵛ.

[92] Here, Camden's deletion affected the metre, and so, to compensate, he introduced a new syllable and word at the beginning of the line, again signalled by a caret. The revised line reads "Hinc' LIND‹VN›VM patrio fit manifesta sono', WAL, CB 7 (14), fo. [7]ᵛ.

[93] Camden, *Britain*, pp. 688, 689–90, 694, 696, 701, 703, 704, 704, 709, 710, 711, 712, and 715 respectively; cf. WAL, CB 7 (14), fos. [7]ᵛ–[8]ʳ, fo. [5]ʳ, fo. [7]ʳ, fo. [6]ᵛ, fo. [7]ʳ⁻ᵛ, fo. [6]ʳ⁻ᵛ, fo. [8]ᵛ, fos. [8]ᵛ–[9]ʳ, fo. [5]ᵛ, fo. [6]ʳ, fo. [9]ʳ, fo. [5]ʳ⁻ᵛ, and fos. [9]ᵛ–[10]ʳ.

printed text follows his emendation. As well as correcting the poems, Camden also reordered them. Whereas there is little discernible sequence in the manuscript, in the *Britannia* the poems follow an obvious south-north axis, in accordance with the larger itinerary principle of the book.

There are also more substantial emendations in the printed text, which were not marked up in the manuscript. The poem on Haddington contains an obvious example. The manuscript reads as follows:

> PLANITIES prætensa jacet prope flumina Tinæ:
>   Fluminis arguti clauditur ista sinu
> Volcani et Martis quæ passa incendia, Fati
>   Ingemit alterno vulnere fracta vices.
> Nempe sacro hæc vates cecinit Sophocardius ore,
>   Quæ ‹prodit› probat eventus prodita ab ore DEI.
> Quæ varias experta vices, rerum*que* potentes,
>   Nunc placidæ gaudet pacis honore frui.[94]

In the *Britannia*, by contrast, the poem reads:

> Planities prætensa iacet prope flumina Tinæ,
>   Fluminis arguti clauditur ista sinu.
> Vulcani & Martis quæ passa incendia, fati
>   Ingemit alterno vulnere fracta vices
> Nunc tandem sæpit icta. Dei præcepta sequuta
>   Præsidio gaudet iam potiore Poli.
>
> Before it, lies a spatious plaine, the Tine his streame hard by,
> In bosome of that river shrill, this towne enclos'd doth lie.
> Which having suffered grievous smart of fire and sword by turnes,
> Grones under those misfortunes much, and for her losses mournes.
> But now at length self-harmes have made it wise, and by Gods lore
> Directed, helpe it hath from heaven which steedeth it much more.[95]

The poem has been substantially revised, with the final two couplets in the manuscript version replaced with a single new couplet in the printed text. Given Camden's reluctance to edit the contributions of his collaborators, we might have expected this revision to have been made by Johnston. In that case, he would presumably have sent Camden another manuscript, which is now lost, with the revised version of the poem. But, in fact, there is every reason to believe that the poem was revised by Camden himself. The fact that the manuscript is bound and preserved with other of his pamphlets means that he cannot have returned it to Johnston for further thought and revision. Perhaps only the length of the revision

---

[94] WAL, CB 7 (14), fos. [7]ᵛ–[8]ʳ.
[95] Camden, *Britannia* (1607), p. 688; *Britain*, sig. 4A6v.

here prevented him from marking up the manuscript in the way that he customarily did for more minor corrections.

Moreover, in a letter of April 1608, Johnston himself spoke of the corrections that Camden had made to the text. From this letter it is apparent that Johnston had not been consulted over any of these. We learn that he had heard from a friend in London that Camden had incorporated the *Urbes Britanniae* in the new edition of the *Britannia*, but that he had not been able to find out how far Camden had edited or revised the poems.[96] He does not identify this friend by name, but it has been suggested that he may have been Jean Castel, the minister of the French Protestant Church in London, who had close ties with the Scottish Presbyterian community there.[97] For this reason, Johnston was eager to get his hands on a copy of the new edition. Scottish booksellers, it seems, were lagging behind, and he had only been able to find a copy of the 1594 edition, which he already owned. He therefore asked Camden, in the nicest possible way, if he might send him the new edition.[98] From a letter of September 1608, it is clear that Camden obliged.[99]

Johnston may have recommended himself to Camden by his series of publications on historical subjects, which had appeared since 1600. In 1602, for example, his *Inscriptiones historicæ regum Scotorum* was published, printed at Amsterdam by Cornelis Claeszoon on behalf of the Edinburgh bookseller Andro Hart. This work contains a series of epitaphs on Scottish monarchs from Fergus, the supposed first king of Scotland, through to James VI and also Prince Henry. For each king or queen, Johnston also gives the date of their accession in three forms: from the age of the world, from the birth of Christ, and from the foundation of the kingdom. In the case of Fergus, he gives the date in Olympiads and from the foundation of Rome. This attention to comparative chronology may have especially recommended the volume. Furthermore, as well as Johnston's poems, it also contains Andrew Melville's 'Gathelus, sive de gentis origine fragmentum', a brief account in verse of the origin of the Scots, which,

---

[96] John Johnston to William Camden, 9 Apr. 1608, *V. cl. Gulielmi Camdeni... epistolæ*, 95: 'Scripsit ad me amicum quidam Londinensis, *Britanniam tuam* excusam typis esse; addit quoque idem de Urbibus nostris, sed quâ formâ & modo illæ editæ sint, non declarat.'

[97] *Letters of John Johnston*, 232 n. 11; see also Charles G. D. Littleton, 'The Strangers, their Churches and the Continent: Continuing and Changing Connexions', in Nigel Goose and Lien Luu (eds.), *Immigrants in Tudor and Early Stuart England* (Brighton: Sussex Academic Press, 2005), 177–91 at 187.

[98] John Johnston to William Camden, 9 Apr. 1608, *V. cl. Gulielmi Camdeni... epistolæ*, 95–6: 'Sed neque Britanniam tuam videre hactenus licuit, quanquam diligentèr eam pervestigari apud bibliopolas nostros curaverim, qui mihi editionem anno 94. quam antea dudum habueram, miserunt... atque peto abs te, ut tuâ operâ exemplar Britanniæ tuæ, si forte adhuc non prostet publicè vænum, mihi per eam procuraretur mittendum, qui solutionem meo nomine præstabit.'

[99] John Johnston to William Camden, 25 Sept. 1608, ibid. 123–4. From an eik to his last will and testament, we discover that he later bequeathed Camden's book to 'Mr. Robert Mauld commisser of St. Androis', along with 'a sand glass quhilk I gat from him selff'; *Letters of John Johnston*, 234 n. 2.

despite its derivativeness, would certainly have advertised the book to antiquarian readers. Melville relied heavily on Hector Boece, tracing the Scots back to one Gathelus, son of Cecrops, the first king of Attica, and his Egyptian wife, the eponymous Scota.[100] And the volume itself came warmly endorsed: it was sent on its way with prefatory material by such luminous voices as Joseph Scaliger, Janus Dousa, and Daniel Heinsius. That same year Claeszoon also printed Johnston's *Vera descriptio augustissimæ stewartorum familiæ* (1602), a series of engraved portraits of the Stuarts, with letterpress Latin verse below.[101]

A year later Johnston's *Heroes ex omni historia scotica lectissimi* (1603) appeared, a collection of potted biographies and eulogies in elegiac couplets of great figures from Scottish history. This volume too was printed on the Continent, emanating from the press of Christoffel Guyot at Leiden, again on behalf of Andro Hart. The *Urbes Britanniae* might be seen as the topographical equivalent, doing for Scottish towns—and, in a few instances, English towns—what the previous volumes had done for Scottish history. We cannot say for certain that Camden commissioned Johnston to write the poems. But, in the light of his eagerness to increase the Scottish section of the *Britannia* for political reasons, and given the nature of his correspondence with other contributors, there is every reason to believe that he strongly encouraged his Scottish friend. There is also no doubt that he had more than just a hand in the version of the poems, which finally appeared in 1607. Johnston himself, incidentally, seems to have continued to work on the *Urbes Britanniae* after this date, perhaps in anticipation of publication in its own right. In the letter of September 1608, for example, he spoke of his wish that Camden scrutinize a new version of the text.[102]

The example of Johnston is suggestive not so much for what he sent Camden as for the extensive accompanying documentation. His contributions are minor in comparison to those of Bainbrigg and Godwin, and his poems are of strictly historical interest. But, for the composition of the *Britannia*, he remains an important and an illustrative figure. For one thing, the correspondence between Camden and Johnston is more extensive than for almost any of the other contributors, and these letters, moreover, address not only Johnston's material, but also the changes or revisions that Camden himself might make to it. For another thing, the manuscript which Johnston presented to Camden is marked up in the author's hand. The example of Johnston can therefore illuminate Camden's working practices, showing the progress of the *Britannia* from scattered contributions to final composition. It also therefore demonstrates how closely Camden worked with—indeed, how he relied upon—his vast network of

---

[100] John Johnston, *Inscriptiones historicæ regum Scotorum, continuata annorum serie a Fergusio primo regni conditore ad nostra tempora* (Amsterdam, 1602), sigs. *4ʳ–*5ᵛ.
[101] For descriptions of the portraits, see Arthur M. Hind, *Engraving in England in the Sixteenth and Seventeenth Centuries*, 3 vols. (Cambridge: Cambridge University Press, 1952–64), ii. 49–50.
[102] John Johnston to William Camden, 25 Sept. 1608, *V. cl. Gulielmi Camdeni... epistolæ*, 124: 'De *vrbibus nostris* nihil statuerim, priusquam censuræ rursus tuæ subjiciantur.'

correspondents. In short, it confirms that, for Camden, collaboration was an integral part of antiquarian method.

Whether his collaborators enabled Camden to answer Ortelius's initial request is another matter. In some ways, the contributions of the likes of Johnston and Bainbrigg take the *Britannia* away from the relatively narrow historical focus which Ortelius envisaged. Camden's project travels in more various directions, although he himself never forgot his friend's request. A lengthy correspondence with the French scholar and librarian Pierre Dupuy over the publication of Nicolas Bergier's history of Roman roads, *Histoire des grands chemins de l'Empire romain* (1622), attests to his continued interest in the geography and itineraries of the Roman Empire, long after he had completed his *magnum opus*.[103] Nevertheless, restoring antiquity to Britain, thanks in no small part to the diversity of contributions that he received, became about more than identifying Roman toponyms and following Roman roads. His canvas was a broader one, reflecting the growing encyclopedism of antiquarian interests. It was also one increasingly understood in ways that Ortelius did not and could not have conceived.

Perhaps the best answer comes from one of Camden's contemporaries. In his poem 'To William Camden', first printed in his *Epigrams* of 1616, Ben Jonson, who had been a pupil at Westminster School under Camden, speaks of the debt that he and the country owe to him:

> Camden, most reverend head, to whom I owe
>   All that I am in arts, all that I know;
> (How nothing's that?) to whom my country owes
>   The great renown and name wherewith she goes.[104]

The poem straddles the personal and the public, for what begins as Jonson's homage to his former schoolmaster becomes praise for the titular excellence of the pre-eminent antiquary of the Jacobean age. Britain, Jonson asserts, owes both her name and her fame to Camden. By identifying the two in this way, Jonson also inevitably speaks of politics. His readers are put in mind of the island as well as Camden's book. The *Britannia* becomes, in Jonson's poem, the literary counterpart to James's project for the union of the two kingdoms. The *Britannia* puts into words what James had tried to effect in law. But whereas his plans had foundered on a groundswell of parliamentary opposition, as he struggled to get further than a union in name, Camden had succeeded in making the island

---

[103] BNF, Dupuy 699, fos. 203ʳ–212ʳ. Dupuy seems to have sent Camden sections of Bergier's book for his perusal and comment. In a letter of 28 Aug. 1619, for example, Camden spoke of the great pleasure that he had taken in reading Bergier's preface (fo. 206ʳ), and in another, undated letter he confessed that he waited for nothing more keenly ('Nihil auidiùs expecto') than the publication of the book (fo. 208ʳ).

[104] Ben Jonson, 'To William Camden', in *Ben Jonson*, ed. Ian Donaldson (Oxford: Oxford University Press, 1985), ll. 1–4.

whole again. As Thomas Browne asked in *Camdeni insignia* (1624), the memorial volume published on Camden's death in November 1623, 'How dost thou, cruel England, / suffer him to die, through whom thou livest whole?'[105] Browne's apostrophe is to England, but his reference is to the *Britannia*, and his allusion is to the reunification of the whole island in the pages of the book. Camden, as the tributes of Jonson and Browne attest, had indeed succeeded in restoring 'antiquity to Britaine, and Britain to his antiquity'—only not in the toponymic way that Ortelius had imagined forty years earlier. Restoration, it seems, was now understood in political as well as historical terms. Whether Camden would have succeeded without his contributors, without their courtesy and collaboration, this chapter, I hope, has amply answered.

[105] Thomas Browne, 'In Honour of Camden', in *The Works of Sir Thomas Browne*, ll. 19–20; see also *Camdeni insignia* (Oxford, 1624), sig. C3ᵛ: 'dura quid pateris mori, / Quo tota vivis, Anglia'.

4

Monuments and Megaliths: From Stonehenge to 'Stonage'

In spring 1635 a curious performance took place at St John's College, Oxford. The occasion was the return of the President, Dr Richard Baylie, from Salisbury, where he had been appointed dean on 22 April that year, probably through the influence of Archbishop Laud, his uncle by marriage. To celebrate his return, a new play was performed, which is variously known today as *The Converted Robber* and *Stonehenge, a Pastoral*.[1] This play is now generally believed to be by Dr John Speed, son of the chronologer and historian of the same name, and fellow of St John's, although it has also been ascribed to George Wilde, another fellow of the college and one of Laud's private chaplains.[2] The play survives in a single manuscript witness in the British Library (Additional MS 14047, fos. 44ᵛ–59ᵛ), where it is titled 'The converted Robber' and described as 'A Pastorall Acted by sᵗ. Johns. Collǣge'. The codex, a small quarto of 159 leaves in various hands, also contains two other plays performed at St John's in the 1630s, 'Loves Hospitall' (fos. 8ʳ–39ʳ) and 'Eumorphus, sive Cupido Adultus' (fos. 60ʳ–96ᵛ), both of which are by Wilde.

Speed's play is a mostly conventional tale of virtue rewarded. A band of robbers, intent on rape and pillage, are converted by the constancy of the faithful shepherdess Castina. What is unusual about the play is the prominence of its setting: Salisbury Plain. This, as Walter Greg pointed out a century ago, was doubtless intended as a compliment to Baylie on his appointment to the deanship.[3] The play ends, after all, by wishing him luck in his new position: 'Lett vs that do noe envy beare 'vm / Wish all felicity to *Sarum*'.[4] But the play also includes a disquisition on Salisbury's attractions. In the opening scene Alcinous,

---

[1] Anthony à Wood, *Athenae oxonienses: An Exact History of All the Writers and Bishops Who Have Had their Education in the University of Oxford*, ed. Philip Bliss, 4 vols. (London, 1813–20), ii. 660; Gerald Eades Bentley, *The Jacobean and Caroline Stage*, 7 vols. (Oxford: Clarendon Press, 1941–68), v. 1181–4; *Records of Early English Drama: Oxford*, ed. John R. Elliott, Jr, Alan H. Nelson, Alexandra F. Johnston, and Diana Wyatt (Toronto: University of Toronto Press, 2004), ii. 807–8.
[2] For the ascription to Wilde, see Josephine Laidler, 'A History of Pastoral Drama in England until 1700', *Englische Studien*, 35 (1905), 193–259 at 234–6.
[3] Walter W. Greg, *Pastoral Poetry and Pastoral Drama: A Literary Inquiry, with Special Reference to the Pre-Restoration Stage in England* (London: A. H. Bullen, 1906), 383.
[4] BL, Additional MS 14047, fo. 59ʳ.

the leader of the robbers, who is disguised as a shepherd, is led across Salisbury Plain by a real shepherd, the garrulous Jarbus. As they walk, Jarbus points out various landmarks. One in particular catches the robber's attention. A stage direction, written in the margin of the manuscript, reveals this to be Stonehenge, the most curious monument of all on the Plain: 'The sceane is opend and it shewes to be like stonage the wonder that is vpon that Playne of Sarum.'[5] This provides an opportunity for Speed to survey popular tales about Stonehenge, to bring various traditions together in a long and confused catalogue. Fittingly, this is spoken by the comic Jarbus, whose rustic speech, inflected with a distinct dialect, contrasts with the easy eloquence of Alcinous and his companions. Jarbus calls Stonehenge 'thilke enchaunted Pile of stones', and mentions that it was once believed to be the 'Diuells dwellinge'. He alludes to the tradition that the stones cannot be counted because they are enchanted: 'The rest stond vnd*er* like A spell / That none thilke number right mought tell.' He also reports the story that the stones were erected by Merlin, transported by magic from Ireland, and he adds the detail that they might be the petrified bones of a giant:

> From *Irish* or from Vayry Lond
> There picket (theyn zay) by Gyants honde.
> Till *Merlin* old by tricke of Arte
> Fot them I wott w*i*thout A Carte.
> Some would (I woss) the were the bones
> of thilke same Gyant turn'd to stones
> Armour in yon hillock mought be zeene
> To vitt zuch limbs as those mought beene.[6]

Speed was poking fun at his old shepherd here, satirizing popular tales about Stonehenge by delivering them in this absurdly rustic voice. His learned audience at St John's would have understood the joke, and they would surely also have recognized the knowing, literary reference to Spenser's 'Vayry Lond'. (Spenser gives his own, divergent explanation for the monument in the chronicle read by Prince Arthur in Eumnestes' chamber in Book 2 of *The Faerie Queene*.[7]) But Jarbus himself is not quite the fool that he seems. His parenthetical reflection, 'theyn zay', distances him from the story that he reports. He never lays claim to historical truth or authority. He is merely a cataloguer of popular memories, a compiler of traditional beliefs. His speech on Stonehenge makes no attempt to reconcile these traditions and privileges no single interpretation.

---

[5] BL, Additional MS 14047, fo. 46ᵛ.
[6] Ibid., fos. 46ᵛ–47ʳ.
[7] Spenser, *The Faerie Queene*, ed. Hamilton, II. x. 66. 6–9: 'Soone after which, three hundred Lordes he slew / Of British bloud, all sitting at his bord; / Whose dolefull moniments who list to rew, / Th'eternall markes of treason may at *Stonheng* vew.'

On one level, Jarbus's speech is nothing more than a droll interlude, designed to amuse the President and fellows of an Oxford college. It is an unusual comic diversion, given relevance by the circumstances of the play, in an otherwise familiar pastoral plot. On another level, though, his speech attests to how widespread curiosity about Stonehenge had become in the early seventeenth century. That curiosity is the subject of this chapter, as I explore the ways in which Stonehenge and other similar monuments were interpreted and imagined by early modern writers. For the antiquaries, the key to understanding such monuments was to measure them—what was known at the time as mensuration. To measure a monument was, in a sense, to know it. Rosemary Hill's recent distinction between architectural and antiquarian approaches to Stonehenge turns out, at least for the period with which this book is concerned, to be a false one.[8] Mensuration was an important weapon in the antiquary's armoury, and for monuments such as Stonehenge, where the documentary evidence was deficient, perhaps the most important one. But if that uncertainty was a source of frustration for the antiquaries, to be tackled with a radius and measuring rod, it was, as 'The converted Robber' shows, an opportunity for poets. Stonehenge—and this is something to which I return later in the chapter—emerges as an important figure in the early modern imagination, a locus for poetic reflections on the limits of historical knowledge and the nature of historical interpretation.

In this way, mensuration offers an example of antiquarian curiosity in practice. This methodology, which sought both to describe material remains in terms of their measurements and through those measurements to certify their 'bigness' and wonder, illustrates the epistemological importance of that curiosity. To measure an ancient monument was a way to describe and order it, and so also to articulate what was curious about it, in terms of its architecture, appearance, or any other respect, and this in turn offered a way of comprehending it. Curiosity was concerned with detailed description and explanation of what was rare and strange about an object, natural or artificial, but, as Katie Whitaker has recently argued, it 'also essentially involved the attempt to understand' that object.[9] The antiquarian responses to Stonehenge illustrate her argument.

As so often with English antiquarianism, the roots of this mensural approach can be traced to the methods of Italian predecessors. By the middle of the sixteenth century, amongst Roman antiquaries in particular, antiquarian expertise had become almost inseparable from architectural practice.[10] One of the first to make this connection had been Raphael, who, in a letter of 1519 to Pope Leo X, proposed a new method of surveying the Roman ruins. Having deplored in familiar rhetorical terms the ruin of the city in the first half of this letter, he then

---

[8] Rosemary Hill, *Stonehenge* (London: Profile, 2008), 21–85.
[9] Katie Whitaker, 'The Culture of Curiosity', in N. Jardine, J. A. Secord, and E. C. Spary (eds.), *Cultures of Natural History* (Cambridge: Cambridge University Press, 1996), 75–90 at 81.
[10] Schnapp, *The Discovery of the Past*, 125–6.

explained his new method, an approach which would encompass accurate representations of all the ancient monuments in plan, internal elevation, and external elevation. He then concluded the letter by recommending himself as the surveyor, contrasting the poor efforts of others with his own unrivalled practice and his superior knowledge of ancient architecture and antique remains.[11]

It is unlikely that Raphael's letter was known in England until the early eighteenth century, when it was printed for the first time. Wrongly attributed to Baldassare Castiglione, the letter appeared in 1733 as an appendix to the edition of Castiglione's works brought out that year by the Volpi brothers.[12] But its architectural method was known, perhaps through the intermediary of later Italian architects such as Andrea Palladio, and by the end of the sixteenth century its mensural approach seems to have taken hold in England as well. It was called upon to fill gaps in knowledge; to illustrate, confirm, or disprove traditions and long-held beliefs; to apprehend the wondrous, the curious, and the rare. Such wonders could be exotic and foreign, as travel writing had long attested. But they could also be nearer at hand, domestic monuments such as the megaliths at Avebury and Stonehenge, which placed similar demands on the powers of the antiquary, and attracted the attention of almost all.

STONE CIRCLES

Stonehenge has been called by one modern writer 'the classic battleground of archaeology, where scholarly reputations are sacrificed and where every new generation massacres the theories of its predecessors'.[13] The monument attracts endless speculation over who built it and why, over where the stones came from and how they were transported, questions which inevitably still await their answers. Things were no different in the early modern period, as Jarbus's speech demonstrates. A plethora of traditions and interpretations circulated, as popular beliefs competed with antiquarian theories based on mensuration and surveying.[14] As an easily visible monument in the landscape, Stonehenge (like

---

[11] Raphael to Pope Leo X, 1519, in *Raffaello nei documenti nelle testemonianze dei contemporanei e nella letteratura del suo secolo*, ed. Vincenzio Golzio (Vatican City: Pontificia Insigne Accademia Artistica dei Virtuosi al Pantheon, 1936), 82–92.

[12] *Opere volgari, e latine del conte Baldessar Castiglione* (Padua, 1733), 429–36. The letter was printed from a manuscript in the possession of Scipione Maffei, the Veronese classicist and antiquary.

[13] John Michell, *Megalithomania: Artists, Antiquarians and Archaeologists at the Old Stone Monuments* (London: Thames and Hudson, 1982), 22; for a more theoretical account, which presents Stonehenge as a landscape where popular beliefs constantly compete with elite authority and control, see Barbara Bender, 'Stonehenge—Contested Landscapes (Medieval to Present Day)', in ead. (ed.), *Landscape: Politics and Perspectives* (Providence and Oxford: Berg, 1993), 245–79.

[14] For a by no means complete list of early modern descriptions of Stonehenge, see W. Jerome Harrison, 'A Bibliography of the Great Stone Monuments of Wiltshire—Stonehenge and Avebury:

other stone circles) was a natural focus of antiquarian attention. The problem, which the antiquaries set out to address, was that no ancient text offered a reliable, or even partially reliable, explanation for the megaliths.

The traditional, and perhaps most popular, explanation derived from the *Historia regum Britanniae* of Geoffrey of Monmouth.[15] But that work, as we have seen elsewhere in this book, was highly suspect, and by 1600 its credibility as a source was in serious doubt. According to Geoffrey, a British king, Aurelius Ambrosius, had wanted to commemorate the 460 British nobles slain by Hengist and his treacherous band of Saxons. The story went that the Britons and the Saxons had met on Salisbury Plain to conclude a peace treaty. The Britons had come unarmed, as the two parties had agreed, but the villainous Saxons had secreted daggers on their bodies. The result was predictable: carnage and all the Britons killed. Some years later Aurelius Ambrosius erected Stonehenge as a memorial to them.[16] Other medieval historians added incidental details to Geoffrey's story, many of which turn up in Jarbus's catalogue.[17] But few medieval sources had anything to say about the monument's origins or purpose—precisely what interested the antiquaries. An alternative approach was therefore needed. If the monument's history could not be established with any certainty, the antiquaries could at least describe it carefully. After all, as a first step, it was vital for them to know exactly what they were talking about. And that knowledge, as we have seen, tended to mean in the first instance detailed measurement.

Most early modern descriptions of Stonehenge are therefore similar, combining a discussion of its origin, necessarily brief given the paucity of sources, with a more detailed survey of the size and alignment of its stones. As so often, Camden was in the vanguard here. He himself had probably visited Stonehenge in 1596 as part of a tour of southern England, when he also travelled to Salisbury, Wells, and Oxford. His description of the monument begins with its geography, locating it in the Wiltshire landscape: 'Towards the North, about six miles from Salisburie, in thie plaines before named, is to be seene a huge and monstrous peece of worke, such as Cicero termeth *Insanam substructionem*.' He then provides a closer physical description and his first series of measurements:

---

with Other References', *Wiltshire Archaeological and Natural History Magazine*, 32 (1901–2), 1–169; see also Piggott, *Ancient Britons and the Antiquarian Imagination*, 102–17; and Christopher Chippindale, *Stonehenge Complete* (London: Thames and Hudson, 1994; first published 1983), 29–81.

[15] Geoffrey is, for example, the source of Spenser's account of the monument in Book 2 of *The Faerie Queene*.

[16] Geoffrey of Monmouth, *The History of the Kings of Britain*, trans. Thorpe, vi. 15. For the origins of Geoffrey's story, see Stuart Piggott, 'The Sources of Geoffrey of Monmouth II: The Stonehenge Story', *Antiquity*, 15 (1941), 305–19; and Glyn Daniel, *Megaliths in History* (London: Thames and Hudson, 1972), 37–8.

[17] See e.g. Henry of Huntingdon, *Historia Anglorum*, ed. and trans. Diana Greenway (Oxford Medieval Texts; Oxford: Clarendon Press, 1996), i. 7 at 22–3.

within the circuit of a Ditch, there are erected in manner of a Crowne, in three ranks or courses one within another certaine mighty and unwrought stones, whereof some are 28. foote high, and seuen foote broad, upon the heads of which, others like ouerthwart peeces do beare and rest crossewise, with a small tenents and mortescis, so as the whole frame seemeth to hang: whereof we call it *Stonehenge*.[18]

These measurements have a threefold purpose: to convey the shape and size of Stonehenge; to explain the origin of its strange name; and to account for its monstrousness and wonder.

But Stonehenge was also a source of frustration for Camden. 'For mine own part, about these points I am not cunningly to argue and dispute,' he asserts, 'but rather to lament with much griefe that the Authors of so notable a monument are thus buried in oblivion.'[19] Its builders lie forgotten, buried under the weight of historical disputation. For Camden, this sense of frustration was only exacerbated by the report of a strange tablet found near Stonehenge in the reign of Henry VIII. According to the report, this tablet might have held the key to the whole mystery. Camden comments that it was 'inscribed with many letters', but 'in so strange a Character' that neither Sir Thomas Elyot nor William Lily, the two scholars to whom it was sent, could decipher its inscription, and it was therefore abandoned. 'Had it been preserved,' he then reflects, 'somewhat happily might have been discovered as concerning *Stoneheng*, which now lieth obscured.'[20] Had it fallen into his own hands, he seems to be implying, there might have been the chance of discovering something more about Stonehenge and its obscure origins.

Camden appears to have approached other stone circles in the same way. On three further occasions, he gives descriptions which follow the model above. His descriptions of the Rollright Stones in Oxfordshire and the stone circles at Lesser Salkeld in Cumbria and Boscawen-un in Cornwall are all strikingly similar to his account of Stonehenge. In each case, he combines a survey of the monument, locating it topographically and describing its architecture, with a report of any folkloric tradition associated with it, and also a reasoned discussion of who built it and why. And in each case, he was moved to describe the monument by curious wonder. His account of the Rollright Stones, for example, begins with him calling them 'an ancient monument', which stands not far from the banks of the river Evenlode, 'to wit, certaine huge stones placed in a round circle'. The description itself which follows lacks the measured precision of his account of Stonehenge. But this is easily explained, since he adds that 'without all forme and shape they be, unæquall, and by long continuance of time much impaired'. He then reports the local tradition that the stones are petrified men: 'the common people usually call them *Rolle-ritch stones*, and dreameth that they were sometimes men, by a wonderfull *Metamorphosis* turned unto hard stones'. The largest stone, 'which without the circle looketh into the earth', is believed to have been

---

[18] Camden, *Britain*, 251.   [19] Ibid. 253.   [20] Ibid. 254.

'*The King*', the 'five standing at the other side', also beyond the circle, 'Knights mounted on horsebacke', and the stones of the circle itself the king's 'army'.[21] But Camden distances himself from this aetiology by calling it a dream of 'the common people'. As such, it typifies the kind of popular wonder, from which he distinguishes his own, more reasoned curiosity. His explanation for the origin of the stones is more sober, and it depends on an old antiquarian standard: 'These would I verily thinke to have beene the monument of some victorie and haply, erected by *Rollo* the Dane, who afterwards conquered Normandie.'[22] Camden falls back on etymology, and his readers, primed for this kind of method by its prevalence at the time, would have detected the implied derivation of Rollright from Rollo the Dane.

Camden's interest in megaliths is reflected by the frontispiece to the *Britannia*. From the fifth edition of 1600 onwards, the *Britannia* had a title page engraved by William Rogers (Fig. 4.1).[23] This frontispiece is architectural in form, with a plinth that breaks forward left and right. On the left side of the plinth stands Neptune, and on the right Ceres. In the centre of the frontispiece is a cartouche with a map of Britain; above the map is another cartouche with the title 'BRITANNIA'; and above that, there is a third cartouche with a personified figure of Albion-Britannia. In the centre of the plinth, a fourth cartouche presents a rural scene of baths, buildings, and a stone circle. Given the date of the frontispiece, that stone circle may well be intended as a depiction of Stonehenge. Not only had Camden travelled in Wiltshire shortly beforehand, but the 1600 edition was also the first to contain an engraving of the stone circle itself, also by Rogers (Fig. 4.2). If so, the frontispiece presents Stonehenge as an illustrative national monument, as easily identified as the iconic figure of Albion-Britannia, and also as a symbol for Camden's broader interests in the work as a whole. Megaliths, the frontispiece implies, matter.

An almost identical description of Stonehenge was provided shortly afterwards by John Speed the elder in his *History of Great Britaine* (1611). Speed begins by repeating the Galfridian explanation for the monument, although he stops short of asserting it for certain: 'Vnto this *Aurelius Ambrosius* is ascribed the erection of that rare and admirable monument, now called *Stonhenge*, in the same place where the *Britaines* had been trecherously slaughtered and interred.'[24] His description of its architecture then follows: 'The Matter being Stones of a great

---

[21] Ibid. 374. This legend is still current today, as the stone circle continues to be known as 'The King's Men', the outlying stone just to the north as 'The King Stone', and the megalithic tomb just to the west as 'The Whispering Knights'; see Nikolaus Pevsner and Jennifer Sherwood, *The Buildings of England: Oxfordshire* (Harmondsworth: Penguin, 1974), 624.
[22] Camden, *Britain*, 375.
[23] For a description, see Hind, *Engraving in England*, i. 273–4.
[24] John Speed, *The History of Great Britaine Under the Conquests of the Romans, Saxons, Danes and Normans* (London, 1611), 314–15. Speed speaks with greater certainty in his *Theatre of the Empire of Great Britaine* (1611), where a cartouche alongside his map of Wiltshire records that '*This ancient Monument was erected By Aurelius surnamed Ambrosius King of the Brittaines.*'

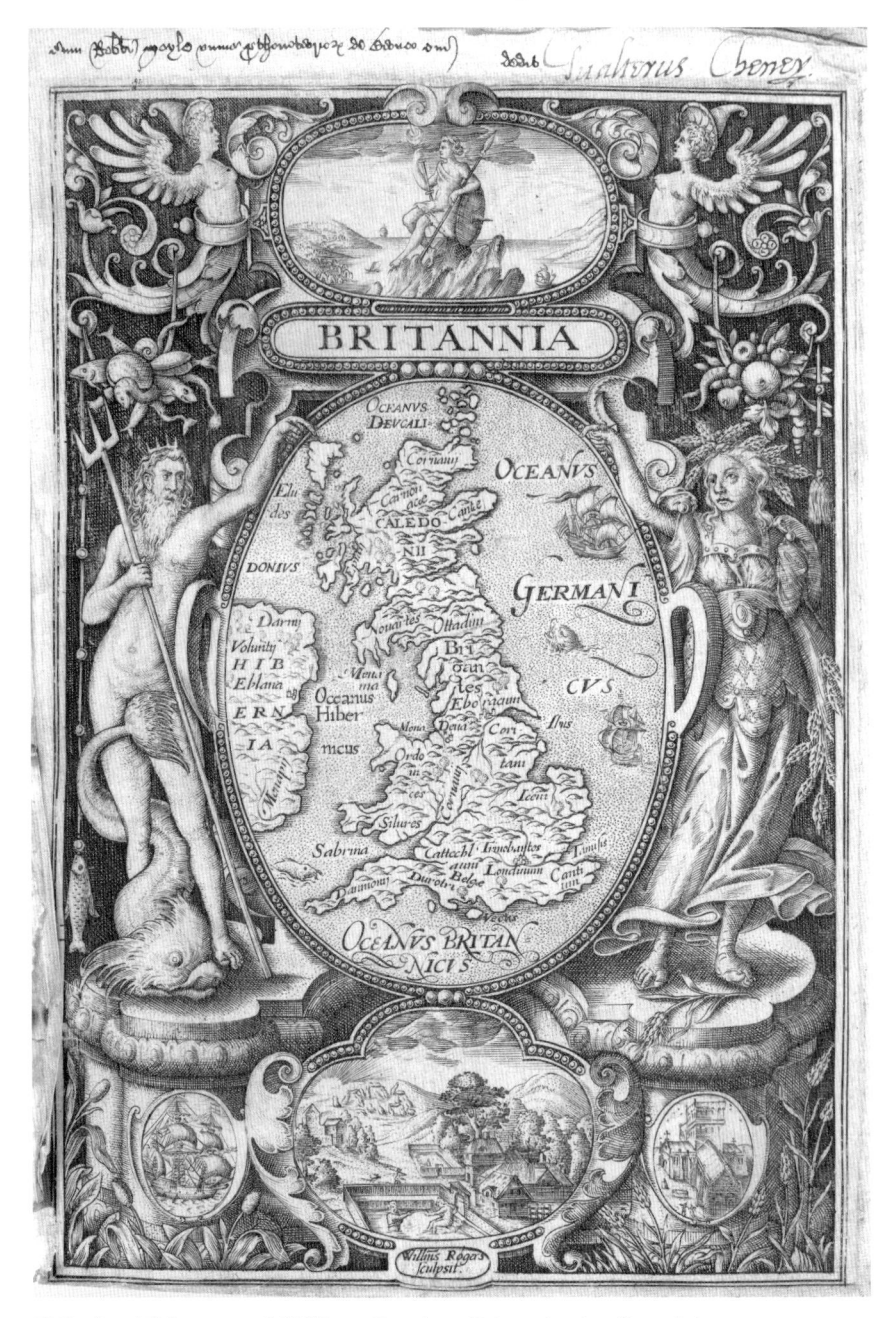

FIG. 4.1. Title page of William Camden, *Britannia sive florentissimorum regnorum, Angliæ, Scotiæ, Hiberniæ, et insularum adiacentium ex intima antiquitate chorographica descriptio* (London, 1600). Cambridge University Library, Peterborough B. 2. 36. Reproduced by kind permission of the Syndics of Cambridge University Library

FIG. 4.2. Stonehenge. William Camden, *Britannia sive florentissimorum regnorum, Angliæ, Scotiæ, Hiberniæ, et insularum adiacentium ex intima antiquitate chorographica descriptio* (London, 1600), 219. Cambridge University Library, Huntingdon 53. 4. Reproduced by kind permission of the Syndics of Cambridge University Library

and huge bignesse, so that some of them contain twelue tunne in waight, and twenty eight foote or more in length, their breadth seuen, and compasse sixteene.' He adds that these stones 'are set in the ground of a good depth, and stand in a round circle by two and two, hauing a third stone somewhat of lesse quantitie laid gate-wise ouerthwart on their toppes, fastned with tenons and mortaises, the one into the other'. Finally, he records the area and size of the monument, asserting that Stonehenge was built on a plot 'about three hundred foot in compasse, in forme almost round, or rather like vnto a horse-shooe, with an entrance in vpon the east-side', and that in its heyday it consisted of three 'rowes of stones', decreasing in scale from outer to inner.[25]

Whether Speed was consciously quoting Camden is hard to say. After all, it is not surprising that his measurements are essentially the same. Nevertheless, his description of the monument's architecture might suggest that he was. His inclusion of the detail that the stones were joined by mortise and tenon, for example, does seem to originate with Camden. This detail was by no means universally given in early modern descriptions of the monument. Moreover, Speed's work, published just a year after the English translation of the *Britannia*, elsewhere openly acknowledges Camden as a source.[26] Either way, Speed's description demonstrates how important the architectural, mensural approach to ancient monuments had become. It also demonstrates that this approach reached beyond just antiquarian circles, for, unlike Camden, Speed was not primarily an antiquary.

The pre-eminent early modern survey of Stonehenge, the most important architectural study of the monument, had to wait for another decade. That survey was carried out by James I's architect general, Inigo Jones, and it was published after Jones's death by his former pupil John Webb under the title *The most notable Antiquity of Great Britain, vulgarly called Stone-Heng on Salisbury Plain* (1655). In his own account of Stonehenge published ten years later, *A Vindication of Stone-Heng Restored* (1665), Webb explains that he was persuaded to publish Jones's survey by 'the best Antiquaries then living', men including John Selden and Sir Justinian Isham of Lamport, for whom he was working at the time.[27] In his preface to Jones's work, Webb reveals that he inherited 'some few indigested notes of the late judicious *Architect*, the *Vitruvius* of his age *Inigo Jones*', which he then 'cast' into the 'rude Form' now in front of his readers' eyes.[28] From Webb's edition we learn that Jones undertook his survey in 1620.

---

[25] Speed, *History*, 315.
[26] For Speed's debt to Camden, and indeed to other earlier antiquaries, including John Leland, see Jennifer Summit, 'Leland's *Itinerary* and the Remains of the Medieval Past', in Gordon McMullan and David Matthews (eds.), *Reading the Medieval in Early Modern England* (Cambridge: Cambridge University Press, 2007), 159–76 at 170–5.
[27] John Webb, *A Vindication of Stone-Heng Restored* (London, 1665), 122.
[28] Inigo Jones, *The most notable Antiquity of Great Britain, vulgarly called Stone-Heng on Salisbury Plain* (London, 1655), sig. A4ʳ. For a discussion of how far Webb revised Jones's survey, see John Bold, *John Webb: Architectural Theory and Practice in the Seventeenth Century* (Oxford: Clarendon Press, 1989), 48.

Whilst staying at Wilton with William Herbert, third earl of Pembroke, James I had become curious about the stone circle and so commissioned his architect general to discover what he could about it.[29]

Jones believed that the only way to make sense of Stonehenge was through its architecture. This is hardly surprising, given his career. He thought, as Rudolf Wittkower pointed out, in precisely the same terms as an antiquary as he did as an architect.[30] Indeed, it is the elegance and invention of Stonehenge's architecture, he argues, that makes it worthy of antiquarian attention in the first place:

Among the ancient monuments whereof, found here, I deemed none more worthy the searching after, then this of *Stoneheng*; not only in regard of the *Founders* thereof, the *Time* when built, the *Work* it self, but also for the rarity of its *Invention*, being different in *Forme* from all I had seen before: likewise, of as beautifull *Proportions*, as elegant in *Order*, and as stately in *Aspect*, as any.[31]

It is also this architecture that allows Jones to dismiss the theory that the Britons built Stonehenge. Stressing their barbarity—they did not, he splutters, even know how to make cheese—Jones argues that it is scarcely credible that such a people could have built so elegant a monument as Stonehenge. 'Now who can, in reason imagine,' he asks, 'that any great knowledge, practice, or delight of Arts and Sciences, wherein the elegancy of Architecture consists, should be in use or esteem, amongst a people, wholly devoted (as I may so say) and given over to such barbarity?'[32] He illustrates the point by citing Tacitus' *Agricola*, noting that, before the arrival of Agricola as governor, the Britons were 'rude', 'dispersed', and 'prone, upon every occasion, to warre', but that thereafter they were gradually mollified and civilized, as Roman arts and fashions took hold.[33]

More than half of *Stone-Heng* is taken up with dismissing previous theories. Having surveyed the literature in this way, Jones then surveys the monument, following the tried and tested approach of the antiquaries. First, he locates Stonehenge geographically. Then, he describes its architecture, noting that it is 'of a circular form' and 'double winged about without a roof', and that it was 'anciently environed with a deep Trench, still appearing about thirty foot broad'.

---

[29] Jones, *Stone-Heng*, 1–2: 'King *James*, in his progresse, the year one thousand six hundred and twenty, being at *Wilton*, and discoursing of this *Antiquity*, I was sent for by the right Honourable *William* then *Earle of Pembrook*, and received there his Majesties commands to produce out of mine own practise in *Architecture*, and experience in *Antiquities* abroad, what possibly I could discover concerning this of Stoneheng.'

[30] Rudolf Wittkower, 'Inigo Jones, Architect and Man of Letters', in id., *Palladio and English Palladianism*, ed. Margot Wittkower (London: Thames and Hudson, 1974), 51–64 at 63.

[31] Jones, *Stone-Heng*, 1.

[32] Ibid. 8–9.

[33] Ibid. 13–14; Tacitus, *Agricola*, trans. M. Hutton, rev. R. M. Ogilvie (Loeb Classical Library; Cambridge, Mass.: Harvard University Press, 1970), 21. 1–2.

He also comments on its interior: 'The inner part of the work, consisting of an *Exagonall* figure, was raised, by due symmetry, upon the bases of four equilaterall triangles, (which formed the whole structure) this inner part likewise was double, having, within it also, another *Exagon* raised.'[34] *Stone-Heng* also includes a series of drawings and plans. In contrast to earlier illustrations, which reproduce Stonehenge as a generic stone circle, Jones aimed at much greater precision in the number and alignment of its megaliths.[35] Crucially, he also produced illustrations 'not onely as the ruine thereof now appears, but as ... it was in its pristine perfection'.[36] His fifth drawing, which shows the whole of Stonehenge in prospective, 'whereby the generall composure of the particular parts of the uprights, are together all seen: and, by which also, the stately Aspect, and magnificent greatnesse thereof, are fully, and more apparently conspicuous', is a case in point (Fig. 4.3).[37] Not only did he map the extant remains, but he also reconstructed them, imagining how Stonehenge would have appeared in its magnificent entirety. He provided the visual equivalent of an antiquary restoring its voice, resurrecting the stone circle in its original and complete state.

From his survey of the monument, Jones proceeds finally to his interpretation of it. His conclusion, to modern ears at least, is a surprising one:

Howsoever, considering what magnificence the *Romans* in prosperous times anciently used in all works, both publick, and private: their knowledge and experience in all *Arts* and *Sciences*: their powerfull means for effecting great works: together with their Order in building, and manner of workmanship amongst them: *Stoneheng* in my judgement was a work, built by the *Romans*, and they the sole *Founders* thereof.[38]

His conclusion may not have been quite so surprising at the time, as he was not the first to propose a Roman origin for the monument. According to the German traveller Herbert Folkerzheimer, John Jewel, bishop of Salisbury in the 1560s, had come to a similar conclusion, believing that 'the Romans formerly erected' the stones here 'as trophies, and that the very disposition of the stones bears some resemblance to a yoke'.[39] From Webb's *Vindication* we learn that the key which

---

[34] Jones, *Stone-Heng*, 55–6.
[35] Earlier illustrations include Rogers's engraving in the *Britannia* (1600) and Lucas de Heere's pen-and-ink drawing in his 'Corte beschryuinghe van D'Enghelandsche gheschiedenissen vergadert uut de beste Chronycschryuers' (c.1570), BL, Additional MS 28330, fo. 36ʳ. De Heere, incidentally, also recorded the dimensions of Stonehenge, noting that its stones 'are around 18 or 20 foot high and around 8 foot wide, across all four sides (for they are square)', and that it 'appears that there were three rows of these stones, of which the largest is around 300 feet in diameter'; see Lucas de Heere, *Beschrijving der Britsche Eilanden*, ed. T. M. Chotzen and A. M. E. Draak (Antwerp: Seven Sinjoren, 1937), fo. 36ᵛ. I am extremely grateful to Dr Maartje Scheltens for translating de Heere's description for me.
[36] Jones, *Stone-Heng*, 56.
[37] Ibid. 63.
[38] Ibid. 66.
[39] Herbert Folkerzheimer to Josiah Simler, 13 Aug. 1562, in *The Zurich Letters (Second Series) Comprising the Correspondence of Several English Bishops and Others with Some of the Helvetian Reformers, during the Reign of Queen Elizabeth*, trans. Hastings Robinson (Cambridge: Parker Society, 1845), 89.

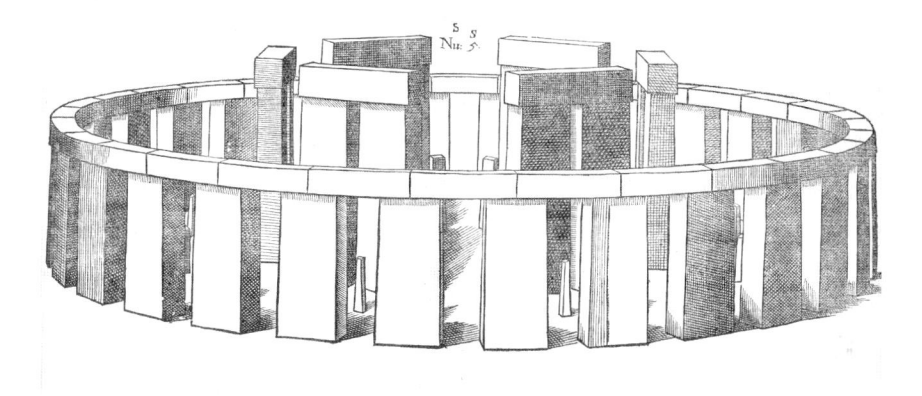

FIG. 4.3. Stonehenge. 'The whole work in *Prospective*, as when entire, whereby the generall composure of the particular parts of the uprights, are together all seen'. Inigo Jones, *The most notable Antiquity of Great Britain, vulgarly called Stone-Heng on Salisbury Plain* (London, 1655), opposite p. 63. Cambridge University Library, Keynes T. 6. 9. Reproduced by kind permission of the Syndics of Cambridge University Library

enabled Jones to unlock the mystery was Andrea Palladio: 'And here I must not omit, but affirm positively, that Mr. *Jones* hath often told me, that that Temple in *Palladio*, gave him the first hint, our *Stone-Heng* might be formed by some *Architectonical Scheme*, and that otherwise he could never without extream difficulty have so exactly found out the ancient form thereof.'[40] The temple in question was Le Galluce (the Temple of Minerva Medica) at Rome, for which Palladio had established a circular scheme, and Jones supposed that something similar might apply to Stonehenge.[41] He reasoned that Stonehenge also was circular in shape, with stones placed within this circle in the form of two hexagons, and the place of these inner stones determined on the basis of four equilateral triangles.[42] On the basis of this architectonical scheme, he concluded that Stonehenge must have been built by the Romans. From here, it was but a short step to his final conclusion that Stonehenge was a temple of mixed Tuscan and Corinthian order dedicated to the god Cœlus.

Jones was a staunch defender of the antiquarian approach to the past. At the end of *Stone-Heng* he restates its principal claim. Whereas history 'affords only *Contemplation*', antiquarianism offers '*Demonstration*'. As well as books and

[40] Webb, *Vindication*, 52.
[41] Andrea Palladio, *I Quattro libri dell'architettura* (Venice, 1570), sig. 4E4^{r-v}.
[42] For more detailed analyses of his application of Palladio, see Frances A. Yates, *Theatre of the World* (London and Henley: Routledge & Kegan Paul, 1969), 176–85; and A. A. Tait, 'Inigo Jones's "Stone-Heng"', *Burlington Magazine*, 120 (1978), 155–8.

records, the antiquary also studies 'ruines', which 'are even yet so many eye-witnesses of their admir'd atchievements'.[43] To set the seal on the virtue of this approach, he then cites the Latin maxim 'Roma *quanta fuit, ipsa ruina docet*' (how great Rome was, her ruin teaches). Jones himself had spent five months in Rome in 1613–14, studying closely the city's ruins, and comparing them with their descriptions in Palladio.[44] He might have taken this maxim from various books, as it was often cited by those humanist scholars in the archaeological vanguard. However, a likely source is the frontispiece to the third book of Sebastiano Serlio's *Tutte l'opere d'architettura*, printed by Giacomo de Franceschi in 1619, where the maxim appears on a strapwork cartouche at the bottom of the page.[45] Jones is said to have owned the copy of this book, which is now in the library of the Royal Institute of British Architects in London (class-mark EW, no. 2974).[46]

Later readers have often been embarrassed by Jones's conclusions, and many have tried to pass them off as Webb's additions to his master's notes. There is little evidence, however, that this is the case. For one thing, Jones's theory seems to have circulated before Webb published his edition. A possible link has been suggested, for instance, with Thomas Carew's masque *Cœlum Britannicum* (1634), for which Jones devised the set, and whose opening scene revealed sundry works of 'the ancient Romanes, or civiliz'd Brittaines'—the proposed builders of Stonehenge in Jones's survey.[47] Jones's theory is also repeated in the miscellany compiled by William Rawley, Francis Bacon's chaplain, at intervals between 1626 and 1641. This volume (Lambeth Palace Library, MS 2086) consists mostly of anecdotes, medical receipts, and notes on gardening and other domestic matters.[48] It also records a tour of the West Country, and this elicits Rawley's comments on Stonehenge: 'Two miles further is stonage. I finde the greatest miracle, the hugenes of the stones, and one stone leaning. As for the stones superimposed, they lay very firme. Affirmed by some to be reared to the God Cœl*us* by

---

[43] Jones, *Stone-Heng*, 108.
[44] Jones recorded his observations in the margins of his copy of Palladio, which he probably acquired on the same trip, and he reproved the Italian more than once. In response to Palladio identifying a temple as dedicated to Neptune, for example, he commented acerbically, 'this is not likly for to neptune being a robustious god they made dorrik temples and not corrinthian nor so adorned'; see *Inigo Jones on Palladio: Being the Notes by Inigo Jones in the Copy of I Quattro libri dell'architettura di Andrea Palladio (1601) in the Library of Worcester College Oxford*, ed. Bruce Allsopp, 2 vols. (Newcastle-upon-Tyne: Oriel Press, 1970), sig. 4Q4ᵛ (i. 66). On Jones's stay in Rome, see J. Alfred Gotch, *Inigo Jones* (London: Methuen, 1928), 72–7.
[45] *Tutte l'opere d'architettura, et prospetiva, di Sebastiano Serlio* (Venice, 1619), sig. G1ʳ.
[46] For the provenance of this volume, see Paul W. Nash et al., *Early Printed Books 1478–1840: Catalogue of the British Architectural Library's Early Imprints Collection*, 5 vols. (Munich: K. G. Saur, 1994–2003), iv. 1821–2.
[47] John Kerrigan, *On Shakespeare and Early Modern Literature: Essays* (Oxford: Oxford University Press, 2001), 213.
[48] See the description in E. G. W. Bill, *A Catalogue of Manuscripts in Lambeth Palace Library MSS. 1907–2340* (Oxford: Clarendon Press, 1976), 90.

the pagans; who was serued, in a temple, sub Dio.'[49] We cannot be certain when Rawley made this tour, as little is known about his movements after Bacon's death in April 1626.[50] But the best guess is that he made it some time before 1629, since, just three leaves later, his miscellany records a gift from the Master of the Rolls, which he received on 22 January that year.[51] So long as the leaves are bound in the correct order—and there is no reason to suspect that they are not— we have a *terminus ad quem* for his tour. But whatever its date, the entry in his miscellany, with its allusion to the pagan god Cœlus, attests to the circulation of Jones's Roman theory, either in manuscript, or simply as a current idea, long before 1655.

Rawley's spelling of Stonehenge, 'stonage', is curious enough to warrant comment. Although this orthography was by no means unique, in Rawley's hands it does take on a certain significance. The name seems to become an etymological joke, an impression lent weight by the fact that his miscellany is elsewhere filled with etymologies and explanations of place names. He notes, for example, that 'A parke called Foglies yaunes, ʽby a K.ʼ because of the yellow Leaues degenerate into Folly Iohn', and that 'Leighton was called Leighton beau Desert, for a braue ʽForestʼ ‹wood›, degenerate now in Leighton Buzzard'.[52] He also records a number of etymological jokes, including the tradition that 'K. H. 8. knighted the Loine of Beefe; Inde Surloine', and a wordplay on the title of Elizabeth Heneage, Viscountess Maidstone and Countess of Winchelsea: 'Viscountesse Maidstone Countesse of Winchelsea. The Latine Name is, *Frigus-Mare-Ventus.*'[53] Moreover, the name Stonehenge was itself subject to extensive etymological speculation. John Leland, for example, had earlier derived the name from the shape of the monument's stone piers, whilst Camden, in one of his notebooks (Bodleian Library, MS Smith 17), alluding to a tradition recorded by the fifteenth-century chronicler Thomas Rudborne of St Swithun's, suggested that the monument was originally called Stanhengest on account of the treachery of Hengist, and that this was then corrupted to Stanheng, and finally to Stonehenge.[54] In this light, 'stonage' might be another kind of etymological explanation. But, unlike the historical etymologies given by Leland and Camden,

---

[49] LPL, MS 2086, fo. 25ʳ.
[50] For the best biography of Rawley, see Graham Rees, 'Introduction' to Francis Bacon, *The Instauratio magna: Last Writings*, ed. Graham Rees (The Oxford Francis Bacon, 13; Oxford: Clarendon Press, 2000), pp. lxxiii–lxxxiii.
[51] LPL, MS 2086, fo. 28ᵛ.
[52] Ibid., fo. 5ʳ.
[53] Ibid., fos. 24ᵛ, 17ʳ. For the tradition that Henry VIII knighted a joint of beef, see *OED*, s.v. 'sirloin', *n*. 2.
[54] John Leland, *Commentarii de scriptoribus Britannicis*, ed. Anthony Hall, 2 vols. (Oxford, 1709), i. 47: '*Chore gaur Britannicum* nomen in Stanheng *Saxonicum* vocabulum degeneravit. sonat autem Stanheng lapides in sublimi pendentes'; Bodleian Library, MS Smith 17, p. 75: 'Saxons Choream Gigantum Stanhengest (quae nunc Stanheng) vocarunt ob proditionem Hengisti ibidem vocarunt ‹qui› vt author est Th. Rudborn Mon. Wint. qui florunt 1412.'

Rawley's name suggests that we cannot say much about Stonehenge other than it is built from stone and is old. Historical explanations for the monument are only ever theories.

The publication of Jones's survey in 1655 sparked immediate controversy. John Aubrey, for instance, admitted that he had read it 'with great delight', but criticized Jones for fitting his theory to the evidence rather than vice versa. He commented, with an appropriate architectural metaphor, that Jones 'had made a Lesbians rule, which is conformed to the stone: that is, he framed the Monument to his own Hypothesis, which is much differing from the Thing it self'.[55] A Lesbian rule was a stone-mason's lead rule, constructed so that it could bend to fit the curves of a moulding.[56] Slightly later, the anonymous author of that scabrous satire *A Fool's Bolt soon shott at Stonage*, usually identified as either John Gibbons or Robert Gay of Nettlecombe, wondered whether, on the basis of his *Stone-Heng*, Jones might have been better called '*out I goe*'.[57] Perhaps the most trenchant criticism, though, came from the natural philosopher and physician-in-ordinary to Charles II, Walter Charleton, who published a sharp riposte in his *Chorea gigantum* (1663). Charleton attributed Jones's theory to his 'ample skill in Architecture' and, less charitably, to his 'fruitfull Imagination'.[58] For Charleton, too, architecture was the key. But heavily influenced by Ole Worm and his *Danicorum monumentorum libri sex* (1643), which proposed a classificatory scheme for ancient monuments, he advocated a more obviously comparative approach. Applying Worm's scheme to Stonehenge, he concluded that the stone circle was a court built by the Danes for the election of their kings and magistrates—in Worm's terminology, one of their *comitalia loca* (assembly places). In *Chorea gigantum*, to illustrate the point, he compares Stonehenge to megaliths in Zealand, Skåne, and Viborg, and presents eight, not terribly convincing, parallels with these *comitalia loca*, concluding that there be 'no one thing in the *Antique Courts of Parliament* yet remaining in *Denmark*, which is not to be found also in our *Stone-heng*'.[59] His readers might feel inclined to repeat Aubrey's criticism of Jones.

In its almost total reliance on bookish learning in the shape of Ole Worm, Charleton's riposte lacks the antiquarian authority which Jones's measured survey can so easily invoke. But it is a typical antiquarian book in one important way. As its title clearly suggests, Charleton conceived himself to be participating in a resurrective project, restoring knowledge of the past (in this case of the Danes) to the present. This resurrective impulse is picked up in his dedicatory

---

[55] Aubrey, *Monumenta Britannica*, i. 19–20 (fos. 23^v–24^r).
[56] *OED*, s.v. 'Lesbian', *a.* 1(a).
[57] *A Fool's Bolt soon shott at Stonage*, in *Stonehenge Antiquaries*, ed. Rodney Legg (Sherborne: Dorset Publishing Company, 1986), 17–51 at 43.
[58] Walter Charleton, *Chorea gigantum; or, The most Famous Antiquity of Great-Britan, Vulgarly called Stone-Heng, Standing on Salisbury Plain, Restored to the Danes* (London, 1663), 17.
[59] Ibid. 49–53.

epistle to Charles II, in which he announces that the book will raise Stonehenge to tell its own story: 'Disdain not, therefore, now to cast an Eye upon it, when it appears to lift up its massive Head again, and offers, in plain Language, to tell You the Story of its Life, from whence it was derived, by whom it was formed, for what noble Use it was intended, and how it hath since been sacrilegiously violated.'[60] Charleton employs a familiar literary device here, as he personifies Stonehenge and restores its voice. That restoration is the argument which follows, and the voice is the Danish origin, the 'Story of its Life', which Charleton trumpets. He sustains this rhetoric throughout the book, as his responses to Stonehenge and other monuments are consistently figured in this kind of language. He cannot write about monuments, except by analogy, and it is this analogical approach which allows him to escape from the historical impasse. Echoing Worm's most basic classification, he proposes a simple twofold division of monuments into literate and illiterate. His first division is 'letter'd Monuments, such as consisted of large stones, with Inscriptions of *Runic*, or *Gothic* Characters, speaking their occasions and intentions'. His second division is 'Unletter'd, which were composed of rude stones, without engravements, but so disposed after a certain manner, as that the Beholder might from the order of their position collect, upon what Accidents, and for what Ends or Uses they had been set up'. That is to say, their architecture was a kind of language, which scholars, as long as they were versed in the comparative approach proposed by Worm and Charleton, might understand. He goes on in the same vein, adding that unlettered monuments, 'though destitute of the Elements of Language, were not absolutely Dumb, but spake their particular purposes in a more obscure Dialect of Figures, and were read in the Alphabet of their proper Platforms'.[61] It was the task of the antiquary, he implies, to learn that dialect and decipher that alphabet.

DUMBE HEAPE, DULL HEAPE

This, then, was the disputatious field into which certain seventeenth-century poets chose to enter, commenting on, and sometimes satirizing, the ceaseless speculation over Stonehenge, but also finding in the enigma of the monument an important moral lesson. For the satirist George Wither, Stonehenge typified man's foolishness in building monuments to perpetuate his fame. In 'Of Vanitie', one of the poems in his *Abuses Stript, and Whipt* (1613), Wither bemoans the ubiquity of this desire, and contrasts it dismissively with the humility of the King of Heaven:

> And though that men to build so curious be,
> How worthy of contempt it is we see,

[60] Ibid., sig. π4^v. [61] Ibid. 37.

> In that th'*arch-King* of heauen, earth and all,
> Was very well contented with a *Stall*.[62]

He goes on, predictably, to assert that '*Time* vtterly decayes' even 'the strongest *Foundation*'. His examples of this are familiar, and they include 'those wondrous high *Pyramides* / That were admired at in former daies' and 'those huge *Colossi* ... Which to erect now were an endlesse paines'. But, for Wither, what is even worse is the deception of these memorials. Even when they do survive, they invariably fail to preserve their builders and origins, as his next example, Stonehenge, admirably demonstrates:

> The wondrous *Heape* that once erected was,
> And yet e'ne at this day doth now remaine
> Not farre from *Sarum* on the *Westerne* plaine,
> Yet who can say directly, (or what story
> Doth absolutely mention) for whose glory
> That was first founded? or by whom? or why?[63]

Stonehenge was wondrous, as the old medieval tradition held, a marvel from the far West which could sit alongside the Seven Wonders of the classical world.[64] Sir Philip Sidney had made this same connection in his poem 'The 7. Wonders of England', where in a Petrarchan conceit he compares the wonder of his love to seven English marvels, including those 'huge heapes of stones' on Salisbury Plain.[65] For Wither, whose poem embodies the staunchly Christian ethos that aspiration must be to heaven alone, this wonder was insufficient. Monuments, however wondrous, cannot escape the ravages of time. As such, they are poor historical witnesses, betraying their founders and origins. In declining to recall these origins, they are also archetypes of foolishness and vanity, material reminders of man's misplaced ambition in seeking earthly remembrance.

Wither's excoriation of earthly desires was hardly original. In arguing that all material remains are subject to the ravages of time, he was drawing on a literary commonplace, which reaches back to Horace and Propertius. In his *Elegies* III. ii Propertius contrasts the contingency of material remains with the immortality that his own poetic genius will attain:

> nec Iovis Elei caelum imitata domus,
> nec Mausolei dives fortuna sepulcri
>   mortis ab extrema condicione vacant.
> aut illis flamma aut imber subducet honores,

---

[62] George Wither, 'Of Vanitie', in *Abuses Stript, and Whipt. Or Satirical Essayes* (London, 1613), sig. M3^v.
[63] Ibid., sig. M4^r.
[64] Daston and Park, *Wonders and the Order of Nature*, 88–9.
[65] Sir Philip Sidney, 'The 7. Wonders of England', in *The Poems of Sir Philip Sidney*, ed. William A. Ringler, Jr (Oxford: Clarendon Press, 1962), l. 1. On the likely Petrarchan source, see Michel Poirier, 'Quelques sources des poèmes de Sidney', *Études anglaises*, 11 (1958), 150–4 at 151.

> annorum aut tacito pondere victa ruent.
> at non ingenio quaesitum nomen ab aevo
> excidet: ingenio stat sine morte decus.

For neither the costly pyramids soaring to the skies, nor the temple of Jove at Elis that mimics heaven, nor the sumptuous magnificence of the tomb of Mausolus are exempt from the ultimate decree of death. Either fire or rain will steal away their glory, or they will collapse under the weight of the silent years. But the fame my genius has won shall not perish with time: genius claims a glory that knows no death.[66]

Verse preserves, where bronze and marble merely deceive. Even the most magnificent wonders of the ancient world, the Pyramids at Giza, the Temple of Jupiter at Olympia, and the Mausoleum at Halicarnassus, cannot escape the ravages of time. No tomb or memorial guarantees immortality; poetry alone, as the monument of wit and invention, can do that.

Wither takes this classical commonplace and then marries it to the ethos which underlies his satire. A literary defence of the primacy of poetry as an art is transformed into a larger moral argument about the vanity of human wishes. Spenser, before him, had done the same thing. In *The Ruines of Time* (1591), for example, he likewise emphasizes that proper aspiration must be to heaven alone, and he too cites the Pyramids and *colossi* as examples of the vanity and baseness of earthly ambition:

> In vaine doo earthly Princes then, in vaine
> Seeke with Pyramides, to heauen aspired;
> Or huge Colosses, built with costlie paine;
> Or brasen Pillours, neuer to be fired,
> Or Shrines, made of the mettall most desired;
> To make their memories for euer liue:
> For how can mortall immortalitie giue?[67]

In his prefatory sonnet to *The Historie of George Castriot* (1596), an English translation probably by Zachary Jones of Jacques de Lavardin's *Histoire de Georges Castriot, surnommé Scanderbeg, roy d'Albanie* (1576), Spenser makes the same point. Scanderbeg's memory resides not in 'statues', 'Colossoes great', 'rich triumphall Arcks', or even 'huge Pyramids', but in a more lasting memorial: 'The scourge of Turkes, and plague of infidels, / Thy acts, ô Scanderbeg, this volume tels.'[68] Shorn of the moral context of *The Ruines of Time*, this sonnet is closer in

---

[66] Propertius, *Elegies*, trans. G. P. Goold (Loeb Classical Library; Cambridge, Mass.: Harvard University Press, 1990), III. ii. 19–26. See also Horace, *Odes*, trans. Niall Rudd (Loeb Classical Library; Cambridge, Mass.: Harvard University Press, 1990), III. xxx. 1–5: 'Exegi monumentum aere perennius / regalique situ pyramidum altius, / quod non imber edax, non Aquilo impotens / possit diruere aut innumerabilis / annorum series et fuga temporum.'

[67] Edmund Spenser, *The Ruines of Time*, in *The Shorter Poems*, ed. Richard A. McCabe (Harmondsworth: Penguin, 1999), ll. 407–13. The *locus classicus* for the modern reader is, of course, not Spenser, but Shakespeare's sonnets, especially Sonnet 55.

[68] Edmund Spenser, 'Vpon the Historie of George Castriot, alias Scanderbeg King of the Epirots, *translated into English*', in Jacques de Lavardin, *The Historie of George Castriot, Surnamed*

sentiment to Horace and Propertius. Scanderbeg lives, and will continue to live, so long as Lavardin's volume continues to be read. Once again, immortality rests in the hands of the poet.

Nor was Wither the first to recognize the potency of Stonehenge as an example. Others too deplored its failure as a memorial and were similarly fascinated and repelled by this apparent defiance of history. Samuel Daniel, for example, in his *Musophilus* (1599), berates those who entrust their memories to monuments, to mere 'deceitfull stones', and he produces Stonehenge as his best example:

> And whereto serue that wondrous *Trophei* now,
> That on the goodly Plaine neere *Wilton* stands?
> That huge dumbe heape, that cannot tell vs how,
> Nor what, nor whence it is, nor with whose hands,
> Nor for whose glory, it was set to shew
> How much our pride mocks that of other lands?[69]

This sounds very much like Wither's complaint. Daniel acknowledges the wonder of Stonehenge, but weighs that against the heap which now stands on Salisbury Plain. He asks the same questions as the satirist, and thereby demonstrates forcibly the monument's failure as a memorial. We know neither when it was built, nor why it was built. Its builders lie forgotten, and so too do those whom they sought to memorialize in the first place. Stonehenge appears to typify man's vainglory in seeking immortality by material means.

But things are not as straightforward as they seem. Daniel, as Philip Schwyzer has rightly pointed out, understood the fascination of the monument.[70] Indeed, as soon as his eponymous speaker has denounced it in the terms above, he retracts somewhat by imagining the responses of a traveller confronted with the sight of Stonehenge for the first time. As Daniel himself had lived in Wiltshire in the 1590s, when he was tutor to William Herbert at Wilton, this passage is likely to be at least partly autobiographical:

> Whereon, whenas the gazing passenger
> Hath greedy lookt with admiration,
> And faine would know his birth, and what he were,
> How there erected, and how long agone:
> Enquires, and asks his fellow traueller,
> What he hath heard, and his opinion:
> And he knowes nothing. Then he turnes againe,

Scanderbeg, King of Albanie. Containing his famous actes, his noble deedes of Armes, and memorable victories against the Turkes, for the Faith of Christ (London, 1596), sig. ¶8ʳ, ll. 5–8, 13–4.

[69] Samuel Daniel, *Musophilus Containing, A generall Defence of all Learning*, in *The Complete Works in Verse and Prose of Samuel Daniel*, ed. Alexander B. Grosart, 5 vols. (New York: Russell & Russell, 1963; first published 1885), ll. 337–42.

[70] Schwyzer, *Archaeologies of English Renaissance Literature*, 82–3.

> And lookes, and sighs, and then admires afresh,
> And in himselfe with sorrow doth complaine
> The misery of darke Forgetfulnesse:
> Angry with Time that nothing should remaine
> Our greatest wonders wonder, to expresse.[71]

The traveller's response is complex, and his initial 'admiration' and thirst for knowledge give way to something more reflective, as he meditates on 'darke Forgetfulnesse', on how little there is to know about the stone circle. But that admiration never disappears. His frustration at the unknowableness of Stonehenge, heard in the strong caesura of the line 'And he knowes nothing. Then he turnes againe', and emphasized by the sense of expectation created by the preceding line, is trumped by his wonder. And that wonder is not just baffled astonishment. Musophilus's traveller, thoroughly familiar with the corpus of ruin literature, as his personification of the monument suggests, embodies the kind of curious wonder which seeks to understand the object and so leads to new knowledge.

Moreover, Daniel's target is much more specific than Wither's. His anger is at 'Time' itself, and his Stonehenge passage is not a satire on the vanity of human wishes, but a reflection on the nature of historical knowledge. The first clue comes in his description of the monument as 'a huge dumbe heape'. Stonehenge is a matter of concern precisely because it cannot speak. What is more, this dumbness has laid it open to 'fabulous discourse'. With barely concealed contempt, Musophilus repeats the most popular explanation of the monument's origins:

> Then Ignorance, with fabulous discourse,
> Robbing faire Arte and Cunning of their right,
> Tels, how those stones, were by the Deuils force,
> From *Affrike* brought to *Ireland* in a night,
> And thence, to *Britannie*, by Magicke course,
> From Gyants hands redeem'd, by *Merlins* sleight.
> And then neere *Ambri* plac'd, in memorie
> Of all those noble Britons murthered there,
> By *Hengist* and his Saxon trecherie,
> Comming to parlee in peace at vnaware.[72]

What Daniel himself thought of the Galfridian tradition is apparent from his later *Collection of the History of England* (1612–17/18). He does not dismiss the story there, but he treats it sceptically and alludes to it only as a report: 'And besides force, they are sayd to haue vsed treachery (in murthering three hundred

---

[71] Daniel, *Musophilus*, ll. 343–54.
[72] Ibid., ll. 355–64.

of the *Brittish* Nobility) at an assembly of peace at *Amesbury*.'[73] Stonehenge, the supposed memorial of that treachery, is not mentioned at all.

Musophilus subsequently extends his charge to 'Antiquitie' herself, so that Stonehenge becomes an illustration of a larger problem about historical knowledge. Antiquity is 'so great a liar', and 'her younger sonnes', historians like Geoffrey, so 'abuse' her 'age' that now even 'her truths hardly beleeued are'.[74] A scepticism about all antiquity, however that word is defined, is the inevitable consequence. The Stonehenge passage concludes with an apostrophe, as Musophilus switches from addressing his respondent, Philocosmus, to addressing the monument itself. His tone becomes altogether more opprobrious, as he attacks it directly in quasi-legal language. He charges it as a 'false' witness 'against their fame / That set thee there, to testifie their right', and calls it 'a Traitour to their name / That trusted thee with all the best they might'.[75] Daniel leaves his readers in little doubt about what this means. Stonehenge's betrayal is total.

A few years later Michael Drayton wrote about Stonehenge in almost the same way in the first part of his *Poly-Olbion* (1612). Just as Daniel does, Drayton personifies the stone circle and charges it directly with traducement and neglect. In the ventriloquized world of *Poly-Olbion*, where rivers, mountains, and monuments speak, this charge is issued by the Wansdyke:

> Dull heape, that thus thy head above the rest doost reare,
> Precisely yet not know'st who first did place thee there;
> But Traytor basely turn'd to *Merlins* skill doost flie,
> And with his Magiques doost thy Makers truth belie:
> Conspirator with Time, now growen so meane and poore,
> Comparing these his spirits with those that went before;
> Yet rather art content thy Builders praise to lose,
> Then passed greatnes should thy present wants disclose.
> Ill did those mightie men to trust thee with their storie,
> That hast forgot their names, who rear'd thee for their glorie:
> For all their wondrous cost, thou that hast serv'd them so,
> What tis to trust to Tombes, by thee we easely know.[76]

Drayton's source is obvious. 'Traytor basely turn'd to *Merlins* skill', 'thy Makers truth belie', 'Conspirator with Time', and 'content thy Builders praise to lose' are all lifted from Daniel's charge-sheet. So too is Wansdyke's notion that

---

[73] Samuel Daniel, *The Collection of the History of England*, in *The Complete Works in Verse and Prose*, iv. 99. On Daniel's scepticism as a historian, see Daniel Woolf, *The Idea of History in Early Stuart England: Erudition, Ideology, and 'The Light of Truth' from the Accession of James I to the Civil War* (Toronto, Buffalo, and London: University of Toronto Press, 1990), 89–94.
[74] Daniel, *Musophilus*, ll. 367–77.
[75] Ibid., ll. 381–4.
[76] Michael Drayton, *Poly-Olbion*, in *The Works of Michael Drayton*, ed. J. William Hebel, Kathleen Tillotson, and Bernard H. Newdigate, 5 vols. (Oxford: Basil Blackwell, 1961; first published 1931–41), iii. 53–64.

Stonehenge is somehow collusive in its own failure, and also his pessimistic conclusion about trusting in monuments and tombs.

Yet in one important way Drayton distinguishes himself from his predecessor. Wansdyke calls Stonehenge not 'dumbe heape', but 'Dull heape'. The change of word may simply be to differentiate the passage from its model; a good imitation, after all, does not slavishly follow its original. But Drayton's word, 'Dull', also introduces an ambiguity that allows him to have it both ways, to hedge his bets over the monument's silence. On the one hand, Stonehenge may be a 'Dull heape' because it is senseless and inanimate, and therefore also, by definition, silent. On the other, Wansdyke's comment may be an architectural one, an observation on the physical characteristics of Stonehenge, a reflection on the dull, blue-grey colour of its megaliths.[77] Elsewhere in the poem, after all, Stonehenge is not silent. Just prior to Wansdyke's speech, we learn that the two monuments have long striven for pre-eminence, and it is to rebuff an insult from his adversary that the earthwork speaks in the first place:

> Who (for a mightie Mound sith long he did remaine
> Betwixt the *Mercians* rule, and the *West-Saxons* raigne,
> And therefore of his place him selfe hee proudly bare)
> Had very oft beene heard with *Stonendge* to compare;
> Whom for a paltry Ditch, when *Stonendge* pleasd t'upbraid,
> The old man taking heart, thus to that Trophy said.[78]

Then follows the invective quoted previously. Moreover, other voices in the poem are in much less doubt than Wansdyke over Stonehenge's origins. '*Stonendge*, that to tell the *British* Princes slaine / By those false *Saxons* fraud, here ever shall remaine', Salisbury Plain announces shortly afterwards.[79] In later songs we hear of '*Merlin* by his skill' and '*Magiques* wondrous might', a deliberate rejoinder to Wansdyke, and also of the Saxon treachery, as they the Britons 'unmercifully slew'.[80] *Poly-Olbion* therefore encompasses competing and irreconcilable interpretations of the monument. The scepticism evinced by Daniel about material evidence, which serves as one of his arguments in his larger case for the primacy of poetry, becomes in *Poly-Olbion* a sideswipe at fruitless historical speculation. Wansdyke and Stonehenge squabble, but Drayton's song lacks the vituperation of *Musophilus*. The tone is less angry and more satirical. Drayton seems to be commenting on historical questions, which, as the conflicting narratives in the poem suggest, cannot be answered for certain. For the more antiquarian-minded Drayton, Stonehenge was not 'dumbe', but a curiosity that was fascinating and frustrating in equal measure.

The dramatist William Rowley seems to have reached a similar conclusion, as he too satirises the debates on Stonehenge in his play *The Birth of Merlin*

---

[77] *OED*, s.v. 'dull', *a.* 2(a) and 7.   [78] Drayton, *Poly-Olbion*, iii. 47–52.
[79] Ibid., iii. 141–2.   [80] Ibid., iv. 329–30, viii. 360–2.

(*c*.1622). This play dramatizes the dynastic struggles between the British kings Vortiger and Aurelius Ambrosius, the Saxon invasions of Hengist and Horsa, and the early life of Merlin. This had been popular subject matter in the theatres in the 1590s, with Henslowe's *Diary* recording twelve performances of a play known as 'valteger' in 1596–7, and also a single performance of a play called 'henges' on 22 June 1597.[81] It seems to have enjoyed a second flowering around 1620: as well as Rowley's play, licensed in 1622 as 'a New Play, acted by the Princes Servants at the Curtayne', but hard to date for certain, there was also Thomas Middleton's *Hengist, King of Kent*, usually dated to between 1616 and 1622.[82] Rowley may therefore have just been chasing theatrical success. Nevertheless, he does give the familiar chronicle material a new treatment. What Middleton dramatizes as a brutal tragedy, Rowley presents as a scurrilous comedy. The subplot of his play is a parodic account of the birth and parentage of Merlin, as Joan Goe-too't, his mother, searches for the man who made her pregnant. Assisted by her corpulent brother the Clown, she eventually discovers this man to be the Devil. Rowley then makes this bawdy diversion his explanation for Stonehenge. In the penultimate scene of the play he connects it with the chronicle tradition, as Merlin intervenes in the nick of time to save his mother from the Devil's lewd advances for a second time. Merlin banishes her to contemplate her offences against the flesh, but mitigates the harshness of his punishment with the promise that on her death he will erect an incomparable monument in memory of her:

Leave this soyl, and Ile conduct you to a place retir'd, which I by art have rais'd, call'd *Merlins Bower*, there shall you dwell with solitary sighs, with grones and passions your companions, to weep away this flesh you have offended with, and leave all bare unto you aierial soul, and when you die, I will erect a Monument upon the verdant Plains of *Salisbury*, no King shall have so high a sepulchre, with pendulous stones that I will hang by art, where neither Lime nor Morter shalbe us'd, a dark *Enigma* to the memory, for none shall have the power to number them, a place that I will hollow for your rest,

> Where no Night-hag shall walk, nor Ware-wolf tread,
> Where *Merlins* Mother shall be sepulcher'd.[83]

With its innumerable stones, that monument is clearly Stonehenge. Its origins, however, are rendered ludicrous: rather than a memorial to the Britons treacherously slain by the Saxons, it becomes a monument to the bawdy and foolish Joan

---

[81] *Henslowe's Diary*, ed. Walter W. Greg, 3 vols. (London: A. H. Bullen, 1904–8), fos. 25^v–26^r, 27^r.
[82] For the licensing of *The Birth of Merlin*, see *The Control and Censorship of Caroline Drama: The Records of Sir Henry Herbert, Master of the Revels 1623–73*, ed. N. W. Bawcutt (Oxford: Clarendon Press, 1996), 136; for its date, see the discussion in the introduction to *A Critical, Old-Spelling Edition of The Birth of Merlin (Q 1662)*, ed. Joanna Udall (London: The Modern Humanities Research Association, 1991), 11.
[83] William Rowley, *The Birth of Merlin: Or, The Child hath found his Father* (London, 1662), sig. G3r.

Goe-too't. The absurdity of the Galfridian tradition is laid bare. But the joke is not only at the expense of Geoffrey. In pronouncing that the monument will be 'a dark *Enigma* to the memory', Merlin preordains the endless speculation over its origins. The joke is therefore also on all those who have laboured to make sense of Stonehenge. More fool you, Rowley is saying, for trying to make those 'pendulous stones' speak. In his commentary to Book 3 of his translation of *Orlando Furioso* (1591), Sir John Harington, also speaking about Stonehenge, wrote that 'the wiser sort can rather marvell at them then tell either why or how they were set there'.[84] Rowley, it seems, would have agreed; he was one of 'the wiser sort'.

All these examples imagine Stonehenge in terms of the human voice. That is to say, they imagine it by recourse to the literary trope known to early modern rhetoricians as prosopopoeia. In *The Garden of Eloquence* (1577) Henry Peacham defines this trope as 'the fayning of a person, that is, when to a thing sencelesse and dumme, wee fayne a fit person, this figure Orators vse as well as Poets'. He adds that 'Somtime to Citties, townes, beastes, byrdes, fyshes, creeping wormes, weapons, stones and to such lyke things doe they attribute speech'.[85] His definition was echoed by George Puttenham, who asserted that 'if ye wil faine any person with such features, qualities & conditions, or if ye wil attribute any humane quality, or reason or speech to dombe creatures or other insensible things, & do study (as one may say) to give them a humane person, it is... *Prosopopoeia*'.[86] To the poet and orator we might be inclined to add the antiquary. Leonard Barkan, after all, has shown the importance of this trope to the antiquarian-minded in Renaissance Rome, arguing that 'the very basis of recuperating ancient sculpture that represented the human form was to endow the object with a voice', and that 'Renaissance viewers responded not only by describing the works in their own voices but also by giving the objects voices of their own'.[87] The examples of Daniel and Drayton, in particular, suggest that a similar argument might be made about early modern England.

In the case of Stonehenge, however, that voice is more often than not absent. For one authority, the Catholic historian Edmund Bolton, that absence was itself the key to the whole mystery. Bolton's explanation of the monument, expounded

---

[84] Lodovico Ariosto, *Orlando Furioso*, trans. Sir John Harington, ed. Robert McNulty (Oxford: Oxford University Press, 1972), 47.
[85] Henry Peacham, *The Garden of Eloquence Conteyning the Figures of Grammer and Rhetorick, from whence maye bee gathered all manner of Flowers, Coulors, Ornaments, Exornations, Formes and Fashions of speech, very profitable for all those that be studious of Eloquence, and that reade most Eloquent Poets and Orators, and also helpeth much for the better vnderstanding of the holy Scriptures* (London, 1577), sig. O3ʳ. See also *OED*, s.v. 'prosopopoeia', *n*. 1: 'A rhetorical device by which an imaginary, absent, or dead person is represented as speaking or acting; the introduction of a pretended speaker'; *sb*. 2(a): 'A figure of speech by which an inanimate or abstract thing is represented as a person, or as having personal characteristics, esp. the power to think or speak.'
[86] George Puttenham, *The Arte of English Poesie*, ed. Gladys Doidge Willcock and Alice Walker (Cambridge: Cambridge University Press, 1970; first published 1936), 239.
[87] Barkan, *Unearthing the Past*, p. xxiv.

in his *Nero Cæsar, or Monarchie depraued* (1624), is novel: he suggests that Stonehenge was, in all likelihood, the tomb of the British queen Boadicea. 'For without auerring any thing precisely, no other toombe seemes to mee so likely to be hers,' he ventures, 'as the admirable moniment of the stones vpon SALISBVRIE *plaine.*'[88] His evidence is the monument's lack of a human voice: 'The dumbnesse of it (vnlesse the letters bee worne quite away) speakes; that it was not any worke of the ROMANS.' They, he adds, 'were wont to make stones vocall by inscriptions'.[89] In other words, Roman remains have a voice because they are inscribed, because they are both artefact and text. As Alison Cooley has pointed out, it is this duality which has long given inscriptions their 'privileged status within the various categories of historical evidence'.[90] But Bolton reverses the argument, finding in uninscribed stones another form of authoritative historical voice. For Bolton, paradoxically, the silence of an ancient monument is telling. An apparently dumb monument such as Stonehenge can in fact speak as eloquently as richly inscribed and splendidly preserved classical remains.

Architecture, as it would do for Walter Charleton, becomes a kind of language, which the antiquary or viewer has to interpret. 'That STONAGE was a worke of the BRITANNS,' Bolton asserts, 'the rudenesse it selfe persuades'.[91] If its lack of inscriptions signals that it was not Roman in origin, the crudeness of its architecture confirms that it was built by the Britons. Bolton supports this argument by turning to literary evidence. He notes, for example, on 'the cleare testimonie of DIO', that 'the BRITANNS entered her pompously, or with much magnificence'.[92] Dio Cassius recorded that, after Boadicea had died, the Britons 'mourned her deeply and gave her a costly burial'.[93] Continuing his reversals of conventional arguments, Bolton concludes by a pair of trademark oxymora that Dio Cassius' argument 'cannot be better verified then by assigning these orderly irregular, and formlesse vniforme heapes of massiue marble, to her euerlasting remembrance'.[94] Finally, he adduces archaeological evidence to support his theory, arguing that the 'bones of men digged vp at times neere this place vnder little banckes, conuince it to haue beene sepulchral'. Less convincingly, he also suggests that ancient weaponry found in the vicinity, 'armours of a large and antique fashion, vpon which the spade, or pickaxe are sometimes said to hit', disproves the Galfridian interpretation, clearing 'the owners from hauing beene

---

[88] Edmund Bolton, *Nero Cæsar, or Monarchie depraued* (London, 1624), 181.
[89] Ibid.
[90] Alison Cooley, 'The Life-Cycle of Inscriptions', in ead. (ed.), *The Afterlife of Inscriptions: Reusing, Rediscovering, Reinventing & Revitalizing Ancient Inscriptions* (London: Institute of Classical Studies, 2000), 1–5 at 1.
[91] Bolton, *Nero Cæsar*, 182.
[92] Ibid.
[93] Dio Cassius, *Roman History*, trans. Earnest Cary, 9 vols. (Loeb Classical Library; Cambridge, Mass.: Harvard University Press, 1961–70), lxii. 12. 6.
[94] Bolton, *Nero Cæsar*, 182.

in the number of those BRITANNS, whom pagan HENGIST wickedly slew: for they came not armed, but weaponlesse'.[95] Thus Bolton marshals a complex, four-pronged defence of his theory of Stonehenge, bringing together an antiquarian argument based on the monument's architecture, an archaeological argument based on bones and weapons buried nearby, an historical argument based on the evidence of Dio Cassius, and a literary argument based on a common rhetorical trope.

In his excitement at his own theory about the origins of Stonehenge, Bolton seems not to have worried about, or even commented upon, the consequences for himself, and indeed humankind, of the silence that he found in and around the stones. This silence, after all, does not hold out much hope for future antiquaries. The case of Boadicea would appear to be a special one; silent monuments, in general, would seem to deny that defiance of time which the antiquaries sought. If monuments cannot speak, restitution of the past becomes a faint possibility indeed. A generation later, Thomas Browne, who was markedly less sanguine about the prospects for the reconstruction of the past, understood the implications of this kind of argument. Like Bolton, he too repeated the paradox of silent antiquities speaking. In the epistle to Thomas Le Gros of Crostwick Hall, which prefaces his *Urne-Buriall* (1658), Browne calls a series of funerary urns found near Walsingham 'sad and sepulchral Pitchers, which have no joyful voices'. Initially, at least, it seems as if he is saying that these urns are silent. He contrasts them, for instance, with the 'Theatrical vessels, and great Hippodrome Urnes in Rome', which 'resound the acclamations and honour due unto you'. But from the next clause we discover that his emphasis is, in fact, not on their 'voices', but on the word 'joyful'. Browne adds that these urns 'silently' express 'old mortality, the ruines of forgotten times, and can only speak with life, how long in this corruptible frame, some parts may be uncorrupted; yet able to out-last bones long unborn, and noblest pyle among us'.[96] These urns, which are at first silent, telling us nothing about who was buried in them, turn out to have a specific articulacy. They may be poor historical witnesses, but they are excellent illustrations of the inexorable march of time. By their very preservation they emphasize the corruptibility of human flesh, the bodies which were once contained in them. Where Bolton finds a novel solution to an age-old historical enigma, Browne finds only pessimistic tokens about the whole antiquarian endeavour.

One curious thing about these poetic responses to Stonehenge is their description of it as a heap. This seems a strange word for the monument, even if the stones themselves were probably less upright than they are today.[97] Indeed, one

---

[95] Ibid. 184.
[96] Thomas Browne, *Hydriotaphia, or Urne-Buriall*, in *The Works of Sir Thomas Browne*, ed. Keynes, i. 131.
[97] In the early 1920s, during excavation work under the direction of William Hawley, a number of the more precariously leaning stones and their lintels were straightened and set in concrete; see Hill, *Stonehenge*, 151–3.

traveller, who visited the monument in the 1560s, made precisely the point that the 'stones are not heaped one upon another, nor even laid together, but are placed upright, in such a way that two of them support a third'.[98] Furthermore, the word seems to convey the opposite to the carefully measured descriptions of the antiquaries, where mathematics and architecture come to the fore. Whilst the likes of Camden and Jones emphasize the regularity and order of the monument, Daniel, Drayton, and Wither all suggest the converse. A heap, after all, is defined as a collection of things gathered together in an irregular or approximate form.[99] A heap, therefore, would seem to be hard to subject to the kind of careful measurement which the antiquaries typically undertook.

Yet the choice of this word is clearly not an accident. Daniel and Drayton both apostrophize the monument as a 'heape', whilst Wither only ever calls it 'wondrous *Heape*'. The explanation for this may lie in the slightly pejorative connotations of the word. Miles Coverdale, for example, had used it memorably and despairingly in his translation of Psalm 79 to describe the sack of Jerusalem: 'O God, the Heithen are fallen into thine heretage: thy holy temples haue they defyled, and made Jerusalem an heape of stones.'[100] Unlike Jerusalem, Stonehenge had, of course, not been reduced to rubble, but the pejorative undertone heard in the psalm does fit the sentiment of the poems of Daniel, Drayton, and Wither. It reflects the frustration heard in Drayton and Daniel at the monument's impenetrability, and also corresponds with the sterner moral argument of Wither about vanity and ambition. Heap, then, becomes not so much an architectural designation, a literal comment on the monument's form, as an expression of its historiographic failure. The stones may not be rubble, but, given their inability to communicate anything certain or significant about their builders and purpose, they may as well be.

In attracting the competing responses outlined in this chapter, Stonehenge was not unique. Other ancient monuments similarly taxed the antiquarian imagination, surprising viewers by their endurance and frustrating them with their historical blankness. When George Sandys, about whom we shall hear more in the next chapter, described the Pyramids at Giza as '(the barbarous monuments of prodigality and vain-glory) so vniuersally celebrated', and called the Great Pyramid of Cheops 'too great a morsell for time to deuoure', he was articulating something similar to Bolton's 'orderly irregular, and formlesse vniforme heapes of massiue marble'.[101] The geographical and historical contexts may have been different, but the contradictions and paradoxes are the same. By the same token,

---

[98] Herbert Folkerzheimer to Josiah Simler, 13 Aug. 1562, in *The Zurich Letters*, 88–9.
[99] *OED*, s.v. 'heap', *n.* 1(a).
[100] *Biblia. The Bible, that is, the holy Scripture of the Olde and New Testament, faithfully and truly translated out of Douche and Latyn in to Englishe* (London, 1535), sig. 2E1ᵛ; cf. Ps. 79: 1: 'O god, the heathen are come into thine inheritance; thy holy temple have they defiled; they have laid Jerusalem on heaps' (AV).
[101] George Sandys, *A Relation of a Iourney begun An: Dom: 1610* (London, 1615), 127, 129.

when the Spanish Jesuit José de Acosta described the great Incan remains at Cuzco, Tiahuanaco, and Tambo in his *Historia natural y moral de las Indias* (1590), a work known in England through Edward Grimeston's translation of 1604, he noted that they were built from 'stones of an vnmeasurable greatnes: so as men cannot conceive how they were cut, brought, and set in their places'.[102] Immediately contradicting himself, he then recorded the dimensions of one of these stones. At Tiahuanaco, we learn, Acosta 'did measure a stone of thirty eight foote long, of eighteene broade, and six thicke', and at Cuzco, he added, 'there are stones of a grater bignes' still.[103] But, like his English contemporaries, he was not just wonderstruck. His description of the Incan remains is also an attempt to understand them, as he articulates precisely what is curious about them:

As these workes were strange, and to amaze the beholders, wherein they vsed no morter nor ciment, neither any yron, or steele, to cut, and set the stones in worke. They had no engines or other instruments to carrie them, and yet were so artificially wrought, that in many places they could not see the ioyntes: and many of these stones are so big, that it were an incredible thing, if one should not see them.[104]

Wonder becomes something to be explained, in this case, as increasingly with Stonehenge, in terms of the monuments' architecture. The 'bigness' of the stones is what impressed Acosta the most, and what better way to convey this to his readers than through a series of prodigious measurements.

But the example of Stonehenge is suggestive. Not only does it show antiquarian methodology in practice: by dint of its ubiquity and hold on the literary and historical imaginations it also raises questions about the limits of that methodology. Mensuration was undoubtedly useful for certifying 'bigness', as the examples discussed in the first part of this chapter demonstrate. Stonehenge could be described, measured, and explained by recourse to its architecture. Moreover, even the barest stones could be made to speak, as Bolton and Charleton in their different ways attest. But that speech was fraught with contradiction and

---

[102] José de Acosta, *The Naturall and Morall Historie of the East and West Indies* (London, 1604), p. 459; id., *Historia natural y moral de las Indias* (Seville, 1590), sig. 2D4r: 'Los edificios y fabricas que los Ingas hizieron en fortalezas, en templos, en caminos, en casas de campo, y otras, fueron muchos y de excessiuo trabajo, como lo manifiestan el dia de oy las ruynas y pedaços que han quedado, como se veen en el Cuzco, y en Tiaguanaco, y en Tambo, y en otras partes, donde ay piedras de immensa grandeza, que no se puede pensar, como se cortaron y traxeron, y assentaron donde estan.'

[103] Acosta, *Naturall and Morall Historie*, 460; id., *Historia natural y moral*, sig. 2D4r–v: 'En Tiaguanaco medi yo vna de treynta y ocho pies de largo, y de diez y ocho en ancho y el gruesso seria de seys pies, y en la muralla de la fortaleza del Cuzco, que està de mamposteria, ay muchas piedras de mucho mayor grandeza.'

[104] Acosta, *Naturall and Morall Historie*, 459–60; id., *Historia natural y moral*, sig. 2D4r: 'porque la labor es estraña, y para espantar: y no vsauan de mezcla, ni tenian hierro, ni azero para cortar y labrar las piedras, ni machinas, ni instrumentos para traellas, y con todo esso estan tan pulidamente labradas, que en muchas partes apenas se vee la juntura de vnas con otras. Y son tan grandes muchas piedras destas, como està dicho, que seria cosa increyble sino se viesse.'

difficulty. In the case of Stonehenge, the imaginative leap, which the early modern antiquary typically made, was a large one indeed. Measurement could not always reach the heart of ancient monuments. Even antiquarianism, it seems, had its limits; some monuments, as the example of Stonehenge suggests, remained just beyond its ken. As we shall see from the next chapter, where I turn to classical remains, which were much more heavily documented in literary and epigraphic records, antiquarian restorations of the past still largely depended on texts or textual evidence. This is what made Stonehenge so frustrating for early modern writers and scholars; it is also what made it so curious, and what ensured that it remained such a source of historiographic speculation.

5
A Peripatetic Education: Antiquarian Travellers and the Apodemic Arts

In 1634 Henry Peacham the younger published a new and revised edition of his courtesy manual *The Compleat Gentleman*. This work had first appeared in 1622, born out of Peacham's belief, arising from a Continental tour that he had made in 1612–13 to France, Germany, and the Low Countries, that the education of English gentlemen lagged far behind that of their European contemporaries. He set out to correct this by prescribing the conduct and practices which an English gentleman needed to master in order to achieve truly gentle status. In his scheme education was as important as birth and blood. His curriculum included fencing, music, and painting, but also more scholarly pursuits such as cosmography, geography, and poetry. From 1634 it also included antiquarian matters, as his new edition added a chapter titled 'Of Antiquities'. Focusing on statues, inscriptions, and coins, this chapter instructed his readers in how they should respond to and interpret antiquities.

Peacham's decision to include this chapter may have had something to do with his patron. *The Compleat Gentleman* was dedicated to William Howard, the future Viscount Stafford, and the fifth son of the greatest collector of antiquities and art in Jacobean England, Thomas Howard, earl of Arundel.[1] In the period between Peacham's two editions, a catalogue of the Greek and Latin inscriptions in Arundel's collection had been published: John Selden's *Marmora Arundelliana* (1628). In the new chapter Peacham directs his readers to the pages of Selden's work and describes Arundel House as 'the chiefe English scene of ancient inscriptions'.[2] But Peacham himself also appears to have shared the antiquarian impulses of the Howard family; the language of his new chapter suggests that he participated fully in their resurrective project. He argues, for example, in a striking echo of Petrarch, that by observing ancient statuary a gentleman might also observe directly, as if it were present, the ancient world. 'For next men and

---

[1] On Arundel as a collector, see David Howarth, *Lord Arundel and his Circle* (New Haven and London: Yale University Press, 1985).
[2] Henry Peacham, *The Compleat Gentleman. Fashioning him absolut, in the most necessary and commendable Qualities concerning Minde or Body, that may be required in a Noble Gentleman* (London, 1634), 112.

manners, there is nothing fairely more delightfull, nothing worthier observation,' he asserts, 'than these Copies, and memorials of men and matter of elder times; whose lively presence is able to perswade a man, that he now seeth two thousand yeeres agoe.'[3] Lively should be understood here in the now obsolete sense of having life.[4] Statues thus allow the educated gentleman, in his mind's eye at least, to defy the passage of time. For Peacham, inscriptions work in the same way, albeit more vocally. In an elaborate, and characteristically antiquarian, prosopopoeia, he writes that visitors to Arundel House can encounter an extraordinary collection of speaking stones, ancient marbles animated by their inscriptions. His readers will find 'all the walles of the house inlayde with them, and speaking Greeke and Latine to you'. The garden at Arundel House, where ancient statuary was also displayed, provides more vocal delights still, affording 'a world of learned lectures in this kinde'.[5] Peacham's third kind of antiquity, coins, are also 'lively', imbued with the same immediacy and presence. Whilst 'bookes and histories and the like are but copyes of Antiquity', imitations at one remove from the past, coins are 'the very Antiquities themselves'. Any reader curious to see ancient temples, altars, aqueducts, and amphitheatres, Peacham directs to 'Repare to the old coynes, and you shall finde them, and all things else that ever they did, made, or used, there you shall see them excellently and lively represented'.[6]

Peacham also provides more practical instructions, and much of his chapter is taken up with how a gentleman should learn to observe antiquities correctly. With statuary, for example, 'he must be able to distinguish them, and tell who and what they be'. To do this, there are four options open to him. First, he can rely on 'generall learning in History and Poetry'. From this 'we are taught to know *Iupiter* by his thunder-bolt, *Mars* by his armour, *Neptune* by his Trident, *Apollo* by his harpe, *Mercury* by his winges on his cap and feet, or by his Caduceus; *Ceres* by a handfull of corne, *Flora* by her flowers'. Second, he can compare statues to coins: 'For if you looke upon them sidewayes and consider well their half-faces, as all coynes shew them you will easily know them.' Third, he can consult Girolamo Franzini's *Icones statuarum antiquarum urbis Romæ*. Franzini's book—one of a series of handbooks on Roman antiquities which he published in the 1580s and 1590s—consists of 111 woodcuts, mostly of statues, including the famous *Laocoön* and the *Apollo Belvedere*, but also of other antiquities, such as the city's obelisks. Its small format (sixteenmo) suggests that it

---

[3] Henry Peacham, *The Compleat Gentleman. Fashioning him absolut, in the most necessary and commendable Qualities concerning Minde or Body, that may be required in a Noble Gentleman* (London, 1634), 105.

[4] *OED*, s.v. 'lively', *a.* I, 1: 'Having life; living, live, animate'.

[5] Peacham, *Compleat Gentleman*, 112. Francis Bacon—at least according to a quip recorded by William Rawley—was similarly impressed by Arundel's garden. In his miscellany Rawley noted: 'My Lo: St. Albans, comming into the Earle of Arundells Garden, whether ther were many statues, of naked Men, and Women, he made a stand, and Said; The Resurrection'; LPL, MS 2086, fo. 33ʳ. For the display of classical statuary in gardens, see the discussion above at p. 87.

[6] Peacham, *Compleat Gentleman*, 123–4.

was intended as a pocket guidebook, displaying the highlights of the Eternal City for the historically minded visitor. Peacham's fourth and final way is 'to visit them in company of such as are learned in them, and by their helpe to grow familiar with them, and so practise their acquaintance'.[7] Peacham's prose here enacts an extraordinary personification, turning inanimate marble statues into lively human bodies, with whom his would-be gentlemen might converse, a transformation that itself imitates the essence of the antiquarian encounter. By travelling with scholars, his aspiring gentlemen could imbibe the knowledge which would enable them to make that imaginative leap which was central to the antiquarian response to the ancient world. Only then could they make sense of ancient statuary; only then could they discover 'the pleasure of seeing, and conversing with these old *Heroes*'.

In connecting travel and the education of a gentleman in this way, Peacham was giving voice to an idea current at the time. From the 1570s the notion that travel might complement the education of young men of rank was widely held. Shortly after Peacham, James Howell, who had himself travelled in the Low Countries, Italy, and Spain, went so far as to pronounce that '*Peregrination*... may be not improperly called a *moving Academy*, or the true *Peripatetique Schoole*'.[8] Modern scholars have long been familiar with this idea, and it has been shown that initially this education was conceived in primarily political and ethical terms. Only later did there emerge competing aesthetic, scientific, and technological motivations for travel.[9] By observing cities, customs, and men, English travellers abroad might evolve a fuller political knowledge of foreign climes. In Peacham's case, the ethical dimensions of this education were brought to the fore. A knowledge of antiquities was requisite for a complete gentleman; to attain that knowledge, the would-be gentleman was best advised to travel abroad.

But Peacham was also giving voice to something more explicitly antiquarian. His chapter attests to the existence in the early modern period of a specifically antiquarian kind of travel. One manifestation of this was the activities of men such as Arundel, who made a series of journeys abroad to add to their burgeoning collections of curiosities. Another, less familiar manifestation was the emergence of an antiquarian mode of travel writing—that is to say, travel writing which sought to extend the methods and approaches of the likes of Camden to the equally rich, if not richer, soil of 'abroad'. Given that antiquarianism had always had a strongly peripatetic element, as Daniel Woolf has shown, this emergence is hardly surprising.[10] As so often, English travellers were following here in the footsteps of their Italian humanist forebears. Earlier Italian examples of this kind

---

[7] Ibid. 109–10.
[8] James Howell, *Instructions for Forreine Travell* (London, 1642), 8.
[9] George B. Parks, 'Travel as Education', in *The Seventeenth Century: Studies in the History of English Thought and Literature from Bacon to Pope by Richard Foster Jones and Others Writing in his Honor* (Stanford: Stanford University Press, 1951), 264–90; see also John Stoye, *English Travellers Abroad 1604–1667* (New Haven and London: Yale University Press, 1989; first published 1952).
[10] Woolf, *The Social Circulation of the Past*, 142.

of antiquarian travel are plentiful, from Flavio Biondo to the autodidact and epigrapher Ciriaco of Ancona. Ciriaco toured Italy, Greece, and the eastern Mediterranean in the early fifteenth century, collecting information and recording ancient monuments and inscriptions, and he presented himself, like all Renaissance and early modern antiquaries, as resurrecting the past.[11] But whilst his activities are well documented, those of later English travellers who engaged in similar antiquarian pursuits are much less known. This kind of travel writing remains an under-studied part of the story of antiquarianism in early modern England. Where scholars have studied it, it has tended to be from the point of view of the history of collecting rather than from the literary and more broadly historical perspectives of this book.

The chapter which follows is an attempt to address that parochialism, to explore some of the connections between antiquarianism and travel writing in early modern England. It proposes that the antiquarian mindset, that urge to gather and reconstitute vestiges of the past, was an important influence on many of the travel accounts written at the time, governing what was included in them, but also how they were organized. To do this, the chapter looks in detail at the works of two of the most celebrated English travellers of the early seventeenth century, George Sandys and Thomas Coryate, two of that group dubbed 'urbane' by Eva Taylor and later Boies Penrose.[12] Taylor defined this kind of traveller as 'the man of culture who was touring Europe to complete his education, or to satisfy his spirit of curiosity, or occasionally just to seek notoriety'.[13] This chapter argues that an antiquarian outlook shaped the published accounts of both men. It explains, for example, the sheer number of inscriptions recorded, monuments described, and references cited, a classicism which has not always been to the taste of their readers. Sandys and Coryate both tended to look to ancient remains, to the traces of the classical world, before they turned to the more recent past or their own day. When Coryate described Padua, for example, which he visited in June 1608, he omitted the city's chief attraction for English travellers, its university and colleges. 'For my minde was so drawen away with the pleasure of other rarities and antiquities,' he wrote, 'that I neglected that which indeed was the principalest of all.'[14] Sandys and Coryate might not have been antiquaries in

---

[11] When Ciriaco visited Vercelli, he told a priest, who was concerned about his digging, 'I go to awake the past', and in Fano he deciphered a Latin inscription on the city gate, 'as if his was the agency by which the half-buried glory of the people of Fano had come to life again'; cited and translated in Paul MacKendrick, 'A Renaissance Odyssey: The Life of Cyriac of Ancona', *Classica et Mediaevalia*, 13 (1952), 131–45 at 133–4. On Ciriaco's antiquarianism, see Weiss, *The Renaissance Discovery of Classical Antiquity*, 137–42.

[12] E. G. R. Taylor, *Late Tudor and Early Stuart Geography 1583–1650* (London: Methuen, 1934), 144–57; and Boies Penrose, *Urbane Travelers 1591–1635* (Philadelphia: University of Pennsylvania Press, 1942).

[13] Taylor, *Late Tudor and Early Stuart Geography*, 144.

[14] Thomas Coryate, *Coryats Crudities* (London, 1611), sig. N6ʳ.

the strictest sense of the term, but there is no doubt that their works, and also their interests and habits of mind, bear the influence of antiquarianism.

The strongest evidence for this antiquarianism lies in the responses of the two men to the ancient remains, inscribed or not, which they encountered in the course of their peregrinations. In his influential book *Collectors and Curiosities* (1990) Krzysztof Pomian argues that ancient remains were given meaning by Renaissance collectors and travellers 'as they were seen in relation to the texts which had come down from antiquity, texts to which they were meant to provide the key'.[15] Ancient texts and objects informed one another, each accruing a more concrete sense through comparison with the other. This process seems to have had a particular resonance for the likes of Sandys and Coryate. They put it into practice, testing what they had read in the classics against what they observed in their travels, as well as making sense of those observations through recourse to their reading. Their works gather together inscriptions and other vestiges of the past, piling them up in an attempt to interpret them and also, more daringly, to restore them to their original splendour. Stephen Bann has written compellingly about the ways in which a collection might be conceived as a kind of literary work, engaging in a form of rhetoric and self-presentation, through a detailed case-study of John Bargrave, the traveller, collector, and canon of Canterbury Cathedral, whose cabinet included such choice titbits as pumice from Mt Etna, a dried chameleon from North Africa, and the finger of a Frenchman.[16] With Sandys and Coryate, both of whom did, incidentally, collect objects as well as words, the opposite question seems to obtain. How far might their works be conceived as a particularly literary kind of collection? Or, put more generally, how far did they participate in the seventeenth-century culture of curiosity and collecting? The rest of this chapter sets out to answer those questions.

THE APODEMIC ARTS

In their focus on antiquities, Sandys and Coryate were following one of the common recommendations in contemporary works and theories about travel. These works sometimes took the form of letters of advice, such as those to Roger Manners, the fifth earl of Rutland, on his travels, written in the name of the earl of Essex, but normally attributed to Francis Bacon, or Sir Philip Sidney's instructions to his younger brother Robert.[17] They sometimes also took the form of short disquisitions, such as Bacon's essay 'Of Travaile', first published in

---

[15] Krzysztof Pomian, *Collectors and Curiosities: Paris and Venice, 1500–1800*, trans. Elizabeth Wiles-Portier (Cambridge: Polity, 1990), 35.

[16] Stephen Bann, *Under the Sign: John Bargrave as Collector, Traveler and Witness* (Ann Arbor: University of Michigan Press, 1994), esp. 20–2.

[17] For a forthright defence of Bacon's authorship of the letters to Rutland, see Brian Vickers, 'The Authenticity of Bacon's Earliest Writings', *Studies in Philology*, 94 (1997), 248–96.

1625. This piece advances on the moral and ethical advice of the letters to Rutland, as it also lists more practically 'The Things to be seene and observed'. These include various subjects of antiquarian interest: 'The Churches, and Monasteries, with the Monuments which are therein extant'; 'The Wals and Fortifications of Cities and Townes'; 'Antiquities, and Ruines'; 'Libraries'; and 'Cabinets, and Rarities'.[18] But they also took the form of printed manuals, formal methods which taught the prospective traveller how to comport himself and what company he should keep. These manuals also tackled problems of knowledge and information, instructing the traveller in what he should observe, what he should note down, and how he should organize and present the mass of material which his journey would inevitably generate. These works, known as the *artes apodemicae* (apodemic arts), first appeared in the 1570s, initially emerging from Protestant presses north of the Alps, and they continued to be published in vast numbers until the end of the eighteenth century. The titles of some 300 such works are known today.[19]

The early *artes apodemicae* are similar in content and structure. Certain topics tend to recur and the works are often organized in the same way, moving from a definition of travel through a subdivision of that concept to moral and practical advice as well as to classical examples; a model or exemplary description might then be appended.[20] One such method was Hieronymus Turler's *De peregrinatione et agro Neapolitano* (1574), first published at Strasbourg. Book 1 of this treatise defines travel and provides moral and practical advice; Book 2 is a model description, taking the kingdom of Naples as its subject. Turler's treatise was quickly translated into English; an anonymous version, titled *The Traveiler*, was printed in 1575 by William How for the bookseller Abraham Veale. It is likely, therefore, that his method was better known in England than some of the other *artes apodemicae*.

Of all the early theorists of travel, Turler was perhaps the most interested in antiquities and collections.[21] Like other theorists, he emphasized first and foremost the educational benefits of travel. These might take the form of a scholar travelling abroad to study medicine or law, as Turler himself had done in his youth at Louvain and Padua. They might take the form of learning the art of navigation through sailing on voyages of discovery. But they might also, as one section of *The Traveiler* makes clear, mean travelling in search of antiquities.

---

[18] Francis Bacon, 'Of Travaile', in *The Essayes or Counsels, Civill and Morall*, ed. Michael Kiernan (The Oxford Francis Bacon, 15; Oxford: Clarendon Press, 2000; first published 1985), 56–7.

[19] For a complete list of titles, see Justin Stagl, *Apodemiken: Eine räsonnierte Bibliographie der reisetheoretischen Literatur des 16., 17. und 18. Jahrhunderts* (Paderborn, Munich, Vienna, and Zurich: Ferdinand Schöningh, 1983).

[20] Justin Stagl, *A History of Curiosity: The Theory of Travel 1550–1800* (Chur: Harwood, 1995), 71–81.

[21] Ibid. 79 n. 140.

Turler turns out to have been a staunch defender of the peripatetic model of antiquarianism.

The reason to adopt such a course was that the experience of observing a place was far superior to merely reading about it. 'For what description of any place can bee so euident, or what interpretacion so plaine and perspicuous,' Turler asks, 'but the beeholding of the thing it self doth far exceede it?'[22] He then cites three examples in illustration of this. All are intended to show why an antiquary should travel beyond his native soil, to demonstrate the riches which might be found abroad. His first example is a classical one, as he recounts the story of Cicero's discovery of the tomb of Archimedes at Syracuse during his quaestorship there: 'Tullie glorieth in a certen place, that he founde out the Sepulcher of Archimedes the Geometrician, . . . which sepulcher was ouergrowne with bushes and briars, and much defaced, for that it was long since he died.'[23] The story comes from the *Tusculan Disputations* (5. 64–6), where Cicero describes the tomb as 'enclosed all round and covered with brambles and thickets'.[24] But the reference to the defacement of time is Turler's own, an addition which allows him to overlay the Ciceronian passage with a Renaissance preoccupation with mutability and also give it a more overtly antiquarian perspective.

Turler's other two examples are more recent. As he notes, 'nothing inferior vnto these, haue bin founde also not much before our age, at which a man may no lesse wonder'.[25] His translator did him few favours here, with the succession of negatives, but the point is clear enough: discoveries, such as Cicero's, might still be made. His second example, the story of the miraculous discovery of the body of a Roman girl (widely believed to be Cicero's daughter Tulliola) buried beneath the Appian Way, illustrates his point. This story was widely bruited at the time, but Turler's source appears to have been the *Commentariorum urbanorum* (1506) of Raffaello Maffei (Volaterranus), perhaps in the 1559 Basle edition, the closest in date to his own work:

Hereof a sufficient witnes is Raphaell Volaterranus, writing, that in his time in the way called Via Appia nigh Rome, there was digged vp the body of a woman, embaulmed with precious oyntments, whole, vncorrupted, layd vp in a Coffin, and couered with a Marble Stone, hauinge beetweene her feete (as he sayth) a burning Candle whom the liquour of the oyntment nourished, but suddenly went out as soone as the Marble coueringe was remooued: adding moreover, that diuers supposed that it was the body of Tulliola, Tullies Daughter whom he loued dearely.[26]

---

[22] *The Traveiler of Ierome Turler, Deuided into two Bookes* (London, 1575), sig. C7ʳ.
[23] Ibid., sig. C7ʳ⁻ᵛ.
[24] Cicero, *Tusculan Disputations*, trans. J. E. King (Loeb Classical Library; Cambridge, Mass.: Harvard University Press, 1966), V. xxii. 64: 'cuius ego quaestor ignoratum ab Syracusanis, cum esse omnino negarent, saeptum undique et vestitum vepribus et dumetis indagavi sepulcrum'.
[25] Turler, *Traveiler*, sig. C7ᵛ.
[26] Ibid., sig. C7ᵛ; *Commentariorum vrbanorum Raphaelis Volaterrani, octo et triginta libri* (Basle, 1559), sigs. Q4ᵛ–Q5ʳ. The body of Tulliola, as Anthony Grafton has pointed out, was discovered

Here Turler was also reflecting on what Jennifer Wallace describes as the fundamental ambivalence of excavation, the dilemma that 'the excavator destroys his material as he discovers it'.[27] That miraculous (and clearly apocryphal) flame is extinguished as the body of Tulliola is brought to light. Part of the story disappears at the very moment of its recovery. It is left to later witnesses, to what I have described in this book as the antiquarian imagination, to invest the corporeal remains with significance, to reinforce the wondrousness of the preservation of such vestiges of the past.

The most significant of Turler's precedents, though, may be his third one: the example of Ciriaco of Ancona, 'a wonderfull searcher of Antiquities, not only concerning his owne cuntrey of Italie, but almost of all Europe, and of a great part of Asia and Africa, whereby hee tooke the name of an Antiquarie, leauinge an euerlastinge renowme of his name vnto posteritie'.[28] Picking up on the resurrection of the two previous examples, Turler notes approvingly Ciriaco's presentation of himself as quickening the dead, restoring the past, defying time:

Who vpon a time, when one demaunded of hym, why hee bestowed so muche labour in search of such matters: answered, that he would gladly raise some dead man to lyfe: rightly weighing how that many things are decaid and forgotten through process of time, which might be restored by dyligence of traueilynge, and by industrie of learned men, preserued from iniurie of obliuion.[29]

Previous chapters in this book have shown that resurrectional metaphors such as these were a common way of conceiving antiquarian activity. But Turler introduces a new perspective, shifting the argument so that the journey itself, the 'dyligence of traueilynge', as much as the 'industrie of learned men' becomes the resurrective act. And this, his book implies, is the greatest recommendation of all for antiquarian travel.

Another *ars apodemica* to specify the observation of antiquities was Albrecht Meier's *Methodus describendi regiones, vrbes & arces* (1587). This method, commissioned by Heinrich Rantzau, lord of Breitenburg, and published at his own expense, was a list of 186 topics after which the traveller should inquire.[30] Meier composed his work along Ramist lines, organizing his list of topics under twelve distinct heads. Amongst his topics there are various which might be conventionally considered as antiquarian. Under 'SCHOLASTICA', for example, his tenth head, Meier includes the following:

---

bewilderingly often in the Renaissance, at places including Florence and Malta, as well as here beneath the Appian Way; see *Forgers and Critics: Creativity and Duplicity in Western Scholarship* (Princeton: Princeton University Press, 1990), 26–8.

[27] Wallace, *Digging the Dirt*, 24.
[28] Turler, *Traveiler*, sigs. C7ᵛ–C8ʳ.
[29] Ibid., sig. C8ʳ.
[30] Parks, 'Travel as Education', 270; Stagl, *History of Curiosity*, 128.

Antiquæ notationes in Rupibus incisæ, aliæque antiquitates & res visu mirabiles.
Antiqua Numismata Rom. Impp. [sic] & similia.
Antiquæ vel recentes artificiosissimæ picturæ, Item columnarum, statuarum, Obeliscorum, Pyramidum, sepulchrorum inscriptiones.

Ancient markings inscribed on rocks, and other antiquities and wondrous things to behold. Ancient coins of Roman emperors and similar pieces. The most skilful paintings, ancient or modern; also inscriptions of columns, statues, obelisks, pyramids, and sepulchres.[31]

Further antiquarian interests follow in the next section, 'HISTORICA (Generalia)'. Here, Meier enjoins the traveller to inquire after the origin of a city, its founders, its name and etymology, its insignia or coat of arms, and its first inhabitants.[32] Taken together, these two heads replicate the matter of an antiquarian primer, covering its broad purview, as the traveller is instructed to look into the history and literature of the places that he visits.

Meier's method was also translated into English, appearing in 1589 under the title *Certaine briefe, and speciall Instructions*. The translator was one Philip Jones, about whom little is else known.[33] Jones prefaces the translation with a dedicatory epistle to Sir Francis Drake. This provides a standard eulogy of travel as political education, instructing travellers to master the laws, customs, and governments of the countries which they visit. They are to return to England with their brains bettered and their spirits quickened in respect of the varieties of the world. The *Instructions* are intended to enable them to do this. At various points in the text Jones expands on Meier's skeletal original. Under the tenth head, for example, he specifies that travellers should look for epitaphs and inscriptions 'cut, grauen, carued, or painted vpon tombes, pillers, gates, Churches, and other buildings'. When it comes to looking at coins, they should attend to 'their stampe, signe, posies, and sentences'.[34] He also adds that they should seek out 'Antiquaries, that is men excellently seene in antiquities and ancient monuments, both of the Church, and kingdome'.[35] This last instruction is Jones's invention; *antiquarii* are not mentioned in Meier's original.[36] Jones might have conceived the benefits of travel as primarily political, but he clearly also recognized the great

---

[31] Albrecht Meier, *Methodus describendi regiones, vrbes & arces, & quid singulis locis præcipuè in peregrinationibus homines nobiles ac docti animaduertere, obseruare & annotare debeant* (Helmstadt, 1587), sig. B1ʳ.
[32] Ibid., sig. B2ᵛ: '1. Vrbis antiquitas seu origo. Quando primùm condi cœpta vrbs, vrbisque partes, Templa, Curiæ, Arces? 2. Primi Conditores. 3. Nomina Appellationesque veteres, ac recentiores, Etymologia seu ratio Nominum. 4. Insignia Regionis, Ciuitatis, & ratio significatioque insignium. 5. Primi Inhabitatores (Incolæ, qui olim eos terras tenuerunt).'
[33] According to *STC*, Jones was also the author of *Certaine sermons preached of late at Ciceter* (1588) (*STC* 14728).
[34] Albrecht Meier, *Certaine briefe, and speciall Instructions for gentlemen, merchants, students, souldiers, Marriners &c. Employed in seruices abrode, or anie way occasioned to conuerse in the kingdomes, and gouernementes of forren Princes*, trans. Philip Jones (London, 1588), sig. D1ᵛ.
[35] Ibid., sig. D2ʳ.
[36] Cf. Meier, *Methodus*, sigs. B1ᵛ–B2ʳ.

opportunity which it presented for learning about history, literature, and antiquities.

There were dissenters: not everyone believed that observation of antiquities was good for the health of young men. Montaigne, for example, complained that, when French gallants visited Italy, they paid too much attention to 'how many paces the Church of *Santa Rotonda* is in length or breadth', and more salaciously to 'what rich garments the curtezan *Signora Livia* weareth, and the worth of her hosen'. Invariably they could dispute 'how much longer or broader the face of *Nero* is, which they have seene in some old ruines of *Italie*, than that which is made for him in some other old monuments elsewhere'. But they could say nothing about the 'humours and fashions of those countries they have seene, that they may the better know how to correct and prepare their wits by those of others'.[37] The problem for Montaigne was not antiquities *per se*, but that young men studied them (and also ladies' lingerie) at the expense of a proper peripatetic education. For Sir Thomas Palmer, author of *An Essay of the Meanes how to make Our Travailes, into forraine Countries, the more profitable and honorable* (1606), the dangers were greater still. Palmer recognized the attraction of antiquities, acknowledging that they were one of the reasons why travellers went to Italy; he described them as 'the speciall gallerie of monuments and olde aged memorials of histories, records of persons and things to bee seene thorowout the Countrey'. But he also described them as 'a fantasticall attracter, and a glutton-feeder of the appetite'.[38] Palmer's views may have been coloured by a profound anti-Italian prejudice, but his description deserves our attention.[39] For one thing, it reflects that voracious consumption, that acquisitiveness, which did indeed come to define the attitude towards antiquities of later travellers and collectors. But it also suggests that Palmer found something injurious in the way that antiquities took hold of the mind, in how they worked on the imagination or fancy.

These comments return us to the satires of Marmion, Earle, and Donne; to their portraits of obsessive, greedy, and doltish antiquaries, who venerate ancient objects above all else. For Palmer, antiquities were at best a distraction, diverting travellers from what they should rightly observe, and at worst a downright delusion. For Montaigne—whose comments might well strike a chord, since many travel accounts, and not just of Frenchmen, were overburdened with just the kind of antiquarian quibbling that he bemoaned—they were also a distraction. The fact that he and Palmer felt the need to comment at all suggests how

---

[37] Michel de Montaigne, 'Of the institution and education of children', in *The Essayes of Michael Lord of Montaigne*, trans. John Florio, 3 vols. (London and Toronto: J. M. Dent, 1928), i. 158–9.

[38] Sir Thomas Palmer, *An Essay of the Meanes how to make Our Travailes, into forraine Countries, the more profitable and honorable* (London, 1606), 43–4.

[39] For Palmer, Italy was the principal 'corrupter of men', and Rome 'the Forge of euery policie, that setteth Princes at oddes, or that continueth them in debates, little or much', 'the tempter of Subiects to ciuil dissensions', 'the seller of all wickednes and heathenish impieties', and, in a nonce-word which tells us everything, 'the machediuell of euill policies and practises', *Essay*, 44.

widespread this distraction had become. Antiquarian travel, as the examples to which I turn in the remainder of this chapter show, was neither the preserve of wealthy collectors, nor just an abstruse byway of early modern historical scholarship.

A RELATION OF RUINS

In early May 1610, at the age of 32, George Sandys set sail for France, embarking on an antiquarian journey which would take him to Italy, Greece, Constantinople, Egypt, the Holy Land, and Malta. We do not hear of him again until March 1612—by which time he had returned to England—when his name was included among the list of adventurers in the third charter of James I to the Virginia Company.[40] In 1615, three years after his return, *A Relation of a Iourney begun An: Dom: 1610* appeared, an account written up and, as will become apparent, greatly augmented from the journals or notebooks which he had evidently kept on that journey. The work was immediately well received, with Bacon, Thomas Browne, and Robert Burton just some of the seventeenth-century writers who drew upon it for observations about the East.[41]

Like other contemporary travellers, Sandys took the advice of the *artes apodemicae* to heart. His observations run their whole gamut. He comments on politics, religion, customs, law, medicine, natural history, geography, and architecture. He has been admired by modern scholars variously for his descriptions of fountains and gardens, his moderate account of the Eastern Churches, and his challenge of a persistent anti-Semitic prejudice.[42] But one subject, one overarching interest, runs through his whole book. That interest is a fascination with ruins, with what has been called 'the contrast between ancient fame and modern desolation'.[43] For Sandys, that contrast is most clearly evidenced in material terms. Throughout his travels he encountered visible traces of the past, which he assiduously observed and recorded. His book becomes a repository of these ruins and remains, an encyclopedia of antiquarian fare, which gives meaning to those traces by bringing them together and interspersing pertinent classical quotations. But Sandys also shared the fundamental anxiety of the antiquaries, their sense of the unequal struggle with time. In his description of an eastern Mediterranean

---

[40] Richard Beale Davis, *George Sandys: Poet-Adventurer* (London: Bodley Head, 1955), 82.
[41] Ibid. 89.
[42] Hester Lees-Jeffries, *England's Helicon: Fountains in Early Modern Literature and Culture* (Oxford: Oxford University Press, 2007), 16–18; John Dixon Hunt, *Garden and Grove: The Italian Renaissance Garden in the English Imagination: 1600–1750* (London and Melbourne: J. M. Dent, 1986), 14–15, 50; James Ellison, *George Sandys: Travel, Colonialism and Tolerance in the Seventeenth Century* (Cambridge: D. S. Brewer, 2002), 69–77; David S. Katz, *Philo-Semitism and the Readmission of Jews to England 1603–1655* (Oxford: Clarendon Press, 1982), 170.
[43] Jonathan Haynes, *The Humanist as Traveler: George Sandys's Relation of a Journey begun An. Dom. 1610* (London and Toronto: Associated University Presses, 1986), 41.

littered with former glories, he captures perfectly the frustration of their project, the inherent problem of dealing in broken knowledge.

The antiquarian tone is set from the outset. In the prefatory epistle to Prince Charles, Sandys categorizes the *Relation* as an account of how the mighty are fallen, of how 'the most renowned countries and kingdomes' now lie in ruins, literally, but also intellectually and spiritually. He comments with sadness:

> Which countries once so glorious, and famous for their happy estate, are now through vice and ingratitude, become the most deplored spectacles of extreme miserie: the wild beasts of mankind hauing broken in vpon them, and rooted out all ciuilitie; and the pride of a sterne and barbarous Tyrant possessing the thrones of ancient and iust dominion.[44]

It is hard not to conclude that he was thinking primarily of Greece, a Christian land now under the sway of the Turk. Others had written about Greece in a similar way, and the Turkish dominion was widely believed to be divine punishment for the iniquities of the Orthodox Church.[45] The Scottish minister Robert Pont, for example, made this connection in his tract *De unione Britanniæ* (1604): 'we cannot without teares remember the fatall success of the Greek churches after they submitted themselves to the slavery of the Romish bishop, and imbraced his heresie in the adoration of the bread and worshipping of images, which now lie ruined and desolate under the most slavish bondage of the Turk'. 'For what other course can be conceaved,' he asked, 'why God should suffer those persistent enemies to Him and His truth so to rage and run over not Hungary alone, but many other parts of Christiandom?'[46] Sandys's position was markedly less doctrinaire, and unlike Pont he found in elements of the Orthodox Church a possible bulwark against Catholicism.[47] But his comment still reflects the widespread cultural reading of the ruination of Greece, and indeed the whole Levant. The end of his epistle, however, suggests that he had a broader historical project in mind: 'I haue not onely related what I saw of their present condition; but so far as conueniency might permit, presented a briefe view of the former estates, and first antiquities of those people and countries.'[48] There could be no clearer

---

[44] Sandys, *A Relation of a Iourney*, sig. $A2^{r-v}$.

[45] Terence Spencer, *Fair Greece Sad Relic: Literary Philhellenism from Shakespeare to Byron* (Athens: Denise Harvey, 1986; first published 1954), 43–7; see also Efterpi Mitsi, 'Painful Pilgrimage: Sixteenth-Century English Travellers to Greece', in *Travels and Translations in the Sixteenth Century: Selected Papers from the Second International Conference of the Tudor Symposium (2000)*, ed. Mike Pincombe (Aldershot: Ashgate, 2004), 19–30.

[46] Robert Pont, *Of the Union of Britayne*, in *The Jacobean Union: Six Tracts of 1604*, ed. Bruce R. Galloway and Brian P. Levack (Edinburgh: The Scottish Historical Society, 1985), 1–38 at 15. I quote from a translation taken from a manuscript in the Royal collection (BL, MS Royal 18 A XIV), which suggests that this translation might have been a presentation copy given to James I.

[47] Sandys describes the Greek Patriarch at Alexandria, for example, as 'a man of approued vertue and learning, a friend to the reformed religion, and opposing the contrary; saying that the differences betweene vs and the *Greeks*, be but shels; but that those are kernels betweene them and the other'; *Relation*, 115.

[48] Ibid., sig. $A2^v$.

statement of his antiquarian intent. But this act of restitution was itself a form of admonition. As Sandys goes on, he has sought to restore the past in order to 'draw a right image of the frailty of man, and mutability of what so euer is worldly; and assurance that as there is nothing vnchangeable sauing God, so nothing stable but by his grace and protection'.

In Book 1 of the *Relation*, which recounts his journey from Venice to Constantinople and his stay in the Imperial city, Sandys keeps his word. The book is a storehouse of antiquarian matter, and as detailed a survey of Greek ruins and remains as any previously published in English. On Kythera, for example, he mentions a temple of Venus, whose 'ruines are now to be seene'.[49] By the same token, when he describes the island of Zante (mod. Zakynthos), which he visited in September 1610, he reports the discovery of a pair of venerable urns buried underground in an ancient sepulchre. These urns had been unearthed in the grounds of a monastery, and they were believed to contain the ashes of Cicero and his wife. Evidently recognizing the importance of inscriptions (albeit ones that are now considered spurious), Sandys also records that 'Vpon a square stone that couered the tombe, was ingrauen M. TVL. CICERO LAVE ET TV IEPTIA ANTONIA and vnder the vrne which containeth the ashes, AVE MAR. TVL. It being supposed that *Cicero* was there buried.'[50] These, as the marginal note '*Iohannes Zuallardus in Itin. l. 1*' alongside indicates, were not inscriptions which he noted at the time. Instead, he took them (and also the story of the discovery of the tomb) from Jean Zuallart's *Il devotissimo viaggio di Gerusalemme* (1587), a book which he presumably read on his return to England, as he was writing his material up. But they were precisely the kind of antiquarian detail which his project demanded, and so he duly inserted them into the course of his travels.

Sandys keeps his other pledge as well. He depicts Greece as a desolate series of ruins, her once great cities reduced to heaps of stones. These are to be catalogued and described, but also bemoaned. The Morea, for example, was once 'so highly celebrated by the ancient Poets: but now presenting nothing but ruines, in a great part desolate, it groneth vnder the Turkish thraldome, being gouerned by a *Sanzacke*, who is vnder the *Beglerbeg* of *Grecia*'. An equally grim fate had befallen the island of Delos, its great temples plundered as common quarries: 'The ruines of *Apollos* temple are here yet to be seene, affoording faire pillars of marble to such as will fetch them, and other stones of price, both in their nature and for their workmanship.'[51] With their insistent *ubi sunt* theme, such comments remind us that, as well as the antiquarian tradition, Sandys was also the heir of an equally strong poetic tradition of lamenting ruins.[52]

---

[49] Ibid. 10.
[50] Ibid. 8; for the inscription, see *Corpus inscriptionum Latinarum*, iii/1, ed. Theodor Mommsen (Berlin: Georgius Reimerus, 1873), 5.
[51] Sandys, *Relation*, 9, 11.
[52] As such, Sandys embodies that ambivalence identified by Rose Macaulay, what she describes as 'the Renaissance desire to build up the ancient ruins into their glorious first state, and to lament their ruin as wreckage of perfection'; see *Pleasure of Ruins*, 192–3.

From an antiquarian perspective, one moment in Book 1 stands out: the description of Troy. This description is important because, unlike many of his contemporaries, Sandys did not believe that the ruins shown to travellers were those of the Homeric city.[53] He was, of course, right, for what travellers saw were in fact the ruins of Alexandria Troas, a later city founded by one of the successors of Alexander the Great. But Sandys was swimming against the historical tide, since most reports—no doubt reflecting what their authors wanted to see—doggedly stuck to the story. William Biddulph, chaplain to the English merchants at Aleppo, who sailed past the site shortly before Sandys, simply commented that 'Ouer against Tenedos is Troy, which is also called Troas or Troada', whilst a later French traveller was confident enough to inscribe epitaphs to Priam, Hecuba, and Hector on three tombstones there.[54] Sandys had little time for such reports, and he doubted that any traces of the Homeric city had survived. Quoting and translating Ovid's lines on the fall of the house of Priam, '*Now prostrate, onely her old ruines showes, / And tombes that famous ancestors inclose*', he comments wryly: 'But those not at this day more then coniecturally extant'.[55]

Sandys visited the Troad on 25 September 1610, when he was put ashore at Cape Sigeum in the company of two or three others. He was, we learn, 'desirous to see those celebrated fields where once stood *Ilium* the glory of *Asia*, that hath affoorded to rarest wits so plentifull an argument'.[56] But, as so often with Sandys, what follows in the *Relation* turns out to have as much to do with literary tradition as any observations that he could possibly have made that day. For Sandys had a particular target in mind: the French naturalist Pierre Belon, who had written a lengthy description of what he took to be Troy in his popular and much reprinted *Les Observations de plusieurs singularitez et choses memorables*,

---

[53] For a useful survey of early travellers' descriptions of Troy, see J. M. Cook, *The Troad: An Archaeological and Topographical Study* (Oxford: Oxford University Press, 1973), 14–51.

[54] William Biddulph, *The Travels of certaine Englishmen into Africa, Asia, Troy, Bythinia, Thracia, and to the Blacke Sea* (London, 1609), 14. The story of the Frenchman is reported by Aaron Hill, who presents the stones as a kind of epigraphic puzzle for later travellers; see *A Full and Just Account of the Present State of the Ottoman Empire In all its Branches: With The Government, and Policy, Religion, Customs, and Way of Living of the Turks in General* (London, 1710), 205: 'there stood three things like *Tomb-Stones*, and upon approach we found 'em really to be such, at least design'd to represent them;... which by the *Inscriptions* on 'em, seem'd to have been done in *Christendom*, to gratifie the Humour of some curious Person, willing to amuse *Posterity*, when they shou'd find such *Tombs* in such a Place, and never know which way they came to be there'.

[55] Sandys, *Relation*, 20; Ovid, *Metamorphoses*, trans. Frank Justus Miller, rev. G. P. Goold (Loeb Classical Library; Cambridge, Mass.: Harvard University Press, 1996; first published in this edition 1916), xv. 424–5: 'Nunc humilis veteres tantummodo Troia ruinas / Et pro divitiis tumulos ostendit avorum.'

[56] Sandys, *Relation*, 19.

trouuées en Grece, Asie, Iudée, Egypte, Arabie, & autres pays estranges (1553).[57] Belon, who had visited in 1546, was one of the greatest enthusiasts for the Trojan ruins, and in his book he takes to task those who deny that any are still standing:

Il ne fault pas adiouster foy a ceulx qui disent que toutes les ruines sont demolies. Les fondements des murailles du circuit de la ville sont encores apparoissants, qui sont renforcez en quelques endoicts de pilliers & esperons larges de deux toises. Ie fuz quatre heures à l'entourner, tant à pied qu'à cheual.[58]

He evidently spent these four hours well, for what follows is an extraordinarily detailed description of what the traveller might see. The attractions include ruins inside the walls, marble tombs outside, and a pair of forts flanking the city. Belon also draws attention to the statues and other antiquities which were periodically turned up there: 'Lon veoit de grands Colosses dede*n*s Troye couchez par terre, taillez à l'antique, & y a vn endroit assez pres du chasteau, de la mer, ou est vn moult grand amas de marbres.'[59] Moreover, although he might have been mistaken in what he was investigating, he did have a shrewd antiquarian eye. He picks out inscriptions, using these to date different parts of the site. One in particular caught his attention, a Roman inscription from the time of Antoninus Pius carved on a white marble pillar stuck fast in the ground. Belon emphasizes the great effort that it had taken to read it: 'Toutes lesquelles parolles estoient d'vn costé du pilier, ta*n*t consummées d'antiquité, qu'à peine les pouoye lire.'[60] This emphasis allows him to present himself in a typically antiquarian fashion: labouring valiantly to recover ruins and remains from the consumption of time.

For Sandys, the key to finding the site of Troy was the identification of that elusive pair, the rivers Simoïs and Scamander. Following Strabo, he locates 'ancient *Ilium*' on the 'ample plaine' between the 'not farre disioyning vallies' of the two rivers.[61] And they give him his first grounds for complaint: 'These riuers, though now poore in streames, are not yet so contemptible, as made by *Bellonius*.' The Frenchman had described the two rivers as tiny streamlets, which in summer were dry, and in winter were barely deep enough for a goose.[62] Sandys

---

[57] Another traveller with antiquarian interests, who read and commented upon Belon, was Ogier Ghiselin de Busbecq. In the first of his Turkish letters to Nicholas Michault, Busbecq corrected Belon's identification of the hyena with the civet; see *Itinera Constantinopolitanum et Amasianum* (Antwerp, 1582), sig. D2[r]: 'fallitur verò Bellonus qui hyænam putat quem Cattum siue felem Zibettum vocant'. Busbecq's copy of Belon may survive today: in the Arcadian Library, London, there is a copy of the second edition of the *Observations* (1554) (record number 08185) which has the inscription 'Busbeq' in a contemporary italic hand on its title page. Alas, I have not yet been able to confirm whether this signature is genuine.

[58] Pierre Belon, *Les Observations de plusieurs singularitez et choses memorables, trouées en Grece, Asie, Iudée, Egypte, Arabie, & autres pays estranges, redigées en trois liures* (Paris, 1553), sigs. x2[v]–x3[r].

[59] Ibid., sig. x3[v].

[60] Ibid.

[61] Sandys, *Relation*, 21.

[62] Belon, *Observations*, sig. x4[r]: 'ce sont si petits ruisselets ... ils sont en esté à sec, & en hyuer vne oye à grand peine y pourroit elle nager dedens'.

then puts the dagger in, adding that 'perhaps' Belon 'mistaketh others for them, (there being sundry riuolets that descend from the mountaines) as by all likelihood he hath done the site of the ancient *Troy*'.[63] He notes that 'the ruines that are now so perspicuous, and by him related, do stand foure miles South-west from the aforesaid place, described by the Poets, and determined of by Geographers'. The clincher, though, and here again he was remembering his Strabo, was that the ruines were simply 'too neare the nauall station, to affoord a field for such dispersed encounters, such long pursuites, interception of scouts . . . and executed strategems, as is declared to haue hapned between the Sea and the Citie'.[64] Strabo had pointed out that Polites, the Trojan sentinel, would not have needed to rely on his speed to escape from the Greeks in Book 2 of the *Iliad*, if the present city were the same as the ancient one, since he could have kept watch over their fleet from the citadel within that city.

The contrast between Sandys and Belon is emphasized by the maps of the Troad in the two books. The woodcut map in the *Observations* locates the ruins of Troy by Cape Sigeum and the seashore at what is clearly the site of Alexandria Troas (Fig. 5.1). They are identified by the caption 'Ruines de Troye'. By

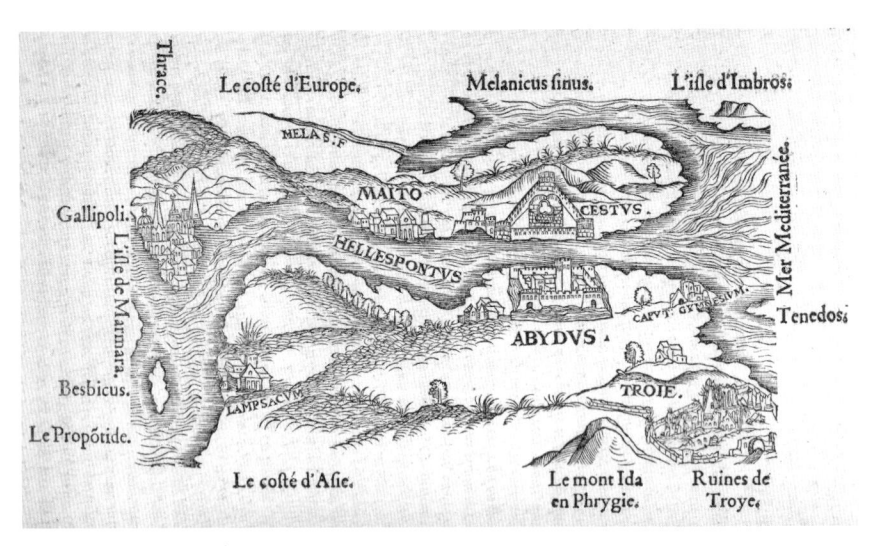

FIG. 5.1. Map of the Troad. Pierre Belon, *Les Observations de plusieurs singularitez et choses memorables, trouées en Grece, Asie, Iudée, Egypte, Arabie, & autres pays estranges, redigées en trois liures* (Paris, 1553), sig. v4ʳ. © British Library Board. All Rights Reserved (shelfmark 567. f. 21. (3))

---

[63] Sandys, *Relation*, 22.
[64] Ibid.; Jack E. Friedman, 'George Sandys' Debt to Strabo in his Remarks on Homeric Troy', *Notes & Queries*, 222 (1977), 203–4.

A Peripatetic Education 155

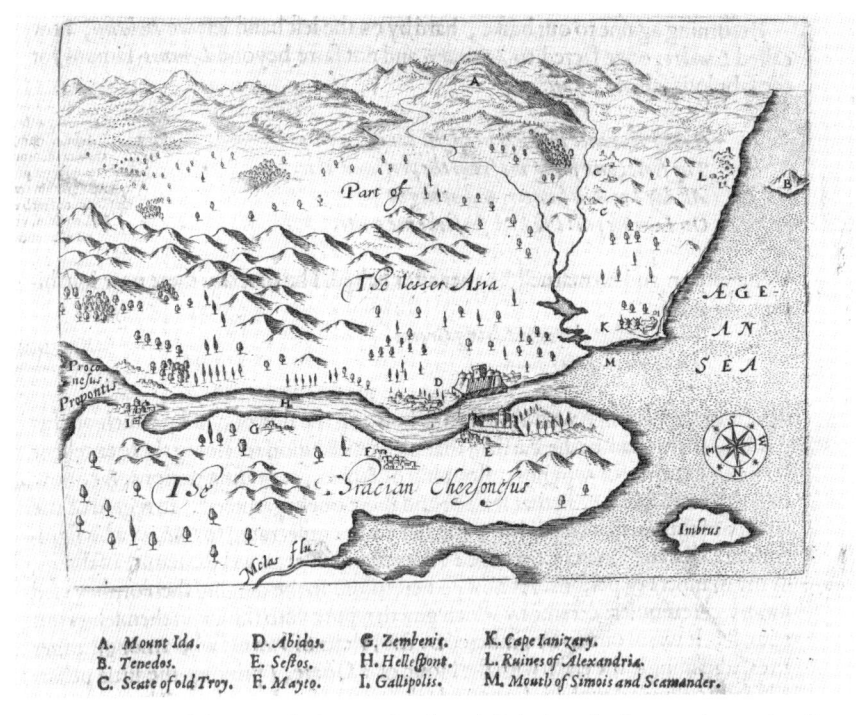

FIG. 5.2. Map of the Troad. George Sandys, *A Relation of a Iourney begun An: Dom: 1610* (London, 1615), 24. Cambridge University Library, Syn. 4. 61. 5. Reproduced by kind permission of the Syndics of Cambridge University Library

contrast, the map in the *Relation*, almost certainly engraved by Francis Delaram, distinguishes between the two Trojan sites (Fig. 5.2).[65] This map is initially confusing as it reverses the customary north–south axis, but it represents a considerable advance on its French predecessor because of the degree of topographical detail. Mount Ida, the Simoïs, and Scamander, all clues to Homer's geography, are marked on it. The map differentiates between the two sites with a simple alphabetical key. At 'C', just to the west of the Simoïs and Scamander, there is the '*Seate of old Troy*', whilst at 'L', on the shore opposite the island of Tenedos, there are the '*Ruines of Alexandria*'. The map represents both sites with the same symbol (rudiments of buildings), but it further distinguishes between them by the extent of this symbol. At 'L' the symbol is repeated frequently and in close proximity, whereas at 'C' it is less fully realized. The map therefore also corresponds with the respective states of preservation of the two sites. One

[65] On Delaram's engravings for the *Relation*, see Hind, *Engraving in England*, ii. 238–9.

consists of ruins to be visited and depicted; the other is a historical conjecture, based on comparison of classical sources.

Sandys's antiquarianism also shines through in Book 4, when he describes his travels in southern Italy. Here, he was travelling through more familiar territory still, a landscape suffused with classical allusions and literary significances. It is reflected, for example, in his description of the plains around Cumae, the seat of the famed Sibyl, just to the north of Naples. Much of this account is taken up with a discussion of the Sibyl's prophecies, principally gleaned from Books 3 and 6 of the *Aeneid*. The Sibyls seem to have had a particular fascination for Sandys, perhaps, as Jonathan Haynes has argued, because they held out the promise of historical continuity, from the Greek to the Roman worlds, but also from classical antiquity to the Christian present.[66] They were important enough for the Cumaean Sibyl to appear on the frontispiece of the *Relation*, on a small lozenge at its foot, apparently as a symbol for Sandys's travels in Italy. But Cumae had other mysteries as well, other attractions for the historically and literarily minded traveller.

The first of these was that old antiquarian chestnut, the problem of the city's name. Sandys tackles this with gusto, giving four explanations for it:

The *Grecians* of *Calchis* a Citie of *Eubœa*; who seeking a habitation, first planted themselues in *Ænaria*, an Iland hard by, and after remoued to this place being then vninhabited. The Generals, *Hippocles Cumeus*, and *Megasthenes* of *Calchis*, agreeing betweene themselues, that the one should haue it, and the other should name it. So the *Calchians* built, and possest it; but named it *Cuma*. Others say that it was so named of the waues of the sea: or of repose (for the name doth signifie the same) then hauing ended their long nauigations: or rather of a woman being great with child, whom they there found sleeping.[67]

In its uncertainty, the etymology allows Sandys to survey some of the broad categories for the explanation of a place name. The first is memorial; the name as a record of its founder. The second is topographical, the name arising from the local landscape. The third is historical; the name as a record of a particular event. The fourth is aetiological, the name finding its origin in a foundation story. By entertaining possible origins, without coming to a definitive conclusion, Sandys's approach here recalls many of the discourses presented to the Elizabethan Society of Antiquaries. This may have been intentional, but it may also simply reflect how widespread that approach to etymology had become.

An even greater draw to Sandys was the ruins. He describes Cumae, in one of his favourite phrases, as 'a confusion of ruines', as nothing but 'peeces of wals, broken down Aquaducts, defaced Temples, foundations of Theaters, to be

[66] Haynes, *Humanist as Traveler*, 132–4.
[67] Sandys, *Relation*, 282.

admired Caues'.⁶⁸ The last is an allusion to the cave of the Sibyl. All the buildings, all the marks of classical civilization, are reduced to their fundaments. But any melancholy is immediately assuaged, as Sandys shifts attention to the surrounding plains. These too are rich in historical treasure. They are 'repleate with ruines: where are to be seene the foundations of Temples, Theaters, &c. vnder which, no doubt but many admirable antiquities haue their sepulture'.⁶⁹ This last clause exemplifies the paradox of the early modern antiquary, stuck between frustration at what has disappeared into the earth and wonder at what has survived the passage of time.

On this occasion, at least, the second impulse seems to have won out. Sandys argues that these admirable antiquities are 'Approued by that triall made by *Alfonsus Pimentellus* the Vice-roy, in the yeare 1606'. That trial was an archaeological dig.⁷⁰ Juan Alonso Pimentel de Herrera, Count of Benavente, and Viceroy of Naples, was a celebrated collector of art and antiquities.⁷¹ By 1605 the fame of his collection had reached England, when the anonymous chronicler of the embassy of Charles Howard, the earl of Nottingham, to Philip III of Spain described the curiosities to be found in his castle at Benavente. These included portraits of Hannibal and Scipio, and also 'one of their thigh bones that was as big as any mans thigh, flesh and all, in anie part'.⁷² In 1606, 'desirous to find out some antique statues to send into *Spaine*', Pimentel sought and obtained permission to dig just outside Cumae. The results were spectacular. According to Sandys, Pimentel discovered 'an entire Temple, although crushed together' and also 'a number of defaced figures excellently wrought: the worke as well of the *Grecians* as Latines'. These included statues of Neptune, 'his beard of a blew colour'; Saturn or Priapus, 'for he held in his hand the heft of a cycle'; Vesta, 'with the top of her haire wound round in a fillet'; Castor, 'hauing a hat on his head, his chin a litle couered with downe'; Apollo, 'with long disheueled haire'; and Hercules, 'with a club crowned with a wreath'.⁷³ Sandys's initial term 'Approued' is highly significant because it indicates the importance which he placed on material remains—in this case, Pimentel's find—as evidence. Pimentel's statues made good his statement that diverse antique remains are buried in the plain beneath Cumae. This evidentiary standard is then reinforced by his concluding remark on the dig: 'Some thinke it to haue bene a Pallace: but

---

⁶⁸ Ibid. 282 3.   ⁶⁹ Ibid. 287.
⁷⁰ For a later account of this dig, see Lorenzo Palatino, *Storia di Pozzuoli, e contorni con breve tratto istorico di Ercolano, Pompei, Stabia, e Pesto* (Naples, 1826), 127–8.
⁷¹ For Pimentel's collections, see J. Miguel Morán and Fernando Checa, *El coleccionismo en España: De la cámara a la galería de pinturas* (Madrid: Cátedra, 1985), 170, 220–2.
⁷² Cited in Gustav Ungerer, 'Juan Pantoja de la Cruz and the Circulation of Gifts between the English and Spanish Courts in 1604/5', *Shakespeare Studies*, 26 (1998), 145–86 at 148.
⁷³ Sandys, *Relation*, 287.

whatsoeuer, it testifieth an admirable building.'[74] Unearthed statues and stones are testimony to, witnesses of, a buried Greek and Roman past.

There is, though, one surprising aspect of Book 4: the almost total omission of Rome itself. Sandys's description of the city is perfunctory and, given the attention which he lavishes on less significant sites, astonishingly brief. He skirts over it in just two comments in the final paragraph of the book. We discover only that he stayed 'foure dayes (as long as I durst)', and that Master Nicholas Fitzherbert, former secretary to Cardinal Allen, accompanied him 'in the suruey-ing of all the antiquities and glories of that Citie'.[75] He has nothing more to say: the antiquities and glories go undescribed. This abruptness is only emphasized when we consider the attention which other travellers paid to the city. Fynes Moryson, who visited Rome in April 1594, distinguished 'the Antiquities into foure daies iournies', whilst even Anthony Munday found time in his extraordinary anti-Catholic polemic, *The English Romayne Lyfe* (1582), to say something about them.[76] He provided one of the first descriptions of the catacombs, the 'darke Vautes vnderneath the ground', of San Pancrazio and Priscilla; the latter were only discovered in 1578, a year before his visit, and they would not be widely known until Antonio Bosio's *Roma sotterranea* (1632).[77] Furthermore, by the time that Sandys visited, following the peace treaties of 1598 and 1604, Rome was a much less dangerous place for English Protestant visitors to be.[78] Thus Arundel could summon his wife Aletheia to Rome in March 1614 with the eulogistic assertion that 'there are no more such places'.[79] Sandys's silence must therefore have been striking to his readers, and it needs further comment.

Two possible explanations suggest themselves. First, Sandys may simply have considered another description of Rome's antiquities to be redundant. As well as travellers' tales, there were any number of books in Italian which enumerated the city's antiquities. At the popular end of the market, for example, there was *La guida romana* (1557), written by an Englishman named Shakerley.[80] This oft reprinted work, as its author makes clear in the preface to the 1562 edition, was intended as a brief and reliable guide to the city's sights.[81] Shakerley arranged his

---

[74] Sandys, *Relation*, 288.   [75] Ibid. 309.
[76] Fynes Moryson, *An Itinerary* (London, 1617), 129.
[77] Anthony Munday, *The English Romayne Lyfe* (London, 1582), sig. G1ʳ; Antonio Bosio, *Roma sotterranea* (Rome, 1632), 479–80.
[78] Stoye, *English Travellers*, 74.
[79] Cited in Howarth, *Lord Arundel and his Circle*, 44; also in HMC, *The Manuscripts of the Earl Cowper, K. G., Preserved at Melbourne Hall, Derbyshire*, 3 vols. (London: HMSO, 1888–9), i. 83.
[80] Shakerley has been variously identified as Peter Shakerley, who produced an English translation of Ecclesiastes in 1551, and Thomas Shakerley, an English organist resident at Rome; see 'A Sixteenth Century Guide Book', *The Connoisseur*, 2 (1902), 204; and Andrea Palladio, *The Churches of Rome*, trans. Eunice D. Howe (Binghamton: Medieval & Renaissance Texts & Studies, 1991), 119.
[81] *La guida romana per tutti i forastieri che vengono per vedere le antichita di Roma, a vna per vna in bellissima forma & breuita* (Rome, 1562), fo. [1]ᵛ: 'Non Pensate Signori, che io cerchi in questa operetta laude, o premio alcuno, ma solamente attendo mostrarui, quello che so hauere a caro,

book as three itineraries, one for each day, and his focus was on the city's ruins. Even a popular book such as this one, incidentally, turns out to share the resurrective impulse, as its revived, personified description of the mutilated statue of the Pasquino shows.[82] There were also the handbooks by Franzini, which we encountered at the beginning of this chapter.[83] Sandys may have felt that there was nothing to add, that an already burgeoning field did not need another contribution. But his silence may admit of another explanation as well. In the final paragraph Sandys moves at breakneck speed, travelling from Anzio to Venice, the end of his journey, via Rome, Florence, Bologna, and Ferrara. He gives the distinct impression that he wanted to finish his book as quickly as possible. His method of composition, that careful and constant embellishment of his original observations with the fruits of his reading, made great demands on him. By the time that he reached Rome, for which the number of literary references to engage with and incorporate would have been overwhelming, he may have lost the energy to put this method into practice. He gives instead the barest record of what he saw and did. But even then, in his 'surueying of all the antiquities and glories of that Citie', his antiquarianism comes to the fore.

CORYATE'S *CRUDITIES*

Shortly before Sandys set out on his journey, his contemporary Thomas Coryate travelled abroad for the first time. Setting out from Odcombe in Somerset in spring 1608, Coryate undertook a five-month walking tour through France, Italy, Switzerland, Germany, and the Netherlands. He published the results as *Coryats Crudities* (1611), a volume which, with its mock encomia by the greatest writers of the day, initially at least seems to live up to Coryate's reputation as a buffoonish wit. On the surface, the *Crudities* would appear to have little to do with the tradition of learned travel described in this chapter. Yet Coryate was aware of the *artes apodemicae*. Indeed, the *Crudities* are prefaced with an *ars apodemica* of their own, Coryate's English translation of an oration in praise of travel by the German humanist and poet Hermann Kirchner, delivered by George Haunschildt at the University of Marburg, where Kirchner held various

---

perche ben si vede che de di in di, nostri Inglesi, & Francesi, Flamenghi, & de molte altre natione vengono a Roma, desiderosissimi veder le cose di quella, & ben cognoscere delle quale molte volte non si vede la terza parte, Però mosso per contentarui, ho preso ardimento esser guida alli desiderij vostri.'

[82] Ibid., fo. [7]ᵛ: 'Et a piedi di questa piazza, sotto il palazzo di Casa Orsina trouerete attaccato. M. Pasquino Romano antichissimo, doue con lui vi lascio fin che haurete pranzato.' This kind of personification and apostrophe was, as Leonard Barkan has shown, the customary way that Renaissance writers described and wrote about the statue; see *Unearthing the Past*, 210–31.

[83] See p. 140 above.

positions.[84] Coryate also included a second of Kirchner's speeches later in the *Crudities*, 'An Oration in praise of the trauell of Germany in particular'. Moreover, Coryate himself was not the fool that he customarily played. Although he did not take a degree, he did enter Gloucester Hall at Oxford, and he was, as his modern biographer has pointed out, reasonably learned in classical literature and history.[85] He was also, as the final part of this chapter shows, well versed in antiquarian matters.

One piece of evidence for Coryate's antiquarian interests comes from his circle of friends. He seems to have known Sir Robert Cotton, whom he greeted in a letter from Ajmer in India as 'that famous Antiquarie', and listed him among his 'louers of vertue, and literature'. In the same letter Coryate describes 'a very curious white marble head of an ancient Heros or Gyant-like Champion, found out very casually by my diligent peruestigation amongst the ruines of the once renowned City of *Cyzicum*', which was now in his possession. Never one for false modesty, Coryate brags that 'to this head wil his best antiquities whatsoeuer veyle bonnet'.[86] What Cotton made of the marble head, or indeed the boast, is unknown.

Coryate's antiquarian interests, however, are best attested by the *Crudities* themselves. In a letter to Sir Michael Hickes, dated 15 November 1610, Coryate spoke revealingly about his intentions for the work. This holograph letter is now bound in the hand-coloured copy of the *Crudities* which Coryate presented to Prince Henry (British Library, class-mark G6750). He wrote to Hickes, secretary to Sir Robert Cecil, to seek his assistance in obtaining a licence for the book, asking him 'to intercede for me vnto my Lord Treasurer, that it would please his Lordship to give order it may be printed in London with some expedition'. But Coryate also commented upon the work itself, describing it as a 'booke containing principally the most remarkable antiquities of those cities that I have described', and he seized the opportunity to emphasize the pains that he had taken over the task. 'I wrote soe many observations in the foresayd countries,' he remarked, 'as have filled very neere 4 quiers of paper having in the space of 5 monenths surveyed 47 cities.' In the seventeenth century a quire normally consisted of twenty-four or twenty-five sheets.[87] If Coryate's comment is true, he must have taken very detailed notes indeed. He goes on to boast that 'no man of our nation since the incarnation of Christe hath observed more for the time in the foresayd countries', and that in Venice he stuck to his task so diligently that

---

[84] For a short life of Kirchner, see Jacob N. Beam, 'Hermann Kirchner's *Coriolanus*', *Publications of the Modern Language Association of America*, 33 (1918), 269–301 at 269–74.

[85] Michael Strachan, *The Life and Adventures of Thomas Coryate* (London: Oxford University Press, 1962), 4–5.

[86] *Thomas Coriate Trauelller for the English VVits: Greeting. From the Court of the Great Mogul, Resident at the Towne of Asmere, in Easterne India* (London, 1616), 44.

[87] Philip Gaskell, *A New Introduction to Bibliography* (New Castle, Del.: Oak Knoll Press, 1995; first published 1972), 59.

he scarce afforded himself '2 howers rest sometimes of the whole 24'. We may afford Coryate a degree of licence here. The letter undoubtedly exaggerates, but no reader of the *Crudities* could deny his indefatigability, the sheer number of sites visited, inscriptions transcribed, and manners observed. His purpose in the letter was to convince Hickes of the closeness and extent of these observations, and thereby expedite publication of the work. He was perhaps attempting to counter that clownish reputation which in other company he so assiduously cultivated.

These 'remarkable antiquities' seem to have taken various forms. Coryate was a keen bibliophile, and throughout the *Crudities* he comments on libraries and collections across Europe. Thus at Lyon he was shown the library of the Jesuit College, where the most notable book was 'the King of Spaines Bible, which was bestowed on them by the French King *Henry* the fourth', whilst at Venice he paid his respects at an even greater bibliographical fane. A Venetian youth, knowing that Coryate 'was a great admirer and curious obseruer of auncient monuments', brought him into 'a fair chamber, which was the next roome to Cardinall *Bessarions* Library, so famous for auncient manuscripts bothe Greeke and Latin'.[88] Coryate knew his history of humanism well enough to recognize the significance of the place. But his greatest bibliographical discovery was at Heidelberg, where he was shown the Palatine Library by Jan Gruter. Coryate's description of this library combines his customary attention to architectural detail with a large dose of bibliophilic awe:

A place most beautifull, and diuided into two very large and stately roomes that are singular well furnished with store of bookes of all faculties. Here are so many auncient manuscripts, especially of the Greeke and Latin Fathers of the Church, as no Librarie of all Christendome, no not that of the Vatican of Rome nor Cardinall *Bessarions* of Venice can compare with it.[89]

One manuscript in particular caught his attention, 'a faire large parchment booke written by the great grandfather of *Fredericke* the fourth that was the Count Palatine when I was there'. But Coryate does not leave his description at that. His fascination with libraries was not simply for what they preserved of the past. It was also for what they might transmit to the future. For Coryate, this fascination was not retrospective at all. Unlike Earle's antiquary, Coryate does not condemn the printed book as 'a nouelty of this latter age'; nor does he share that

---

[88] Coryate, *Crudities*, sigs. G8ᵛ, P2ᵛ. Cardinal Bessarion's library contained important manuscripts which he brought to Italy from Constantinople, and which made a number of Greek works, including Platonic and Neoplatonic texts, available once again in western Europe. Following Bessarion's donation of the manuscripts to the senate of Venice in 1468, the collection formed the nucleus of the Biblioteca Marciana in the city; see Lotte Labowsky, *Bessarion's Library and the Biblioteca Marciana: Six Early Inventories* (Rome: Edizioni di storia e letteratura, 1979).
[89] Coryate, *Crudities*, sig. 2N4ᵛ.

unfortunate taste for 'Moth-eaten' manuscripts and 'dust'.[90] He draws a contrast between libraries in antiquity and the present day:

> I beleeue none of those notable Libraries in ancient times so celebrated by many worthy historians, neither that of the royall *Ptolomies* of Alexandria burnt by *Iulius Cæsar*, nor that of King *Eumenes* at Pergamum in Greece, nor *Augustus* his Palatine in Rome, nor *Traians* Vlpian, nor that of *Serenus Sammonicus*, which he left to the Emperor *Gordianus* the younger, nor any other whatsoeuer in the whole world before the time of the inuention of printing, could compare with this Palatine.[91]

Present and future preservation is contrasted with antique loss. It is not a coincidence that the first ancient library in Coryate's list is the most famous lost library of them all.[92] Coryate's celebration of the Palatine Library also becomes a triumphant heralding of its modernity. It is the presence of printed books which marks it off from its illustrious predecessors, the invention of printing which guarantees its repository pre-eminence.

Coryate's 'remarkable antiquities' also encompass inscriptions, an interest which he shared with his guide at Heidelberg. Monumental inscriptions, which he gathered on his travels, are scattered throughout the *Crudities*, so that the work becomes a kind of elaborate epigraphic collection. It is the literary equivalent of Gruter's massive *Inscriptiones antiquae totius orbi Romani* (1602–3). Coryate's epigraphic interest is apparent from the first stage of his journey. At Calais, where he arrived on the afternoon of 14 May 1608 after a particularly rough crossing from Dover, he notes little apart from the 'faire monument of an English Lady', Mary Wentworth, who had died there in 1554. After transcribing the 'Epitaph cut in the stone vpon it', he comments: 'These were the words that were ingrauen vpon her Tombe, but so intricate and harsh, that euery Latinist cannot vnderstand them.'[93] In the rest of the book he follows suit, liberally sprinkling his descriptions of the towns visited with ancient and modern inscriptions.

At Padua, which Coryate visited over four days in June 1608, and one of the longest sections in the *Crudities*, this interest threatens to overwhelm. One of the attractions of the city for him was its association with the Roman historian Livy. Thus his visit to what was known as Livy's House was a highlight of his time in the city. 'For had it beene much worse then it was,' he asserts, 'I should haue esteemed it pretious, because it bred that man whom I doe as much esteeme, and whose memory I as greatly honour as any Ethnick Historiographer whatsoeuer, either Greeke or Latin.' Coryate acknowledges that 'some carping criticke' may object to his claim that Livy's House still stood, when he had already noted more

---

[90] Earle, *Micro-cosmographie*, sigs. C2ᵛ–C3ʳ.
[91] Coryate, *Crudities*, sigs. 2N4ᵛ–2N5ʳ.
[92] For a brief history of the library of Alexandria, see Lionel Casson, *Libraries in the Ancient World* (New Haven and London: Yale University Press, 2001), 31–47.
[93] Coryate, *Crudities*, sig. D3ʳ⁻ᵛ.

than once that Padua 'hath beene eftsoones sacked, and consumed with fire'. He therefore tries to pre-empt such criticism, but his response is hardly convincing, as it ranges from the conjectural to the frankly absurd. First, he notes that 'the very antiquity of the structure doth signifie it is very ancient'. Next, he reports that 'it is a receiued opinion of the Citizens of Padua, and the learned men of the Vniuersity that *Liuie* dwelt therein'. Third, and an extraordinary argument, he is 'persuaded that the most barbarous people that euer wasted Padua, as the Hunnes and the Longobardes, were not so voide of humanity, but that in the very middest of their depopulating and fiering of the City, they would endeuour to spare the house of *Liuie* (at least if they knew which was his) and to preserve it to posterity for a monument of so famous a man'.[94] The parenthetical aside suggests that Coryate recognized the fatuousness of his last argument. His tongue is firmly in his cheek. The reflection is just the kind of witty remark which characterizes the *Crudities*, interspersed with and enlivening the antiquities and observations gathered therein.

Livy's House, which belonged to a Paduan gentleman named Bassano, is presented as a repository of inscribed statuary. By the gate, 'there is erected a stony statue of *Caius Sempronius* and his wife, with very auncient letters ingrauen in the stone vnder the statues'. Coryate imagines this statue in terms of that fundamental struggle between art and time. Thus its inscription was 'so eaten and consumed' by 'deuouring time' that he 'could vnderstand but little of it'. But time had not vanquished the statue altogether, and Coryate was able to recover snatches of the inscription and thereby identify it: 'But this I am sure was at the beginning *C. Sempronius*. Also in the same inscription I read *Vxori Clodiæ*. And these figures XXXVI. and these a little after XXVI.'[95] Within Livy's House there were greater riches still, as Coryate found 'many ancient monuments, and sundry Greeke and Latin inscriptions of great antiquity in stones'. These included 'a fine peece of marble in great capitall letters; VRATORIS ILLYRICI', 'a spread eagle fairely displayed in an olde peece of free stone', and 'a stately armes of some worthy auncient Romane Gentleman ... made in stone'. Most remarkable of all was 'a very auncient little pillar of free stone square' with a Greek inscription, which Coryate describes as 'one of the auncientest monuments of all Christendome', believing it to have been 'made in the time of *Æneas*'. The evidence is the inscription itself: 'the very wordes themselues seeme to import so much, which I literally interpret thus: The end of *Æneas* passing or sayling ouer the sea.' Finally, Coryate provides an ingenious back story to explain how the inscription came to be in the house: 'This beeing so remarkable a monument, I thinke some one of the auncient Roman Emperors might get it into his handes; and so finally *Liuie* being a great louer and searcher of antiquities, and very gracious with the Emperors *Augustus* and *Tiberius*, might request it of them, and bring it to his

---

[94] Ibid., sig. M6^{r-v}.   [95] Ibid., sig. M7^r.

house at Padua.'[96] We are, remarkably, back where we started: with Livy and his ownership of the house.

It is hard to know how seriously Coryate intended this to be taken. The story of Livy's House was an old and persistent one, and certainly not Coryate's invention—a nineteenth-century guidebook calls it 'an immemorial tradition'[97]—but his description of the house and its gardens is undercut by his reflections and inferences. His endorsement of the Greek inscription, 'Surely it is probable enough that this might be in the time of *Æneas*', is hardly ringing. And his tale of Livy's acquisition of the inscription is surely a tall one. There are any number of more obvious explanations for how this inscription came to be in a collection of antiquities in a house in Padua. Coryate cannot, therefore, be said to share the purely documentary purpose of some of the antiquaries. He wanted to amuse his readers as well as inform them.

But Coryate did nonetheless share the antiquarian urge to gather and collect traces of the past. His inscriptions are only the most obvious illustration of this. He also shared the antiquarian response to ruins, and it is to an example of this that I turn in the last part of the chapter. Six weeks after leaving Padua, Coryate arrived at Verona. As always, his description of the city is larded with inscriptions. But Verona offered greater treasures than inscribed stones, and for once Coryate's attention shifted away from epigraphy. 'So many notable memorable monuments are to be seene in this noble city of Verona,' he asseverates, 'as no Italian citie whatsoeuer (Rome excepted) can shew the like.'[98] One monument, though, quickly emerges as 'the worthiest and most remarkable of all': the Roman amphitheatre. The amphitheatre therefore becomes the focus, the central point, of his account of Verona. Few other monuments in the *Crudities* are afforded such a detailed or long description.

Throughout the description Coryate vacillates between bemoaning the ruin of the amphitheatre and restoring it to its former glory. The accompanying engraving by William Hole is a triumphant, if fundamentally flawed, restoration (Fig. 5.3). 'I haue expressed a picture in this place,' Coryate writes, 'according to the forme of it, as it flourished in the time of the Roman Mornarchy.'[99] He presents to his readers not the ruin which he visited in August 1608, but a reconstruction of the monument, as he imagined it in its heyday. This is reinforced by the caption to the engraving: 'A Delineation of the Amphitheater of Verona expressed in that forme wherein it flourished in the tyme of the Roman Monarchie, only the greatest part of the outward wall which inclosed it round about, is omitted'. Unfortunately, Hole seems to have confused the amphitheatre

---

[96] Coryate, *Crudities*, sigs. M7ʳ–M8ᵛ.
[97] *Hand-Book for Travellers in Northern Italy: States of Sardinia, Lombardy and Venice, Parma and Piacenza, Modena, Lucca, Massa-Carrara, and Tuscany, as far as the Val d'Arno* (London: John Murray, 1842), 308.
[98] Coryate, *Crudities*, sig. Z5ʳ.
[99] Ibid.

with the Roman theatre, three-quarters of a mile away on the opposite bank of the river Adige, and his engraving, which follows a woodcut in Torello Saraina's *De origine et amplitudine ciuitatis Veronæ* (1540) (Fig. 5.4), depicts the latter.[100] The description which follows tells a different story. The confidence in the antiquarian project, implicit in the engraving, is kept in check, as Coryate turns to what he had actually seen: 'Neyther doe I thinke that antiquity could euer shew a fayrer piece of worke for an Amphitheater; but it is very ruinous at this time.' Initially, it seems as if he is thinking about the physical state of the monument. He turns out, though, to have had a broader target in mind: 'So that it hath lost more then halfe of his pristine glory: it is vncertaine who was the first founder thereof. That it was built by one of the Roman Emperours euery man beleeueth, but by whom no Chronicle, Annals, or ancient History doth certainly record.'[101] The first clause here is the pivot, as Coryate moves from the physical destruction of the amphitheatre to the more profound loss, which is the forgetting of its founder. There is no text, 'no Chronicle, Annals, or ancient History',

FIG. 5.3. 'A Delineation of the Amphitheater of Verona'. Thomas Coryate, *Coryats Crudities* (London, 1611), opposite p. 311. Cambridge University Library, SSS. 29. 17. Reproduced by kind permission of the Syndics of Cambridge University Library

---

[100] Strachan, *Life and Adventures*, 60. Saraina's woodcut is correctly titled 'THEATRVM IN RIPA ATHESIS POSITVM'.
[101] Coryate, *Crudities*, sig. Z5^v.

FIG. 5.4. The theatre at Verona. *T. Saraynæ . . . de origine et amplitudine ciuitatis Veronæ* (Verona, 1540). Cambridge University Library, F154. a. 2. 1. Reproduced by kind permission of the Syndics of Cambridge University Library

to provide the key. The tried and tested method is rendered impotent. The amphitheatre is saved from total oblivion only by '*Torellus Sariana* a learned man borne in Verona, who hath written certaine bookes of the antiquities of this city'. The antiquary Saraina has saved the monument from time; his books have preserved it for posterity.

The remainder of Coryate's description is taken up with surveying the remains of the amphitheatre and imagining it in its pomp, conjoining a confidence in the testamentary and affective power of material remains with that age-old lament at the ravages of time. On the one hand, he asserts that the amphitheatre 'hath as yet many notable things to be seene, which doe argue the singuler beauty thereof when it flourished in his prime'. Not only can the ruins be restored, but they also have a voice, as they 'argue' or betoken the splendour of the original building. Yet, on the other, he emphasizes how illusory this restoration is. It is an act of conjuration, a visual projection, and a rhetorical trick. He understands that restitution can only go so far. Nevertheless, he does seem to have believed that the antiquary and traveller had important preservative roles, and this may be the explanation for the wealth and precision of architectural detail that he then provides. Like the writers discussed in Chapter 4, Coryate set great store by mensuration, and he took particular care over measuring the amphitheatre. The *cavea* (the auditorium) is described as 'in the forme of an egge, sharpe at the ends, and broade at the sides' and 'in length nine & thirty perches, in bredth two and twenty and halfe'. Lest any reader question these measurements, Coryate adds that he 'did exactly obserue the length and bredth of it'. He also cites the measurements of others. We learn, for instance, that 'from north to south it is thought to be three hundred and threescore foote long: and from east to west three hundred and forty foote broad'.[102] He is equally precise about the different kinds of marble used in its construction and also by the Veronese in their restoration work. A distinctive pink marble seems to have particularly caught his eye. If Coryate regrets the ruin of the amphitheatre—its outer wall, for example, is described as 'but a little fragment'—he concludes his description with a triumphant statement of its unique wonder. 'It is a worke of such admirable magnificence,' he writes, 'that as I neuer saw the like before, so I thinke in all my future trauels (which I determine God willing to vndertake both in Christendome & Paganisme) I shall neuer see a fairer.'[103]

Just as in Moscardo's catalogue, which I discussed in the Introduction, the amphitheatre at Verona becomes a locus for reflection on antiquarian activity.[104] Coryate meditates on the nature of preservation and the passage of time, on what the antiquary could recover and what was irrevocably lost. His description also illustrates the approaches that he took to the monuments which he encountered on his travels and the strategies that he employed in writing about them. If his meditation is contradictory and sometimes confusing, this may simply reflect the relatively undigested nature of the *Crudities*. Coryate seems to have revised his travel notes far less than Sandys, although his work is more artful than its title suggests. He too embellished his observations with his reading. In the case of the Verona amphitheatre, this meant primarily Saraina, but also the short description in Franciscus Schottus's *Itinerari Italiae* (1600), a small duodecimo travel guide to Italy and its antiquities.[105] Moreover, the contradictions may also reflect a peculiar duality of the antiquarian mindset, the coexistence of imaginative and documentary ends, impulses which, to modern eyes at least, seem to pull in different directions.

Coryate and Sandys are just two examples of a larger phenomenon. This chapter could have also considered Fynes Moryson, for instance, whose *Itinerary* (1617) recounts four journeys which he made in the 1590s, and manifests a similar concern to document antiquities. Moryson did not travel abroad specifically, or even primarily, for this reason. But like Coryate and Sandys, in his published account he faithfully records unearthed ruins, remains, and statues. Antiquities, after all, as Bacon argued, were fit matter for any traveller and were to be observed by all. The peripatetic education of young men had an antiquarian element as well as the more important political and ethical ones. And this element would only increase, as the seventeenth century went on. Peacham's prescription, just a few years later, is proof of that. But Coryate and Sandys also attest to a broader concern of this book, the permeation of antiquarian thought in the wider literary culture of early modern England. From Coryate's epitaphs

---

[102] Ibid., sig. Z7^{r-v}. [103] Ibid., sig. Z8^r.
[104] For Moscardo and his catalogue, see p. 7 above.
[105] Franciscus Schottus, *Itinerari Italiae rerumque Romanarum libri tres* (Antwerp, 1600), 36–41.

to Sandys's etymologies, these travellers shared in that project to rescue fragments of history from the shipwreck of time. Travel, always an important part of antiquarian activity, started to take on a new significance. What had begun in the sixteenth century as an essentially national project, in response to a set of specific historical and political circumstances, now reached far beyond the shores of Albion.

6

Antiquarian Readers: The Case of Drayton and Selden

The previous chapters of this book have focused on writers, on the methods used by antiquaries to organize, support, and interpret their material. They have explored antiquarian interests and methodologies, and have examined the practice of antiquarian writing. In this chapter I shift attention from writing to reading, in order to consider some of the ways in which antiquaries spoke to their readers and also some of the ways in which those readers in turn interpreted and responded to their books. Any account of the reception of antiquarianism in early modern England, let alone any account such as this book, which argues for its ubiquity in the literary and intellectual cultures of that time, has to take account of antiquarian readers as well as writers. To examine these issues, I therefore turn in this chapter to the most antiquarian of seventeenth-century poets, Michael Drayton, and explore both how his works responded to and might be conceived as a reading of antiquarian scholarship, and how they themselves were read and interpreted by subsequent scholars.

There are a number of reasons why Drayton makes a compelling case study in antiquarian reading. First and foremost, his major work, *Poly-Olbion* (1612 and 1622), that extraordinary evocation of the historical landscape of early modern England and Wales, offers the most consistent literary engagement with antiquarian scholarship and methodology in the period. Drayton, as Fritz Levy and George Boon argue, was an astute and assiduous reader of the antiquaries, although his work is also more than just the spin-off, the *Britannia* in alexandrines, that they suggest.[1] Second, when the first part of *Poly-Olbion* was printed in 1612, it appeared with an antiquarian commentary of its own, with the annotations of an antiquarian reader. Drayton had commissioned his friend John Selden, the scholar famously described by John Lightfoot, Master of St Catharine's College, Cambridge, as 'the learnedst man on earth', to provide a commentary to the poem, to explicate historical uncertainties and illuminate historical difficulties.[2] In this way, from the outset Drayton foregrounds reading

---

[1] Levy, *Tudor Historical Thought*, 222; Boon, 'Camden and the *Britannia*', 17.
[2] Quoted in Parry, *The Trophies of Time*, 95. Our knowledge of this remarkable scholar has been transformed by G. J. Toomer's intellectual biography *John Selden: A Life in Scholarship* (Oxford: Oxford University Press, 2009).

as part of the antiquarian project. Just as his own work can be said to read Camden, Stow, and the others, so that work is in turn read by their greatest seventeenth-century successor, Selden. Third, despite the perception of some scholars, Drayton's works turn out to have been both read and used as sources by later antiquaries.[3] In short, therefore, Drayton was both an antiquarian reader in his own right and the subject of antiquarian reading.

Nevertheless, this antiquarianism has not always been recognized or appreciated. Drayton has often been characterized as an intellectually conservative writer, derided as an awkward Elizabethan throwback, who, by the time of his death in 1631, was badly out of kilter with the times.[4] Historians, in particular, have been critical, attacking his works for not being antiquarian enough. T. D. Kendrick, for example, described *Poly-Olbion* as 'the most spirited and the most direct exposition in the seventeenth century of the factual content of the Trojan legend'.[5] For those critical of Drayton's scholarship, Selden's annotations come as a welcome corrective, saving the work from its most fanciful excesses, and carefully and consistently emending its many errors.[6] These scholars describe a dispute between the poem and its annotations, a struggle between poetic fancy and historical truth. In this scheme, Drayton represents the last bastion of medieval tradition, clinging to the now discredited matter of Britain and other similarly dubious legends; Selden, by contrast, is in the antiquarian vanguard, typifying the new scholarship inflected by humanist philological tradition.

These kinds of attack reflect that unfortunate teleology which pervades much recent scholarship on antiquarianism. To criticize Drayton for not being antiquarian enough, for giving too much credit to his Galfridian material, is an anachronism which says more about the modern practice of history than it does about early modern ideas of antiquarian scholarship. But to criticize Drayton for being too antiquarian, as literary critics such as Mario Praz have done, is also an anachronism.[7] We need to assess Drayton's antiquarianism on its own terms, not according to modern aesthetic and historical standards. Besides, as more recent

---

[3] For the argument that Drayton was little read and less influential, see Oliver Elton, *An Introduction to Michael Drayton* (Manchester: Spenser Society, 1895), 52; and Russell Noyes, 'Drayton's Literary Vogue Since 1631', *Indiana University Studies*, 22 (1935), 3–23. For a recent challenge to this assumption, see Jean R. Brink, *Michael Drayton Revisited* (Boston: Twayne, 1990), 129–37.

[4] Alice d'Haussy, *Poly-Olbion ou l'Angleterre vue par un élisabéthain* (Paris: Klincksieck, 1972); Richard Hardin, *Michael Drayton and the Passing of Elizabethan England* (Lawrence, Kans.: University of Kansas Press, 1973).

[5] Kendrick, *British Antiquity*, 103.

[6] Ibid.; F. Smith Fussner, *The Historical Revolution: English Historical Writing and Thought 1580–1640* (London: Routledge and Kegan Paul, 1962), 46–7; David Sandler Berkowitz, *John Selden's Formative Years: Politics and Society in Early Seventeenth-Century England* (Washington, DC: Folger Shakespeare Library, 1988), 39; and Levy, *Tudor Historical Thought*, 223.

[7] Praz, 'Michael Drayton', 107. Jack B. Oruch makes a similar argument when he asserts that antiquarian matter is 'inappropriate' for poetry; see his 'Spenser, Camden and the Poetic Marriage of Rivers', *Studies in Philology*, 64 (1967), 606–24 at 624.

scholars have shown, Drayton's relationship with Selden is more complex than these attacks would suggest. For Paul Christianson, *Poly-Olbion* is 'a lovely baroque conceit', with Drayton and Selden 'engaged in friendly discourse and debate', whilst Anne Lake Prescott emphasizes the work's dialogic qualities and the engagement between its two constituent parts.[8] The poet and annotator, they suggest, are never in straightforward opposition to one another.

To early modern readers, schooled in the dialogues of Lucian, and attuned to the dynamics of glossing and annotation, this relationship would have been more apparent. Likewise, the idea that the poems and the notes might be complementary rather than competing elements in a larger antiquarian project would have been less surprising. Collaboration, after all, as I showed in Chapter 3, was an important element of antiquarian methodology. But whereas Camden's collaborators, for instance, enabled him to make a virtue out of his ever more comprehensive repository of antiquarian knowledge, Drayton's collaboration only seems to emphasize the impossibility of completeness. In calling on Selden's help, he draws attention to the incompleteness of his own contributions. Where Camden holds out the hope of successfully restoring Britain to its antiquity, Drayton's version of the antiquarian project is altogether more effacing and much less optimistic. The antiquary, Drayton suggests, can but offer one part of the whole. There is always more to be unearthed, more to be discovered, more to be restored. There is, in short, always another voice.

In the chapter which follows, I explore the significance of Drayton's emphasis on polyphony for his reading of the antiquarian project. The chapter begins by locating Drayton in an antiquarian milieu, tracing his connections with those associated with the Elizabethan Society of Antiquaries, and demonstrating how through his early works he sought to position himself as an integral part of that circle. I then turn to *Poly-Olbion*, first showing why it should be read as an antiquarian poem, and then arguing that in its polyphony, its multiple voices and narrators, Drayton's own version of antiquarianism is to be found, a version which revels in the copiousness of antiquarian books, but which also highlights the uncertainties and irresolution that that copiousness inevitably entails. In the second part of the chapter I turn to the ways in which Drayton encodes this multifariousness in the physical structure of his printed book, in the material counterparts to the poem's many narrators: William Hole's engraved

---

[8] Paul Christianson, *Discourse on History, Law, and Governance in the Public Career of John Selden 1610–1635* (Toronto, Buffalo, and London: University of Toronto Press, 1996), 32; Anne Lake Prescott, 'Drayton's Muse and Selden's "Story": The Interfacing of Poetry and History in *Poly-Olbion*', *Studies in Philology*, 87 (1990), 128–35; and ead., 'Marginal Discourse: Drayton's Muse and Selden's "Story"', *Studies in Philology*, 88 (1991), 307–28. See also Christianson's earlier 'Young John Selden and the Ancient Constitution, ca.1610–1618', *Proceedings of the American Philosophical Society*, 128 (1984), 271–315 at 284; and Alessandra P. Maccioni, 'Il *Poly-Olbion* di Michael Drayton fra il mito dei Tudor e il *New Learning*', *Studi dell'Istituto linguistico*, 7 (1984), 17–63.

frontispiece, which appeared in every edition from the first of 1612 onwards, and, perhaps more strikingly, the annotations of Selden. In the last part of the chapter I then reflect on both what this polyphony said to Drayton's readers and imitators and what it might say about antiquarianism more generally.

'HIS TOPO-CHRONO-GRAPHICALL POEME'

In writing antiquarian poetry Drayton had a number of models to follow, albeit none conceived on as grand a scale as his *Poly-Olbion*. One possibility was Thomas Churchyard's *The Worthines of Wales* (1587), a work which in its ambition to record Welsh history and traditions clearly anticipates Drayton's project. In his epistle to the reader Churchyard summarizes the diversity of his subject matter, what he calls the 'seuerall discourses' which make up his work. These include 'the beautie & blessednes of the Countrey', 'the strength and statelynesse of their inpregnable Castles', 'their trim Townes and fine situation', 'their antiquitie, shewing from what Kings and Princes they tooke their first name and prerogatiue', and 'all maner of matters belonging to that Soyle, as Churches, Monuments, Mountaynes, Valleys, Waters, Bridges, fayre Gentlemens houses, and the rest of things whatsoeuer, may become a writers pen to touch, or a readers iudgement to knowe'.[9] The scope is intended to remind his readers that the poem belongs firmly to the antiquarian tradition; its virtue lies in its inclusiveness and encyclopedism. Thus Churchyard's text also includes actual documentary evidence, as he intersperses the poem with deeds, charters, and other records. Early in the work, for example, he recounts Edward IV's creation of Sir William Herbert as the first earl of Pembroke following the attainder of Jasper Tudor in 1468. In an act of historical ventriloquism, which anticipates Drayton's own much larger acts of ventriloquism, Churchyard begins by imagining the king's voice when he created the earldom in a succession of archaic fourteeners:

> We by this Charter, that for ours shall firme for euer remaine
> Of speciall grace and knowledge sure, sound and determinate,
> And motio*n* meere him William doe, of *Penbroke* Count create
> Erect, preferre, and vnto him the Title stile and state,
> And name thereof and dignitie, foreuer appropriate,
> As Earle of *Penbroke* and withall, we giue all rights that do
> All honors and preheminence, that state perteyne vnto:
> With which estate, stile, honor, great, and worthie dignitie,
> By cincture of a Sword, we him ennoble reallie.[10]

---

[9] Thomas Churchyard, *The Worthines of Wales* (London, 1587), sig. A2^r.
[10] Ibid., sig. B4^v.

Churchyard then switches to three stanzas of decasyllables, as he proceeds to give his own reflections on the events; the difference in metre enables him to separate historical comment from historical reconstruction. Finally, he shifts form altogether, moving from verse back to the charter itself, as he publishes the Latin text in its entirety. Without this text he fears that his readers will consider his ventriloquism just 'a tale, devisde to please the eare'. As he comments, 'The world beleeues, no more than it hath seene'.[11]

Churchyard, it seems, shared the antiquarian preference for ocular evidence of the past. He also shared the antiquarian impulse to gather together its scattered remains. *The Worthines of Wales* is haunted by a fear of loss and is knit together by a series of meditations on time. As he makes his literary progress through Wales, Churchyard encounters numerous castles and churches fallen into ruin. At Abergavenny, for example, he laments the stately castle, 'Which loe to ruyne, and wretched wracke it goes', whose 'goodly Towers, are bare and naked laft, / That cou'red were, with timber and good lead'.[12] Towards the end of the work he muses at greater length on the ravages of time, picking up in his '*A discourse of Tyme*' on the localized exempla which have run through the poem.[13] Here, he derides time in familiar language as the canker 'that all consumes to dust', the 'glutton great, that feedes on each mans store'. His anger is then channelled through his description of the town of Ruthin in Denbighshire, with which he concludes the '*Discourse*'. Where there once stood 'a noble Castle' and 'Towers most fayre', there now 'growes nothing but grasse'; the 'stones lye waste' and 'the walles seemes [*sic*] but a shell'. Yet Churchyard also challenges time, as the longer description of Ruthin which follows, 'Of Wrythen, both the Castle *and the Towne*', catalogues with precision the buildings which actually remain.[14] If time does vanquish all material remains, as Churchyard suggests, the task of the antiquary and poet is to provide a textual record for posterity. If the buildings themselves will inevitably fall into ruin, they will at least survive in the words of Churchyard's poem.

An even closer model for Drayton may have been William Vallans's *A Tale of Two Swannes* (1590). Vallans's poem, which was written in imitation of John Leland's *Cygnea cantio* (1545) and ultimately of Ausonius' *Mosella*, traces the progress of two swans down the river Lea from Ware Park in Hertfordshire to the river's mouth in the Thames.[15] As they swim, Vallans traces the course of the river and notes antiquarian curiosities on its banks:

---

[11] Ibid., sig. C1ʳ.   [12] Ibid., sig. F3ᵛ.   [13] Ibid., sig. M4ʳ⁻ᵛ.

[14] For Churchyard's perhaps surprising eye for detail, see Barbara Brown, 'Thomas Churchyard and *The Worthines of Wales*', *Anglo-Welsh Review*, 18 (1970), 131–9 at 134.

[15] For this tradition of river poetry and Drayton's position in it, see Wyman H. Herendeen, *From Landscape to Literature: The River and the Myth of Geography* (Pittsburgh, Pa.: Duquesne University Press, 1986), 288–318; for Leland's poem, see James P. Carley, 'John Leland's *Cygnea Cantio*: A Neglected Tudor River Poem', *Humanistica Lovaniensia*, 32 (1983), 225–41.

>And in this pompe, they hie them to the head,
>Whence *Lee* doth spring, not farre from *Kempton* towne,
>And swiftly coming downe through *Brooke-hall* parke,
>Leaues *Whethamsted*, so called of the corne:
>By *Bishops-Hatfield* then they come along,
>Seated not farre from antient *Verolane*:
>His Citie, that first did spend his blessed life,
>In iust maintaining of our Christian faith.[16]

It is noticeable here how Vallans augments his geography with both etymological speculation, reflecting on the origin of the name Whethamstede, and historical comment, alluding to the story of St Alban, the proto-martyr killed by the Romans at Verulamium. These are just the sorts of matter upon which the antiquaries (and also Drayton) comment.[17] With his consistent attention to antiquarian matter Vallans does for the river Lea what Drayton attempts to do on a much larger scale. He even provides a model for the annotations, as *A Tale of Two Swannes* also includes a historical commentary or glossary, titled 'A Commentarie Or Exposition of certain proper names vsed in this Tale'. This purports to explain the etymologies of various place names, but, like Selden's annotations, it quickly exceeds its remit. Thus for Verulamium, for example, Vallans expounds his allusion to the martyrdom of St Alban and explains the consequent etymology, but also goes beyond his glossatorial intention to record that 'there be nothing left' of the ancient city 'but the ruins and rubbish of the walles'.[18]

Another formative influence on Drayton may have been Edmund Spenser's projected topographical poem *Epithamalion Thamesis*. Spenser described this project in the third of his *Three Proper, and wittie, familiar Letters* (1580) to Gabriel Harvey. The poem was to be an account of the marriage of the Thames and Medway, and it would 'describe all the Rivers throughout Englande, whyche came to this Wedding, and their righte names, and right passage, etc'.[19] The poem itself never appeared, although Spenser did go some way to fulfilling his plan in his description of the marriage of the Thames and Medway in Book 4 of

---

[16] William Vallans, *A Tale of Two Swannes. Wherein is comprehended the original and increase of the riuer Lee commonly called Ware-riuer: together, with the antiquitie of sundrie places and townes seated vpon the same* (London, 1590), sig. A4^r.

[17] Vallans himself seems to have admired his antiquarian contemporaries, praising Stow, for example, in a different poem for his 'paynes to seeke olde wrytten bookes' and 'care to kepe old monumen*tes* / that els had bene but lost'; see a 'Short Poem of Will. Vallans, Salter; as it seems, upon John Stowes lack of Reward, for compiling his Survey of London', BL, MS Harley 367, fo. 129^r (ll. 21, 23–4).

[18] Vallans, *Tale of Two Swannes*, sig. B4^r.

[19] Edmund Spenser, *Three Proper, and wittie, familiar Letters: lately passed betweene two Vniuersitie men: touching the Earthquake in Aprill last, and our English refourmed Versifying*, in *Spenser's Prose Works*, 17.

The Faerie Queene (1596). Here, his focus is firmly etymological, as he lists the rivers in attendance at the marriage and explains the origins of their names. They range from the humble Mole, 'that like a nousling Mole doth make / His way still vnder ground', to 'that huge Riuer, which doth beare his name / Of warlike Amazons, which does possesse the same'.[20] *Poly-Olbion*, which includes a river marriage of its own in the form of the nuptials of the Thame and Isis in Song XV, may have taken its inspiration from here. Drayton may also have taken inspiration from Spenser's source: Camden's fragmentary poem *De connubia Tamae et Isis*, which was published in different versions in successive editions of the *Britannia*.

Drayton seems to have been at work on *Poly-Olbion* for a considerable period of time. As early as 1594 the germ of his idea for the poem was born. That year the first edition of his sonnet sequence *Idea* appeared, and amongst its fifty-one poems there is one, 'Amour 24', which has been described aptly as 'a miniature *Poly-Olbion* in sonnet form'.[21] This poem is a catalogue of fourteen English rivers, each of which is defined by a geographical or historical association. The river Lea, for example, 'brags of *Danish* blood', an allusion to the defeat of the Danes by King Alfred at Ware, whilst the Thames 'for shyps & Swans is crowned' and the Trent 'for Foords & fishe renowned'.[22] By the end of the decade Drayton's friends seem to have known about his project. Thus in 1598 Francis Meres, for example, who may well have seen drafts of *Poly-Olbion*, mentions it by name in his *Palladis Tamia*: 'As Joan. Honterus in Latin verse writ 3. Bookes of Cosmography with Geographicall Tables: so Michael Drayton is now penning in English verse a Poem called Polu-olbion Geographical and Hydrographicall of all the forests, woods, mountaines, fountaines, rivers, lakes, flouds, bathes and springs that be in England.'[23] Johannes Honter, a cartographer and cosmographer from Kronstadt, was the author of the *Rudimenta cosmographica* (1530), a work originally written in prose, but later revised as four (*pace* Meres) books of Latin hexameters. The *Rudimenta cosmographica* provides a taxonomy of the natural and celestial worlds, as Honter catalogues the stars, maps the heavens, classifies the cities, peoples, rivers, mountains, animals, and plants of the earth, lists various parts of the human anatomy, and enumerates different illnesses and diseases. Meres's comparison is certainly learned, placing Drayton's work in a very particular tradition of scholarly poetry, but in its encyclopedism the *Rudimenta cosmographica* does provide an

---

[20] Edmund Spenser, *The Faerie Queene*, ed. Hamilton, IV. xi. 32. 8–9, and IV. xi. 21. 8–9.
[21] Robert Arnold Aubin, *Topographical Poetry in XVIII-Century England* (New York: The Modern Language Association, 1936), 19.
[22] Michael Drayton, 'Amour 24', *Ideas Mirrour*, in *The Works of Michael Drayton*, i, ll. 12, 1, and 3.
[23] Francis Meres, *Palladis Tamia* (London, 1598), sig. 2O1ʳ. For Drayton's friendship with Meres, see Bernard H. Newdigate, *Michael Drayton and his Circle* (Oxford: Basil Blackwell, 1961; first published 1941), 93.

illuminating parallel for Drayton's monument to the history and topography of Britain.

Moreover, Drayton himself seems to have invited this kind of scholarly association for all his historical works. Thus even *Peirs Gaveston* (1593–4), the first of his historical poems and only his third work to appear in print, elicits this type of reading. The work is one of his four *Legends*, long narrative poems on historical subjects which subscribe to the Ciceronian idea of history as *magistra vitae*.[24] It is written in the style of the *Mirror for Magistrates*, as the ghost of Gaveston rises from hell to narrate a life of vanity, dissoluteness, and effeminacy, and to warn the poem's readers not to follow the same course. *Peirs Gaveston* is the opposite of one of Plutarch's exemplary lives: it is a moralizing lesson in the dangers of self-serving careerism, blind ambition, and sexual excess. In a later edition, *The Legend of Pierce Gaveston* (1619), Drayton makes the lesson even clearer through a comment in his prefatory epistle: 'In PIERCE of Gaveston there is given to the Minions, and Creatures of Princes, a very faire warning, to use their Grace with their Royall Patrons, modestly.'[25] On the face of it, therefore, the poem would seem to have little in the way of scholarly or antiquarian credentials. Yet in a note appended to the poem Drayton emphasizes his exhaustive research and his use of authentic, original material, asserting that he has relied upon sources only from 'the tyme of Edward the second, wherein he only florisht, or immediatly after, in the golden raigne of Edward the third, when as yet his memory was fresh in every mans mouthe'.[26] These sources include early chronicles such as the *Annales Paulini*, the *Vita Edwardi*, and Johannes de Trokolowe's *Annales*.[27] Importantly, Drayton also informs his readers of where he got hold of these manuscripts. When researching the poem he had, we discover, 'recourse to some especiall collections, gathered by the industrious labours of John Stow, a diligent Chronigrapher of our time'.[28] Stow had amassed a vast library of books and manuscripts, which he put at the disposal of a large network of friends and habitually lent to antiquaries, historians, lawyers, and poets.[29] Drayton's note signals to his readers that he too was part of this scholarly network.

---

[24] Cicero, *De oratore*, trans. E. W. Sutton and H. Rackham, 3 vols. (Loeb Classical Library; Cambridge, Mass.: Harvard University Press, 1967; first published in this edition 1942), II. ix. 36.
[25] Michael Drayton, *The Legends of Robert, Duke of Normandie. Matilda the Faire. Pierce Gaveston, Earle of Cornwall. Thomas Cromwell, Earle of Essex*, in *The Works of Michael Drayton*, ii. 382.
[26] Michael Drayton, *Peirs Gaveston*, in *The Works of Michael Drayton*, i. 208.
[27] See Kathleen Tillotson's commentary on the poem in *The Works of Michael Drayton*, v. 25.
[28] Drayton, *Peirs Gaveston*, 208.
[29] Barrett L. Beer, *Tudor England Observed: The World of John Stow* (Stroud: Sutton, 1998), 9–13; and Oliver Harris, 'Stow and the Contemporary Antiquarian Network', in Ian Gadd and Alexandra Gillespie (eds.), *John Stow (1525–1605) and the Making of the English Past* (London: British Library, 2004), 27–35.

There are obvious reasons why Drayton might have wanted the cachet that tapping into this network could bring. For one thing, it bestows an intellectual authority upon his poem which it would otherwise undoubtedly lack. For another, it gives an authenticity to his boast of his research *ad fontes*. Most importantly, it also allows him to reify through the fixity of print his connections with antiquarian circles. Almost as soon as he had arrived in London in 1590, Drayton seems to have moved in an antiquarian milieu, and he numbered Camden, William Lambarde, and Stow himself as three of his earliest London friends.[30] By alluding to his easy access to Stow's library, Drayton positions himself alongside those luminaries as a credible antiquarian writer. He can, therefore, both indicate his conception of the work at hand and, perhaps as importantly, generate certain expectations for any forthcoming or future works. Almost in spite of the poem, in spite of its material and genre, the figure of Drayton the antiquary begins to emerge from his first historical text.

That figure fully emerged some twenty years later in *Poly-Olbion*. This work announces itself on its letterpress title page as 'A Chorographicall Description of Tracts, Rivers, Mountaines, Forests, and other Parts of this renowned Isle of Great Britaine, With intermixture of the most Remarquable Stories, Antiquities, Wonders, Rarityes, Pleasures, and Commodities of the same'.[31] *Poly-Olbion*, in other words, promises a description of the geography and history of Britain, a survey of natural and artificial wonders, an account of rarities past and present. The poem 'Geographicall and Hydrographicall' described by Meres has become a poem chorographical and antiquarian instead.[32] The copiousness heralded by the title page was later emphasized by George Wither in 'To his Noble Friend, Michael Drayton, upon his Topo-chrono-graphicall Poeme', the commendatory verses which he wrote for the second part of *Poly-Olbion*, published in 1622. Wither's coinage, 'Topo-chrono-graphicall', encapsulates the multifariousness of Drayton's work, its blending of geography and history, and its mapping of space and time. Wither's poem imagines the readers of *Poly-Olbion* travelling 'From CORNWAL's Foreland to the Cliffs of DOVER', transported in their minds'

---

[30] Newdigate, *Michael Drayton and his Circle*, 92–4.

[31] Michael Drayton, *Poly-Olbion*, in *The Works of Michael Drayton*, iv, p. i*. The letterpress title page did not appear until the second issue of 1613 (*STC* 7227); see Bent Juel-Jensen, 'Bibliography of the Early Editions of the Writings of Michael Drayton', in *Works of Michael Drayton*, v. 265–306 at 300–2.

[32] The Greek mathematician and geographer Ptolemy defined chorography as the discipline which 'sets out the individual localities, each one independently and by itself, registering practically everything down to the least thing therein (for example, harbours, towns, districts, branches of principal rivers, and so on)', see Claudius Ptolemy, *Geography: An Annotated Translation of the Theoretical Chapters*, trans. J. Lennart Berggren and Alexander Jones (Princeton and Oxford: Princeton University Press, 2000), 1. i. For chorography in the early modern period, see Richard Helgerson, *Forms of Nationhood: The Elizabethan Writing of England* (Chicago and London: University of Chicago Press, 1992), 107–47; and William Keith Hall, 'From Chronicle to Chorography: Truth, Narrative, and the Antiquarian Enterprise in Renaissance England' (Ph.D. diss., University of North Carolina, Chapel Hill, 1995).

eyes by this 'winged PEGASUS'. With its diverse subject matter Wither has seen 'More goodly Prospects' in four days reading than he 'could have known / In foure yeares Travailes'.[33] The poem is the perfect material for the armchair traveller, a superabundant travel guide which enables its readers to journey back and forth across the country without having to move from their seats, without the hassle of having to make their own antiquarian tours.

Wither emphasizes the diversity of *Poly-Olbion* in the catalogue of its subject matter which immediately follows:

> The famous Rivers, the delightsome Fountaines;
> The fruitfull Vallies, the steepe-rising Mountaines;
> The new-built Towres, the ancient-ruin'd Walls;
> The wholsome Baths, the bedds of Mineralls;
> The nigh-worne Monuments of former Ages;
> The Workes of Peace, the Marks of Civill-rages;
> The Woods, the Forrests, and the open Plaines,
> With whatsoe're this spacious Land containes,
> For Profit, or for Pleasure: I o're looke,
> (As from one Station) when I read thy Booke.[34]

As Wither reads *Poly-Olbion*, he travels geographically and also historically. He encounters 'famous Rivers', 'delightsome Fountaines', 'fruitfull Vallies', and 'steepe-rising Mountaines', but he also observes the monuments of men, the 'new-built Towres', 'ancient-ruin'd Walls', and 'wholsome Baths'. What is striking here is his emphasis upon the organization of his journey. For all its mass of material, *Poly-Olbion* is not without direction; the reader does not travel in the dark. This organization is mirrored in the verse itself, as both the rhyme scheme and the succession of strong caesurae highlight the things that Wither encounters as he reads. Just as the catalogue itself is ordered by its form, so that catalogue in turns bestows order upon the much longer poem which follows. Wither's poem draws attention to the encyclopedism of *Poly-Olbion*, and therefore also to its kinship with early modern antiquarian books, but also underscores that the work is more than just an amorphous repository of topographical and historical knowledge, more than just a reference work for readers to consult on a specific subject. It might take 'foure dayes' to read *Poly-Olbion* from start to finish, but Wither's poem advocates precisely that time-consuming approach.

The multifariousness which Wither highlights is perhaps best illustrated by the poem's abundant historical voices. Invariably these are voices inflected by the localism which Claire McEachern has called one of the hallmarks of the poem.[35]

---

[33] George Wither, 'To his Noble Friend, Michael Drayton, Esquire, upon his Topo-chronographicall Poeme', in *Poly-Olbion*, ll. 1–6.
[34] Ibid., ll. 7–16.
[35] Claire McEachern, *The Poetics of English Nationhood, 1590–1612* (Cambridge: Cambridge University Press, 1996), 139.

Welsh nymphs, for example, sing of British and Welsh history, whilst Welsh rivers recite the bardic songs of yore. The river Wye, the most loquacious of Drayton's Welsh rivers, praises the bards for preserving traditions, for transmitting the deeds and descents of long dead ancestors, for saving the past from the destructive ravages of time:

> O memorable Bards, of mixt blood, which still
> Posteritie shall praise for your so wondrous skill,
> That in your noble Songs, the long Descents have kept
> Of your great Heroës, else in Lethe that had slept,
> With theirs whose ignorant pride your labours have disdain'd;
> How much from time, and them, how bravelie have you gain'd![36]

Drayton fashions the Wye here as a recognizably Welsh voice. Her song reflects the concerns of her compatriots, a localism which says less about Drayton's own historical beliefs and more about Welsh traditions. Her words recall, for example, Lodowick Lloyd's praise of the bards in his commendatory verses for Henry Perry's *Egluryn Phraethineb* (1595), a Welsh treatise on rhetoric. For Lloyd, the 'Brittaines may their Bardi brag, and yeeld them guerdon due; / which pend their praise, advanc'd their fame, & did their names renue'.[37] His words speak of a fierce local pride, a specifically Welsh interest in the bards as record-keepers and guardians of genealogical descent, as preservers of the national past. Thus when the river Wye proceeds to draw on their songs to defend the matter of Britain, it is because she is Welsh, not because Drayton is a poor or old-fashioned historian. As a Welsh river, and a river concerned specifically with Welsh history, the Wye's use of bardic songs is entirely fitting.

Drayton's own interest in the bards is well documented.[38] Elsewhere in *Poly-Olbion* he praises them as musicians who 'in their sacred rage / Recorded the Descents, and acts of everie Age', and revels in the strange rhythms ('Englins', 'Cowiths', and 'Owdells'), the 'Silver Harpe', and eisteddfodau of their sixteenth-century descendants.[39] For one scholar, John Curran, this interest stems from Drayton's determination to defend the matter of Britain at all costs. Thus he portrays Drayton as a writer resisting the incursions of antiquarianism with 'the

---

[36] Drayton, *Poly-Olbion*, VI. 259–64. For Drayton's Welsh sources, see Robert Ralston Cawley, 'Drayton's Use of Welsh History', *Studies in Philology*, 22 (1925), 234–55; and I. Gourvitch, 'The Welsh Element in the *Poly-Olbion*: Drayton's Sources', *Review of English Studies*, 4 (1928), 69–77.

[37] Henry Perry, *Egluryn Phraethineb. sebh, Dosparth ar Retoreg, vn o'r saith gelbhydhyd, yn dysculhuniaith ymadrodd, a'i pherthynassau* (London, 1595), sig. b2ʳ.

[38] See Paul Gerhard Buchloh, *Michael Drayton: Barde und Historiker, Politiker und Prophet* (Neumünster: Karl Wachholtz, 1964).

[39] Drayton, *Poly-Olbion*, IV. 171–2, 181–4. At the eisteddfodau of 1523 and 1567 a silver harp had been the prize for the top performer; see Richard Suggett, 'Vagabonds and Minstrels in Sixteenth-Century Wales', in Adam Fox and Daniel Woolf (eds.), *The Spoken Word: Oral Culture in Britain 1500–1750* (Manchester and New York: Manchester University Press, 2002), 138–72 at 153–5.

best tools at his command: bards and druids'.[40] But this argument ignores the localism of *Poly-Olbion*, the importance which Drayton attached to establishing authentic regional voices. To identify Drayton with his narrator, to take the river Wye as the authorial mouthpiece, is to miss the point of his polyphonic poem and underestimate the complexity and variety of the historical voices at play. The Wye is a carefully ventriloquized regional voice, and as such she represents just one perspective on the past.

Curran's argument also ignores the interest of the antiquaries themselves in the bards. The bards' origins and name, their roles and duties, all attracted antiquarian attention. Thomas Hearne, for example, included a fragment on the bards in his *Curious Discourses*, which he titled '*Mr.* JONES *his Answeares to Mr.* TATE's *Questions*'. Hearne identified the author of this fragment as either Sir William Jones, the judge who sat for Beaumaris in the parliaments of 1597, 1604, and 1614, and was 'a person of admirable Learning, particularly in the Municipal Laws and in the British Antiquities', or John Jones of Flintshire, 'a great Antiquary and a curious Collector of British MSS'.[41] Francis Tate seems to have asked a series of questions about the Britons at a meeting of the Elizabethan Society of Antiquaries, three of which concerned their bards: 'Whether the *Barth* had anie office in warre answeringe our Herolds, their garments and enseignes, and whether they used the *Caduceum*, many fetching the original thereof from the Brittons charminge of Serpents?'[42] Jones took to the task enthusiastically, and began his answer by delimiting the extent of their heraldic duties: 'I say the *Bardd* was a Herald to record all the Acts of the Princes and Nobles, and to give armes according to the sorts.' Perhaps because of his Welsh heritage and knowledge of the Welsh language, he was then able to give a more precise answer, dividing the bards into three categories: *privardd*, *posvardd*, and *arroyddvard*. The first 'invented, found out and taught such Philosophie and Learninge, as was never hard of or read by any men before'; the second 'did but imitate, followe and teache that which the *Priveirdd* had set fourth, and must take there author from one of them'; and the third was 'an *ensive Bardd* or *learned man*, and indeed is a Herald at Arms, and his dutie was to declare the genealogie and blaze the armes of Nobles and Princes, and to keepe the record of them, and to alter there armes according to there dignities and deserts'. As for their garb, Jones described it as 'long garments'. His answer then concluded with a robust dismissal of a popular

---

[40] John E. Curran, Jr, 'The History Never Written: Bards, Druids, and the Problem of Antiquarianism in *Poly-Olbion*', *Renaissance Quarterly*, 51 (1998), 498–525 at 524.

[41] *A Collection of Curious Discourses Written by Eminent Antiquaries upon Several Heads in our English Antiquities*, ed. Thomas Hearne (Oxford, 1720), pp. x–xi. For an account of John Jones's collection of manuscripts, see Edward Lhuyd, *Archæologia Britannica, Giving some Account Additional to what has been hitherto Publish'd, of the Languages, Histories and Customs Of the Original Inhabitants of Great Britain: From Collections and Observations in Travels through Wales, Cornwal, Bas-Bretagne, Ireland and Scotland* (Oxford, 1707), 225.

[42] *Curious Discourses*, ed. Hearne, 209.

etymology, the 'most false, erroneous, and fabulous surmise' that the word 'bard' derives from Bardus, fifth king of the Celts and supposed inventor of music.[43] He pointed out that 'there never was any of that name, that ever was either King or King's son of Brittaine', and argued instead that bard 'is a primitive Brittish word which hath the aforesaid significations and interpretations'.[44] Perhaps wisely, he passed over the final question of whether the bards ever used the caduceus.

In tracing the history of the bards the song of the river Wye should not therefore be seen as a counterblast to antiquarian attacks on the matter of Britain. Instead, it is testimony to a particularly Welsh historical consciousness, a strand which runs through her song as a whole. Thus later, for example, when she berates Protestant iconoclasts, 'Who for some Crosse or Saint they in the window see / Will pluck downe all the Church', and castigates them as 'Soule-blinded Sots that creepe / In durt, and never saw the wonders of the Deepe', she may echo Drayton's own views (and an old antiquarian grudge to boot), but she again speaks as an authentically Welsh voice.[45] Sixteenth-century Welsh poets such as Siôn Brwynog and Thomas ab Ieuan ap Rhys had also sung of the bareness of Welsh churches, stripped of their candles, altars, and saints, and had similarly berated the Protestant Reformers as iconoclastic precisians.[46] The Wye, in short, offers an unabashedly Welsh perspective on the past, and her song is an identifiably Welsh intervention in the larger historical project that is *Poly-Olbion*.

If the Wye sings primarily as a Welsh historian, elsewhere in the work there are more obviously antiquarian voices. The river Colne, whose song appears in the second part of *Poly-Olbion*, is one example. She begins her song by praising the fertility of the soil on her banks, and then shifts attention to the antiquities unearthed in the vicinity:

> If you esteeme not these, as things above the ground,
> Looke under, where the Urnes of ancient times are found:
> The Roman Emp'rours Coynes, oft dig'd out of the dust,
> And warlike Weapons, now consum'd with cankring rust:
> The huge and massy Bones, of mighty fearefull men,
> To tell the worlds full strength, what creatures lived then;

---

[43] This etymology originated with the forgeries of Annius of Viterbo; see *Commentaria fratris Ioannis Annii Viterbensis ordinis prædicatorum theologiæ professoris super opera diuersorum auctorum de antiquitatibus loquentium confecta* (Rome, 1498), sig. T2ʳ: 'Apud Tuyscones regnabat Herminon uir ferox armis: & apud Celtas Bardus: inuentione carminum & musice apud illos inclytus.'
[44] *Curious Discourses*, ed. Hearne, 216–19.
[45] Drayton, *Poly-Olbion*, VI. 275–8.
[46] Glanmor Williams, *The Reformation in Wales* (Bangor: Headstart, 1991), 14–17. The classic studies of 16th-c. iconoclasm are Margaret Aston, *England's Iconoclasts*, i: *Laws against Images* (Oxford: Clarendon Press, 1988), and Eamon Duffy, *The Stripping of the Altars: Traditional Religion in England, c.1400–1580* (New Haven and London: Yale University Press, 1992).

> When in her height of youth, the lustie fruitfull earth
> Brought foorth her big-limb'd brood, even Gyants in their birth.[47]

In imitation of the antiquaries, the Colne catalogues the urns, coins, weapons, and bones that have been discovered through the ages. Drayton's source here is probably the *Britannia*, which also details a number of archaeological finds in this part of Essex. Camden writes that an 'infinite deale of auncient coine' is 'daily gotten out of the ground there', and concludes on the basis of these coins that the area 'flourished in the Roman time in happy estate'.[48] He also records the giants' bones, noting that the thirteenth-century chronicler Ralph of Coggeshall discovered 'two teeth of a certaine Giant' in the village of Eadulphness near the mouth of the Colne, and that in the 1560s the Suffolk gentleman Richard Cavendish unearthed 'another Giantlike thing' there.[49] Camden, however, is more circumspect than Drayton's narrator, suggesting instead that the bones may have been the skeletal remains of prodigious sea-creatures. 'Yet may we very well thinke,' he writes, 'that which Suetonius hath writeth, namely that the huge limmes of monstrous Sea-creatures else where, and in this kingdome also, were commonly said and taken to have beene Giants bones.'[50]

Another antiquarian voice in the poem is Hadrian's Wall, who sings not only of battles and history, but also of towns, forts, and architecture:

> Townes stood upon my length, where Garrisons were laid,
> Their limits to defend; and for my greater ayd,
> With Turrets I was built, where Sentinels were plac'd,
> To watch upon the Pict; so me my Makers grac'd,
> With hollow Pipes of Brasse, along me still that went,
> By which they in one Fort still to another sent,
> By speaking in the same, to tell them what to doe,
> And so from Sea to Sea could I be whispered through:
> Upon my thicknesse, three march'd eas'ly breast to breast,
> Twelve foot was I in height, such glory I possest.[51]

This song is itself an act of historical recuperation, as the anthropomorphized wall remembers his Roman heyday. His verbs are all in the past tense, and they therefore signal what has been lost to time, but the speaker also has the ability to conjure and revive his former glories. Unlike Stonehenge, for instance, his past has not been erased. Hadrian's Wall still has a voice—and he has it because of the wealth of surviving sources. Thus he also contrasts himself with the Devil's Dyke, that long traduced Newmarket earthwork, 'Who for the Deuils worke the vulgar dare auow, / Tradition telling none, who truly it began'. His own fate is more

---

[47] Drayton, *Poly-Olbion*, XIX. 131–8.
[48] Camden, *Britain*, 450.
[49] Ibid. 451. For gigantic bones, see the discussion above at p. 72.
[50] Ibid.
[51] Drayton, *Poly-Olbion*, XXIX. 343–52.

Antiquarian Readers 183

secure, as it lies in the hands of 'many a reuerent Booke'.[52] These sources doubtless number Eutropius' *Breviarium historiae Romanae*, which had appeared in various editions in the sixteenth century, including those of Antonius Schonhovius at Basle in 1546, 1552, and 1559, and Aelius Lampridius, whose history had recently been published in Isaac Casaubon's 1603 edition of the *Scriptores historiae Augustae*. Both texts give full accounts of the various fortifications which make up Hadrian's Wall.

By anthropomorphizing ancient remains, by giving them a voice in this way, Drayton comments on the historiographic process itself. Hadrian's Wall is fashioned as an antiquary, but his song is also a reflection upon the claims and potential of antiquarian methodology. To restore the past was the antiquarian goal; to find authoritative historical voices in its traces and remains was its principal approach. Through his insistent use of prosopopoeia Drayton sets out to examine the assumptions and consequences of both. He takes the resurrective impulse of Camden and the other antiquaries to its imaginative extreme. He not only gathers together the scattered remains of the past, but he also brings that past into the present, realizing it by giving those remains voices of their own. In Drayton's poem, stones really can speak, and when they do they are all the more compelling as historical witnesses. The first-person narration brings a continuity between past and present that even the most compendious antiquarian catalogues and descriptions cannot achieve. In *Poly-Olbion* the defiance of time comes tantalizingly close.

ANNOTATING DRAYTON

The multiple voices of Drayton's poem, historical, antiquarian, and otherwise, find a parallel in the structure of the printed book itself. *Poly-Olbion* offers multiple perspectives on the past, and also various supplements and alternatives to Drayton's songs. The first that the reader encounters is the monumental frontispiece (Fig. 6.1). Engraved by William Hole, this frontispiece first appeared in 1612 and was printed in all subsequent editions of the work.[53] The design is architectural, with a central arch springing from square pillars on a continuous plinth decorated with a frieze of scallop shells. Seated underneath the arch is the figure of Albion, a maiden dressed in a splendid cloak with an elaborate cartographic design that incorporates rivers, trees, mountains, churches, and towns. The cloak itself is shaped to recall the outline of Britain; the three-strand pearl necklace around her neck, perhaps an allusion to England, Scotland, and

---

[52] Ibid., ll. 335–42.
[53] For descriptions of the frontispiece, see Hind, *Engraving in England*, ii. 330; and Margery Corbett and Ronald Lightbown, *The Comely Frontispiece: The Emblematic Title-Page in England, 1550–1660* (London, Henley, and Boston: Routledge & Kegan Paul, 1979), 153–61.

Wales, may reinforce this. With her apparel the maiden recalls both the figure of Albion-Britannia, who appears seated on a rock and holding a standard and spear aloft on the title pages of later editions of the *Britannia*, and also the work of Elizabethan cartographers such as John Norden and Christopher Saxton.[54] On the capitals stand two other figures, Brutus and Julius Caesar, and on the plinth itself two more, Hengist and William the Conqueror. The four figures represent the four conquerors of Britain, the 'Princes Time hath seene / Ambitious of her', as Drayton's explanatory poem on the frontispiece puts it.[55]

In this way the frontispiece foregrounds both geography and history, the two disciplines which lie at the heart of Drayton's project. The frontispiece, therefore, creates certain expectations: unlike his collected *Poems* (1619), for example, where the focal point of the title page is a portrait of Drayton himself, *Poly-Olbion* puts the nation to the fore in the shape of Albion and its various histories.[56] The singularity of the maiden at the centre of page is counterbalanced by the four figures who surround her, and who together represent the multiple and perhaps irreconcilable traditions that make up her past. The frontispiece also creates expectations about the genre of the book which follows. Just as the figure of Albion recalls Camden and the *Britannia*, so the four historical figures also speak of that antiquarian tradition. As Corbett and Lightbown point out, the figure of Caesar ultimately derives from an antique coin or medal, probably from an illustration in a popular numismatic collection such as Guillaume Rouillé's frequently reprinted *Promptuarii iconum insignium à seculo hominum, subiectis eorum vitis, per compendium ex probatissimis autoribus desumptis* (1553), or indeed one of the Goltzius volumes discussed in Chapter 1.[57] The fact that all four figures appear with their coats of arms, despite the obvious anachronism, also identifies *Poly-Olbion* with the antiquarian tradition; genealogy and heraldry were staples of antiquarian books. Drayton may therefore have intended his frontispiece to work in a similar way to the note appended to *Peirs Gaveston*: to advertise his antiquarianism, signal his ties with scholars such as Camden, and illustrate the connections of his book with works such as the *Britannia*. That is to say, he may have intended the frontispiece as a pre-emptive strike, a means to market the book to antiquarian readers and ensure that they recognized its antiquarian models and antecedents.

---

[54] For the title page to the *Britannia*, see the discussion above at p. 115. For an introduction to Elizabethan cartography, see Sarah Tyacke and John Huddy, *Christopher Saxton and Tudor Map-Making* (London: British Library, 1980).

[55] Michael Drayton, 'Upon the *Frontispice*', in *Poly-Olbion*, ll. 6–7. The presence of this explanatory poem suggests that Drayton had significant influence over what Hole engraved.

[56] For a discussion of the title page to Drayton's *Poems* (1619), see Wendy Wall, *The Imprint of Gender: Authorship and Publication in the English Renaissance* (Ithaca and London: Cornell University Press, 1993), 82.

[57] Corbett and Lightbown, *The Comely Frontispiece*, 158. For the Goltzius volumes, see p. 30 above.

FIG. 6.1. The frontispiece to Michael Drayton, *Poly-Olbion* (London, 1612). © British Library Board. All Rights Reserved (shelfmark 79. h. 2)

The text which follows contains three further types of supplementary material. In his prefatory epistle Drayton explains why these are included. Afraid that his readers might otherwise struggle with the poem's 'difficult' matter, he decides to provide 'three especiall helps'. These are the arguments which precede each of the thirty songs, 'to direct thee still, where thou art, and through what Shires the Muse makes her journey'; the maps which also precede each of the songs, 'lively delineating to thee, every Mountaine, Forrest, River, and Valley'; and the annotations, or 'Illustrations', which Selden prepared for the eighteen songs of the first part, 'to explaine every hard matter of history, that, lying farre from the way of common reading, may (without question) seem difficult unto thee'.[58] The explanation is straightforward enough: the elaborate paratext is intended to clarify matters, to direct the reader geographically, and to elucidate any historical difficulties or obscurities. Selden himself sheds further light on this commentatorial role in his own epistle to the reader, which follows immediately, as he explains in more detail the purpose of his illustrations:

PERMIT mee thus much of these Notes to My Friend. What the Verse oft, with allusion, as supposing a full knowing Reader, lets slip; or in winding steps of Personating Fictions (as some times) so infolds, that suddaine conceipt cannot abstract a Forme of the clothed Truth, I have, as I might, *Illustrated*.[59]

Selden's task, as he puts it, is to inform where Drayton speaks allusively or elliptically and to reveal the truths hidden behind his many personifications. The task, then, appears to be primarily to aid the reader. The explanations, as given by both Drayton and Selden, are simple and unambiguous. But the illustrations themselves tell a different story.

Selden seems to have prepared his illustrations in a remarkably short period of time. They were, as he admits in his epistle, 'undertaken at request of my kinde friend the Author...but little more then since the Poem first went to the Presse'.[60] Since *Poly-Olbion* was entered in the Stationers' Register on 7 February 1612, and Selden's preface is subscribed 9 May, he must have written the illustrations in less than three months.[61] This hurriedness explains why the illustrations frequently recycle material which had appeared in his earlier works. Selden lifts passages wholesale from tracts such as the *Jani Anglorum facies altera* (1610) and the unpublished *Analecton Anglo-Britannicon* of 1607, pausing only to render them in English.[62] This hurriedness also explains why his

---

[58] Drayton, 'TO THE GENERALL *READER*', in *Poly-Olbion*, p. vi*.
[59] John Selden, 'FROM THE AUTHOR OF THE *ILLUSTRATIONS*', in *Poly-Olbion*, p. viii*.
[60] Ibid., p. xii*.
[61] Edward Arber, *A Transcript of the Registers of the Company of Stationers of London; 1554–1640 A.D.*, 5 vols. (Birmingham: privately printed, 1894), iii. 477; Selden, 'FROM THE AUTHOR OF THE *ILLUSTRATIONS*', p. xiv*.
[62] Christianson, *Discourse on History, Law, and Governance*, 34; G. J. Toomer, 'Selden's *Historie of Tithes*: Genesis, Publication, Aftermath', *Huntington Library Quarterly*, 65 (2002), 345–79 at 346–7.

illustrations are occasionally botched. In the epistle Selden himself apologizes for the many faults, attributing these to that unwelcome trio of 'Compell'd *Absence*, endevor'd *Dispatch*, and want of *Revises*.[63] He was so pressed for time, he goes on, that he was unable to revise or correct his text. As a result, he has to include the lengthy table of errata, which follows his epistle.

The rushed circumstances also shed light on two errors by the printer Humphrey Lownes. Twice he seems to have misjudged the space that Selden's material would require. The illustrations to Song IX, for example, end with a genealogical table of the succession of Welsh kings, but this is included, as Selden himself admits, not so much for intellectual reasons as for filling what would otherwise be blank pages: 'Least (by reason of the Composition in Print) some pages should have beene idle, and because also here is so much of the *Welsh* Storie, I inserted this Chronologie of the Kings and Princes of *Wales*, from *Arthur*, vntill the end of the *British* bloud in them.'[64] The table, in other words, is an elaborate typographical filler, a suitably antiquarian equivalent to the woodblocks and endpieces customarily used by printers. Presumably when casting off—that is, when calculating what would be printed on either side of the sheet—Lownes misjudged how much space Selden's annotations to this song would require. At the end of Song XV, by contrast, when casting off, he did not leave enough space for Selden. The result is that the illustrations here are curtailed, if not in content, certainly in their appearance on the printed page, as they are squashed into a space at the foot of what in the first issue of 1612 is sig. Y2^v. Here, the typography differs from elsewhere in the volume: normally, the heading '*Illustrations*' is printed in double pica, the lemmata in english, and the glosses in pica.[65] Here, however, the heading is printed in the smaller type size of english, and the lemma and gloss—there is only one of each—are in pica; the page is also inconsistently set with interlinear leads. This time Lownes had to squeeze the illustrations into too small a space, and the solution was to alter his otherwise consistent typography.

For all the straightforwardness of Drayton and Selden's explanations, the illustrations themselves are much more ambiguous. The clarity which their epistles promise is not matched in the often digressive, frequently allusive, and always fiendishly learned illustrations that Selden provides. Despite the pledge of his epistle, Selden is uncompromising in the intellectual demands which he places on the reader. These demands are historical, literary, and, perhaps most of all, linguistic. This is apparent as early as the epistle itself, when Selden diverts from his course to enter into a long discussion of the etymology of the Chaucerian word 'dulcarnon'. This digression is occasioned by a passing reference to

---

[63] Selden, 'FROM THE AUTHOR OF THE *ILLUSTRATIONS*', p. xiii*.
[64] Michael Drayton, *Poly-Olbion* (London, 1612), sig. O6^r. Selden's table follows, printed on both sides of this leaf.
[65] For a discussion and table of type size in the hand-press period, see Gaskell, *A New Introduction to Bibliography*, 12–16.

Chaucer: 'whose name by the way Occuring, and my worke here being but to adde plaine song after Muses descanting, I cannot but digresse to admonition of abuse which this Learned allusion, in his *Troilus*, by ignorance hath indured'.[66] Selden's tongue is firmly in his cheek here, since his subsequent riff on dulcarnon is very far from plain. The word itself, which by the seventeenth century was archaic, was a *terminus technicus* of the high medieval mathematical curriculum, used to refer specifically to the exposition of the Pythagorean theorem in Euclid's *Elements* (Book 1, Proposition 47).[67] Chaucer, however, uses the word figuratively, as Criseyde likens her dilemma to the state of perplexity which the theorem typically engenders in students: 'I am, til God me bettre mynde sende, / At dulcarnoun, right at my wittes ende.'[68] Selden supplies an etymology for the word, tracing it to the Arabic epithet *Dhū al-Qarnayn*, which was usually applied to Alexander the Great, and in the process gives one of the first tasters of his prodigious Oriental learning:

Its not *Necham*, or any one else, that can make mee entertaine the least thought of the signification of *Dulcarnon* to be *Pythagoras* his sacrifice after his Geometricall Theorem in finding the Squares of an Orthogonall Triangles sides . . . ; but indeed by easier pronunciation it was made of .i. ذُو القَرنين. *Two horned*: which the *Mahometan Arabians* use for a Root in Calculation, meaning *Alexander*.[69]

This etymology in turn occasions a further Arabic digression, as Selden then points out that Chaucer's *A Treatise on the Astrolabe* 'was chiefly learned out of *Messahalah*'. Selden himself owned a manuscript of Messahala's *De compositione et utilitate astrolabii*, now in the Bodleian Library (MS Selden Supra 78), and he seems to have been the first to suggest this Arabic text as a source for Chaucer's treatise.[70] Selden's digressions, whilst correct, have little to do with the rest of the epistle and no bearing at all on Drayton's songs; they also flatly deny his stated principle earlier in the epistle of 'purposely avoyding frequent commixture of different language'.[71] They instead herald the bravura, even ostentatious, display which will follow, offering an exuberant prelude to the equally digressive illustrations. The showiness is only emphasized by the use of Arabic script, rendered

---

[66] Selden, 'FROM THE AUTHOR OF THE *ILLUSTRATIONS*', pp. x*–xi*. This is a neat musical pun on the relationship between the two parts of *Poly-Olbion*. In early music the descant was the melodious, usually improvised, accompaniment to a simple musical theme (the plainsong or chant). Here, the 'plaine song' is Selden's annotations and the 'descanting' Drayton's polyphonous songs.
[67] Thomas Elwood Hart, 'Medieval Structuralism: "Dulcarnoun" and the Five-Book Design of Chaucer's *Troilus*', *Chaucer Review*, 16 (1981), 129–70.
[68] *Troilus and Criseyde*, in *The Riverside Chaucer*, III. 930–1.
[69] Selden, 'FROM THE AUTHOR OF THE *ILLUSTRATIONS*', p. xi*. For Selden as an Arabist, see G. J. Toomer, *Eastern Wisedome and Learning: The Study of Arabic in Seventeenth-Century England* (Oxford: Clarendon Press, 1996), 64–71.
[70] Michael Masi, 'Chaucer, Messahala and Bodleian Selden Supra 78', *Manuscripta*, 19 (1975), 36–47.
[71] Selden, 'FROM THE AUTHOR OF THE *ILLUSTRATIONS*', p. viii*.

accurately and legibly by Lownes by means of a woodblock.[72] The Arabic digressions are also the first hint that Drayton and Selden may have been playing an elaborate game with their readers.

Contemporary readers would certainly have been used to this kind of game. For all their stated intention of clarifying matters, Renaissance commentaries, as William Slights has shown, often complicate and obfuscate the texts that they gloss. For Slights, this paradox arises from the characteristic playfulness of humanist commentators, and he cites as the archetypal example the 1515 edition of Erasmus's *Encomium moriae*, which was printed with substantial marginal glosses probably by the Dutch scholar Gerardus Listrius, describing these annotations as 'a highly convoluted parodic commentary on an already ironic text'.[73] Closer to home, and perhaps closer in style and form to *Poly-Olbion*, there is also the extraordinary commentary to Spenser's *The Shepheardes Calender* (1579) by the mysterious E.K., the annotator whose identity remains one of that text's many undisclosed secrets.[74] In his prefatory epistle to Gabriel Harvey, E.K. defends his glosses on the grounds of his privy knowledge of the author, arguing that his friendship with Spenser affords him access to the hidden meanings of the poem's allegory. 'I thought good to take the paines vpon me,' he asserts, 'the rather for that by meanes of some familiar acquaintaunce I was made priuie to his counsell and secret meaning in them, as also in sundry other works of his'.[75] E.K., like Selden, promises clarification: his epistle suggests that his glosses will open things up for the reader. Yet, as scholars have pointed out, the glosses themselves are pedantic, obscurantist, and often obfuscatory. The reader who turns to E.K. for clarification is bound to be disappointed. The much cited gloss on Hobbinol's 'frendly Faeries' in the sixth eclogue, which takes the reader via a fanciful etymology from 'Elfes' and 'Goblins' to Florentine factionalism and the houses of the 'Guelfes' and 'Gibelins', is a case in point.[76]

---

[72] *Poly-Olbion* may be only the third English book to contain printed Arabic. For Selden's role in the development of Arabic printing in England, see Miroslav Krek, *Typographica Arabica: The Development of Arabic Printing as Illustrated by Arabic Type Specimens* (Waltham: Brandeis University Library, 1971), 20; and Geoffrey Roper, 'Arabic Printing and Publishing in England before 1820', *British Society for Middle Eastern Studies Bulletin*, 12 (1985), 12–32. I am indebted to Dr Roper for his advice on this subject.

[73] William W. E. Slights, 'The Edifying Margins of Renaissance English Books', *Renaissance Quarterly*, 42 (1989), 682–716 at 716. For a discussion of the potential unreliability of Renaissance annotation and commentary, see A. C. Hamilton, 'The Philosophy of the Footnote', in *Editing Poetry from Spenser to Dryden: Papers Given at the Sixteenth Annual Conference on Editorial Problems, University of Toronto, 31 October–1 November 1980*, ed. A. H. de Quehen (New York and London: Garland, 1981), 127–63.

[74] Any number of suggestions have been made about E.K.'s identity: candidates include Edward Kirke, a sizar at Pembroke Hall at the same time as Spenser, Gabriel Harvey, and indeed Spenser himself. For an introduction to this annotator and his uncertain identity, see David R. Shore, 'E.K.', in A. C. Hamilton (ed.), *The Spenser Encyclopedia* (Toronto: University of Toronto Press, 1990), 231.

[75] Edmund Spenser, *The Shepheardes Calender*, in *The Shorter Poems*, 29 (ll. 176–9).

[76] Edmund Spenser, 'June', in *The Shepheardes Calender*, l. 25 and p. 92.

Selden's illustrations adopt a similar tack, taking the reader far from the songs and lemmata, as the antiquarian urge to compile and complete threatens to overrun Drayton's original text.[77] As the herald Sir Edward Bysshe quipped, it is not always clear who is annotating whom. He once asked Selden jestingly 'whether he wrote the commentary to his "Polyolbion" and "Epistles", or Mr. Drayton made those verses to his notes'.[78] Indeed, at one point the glosses really do exceed the glossed: Song XI. In the first edition this song is printed on five leaves, but the illustrations take up seven.[79] Their length means that they run the full gamut of subjects discussed by Selden in the illustrations more generally. An early gloss, for example, on the line 'And of our Countries, place of Palatine doth hold' (XI. 10), explains this allusion in the manner that the prefatory epistle promises. First, Selden comments that 'We have in *England III.* more of that title, *Lancaster, Durham,* and *Ely*: and, untill later time, *Hexamshire* in the Westerne part of *Northumberland*, was so reputed'. Then he turns more specifically to Cheshire, the geographical context for Drayton's song: '*William* the *Conqueror*, first created one *Hugh Wolfe* a *Norman*, Count *Palatine* of *Chester*, and gave the Earledome to hold, *as freely as the King held his Crowne*', citing a charter from the Monastery of St Werburga at Chester as his evidence. Finally, he discusses the derivation of palatine, moving away from the confines of Drayton's song to the origins of the word: 'For the Name of *Palatine*, know, that in ancient time under the Emperours of declining *Rome*, the title of *Count Palatine* was.'[80] He then gives a lengthy etymology, which traces the spread of this Roman title in various European countries. He seems to have been aware of the laboriousness of this explanation, as he ends the gloss with what seems to be a self-deprecating allusion to its digressiveness: 'To adde the royalties of the Earledom, as Courts, Officers, Franchises, formes of Proceeding, even as at *Westminster*, or the diminution of its large liberties by the Statute of Resumption, were to trouble you with a harsh digression.'[81] The reader, who has travelled far from Drayton's comment on the history of Cheshire, would doubtless agree.

Another early gloss comments on Drayton's scholarship, commending him for his genealogical and antiquarian learning, and thereby offering an important

---

[77] Selden's illustrations may be compared to the similarly overblown commentary that he wrote the same year for his commendatory poem to Arthur Hopton's almanac; see John Selden, 'Ad Arcturium Hopton...Encomium', in Arthur Hopton, *A Concordancy of Yeares* (London, 1612), sig. A8ʳ.

[78] Quoted in Aubrey, '*Brief Lives*', i. 239. 'Epistles' refers to Drayton's *Englands Heroicall Epistles* (1597). Bysshe was mistaken in thinking that Selden wrote the annotations to that work, as is apparent from its prefatory epistle in which Drayton explains why he himself has 'annexed Notes to every Epistles end'; see Michael Drayton, *Englands Heroicall Epistles*, in *The Works of Michael Drayton*, ii. 130.

[79] Drayton, *Poly-Olbion* (1612), sigs. Q2, Q3, Q4, Q5, and Q6, and R1, R2, R3, R4, R5, R6, and S1 respectively.

[80] Drayton, *Poly-Olbion*, ed. Hebel, Tillotson, and Newdigate, 230–1. Selden would again discuss the etymology of palatine in his *Titles of Honour* (1614); see the discussion at p. 76 above.

[81] Ibid. 230–1.

corrective to the perception that Selden spent his time chiding the poet for his credulousness and errors. In response to the line 'Our Leopards they so long and bravely did advance' (XI. 30), an allusion to the coats of arms worn by medieval English soldiers, Selden praises the poet's attention to heraldry: 'He well call's the Coate of *England, Leopards*.'[82] Inevitably, Selden cannot then resist the opportunity of taking previous scholars to task for their heraldic blunders, and he reserves particular criticism for Polydore Vergil:

Neither can you justly object the common blazon of it, by name of Lions, or that assertion of *Polydores* ignorance, telling us that the Conqueror bare three *Fleurs de lis*, and *three Lions*, as quartred for one coat, which hath bin, & is as al men know, at this present born in our Soveraignes armes for *France* and *England*; and so, that the quartering of the *Fleurs* was not at all untill *Ed*. III. to publish his title, and gaine the *Flemish* forces (as you have it in *Froissart*) bare the *French* armes, being then *Azure semy with Fleurs de lis*.[83]

And Selden does not stop there: this convoluted account of French and English heraldry, which takes the reader from a commendation of Drayton's poetry to the chronicles of Jean Froissart, occasions a further genealogical digression, as Selden then explains why the French arms were reduced from four fleurs-de-lis to three. It is only then that he returns to the matter at hand, offering two pieces of evidence in support of Drayton's pardine reference: the thirteenth-century historian Matthew Paris and two lines in a manuscript of John Gower's *Confessio amantis*, 'which the Printed books have not'.[84]

Most of Song XI is taken up with a catalogue of 'the religious Saxon Kings', sung by the river Weaver. As with the Colne, Drayton presents this river as an antiquary, calling him 'one that gave him selfe industriously to know / What Monuments our Kings erected long agoe'.[85] With his focus on ecclesiastical history, the Weaver may well be intended to recall the circle of Matthew Parker, scholars and antiquaries whose researches focused on Anglo-Saxon and the history of the English Church.[86] The Weaver begins his catalogue with a genealogy, asserting that the Saxons 'brought their blood' from '*Woden*, by which name they stiled *Mercurie*'.[87] Selden, unsurprisingly, intervenes, and the poor regard in which he held this genealogy is apparent from his subsequent comment:

Woden, in *Saxon* Genealogies, is ascended to, as the chiefe Ancestor of their most Roiall Progenies; so you may see in *Nennius, Bede, Ethelward, Florence* of *Worcester*, an

---

[82] Ibid. 231.
[83] Ibid. 231–2.
[84] Ibid. 232. Selden owned a manuscript of Gower's poem (now Bodleian Library, MS Arch. Selden B. 11), a mid-15th-c. copy in the first recension; printed texts include Caxton's edition of 1483 (*STC* 12142) and Thomas Berthelet's editions of 1532 and 1554 (*STC* 12143 and 12144).
[85] Drayton, *Poly-Olbion*, XI. 145–6.
[86] For Parker and his circle, see McKisack, *Medieval History in the Tudor Age*, 26–49.
[87] Drayton, *Poly-Olbion*, XI. 173–4.

Anonymus de Regali Prosapia, *Huntingdon*, and *Hoveden*, yet in such sort that in some of them they goe beyond him, through *Frithwald, Frealaf, Frithulf, Fin, Godulph, Geta*, and others, to *Seth*; But with so much uncertainty, that I imagine many of their descents were just as true as the *Theogonie* in *Hesiod, Appollodorus*, or that of *Prester Johns*, sometimes deriving himselfe very neere from the loines of *Salomon*.[88]

Prester John, with whom Selden concludes his list of mythical counterexamples, was the legendary and endlessly fascinating king of Ethiopia; here, he is clearly intended to designate the wilder shores of historical fancy.[89] This kind of intervention, curbing the excesses of Drayton's narrator, is typical. Slightly later in the song Selden has to intervene again, this time to query the Weaver's bold claim of a Saxon origin for the practice of fasting during Lent. (The river attributes this to the Kentish king Eorcenbehrt.) Selden comments wryly: 'Began it here, (so understand him; for plainly that fasting time was long before in other Churches, as appears in the Decreeing Epistle of PP. *Telesphorus*.' The rest of the gloss follows this papal pathway, as Selden digresses into diktats on fasting from the Holy See more generally. Almost as an afterthought, the gloss ends with a return to Drayton's song and Eorcenbehrt: 'For proofe of this in *Erconbert*, both *Bede* and *Malmesbury*, beside their later followers, are witnesses.'[90]

Selden's historical method combines interrogation of Drayton's songs with examination of his sources (and undoubtedly also of sources which he did not use). In his prefatory epistle Selden explains that, when examining sources, he relies upon three principal criteria: 'the Reporters credit', 'Comparison with more perswading authority', and '*Synchronisme* (the best Touch-stone in this kind of Triall)'.[91] By synchronism Selden seems to have meant both agreement in relation to the time of the events described and a form of comparative chronology. Both senses, for instance, seem to be in play in a later gloss to Song XI, when Selden explores the Saxon heptarchy. Having illustrated the 'VII. Kingdomes, their beginnings, territory, and first Christianity' by means of a diagram, he admits that 'as good authority may be given against some of [his] proposed Chronologie, as [he] can justifie [him] selfe with'. Nevertheless, he defends his diagram on the basis that 'our old Monkes', the sources upon which he has to rely, are 'corrupted, or deficient', and therefore 'affoord nothing able to rectifie'. He adds by way of illustration: 'I know the *East-Angles*, by both ancient and later authority, begin above C. yeares before; but if with Synchronisme you examine it, it will be found most absurd.'[92] Selden's best touchstone,

---

[88] Ibid. 234.
[89] A marginal note alongside indicates that Selden's source for the legend of Prester John was the Portuguese humanist Damião de Goes, author of an important description of Ethiopia, *Fides, religio, moresque Aethiopum sub imperio Pretiosi Joannis*, published at Louvain in 1540.
[90] Drayton, *Poly-Olbion*, 236–7.   [91] Ibid., p. viii*.   [92] Ibid. 246.

synchronism, demonstrates the absurdity of his sources, and also therefore justifies his discrepancy from them. The result is that by the end of his gloss, and the thorough exposure to his historical methodology that it brings, the reader is no more certain about the Saxon heptarchy than at its beginning.

Throughout the poem, in the 1612 edition at least, the illustrations are keyed to the songs by a series of section marks ('§'), one of the sorts normally found in a compositor's case. At the beginning of each line which has been glossed is a section mark, followed by a point and a thick space. The result is that the glossed lines are slightly offset and the reader's eyes are inevitably drawn to them. The presence of the section marks suggests that *Poly-Olbion* was printed with a particular manner of reading in mind. Readers were intended to flick back and forth between song and illustration, to read them concurrently, not sequentially. The structure is dialogic, and the section mark is the typographical signal to undertake this kind of circular, non-linear reading. The songs and illustrations are competing, but not alternative, modes of historical expression, and the reader must take account of both. But Drayton does not leave it there. His reader has to contend with a second kind of annotation as well: shorter glosses printed in the ruled margins of the pages. These glosses are lexicographical, defining unfamiliar words, prosopographical, identifying the succession of historical personages, and organizational, directing the reader to similar passages elsewhere in the poem. Alongside the Weaver's first mention of Hengist and Horsa, for example, the following note is printed: 'See concer- | ning their cō- | ming, to the I. | IV. and VIII. | Songs'.[93] These notes are keyed to Drayton's text by superscript letters and asterisks. Once again, therefore, the principle of circularity is represented in the work's typography, as the reader's gaze shifts back and forth from text block to margin, and also from song to song. Whilst Drayton's motivation here may have been partly economical—to save on paper, space, and time, and thereby also avoid repetition—the structural effects of these marginal glosses are quite in keeping with the dialogic nature and ambitions of the work as a whole.

The circularity of Selden's illustrations is also mirrored in the work's extraordinary maps.[94] As with the illustrations, the prefatory material treats the maps in a sober fashion. The maps are presented as a geographical guide, and they stand in lieu of the index which the first part of the poem lacks. As Thomas Corns puts it, 'you can find the song you want by the maps that preface them'.[95] Yet the maps themselves are next to useless cartographically. The reader who wants to map Drayton's progress across the island has a difficult task. Missing both the signs of humanity's shaping influences on the landscape and many of its

---

[93] Ibid. (1612), sig. Q4ʳ.
[94] Like the frontispiece, the maps were probably engraved by William Hole; see Herendeen, *From Landscape to Literature*, 294.
[95] Thomas N. Corns, 'The Early Modern Search Engine: Indices, Title Pages, Marginalia and Contents', in Neil Rhodes and Jonathan Sawday (eds.), *The Renaissance Computer: Knowledge Technology in the First Age of Printing* (London and New York: Routledge, 2000), 95–105 at 99.

topographical features, the maps are instead depictions of a metamorphosed Ovidian landscape. Rather than towns, roads, and churches, they show naiads, dryads, and other nymphs. They are also depictions of a metamorphosed historical landscape: the map to Song XVI, for example, depicts the Roman site of Verulamium as an elderly man, sprawling on a pile of rubble, pillars, and columns, but also as a winsome, fecund nymph, who stands opposite him (Fig. 6.2). The nymph, who is the spirit of Verulamium, points in pity at the old man and bemoans her fate, and thereby demonstrates what the city has become. This is the iconic equivalent of Drayton's description of the once glorious Verulamium now reduced to ashes and dust: 'Thou saw'st when Verlam once her head aloft did beare, / (Which in her cinders now sadly lies buried heere).'[96] The maps, in short, are part of the same interpretative game as the illustrations, frustrating and delighting the reader in equal measure, as they end up doing something quite other than what is initially promised.

One effect of this circularity is that it emphasizes the incompleteness and contestation of Drayton's text. Writing of *The Shepheardes Calender*, Evelyn Tribble observes that E.K.'s commentary, whilst claiming to complete the work, in fact 'produces its incompleteness, positioning a reader with both perfect and imperfect knowledge of the text'.[97] The same is the case with *Poly-Olbion* and its even more complex textual apparatus. Drayton invokes the authority of the antiquaries through his paratext, but also challenges the uniqueness of that authority by his provision of so many alternative voices and perspectives. He shares, as we have seen, the antiquarian confidence in the defiance of time, but he is much less confident about the possibility of completing the antiquarian project.[98] That sense of pessimism is only augmented for the reader by the fact that *Poly-Olbion* itself is incomplete. For one thing, the second part appears without annotations by Selden, a fact for which no scholar has adequately accounted. Possible reasons include the relative commercial failure of the first part, Selden's brief imprisonment in 1621, and his considerable volume of other scholarly projects.[99] If the presence of the illustrations in the first part draws attention to the incompleteness of Drayton's songs, their absence in the second part paradoxically has the same effect. Without illustrations, the second part

---

[96] Drayton, *Poly-Olbion*, XVI. 43–4.

[97] Evelyn B. Tribble, *Margins and Marginality: The Printed Page in Early Modern England* (Charlottesville, Va. and London: University Press of Virginia, 1993), 73.

[98] My reading of the poem here runs counter to that of Barbara Ewell, who sees in the work's multifariousness an attempt by Drayton to encapsulate the totality of the English nation in a single poetic body; see 'Drayton's *Poly-Olbion*: England's Body Immortalized', *Studies in Philology*, 75 (1978), 297–315.

[99] The first part of *Poly-Olbion* did not sell particularly well: the 1622 text was partly made up of its unsold sheets; see Juel-Jensen, 'Bibliography', 302. Drayton himself acknowledges this in his preface to the second part, in which he admits that a 'small number' of copies are 'yet remaining' with the original booksellers (Matthew Lownes, John Browne, John Helme, and John Busbie); see Drayton, *Poly-Olbion*, 391.

FIG. 6.2. Map to Song XVI (Hertfordshire). Michael Drayton, *Poly-Olbion* (London, 1612), 244. Cambridge University Library, Keynes H. 4. 17. Reproduced by kind permission of the Syndics of Cambridge University Library

appears bare and unfinished. For another thing, the poem itself is also literally incomplete. Drayton, unlike Camden, did not even gesture towards north of the border; Scotland, despite the inclusivity of the poem's title, is missing entirely from it. The antiquary, the second part of *Poly-Olbion* seems to suggest, cannot hope to resurrect all traces of the past; the antiquarian project will therefore always have another stage or part.

For one reader of the 1622 edition, this bareness was something that needed to be rectified. This reader, who signed his name 'Iohannis Blaidon', owned the copy of the edition now in the library of St John's College, Cambridge (classmark Bb.4.14).[100] He was probably the John Bladen of Hemsworth in Yorkshire, whose son Nathaniel was admitted to St John's as a pensioner on 6 May 1661.[101] It was presumably through his son that Bladen's copy came to the college. The

---

[100] For the provenance of this copy, see Geoffrey Tillotson, 'Contemporary Praise of *Polyolbion*', *Review of English Studies*, 16 (1940), 181–3.
[101] For Nathaniel Bladen, see John Venn and J. A. Venn, *Alumni Cantabrigienses: A Biographical List of All Known Students, Graduates and Holders of Office at the University of Cambridge from the Earliest Times to 1900*, 10 vols. (Cambridge: Cambridge University Press, 1922–54), i. 162.

copy is annotated throughout, and Bladen's notes include 'An Elogye upon the Author in this 13th song', a poem in praise of Drayton for his description of hunting, a comment on Selden's gloss on the town of Stamford, and an index to the catalogue of English kings in Song XVII.[102] The most extensive annotations, though, are to Song XXVIII, which concerns the county of Yorkshire. On the verso of the map of Yorkshire, for example, our annotator drew a table which he called 'The title of the house of yorke in Edwarde the fowrth' (Fig. 6.3). This table is a genealogy of the House of York, and it illustrates the song of the river Ouse that follows, providing a diagrammatic defence of the Yorkist claim to the throne of England.[103] In providing this table our annotator follows the genealogies that Selden customarily adds to the first part. Elsewhere in the song, this time in the 'Catalogue of the Wonders of the *North-Riding*', the annotator again reprises Selden's role when he adds a gloss on the line 'O'r whose attractiue earth there may no Wild geese flie' (XXVIII. 326):

> The Inhabitants attribute the reason to the Monkes of Whitbye, for the strand whereon grew theire corne & fruites were much troubled with all manner of foule but especially with wild geese, where vpon the Abbot cursed them, & it seemes as probable as that A bishopp should excomunicate sparrowes for defilying St Vincents Church & all that came there afterward dyed, or that St Tho. Becket preaching in the bole of an old oake tree commaunded the pismires to departe.[104]

The note explains why proverbially there are no wild geese in the Yorkshire town of Whitby, with Bladen providing just the kind of material that Selden's epistle promises. He even imitates the gently ironic tone of Selden's illustrations, when he comments disparagingly upon the likelihood of the tale by comparing it to a bishop excommunicating sparrows and St Thomas à Becket preaching to pismires. Our annotator, in short, steps into the glossatory breach, providing additional annotations whenever he can. His Yorkshire roots perhaps explain why these invariably relate to Yorkshire material.

Most of Drayton's other readers, however, seem to have read the poem in a more straightforward way. Contrary to the sage advice of Wither in his commendatory poem, they seem to have consulted it as a source, using it in the manner that they might have used any other historical or antiquarian book.[105]

---

[102] At sigs T5^r, M2^r, and Z4^r–Z6^v respectively.

[103] For the Ouse's song, see Drayton, *Poly-Olbion*, XXVIII. 413–34. With its Yorkist manœuvrings and suggestion of political chicanery the river's song may be compared to the prolix and confusing speech of the Duke of York in *2 Henry VI*, in which he seeks to 'satisfy' himself over his title to the throne; see William Shakespeare, *The Second Part of King Henry VI*, ed. Michael Hattaway (Cambridge: Cambridge University Press, 1991), II. ii. 1–52. For a stimulating discussion of this kind of genealogy in Shakespeare, see Roberto Bizzocchi, *Genealogie incredibili: Scritti di storia dell'Europa moderna* (Bologna: Il Mulino, 1995), 71–4.

[104] At sig. ²V3^v.

[105] One obvious exception was Drayton's friend William Drummond of Hawthornden, who copied voluminous extracts from *Poly-Olbion* into one of his notebooks, but ignored the poem's antiquarian matter in favour of its classical and metamorphic elements; see NLS, MS 2060

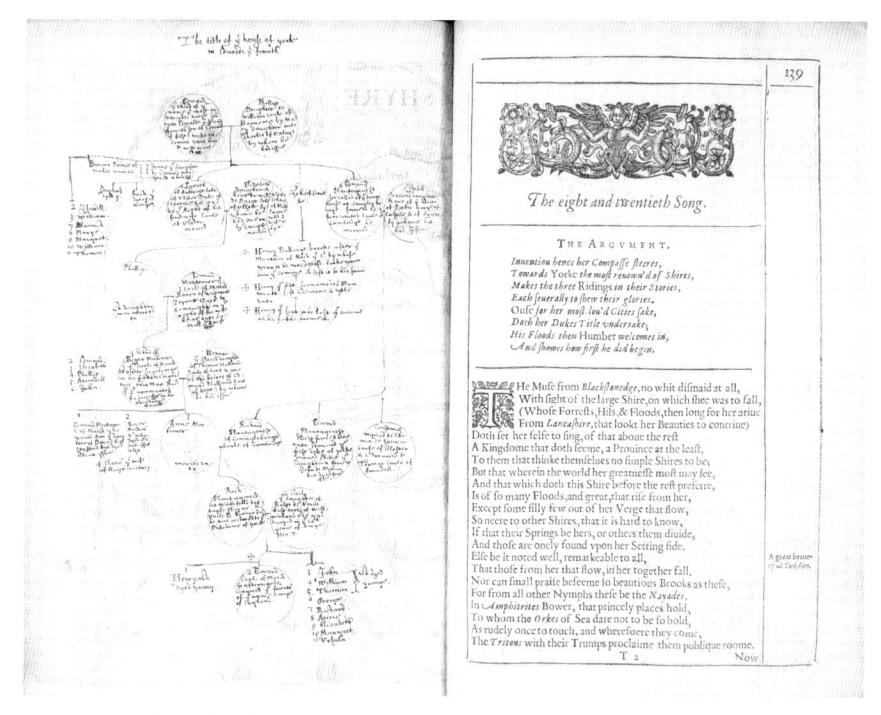

FIG. 6.3. 'The title of the house of yorke in Edwarde the fowrth'. John Bladen's annotations to Song XXVIII in his copy of Michael Drayton's *Poly-Olbion* (London, 1622), opposite p. 139. St John's College, Cambridge, Bb. 4. 14. By permission of the Master and Fellows of St John's College, Cambridge

John Weever, for example, cites the poem as a source on a number of occasions in his *Ancient Funerall Monuments* (1631). He quotes Drayton's description of Verulamium, his account of the four roads supposedly built by the British king Mulmutius, his version of the reign of the Saxon king Sebba, his account of the arrival of Brutus on the Devon coast, his potted history of the reign of Edward I, and his report of the antiquities unearthed on the banks of the river Colne, as well as quoting extensively from his catalogue of British and English saints in Song XXIV.[106] A decade later John Shrimpton used *Poly-Olbion* in a similar way in his

---

(Hawthornden Vol. VIII), fos. 268–75. Drummond's reading accords with his judgement that he found in Drayton, 'which is in most part of my Compatriots, too great an Admiration of their Country; on the History of which, whilst they muse, as wondering, they forget sometimes to be good Poets'; see William Drummond, 'Character of Several Authors', in *The Works of William Drummond of Hawthornden* (Edinburgh, 1711), 226–7.

[106] John Weever, *Ancient Funerall Monuments With In The vnited Monarchie of Great Britaine, Ireland and the Ilands adiacent, with the dissolued Monasteries therein contained; their Founders, and what eminent persons haue beene in the same interred* (London, 1631), 4, 181, 357, 374–5, 459, and

'History of St Albans'. Shrimpton includes Drayton in his list of 'Authors names from whence this Historye is extracte', alongside more obvious sources such as Gildas, Bede, Tacitus, Florilegus, Alexander Neckham, John Whethamstede, Camden, and Weever.[107] He also cites extensively from the poem. His description of the Abbey of St Albans, for example, depends on *Poly-Olbion*: 'This Abbye churche likewise hath bin honored with the sepulchres of many braue men both before & since the conquest as appears by some Verses of m^r Draytons in his poliol: Songe 16'.[108] Later in the seventeenth century the antiquary Roger Gale likewise mined Drayton's poem. In his unpublished 'Essay Towards the Recovery of the Courses of the Four Great Roman Ways' Gale cites passages from *Poly-Olbion* as evidence for his reconstruction of the routes of the four Roman roads, as the introduction to his first extract from the poem attests:

The next is *Wattlingstreet*, according to *Mr Drayton* in his *Polyolbion* of more note thô lesse extent than *Fosse*. And since his Verses may give us some direction in both their courses it will not be amiss if we here insert them, as we shall also do those relating to the *Icknild* and *Ermingstreets* in due time and place.[109]

The examples of Weever, Shrimpton, and Gale suggest that, despite its own interrogation of the form, *Poly-Olbion* was read in the later seventeenth century as an antiquarian encyclopedia, and considered as a repository of all sorts of historical information. *Poly-Olbion*, in short, seems to have been read primarily for its documentary credentials.

These credentials may well explain the book's presence in the library of Brian Twyne, a collection which is not otherwise noted for its attention to English poetry.[110] They may also explain why the 1658 catalogue of the Newcastle-upon-Tyne bookseller William London lists the work under the head 'HISTORY With other Pieces of Humane Learning Intermixed' and calls it 'The History of great *Brittain*'.[111] And they may also explain a strange interleaved copy, which

---

707, and 298–303, 311, 716, and 868. Weever also quotes from Drayton's *The Legend of Great Cromwell* (1607); see pp. 509–13. For Weever's reading of Drayton, see E. A. J. Honigmann, *John Weever: A Biography of a Literary Associate of Shakespeare and Jonson* (Manchester: Manchester University Press, 1987), 71–2.

[107] John Shrimpton, 'The History of the Ancient & free cittie of Verulamium from the first buildinge of it by the Romans vnto the Dilstruction & Vtter Demollishing of the same, the mairtyrdom of St Alban, the first buylding of the towne & monasterye bearinge his name with manye ancient funerall monument*es* some tymes thereto belonging writt in verse & prose', Bodleian Library, MS Gough Herts 3, fo. 4^v.

[108] Ibid., fo. 79^r.

[109] Roger Gale, 'An Essay Towards the Recovery of the Courses of the Four Great Roman Ways', Bodleian Library, MS Rawlinson D. 400, fo. 14^v.

[110] See Ovenell, 'Brian Twyne's Library', 21.

[111] *A Catalogue of The most vendible Books in England, Orderly and Alphabetically Digested; Under the Heads of Divinity, History, Physick, and Chyrurgery, Law, Arithmetick, Geometry, Astrologie, Dialling, Measuring Land and Timber, Gageing, Navigation, Architecture, Horsmanship, Faulconry, Merchandize, Limning, Military Discipline, Heraldry, Fortification and Fire-Works, Husbandry,*

formerly belonged to Sir Robert Carr, the earl of Somerset and James I's favourite.[112] Although it has been rebacked, the covers of this copy are still in their original dark calf binding. The binding is decorated with a single gold fillet and has Carr's arms stamped in the middle.[113] This volume is interleaved with nineteen engraved maps by William Kip and William Hole, after drawings by Saxton and Norden. These maps seem to correct *Poly-Olbion*'s own metamorphic maps, providing the reliable geographical guide that Drayton's work signally fails to give. More importantly, they also provide a strong sense of how one reader, or at least one owner, perceived Drayton's magnum opus: as a work of primarily geographical interest. Carr's copy, in short, turns *Poly-Olbion* into a cartographical repository and a grand collection of seventeenth-century maps.

Such readings tend to close down the multifariousness of *Poly-Olbion*. They also suggest that Drayton's text was mostly read selectively. Given the poem's length, difficulty, and diversity, this is hardly surprising. Drayton's songs, after all, place almost as many demands on the reader as Selden's illustrations do. To use *Poly-Olbion* as an antiquarian gazetteer, as a convenient English alternative to the mostly Latin works that had come before, must therefore have been attractive. But one of the consequences of this kind of reading was that the polyphony of Drayton's poem was increasingly sidelined. Even Drayton's most devoted imitator, the slavish William Slatyer, did not attempt to replicate the multiplicity and extent of his historical voices.[114] And this in turn may speak of a larger shift than just the changing fortunes and reputation of a seventeenth-century poet. The idea of imaginative antiquarianism which *In Defiance of Time* has explored had, by the second half of the seventeenth century, started to wane. With its confident historical voices and eloquent stones and monuments, but also its disavowal of ever completing its own task, *Poly-Olbion* may represent the high-water mark for that triumphant, resurrective, recuperative impulse. The shift away from the imagination and back to the document and record is the concern of my concluding chapter.

Gardening, Romances, Poems, Playes, &c. With Hebrew, Greek, and Latin Books, for Schools and Scholars (London, 1658), sig. U2ᵛ.

[112] Now Bodleian Library, Juel-Jensen Drayton d. 31; see Bent Juel-Jensen, 'A Drayton Collection', *The Book Collector*, 4 (1955), 133–43 at 136.

[113] Carr's stamp here incorporates a stag's head and the motto 'Probitas sibi ipsi securitas'; cf. Dennis Woodfield, *An Ordinary of British Armorial Bookbindings in the Clements Collection, Victoria and Albert Museum* (London: Victoria and Albert Museum, 1958), no. 1330.

[114] Slatyer was the author of the execrable *The History of Great Britanie*, better known in the 17th c. as *Palæ-Albion*. In a typically contrived commendatory poem Slatyer acknowledges his debt to Drayton: 'I / Thy Poly-Olbion did invite, / My Palæ-Albion, thus to write'; see 'Poetarum facilè principi, ac coriphæo, Michaeli Drayton', in *The History of Great Britanie from the first peopling of this Iland to this present Raigne of o*ʳ *hapy and peacefull Monarke K: Iames* (London, 1621), sig. 2D4ʳ (ll. 10–12).

Conclusion

In 1638 a new translation of the popular classical romance *The Loves of Clitophon and Leucippe* was published. This translation, like most printed books at the time, appeared with an impressive array of prefatory and commendatory verse. Most of this material is unremarkable, praising the translator, Anthony Hodges, for his labours and recommending the work as suitable fare for those satiated with English romances. One poem, though, speaks in a more unusual vein:

> To make the dumbe to speake, or raise the dead,
> The chief'st of miracles tis reckoned:
> A wonder then thy powerfull pen hath showne,
> 'Mongst many wonders worthie to be knowne;
> That this dumbe Author, who hath tongue-tied bin
> For many yeares, should now at last begin
> To speake our language: and that he likewise,
> Who had so long layne dead, should now arise.
>   O let him live then, and with him thy praise,
>   Who for thy worth and work deserv'st the bayes.[1]

This, then, is what is at stake with translation: an ancient author, who 'hath tongue-tied bin', who 'had so long layne dead', may in the right hands be resurrected. Translation ensures a new life for an old text, as the author, in this case Achilles Tatius, is revived for new readers. But that success is hard won: the poet reckons this kind of literary resurrection the 'cheif'st of miracles', the wonder most 'worthie to be knowne'. Thus, for all his praise of Hodges, he also ends on a less certain note. Hodges's translation may have revived the classical author, but the continuation of that revival depends on something more capricious, on the vagaries of literary reputation and reception. The poem's final couplet, after all, switches from praise to command, and therefore immediately casts doubt on the endurance of the author's new life. The couplet also appears to switch addressee: the 'praise', 'worth', and 'bayes' all refer to Hodges, whose own fame depends on the translation, but the imploring 'O let him live then' speaks to a more fickle addressee as well, the reader. The revival hangs in the balance; the

---

[1] Joseph Forde, 'In the Translators praise', in *The Loves of Clitophon and Leucippe. A most elegant History, written in Greeke by Achilles Tatius: And now Englished*, trans. Anthony Hodges (Oxford, 1638), sig. A5^r, ll. 1–10.

author's life is now in the uncertain hands of his new readers. Raising the dead, making the dumb to speak: these are only the first hurdles for his translator to overcome.

Many of these same issues are those which have been at stake in this book. *In Defiance of Time* has also been about the urge to resurrect, the impulse to revive the past and restore it to the present. Where Forde's prefatory poem is concerned with one activity associated with humanism, the translation of the classics, *In Defiance of Time* has explored the offshoot of another, perhaps less familiar one, the study of the physical traces of antiquity. That offshoot, in England at least, found its home in the increasingly large number of books on antiquarian subjects—archaeology, epigraphy, etymology, numismatics—written and published at the time. Those books in turn were typically animated by the resurrective spirit that Forde invokes. John Aubrey may be more explicit than most when he describes the task of the antiquary as waking the dead, as making those that have lain in their graves for centuries walk and appear, but his description is not outlandish, and his comparison merely brings to the fore the resurrective vein that runs through early English antiquarianism. Likewise, he may be more explicit about making the dumb speak than many of his predecessors or contemporaries: in his unpublished *Monumenta Britannica*, for example, he asserts that one of the goals of that work is 'to make the Stones give Evidence for themselves', and in an earlier draft 'to make the Stones speak for themselves'.[2] But in establishing these lapidary voices, in conceiving his project in this fashion and personifying his materials in this way, he follows a long-established antiquarian tradition. The forward march of time, this tradition suggests, may in the right circumstances be arrested.

To defy time, however, is a difficult task, as Shakespeare's nineteenth sonnet attests. Having implored and cajoled time to spare his 'love's fair brow', to leave the beloved 'untainted', in the first twelve lines of that sonnet, Shakespeare seems to turn the tables in the final couplet: 'Yet do thy worst, old Time: despite thy wrong, / My love shall in my verse ever live young.'[3] The edacious time of the opening line of the sonnet appears to have been tamed. While the poem begins by inviting devouring time to do its worst, it ends with poetry's triumph over time. 'Devouring Time' becomes plain 'old Time', and the beloved is preserved for ever, and for ever young, in Shakespeare's poem. But that defiance has a slightly hollow ring to it: the triumph, the promise of immortality of the final line, is compromised by the proverbial and greenhorn boast, 'do thy worst', that precedes it. To challenge time is one thing; to overcome it is a different matter entirely. And the antiquaries too recognized this. When an antiquary recovered the past through his books and collections, he performed, as Aubrey suggests, a

---

[2] Aubrey, *Monumenta Britannica*, i. 32 (fo. 30ʳ).
[3] William Shakespeare, 'Sonnet 19', in *The Complete Sonnets and Poems*, ed. Colin Burrow (Oxford: Oxford University Press, 2002), ll. 13–14.

historical sleight of hand. What appeared as a defeat of time was in fact only defiance. The antiquary, as Drayton adroitly shows in *Poly-Olbion*, traded in fragments; he could not hope to recover the past in its entirety.

This sleight of hand became less accomplished, less certain, and less common as the seventeenth century progressed. Aubrey's was an increasingly rare voice, and in his emphasis on the imagination and his faith in its powers of reconstruction he was perhaps more typical of previous generations of antiquaries than his own. Various factors might be suggested to explain this decline, ranging from changing reading habits to the increasing distance from the Reformation context in which antiquarianism originally flourished. The likeliest explanation, though, may be its increasing orientation towards natural history and the new philosophy. Following the foundation of the Royal Society in 1660, these connections became more and more apparent, with various members of that institution having antiquarian as well as scientific interests.[4] Edward Lhuyd, Charles Leigh, Robert Plot, and Aubrey himself are just four examples. One obvious manifestation of this new direction was the shift in antiquarianism back to an essentially documentary enterprise, concerned with recovery rather than restoration, which I described in the previous chapter.

Another related consequence was the emergence of what Michael Hunter has dubbed 'the modern excavation report, in the sense that deliberate excavation was described in a detailed published record'.[5] Hunter cites as his prime example the report by John Lyster of a Roman bath discovered at Wroxeter in Shropshire, published in the *Philosophical Transactions of the Royal Society of London* in 1706–7. Lyster's report begins by locating the site, 'About 40 Perches distant North from a ruinous Wall, call'd the *Old-Work of Wroxeter*, once *Vriconium*, a famous City in *Shropshire*, in a piece of Arable Land, in the Tenure of Mr *Bennet*', and then reporting the circumstances of its discovery. A man of archaeological bent, this Mr Bennet noticed that one part of his land remained barren, failing to support any plants or crops, and he ordered his men to investigate. Eventually, after various misadventures and unearthing much of their own rubbish, they discovered 'a little Doorplace, which, when cleansed, gave Entrance into the Vacancy of a square Room, walled about, and floor'd under and over, with some Ashes and Earth therein'. The first half of Lyster's report, then, is narrative, giving the history of the excavation. The second half presents at greater length what was discovered. First, Lyster adds cautiously that the room 'was built in times past (as some suppose) for a *Sudatory* or *Sweating-house* for *Roman Souldiers*'. Then, he enumerates more confidently and precisely what was found inside:

---

[4] For these connections, see Mendyk, *'Speculum Britanniae'*.
[5] Hunter, 'The Royal Society and the Origins of British Archaeology: I', 116; see also his follow-up article 'The Royal Society and the Origins of British Archaeology: II', *Antiquity*, 45 (1971), 187–92.

4 Rankes of small Brick Pillars, 8 inches square, and laid in a strong sort of very fine Red Clay; each Pillar being founded upon a foot square Quarry of Brick; and upon the head of every Pillar was fixed a large Quarry of 2 foot square, hard almost as Flint, as most of those *Roman* Bricks are, and within as Red as Scarlet, and fine as Chalk.[6]

Lyster explains that these pillars 'were to support a double Floor, made of very strong Mortar, mixed with course [*sic*] Gravel, and bruised or broken Bricks'. The reliability of his report is then vouched for by another correspondent, John Harwood, who wrote to Sir Hans Sloane, secretary of the Royal Society, shortly afterwards, and commended the account as an 'accurate Model and Description'. He also praised Lyster for recovering the ruin and preserving the memory of it: 'sure I am, had it not been for this Worthy Person, the Memory of so remarkable a Piece of Antiquity wou'd in all probability have been lost to Posterity'.[7]

This shift in antiquarianism is perhaps best observed in a writer who has often been seen as a transitional figure between one generation and the next, a writer whose works span the wide range of disciplines and practices associated with both antiquarianism and natural philosophy: Thomas Browne. Browne was certainly an enthusiastic reader of the works of earlier antiquaries, admiring those of Camden in particular, and his own writings share their interest in resurrection, successful or otherwise.[8] But he was also markedly more sceptical than previous antiquaries about the prospects for the preservation, let alone the reconstruction, of the past. Browne's interest, as Claire Preston rightly notes, was 'in oblivion and its effects rather than in re-collecting the past from the grave of time'.[9] In his works, therefore, the resurrective impulse often meets with failure. Browne partook of the antiquarian project, but in the traces of the past he found not so much the potential to restore that past as reminders of what had been irrevocably lost. If the works of Drayton represent the high point for that impulse, Browne's works, written just a few decades later, may sound its death-knell. For Browne, the defiance of time is a remote possibility indeed.

This scepticism runs through Browne's most extended antiquarian meditation, his *Hydriotaphia, or Urne-Buriall* (1658), that extraordinary discussion on urns, archaeology, and ancient funerary practice. Probably written in 1656, and

---

[6] John Lyster, '*A Description of a* Roman *Sudatory, or* Hypocaustum, *found at* Wroxeter *in* Shropshire, Anno 1701', *Philosophical Transactions of the Royal Society of London*, 25 (1706–7), 2226–7. 'Hypocaustum' here should be understood as a Roman bath, or at least part of a Roman bath, not in the more usual sense of the Roman system of underfloor heating.

[7] John Harwood to Sir Hans Sloane, in *Philosophical Transactions of the Royal Society of London*, 25 (1706–7), 2228.

[8] Camden was among the list of authors read to Browne by his daughter Elizabeth Lyttelton; see 'The books which my daughter Elizabeth hath read unto me at nights till she read them all out', CUL, MS Add. 8460, p. 44. The list is in Elizabeth's hand and was probably copied from one of Browne's notebooks. For a description of Lyttelton's manuscript, see Victoria E. Burke, 'Contexts for Women's Manuscript Miscellanies: The Case of Elizabeth Lyttelton and Sir Thomas Browne', *Yearbook of English Studies*, 33 (2003), 316–28.

[9] Preston, *Thomas Browne and the Writing of Early Modern Science*, 132.

printed two years later as a small octavo alongside *The Garden of Cyrus*, his equally astounding account of the quincunx, *Urne-Buriall* oscillates between documenting a series of ancient urns found near Walsingham and reflecting more generally on mortality, ruin, and loss. The work begins with an archaeological conceit, as Browne evokes the rich historical stratum immediately below the surface:

> In the deep discovery of the Subterranean world, a shallow part would satisfie some enquirers; who, if two or three yards were open about the surface, would not care to rake the bowels of *Potosi*, and regions towards the Centre. Nature hath furnished one part of the Earth, and man another. The treasures of time lie high, in Urnes, Coynes, and Monuments, scarce below the roots of some vegetables. Time hath endlesse rarities, and shows all varieties; which reveals old things in heaven, makes new discoveries in earth, and even earth it self a discovery.[10]

For all the grandiloquence of the prose, the strangeness of the allusions, and the dizzying shifts in subject and tone, which take the reader from raking the 'bowels' of a Peruvian mountain to grubbing around leguminous 'roots', Browne's point here is a straightforward one. The antiquary's curiosity should be directed downwards: the earth itself contains endless rarities and treasures. His own curiosity about what lies beneath is apparent from the chapters that follow, and initially at least this seems to be couched in recognizably antiquarian terms. His account of the urns' discovery, for example, takes the same form as Lyster's report: 'In a Field of old *Walsingham*, not many moneths past, were digged up between fourty and fifty Urnes, deposited in a dry and sandy soile, not a yard deep, nor farre from one another.' He then embellishes this account with a precise report of the grisly contents of the urns, 'two pounds of bones, distinguishable in skulls, ribs, jawes, thigh-bones, and teeth, with fresh impressions of their combustion', and of sundry other objects found alongside, from 'coals and incinerated substances' to 'peeces of small boxes', 'combes handsomely wrought', 'handles of small brasse instruments', and 'brazen nippers'.[11] This careful enumeration is then followed by an equally careful interpretation of the urns. Drawing upon an old antiquarian stand-by, etymology, Browne concludes on the basis of place names that the urns must be Roman in origin: 'That these were the Urnes of *Romanes* from the common custome and place where they were found, is no obscure conjecture, not farre from a *Romane* Garrison, and but five Miles from *Brancaster*, set down by ancient Record under the name of *Brannodunum*.' He also notes that 'the adjoyning Towne, containing seven Parishes, in no very different sound, but Saxon Termination, still retains the Name of *Burnham*'.[12] Browne's description thus resembles both the archaeological

---

[10] Browne, *Hydriotaphia, or Urne-Buriall*, in *The Works of Sir Thomas Browne*, i. 135.
[11] Ibid. 140–1.   [12] Ibid. 141.

passages in the works of earlier antiquaries such as Camden and Stow and the detailed archaeological reports published later in the seventeenth century.

Elsewhere, however, *Urne-Buriall* tells a different story. Its fifth chapter, for example, speaks of Browne's pessimism about the antiquarian endeavour, his gloominess in the face of the ravages of time and the unknowableness of much of the past. The Walsingham urns, with their strange ashes and unknown bones, are a case in point: 'But who were the proprietaries of these bones, or what bodies these ashes made up, were a question above Antiquarism.' Some gaps, it seems, even the antiquary cannot bridge. As Browne goes on: 'Had they made as good provision for their names, as they have done for their Reliques, they had not so grosly erred in the art of perpetuation. But to subsist in bones, and be but Pyramidally extant, is a fallacy in duration.'[13] The urns may have survived, but they remain as much of an enigma as the Pyramids at Giza, which by the seventeenth century had become a byword for historical frustration. When George Sandys called the Pyramids 'the barbarous monuments of prodigality and vain-glory', he was commenting upon the same failure in the art of perpetuation.[14] To be 'Pyramidally extant' is to survive outside the realm of history, to be poorly documented and inadequately explained. Browne's point is that it is not enough for a memorial simply to survive; it also has to preserve the identity of those memorialized. As he goes on, 'in the oblivion of names, persons, times, and sexes' the Walsingham urns 'only arise unto late posterity, as Emblemes of mortall vanities; Antidotes against pride, vain-glory, and madding vices'.[15] Instead of perpetuating the deceased, instead of preserving their memory, the funerary urns serve only to highlight their oblivion. What were built as memorials become tokens of man's vanity in seeking immortality by material means. Browne puts into words what the frontispiece to the *Museo Moscardo* had illustrated two years earlier: 'In vain do individuals hope for Immortality, or any patent from oblivion, in preservations below the Moon.'[16] Perpetuation does not lie in man's sublunary hands; the passage of time is not that easily resisted. For Browne, as always, the emphasis is on oblivion: some memories, some histories, some knowledge, he suggests, will never be resurrected.

Ten years later Browne returned to the same subject in 'Brampton Urnes' (1667), but this time he changed tack. Whereas *Urne-Buriall* is clearly shaped by a resurrective impulse, even if it casts doubt on man's capacity to make the fragments of the past whole again, 'Brampton Urnes' has a much humbler objective. Occasioned by the discovery of a series of urns in a field near Brampton in Norfolk, this work simply reports what Browne himself discovered when he travelled there to examine the find. He describes the size, shape, and colour of the

---

[13] Ibid. 165.
[14] Sandys, *A Relation of a Iourney*, 127.
[15] Browne, *Urne-Buriall*, 165.
[16] Ibid. 168. For the *Museo Moscardo* frontispiece, see p. 7 above.

urns, likens them to similar discoveries at Newington in Kent, Yarmouth, and on Anglesey, and reflects on ancient funerary practice. He then turns in more detail to the urns themselves, commenting on the significance of their inscriptions:

> Some had inscriptions, the greatest part none. Those with inscriptions were of the larger sort wch were upon the reverted verges thereof; the greatest part of those wch I could obtaine were somewhat obliterated, yet some of the letters to bee made out; the letters were between lines ether single or double, the letters of some fewe after a fayre Roman stroake, others more rudely and illegibly drawne wherin there seemed no great varietie, NUON being upon very many of them; only upon the inside of the bottome of a smooth red pan-like vessell were legibly sett downe in embossed letters CRACVNA F., which might imply *Cracuna figuli* or the name of the manufactor, for Inscriptions commonly signified the name of the person interred, the names of servants officiall to such provisions or the name of the Artificer or manufactor of such vessels, all which are particularly exemplified by the learned Licetus.[17]

Browne's description reports where the urns are inscribed, comments on the form of the inscriptions and the quality of their workmanship, and then transcribes them, before finally establishing a history for the artefacts on the evidence of these inscriptions and also the epigraphic observations of the seventeenth-century Italian physician Fortunius Licetus. His account, in short, is another example of the 'modern excavation report', albeit one that remained in manuscript until after his death. Furthermore, unlike *Urne-Buriall*, 'Brampton Urnes' has little to say about restoration, preservation, or oblivion. The work speaks of a new set of historiographic concerns and a different kind of engagement with the traces of the past. 'Brampton Urnes' is clearly a successor to *Urne-Buriall*, but in the intervening decade Browne appears to have modified his aims. By the time of the later work a detailed archaeological report seems to have sufficed.

The link between antiquarianism and the imagination did not, however, disappear entirely after Browne. In the early eighteenth century, for example, the antiquary and bibliophile Thomas Carte made a startling claim for the affective power of documents and remains. Speaking of his edition of letters relating to the English Civil War and Protectorate, Carte describes the material therein as 'generally more enlivening than narrations purely historical on the same subject, representing things (which Poets choose to do to render them more agreeable as well as moving) in the very action, bringing us as it were either back to those times, or exposing them so naturally to our view, that we are in a manner present at them'.[18] Carte's point is that contemporary documents, as opposed to later histories, re-*present* the past. When we read these documents, we are

---

[17] Browne, 'Concerning some Urnes Found in Brampton Feild in Norfolk 1667', in *The Works of Sir Thomas Browne*, i. 235.

[18] *A Collection of Original Letters and Papers, concerning the Affairs of England, from the year 1641 to 1660. Found among the Duke of Ormonde's Papers*, ed. Thomas Carte, 2 vols. (London, 1739), i, pp. iii–iv.

transported back in time and we re-enact former events in our heads. These documents are enlivening in the literal and early modern sense of the word: they not only record the past, but they also bring it back to life. For the reader of Carte's edition, momentarily at least, past and present are therefore elided.

To elide the past and present in the way that Carte suggests taxes the imagination as much as the intellect: both the antiquary and the antiquarian reader have to plug gaps and make fragments whole once again. This involves remembering things that they have read, filling historical gaps with literary memories, but it also incorporates rhetorical play and the imaginative capacity to re-enact and reanimate former times. Antiquarianism, in this light, seems a long way from the fusty obsolescence of popular satire, and the antiquary a very different figure from the old satirical types of the bumbling amateur, infatuated collector, and fixated scholar. Carte himself suggests this when he compares the representational powers of letters and documents, the very stuff of antiquarian books, to what 'Poets choose to do'. To a modern reader Carte's comparison with poetry is striking; even the most ardent bibliophile today would be hard pressed to make such a grand claim for the imaginative potential of a historical archive. But, as this book has shown, such a claim would not always have been quite so surprising. In early modern England, poets and antiquaries did respond alike to historical traces and remains. For a brief period, restitution of the past did seem possible—to both poet and antiquary. For a brief period, in other words, the defiance of time was just conceivable.

APPENDIX

List of Contents of Westminster Abbey Library and Muniment Room, CB 7 (14) (the *Urbes Britanniae* manuscript)

(i) 'Vrbes Britanniæ'

1. 'LONDINVM' (fo. [2]ʳ)
2. 'EBORACVM' (fo. [2]ᵛ)
3. 'OXONIA et CANTABRIGIA' (fo. [2]ᵛ)
4. 'CANTVARIA' (fo. [3]ʳ)
5. 'SARISBVRIA' (fo. [3]ʳ)
6. 'NORDOVICVS' (fo. [3]ʳ⁻ᵛ)
7. 'BRISTOLIA' (fo. [3]ᵛ)
8. 'DVNELMVM' (fos. [3]v–[4]r)
9. 'NOVVM CASTRVM' (fo. [4]ʳ)
10. 'COVENTRIA' (fo. [4]ʳ⁻ᵛ)
11. 'CARLEOLVM' (fo. [4]ᵛ)
12. 'EDINBVRGVM' (fo. [5]ʳ)
13. 'ABREDONIA' (fo. [5]ʳ⁻ᵛ)
14. 'PERTHVM' (fo. [5]ᵛ)
15. 'TAODVNVM SIVE DEIDONVM' (fo. [6]ʳ)
16. 'FANVM REGVLI SIVE ANDREAPOLIS' (fo. [6]ʳ⁻ᵛ)
17. 'GLASCVA' (fo. [6]ᵛ)
18. 'BRITANNODVNVM' (fos. [6]ᵛ–[7]ʳ)
19. 'ÆRA SIVE AËRIA' (fo. [7]ʳ)
20. 'STERLINVM' (fo. [7]ʳ⁻ᵛ)
21. 'LIMNVCHVS SIVE LINDVM' (fo. [7]ᵛ)
22. 'HADINA' (fos. [7]ᵛ–[8]ʳ)
23. 'BERVICVM' (fo. [8]ʳ)
24. 'FERMELINODVNVM' (fo. [8]ᵛ)
25. 'CVPRVM FIFAE' (fo. [8]ᵛ)
26. 'OPPIDA AD FORTHAM' (fos. [8]ᵛ–[9]ʳ)

27. 'CELVRCA, SIVE MONS-ROSARVM' (fo. [9]^r)
28. 'ELGINVM' (fo. [9]^v)
29. 'ENNERNESSVS, ET ENNERLOTHEA' (fos. [9]^v–[10]^r)

          (ii) 'APPENDIX Urbium Britanniae'

1. 'DVROVERNVM quæ CANTVARIA' (fo. [10]^v)
2. 'CESTRIA' (fos. [10]^v–[11]^r)
3. 'DVBRIS quæ DOVER' (fo. [11]^r)
4. 'GARIANONVM quæ YERMONTH' (fo. [11]^v)

Bibliography

MANUSCRIPTS

Bibliothèque nationale de France, Paris
  Dupuy 632
  Dupuy 699
  Dupuy 951
Bodleian Library, Oxford
  MS Arch. Selden B. 11
  MS Gough Herts 3
  MS Gough Ireland 2
  MS Rawlinson D. 400
  MS Smith 17
British Library, London
  Additional MS 14047
  Additional MS 21088
  Additional MS 28330
  MS Burney 370
  MS Cotton Julius C. V
  MS Cotton Julius F. VI
  MS Cotton Titus F. X
  MS Harley 367
  MS Harley 374
  MS Harley 530
  MS Harley 2202
  MS Harley 6990
  MS Royal 18 A XIV
  MS Stowe 1045
Cambridge University Library, Cambridge
  MS Add. 3041
  MS Add. 8460
College of Arms, London
  MS L. 14
Lambeth Palace Library, London
  MS 2086
National Library of Scotland, Edinburgh

MS 2060
MS Pont 36
Westminster Abbey Library, London
CB 7 (14)

PRIMARY SOURCES

Acosta, José de, *Historia natural y moral de las Indias* (Seville, 1590).
—— *The Naturall and Morall Historie of the East and West Indies* (London, 1604).
Annius of Viterbo, *Commentaria fratris Ioannis Annii Viterbensis ordinis prædicatorum theologiæ professoris super opera diuersorum auctorum de antiquitatibus loquentium confecta* (Rome, 1498).
The Anonymous Life of William Cecil, Lord Burghley, ed. Alan G. R. Smith (Lampeter: Edwin Mellen Press, 1990).
Arber, Edward, *A Transcript of the Registers of the Company of Stationers of London; 1554–1640 A.D.*, 5 vols. (Birmingham: privately printed, 1894).
Ariosto, Lodovico, *Orlando Furioso*, trans. Sir John Harington, ed. Robert McNulty (Oxford: Oxford University Press, 1972).
Aristotle, *Meteorologica*, trans. H. D. P. Lee (Loeb Classical Library; Cambridge, Mass.: Harvard University Press, 1962; first published in this edition 1952).
—— *Poetics*, ed. and trans. Stephen Halliwell (Loeb Classical Library; Cambridge, Mass., and London: Harvard University Press, 1995).
Aubrey, John, *'Brief Lives', Chiefly of Contemporaries, Set Down by John Aubrey, Between the Years 1669 & 1696*, ed. Andrew Clark, 2 vols. (Oxford: Clarendon Press, 1898).
—— *Monumenta Britannica: or A Miscellany of British Antiquities*, ed. John Fowles and Rodney Legg, 2 vols. (Sherborne: Dorset Publishing Company, 1980–2).
—— *Wiltshire: The Topographical Collections of John Aubrey*, ed. John Edward Jackson (Devizes: The Wiltshire Archaeological and Natural History Society, 1862).
The Works of Ausonius, ed. R. P. H. Green (Oxford: Clarendon Press, 1991).
Auctarium bibliothecæ Edinburgenæ, sive catalogus librorum quos Guilielmus Drummondus ab Hawthornden bibliothecæ D.D.Q. anno. 1627 (Edinburgh, 1627).
Bacon, Francis, *The Advancement of Learning*, ed. Michael Kiernan (The Oxford Francis Bacon, 4; Oxford: Clarendon Press, 2000).
—— *The Essayes or Counsels, Civill and Morall*, ed. Michael Kiernan (The Oxford Francis Bacon, 15; Oxford: Clarendon Press, 2000; first published 1985).
—— *The Instauratio magna: Last Writings*, ed. Graham Rees (The Oxford Francis Bacon, 13; Oxford: Clarendon Press, 2000).
—— *The Instauratio magna Part II: Novum organum and Associated Texts*, ed. Graham Rees with Maria Wakely (The Oxford Francis Bacon, 11; Oxford: Clarendon Press, 2004).
—— *The Major Works*, ed. Brian Vickers (Oxford: Oxford University Press, 1996).
Bagford, John, 'A Letter to the Publisher, Written by the Ingenious Mr. John Bagford, in which are many Curious Remarks Relating to the City of London, and some Things about Leland', in John Leland, *De rebus Britannicis collectanea*, ed. Thomas Hearne, 6 vols. (Oxford, 1715), i, pp. lviii–lxxxvi.

Belon, Pierre, *Les Observations de plusieurs singularitez et choses memorables, trouuées en Grece, Asie, Iudée, Egypte, Arabie, & autres pays estranges* (Paris, 1553).
Biddulph, William, *The Travels of certaine Englishmen into Africa, Asia, Troy, Bythinia, Thracia, and to the Blacke Sea* (London, 1609).
Biblia. The Bible, that is, the holy Scripture of the Olde and New Testament, faithfully and truly translated out of Douche and Latyn in to Englishe (London, 1535).
Bodin, Jean, *Method for the Easy Comprehension of History*, ed. Beatrice Reynolds (New York: Columbia University Press, 1945).
Bolton, Edmund, *Nero Cæsar, or Monarchie depraued* (London, 1624).
The Book of Common Prayer in Manx Gaelic, ed. A. W. Moore and John Rhys, 2 vols. (Oxford: The Manx Society, 1895).
Borel, Pierre, *Les Antiquitez, raretez, plantes, mineraux, & autres choses considerables de la ville, & comté de Castres d'Albigeois, & des lieux qui sont à ses enuirons, auec l'Histoire de ses Comtes, Euesques, &c. Et un recueil des inscriptions Romaines, & autres antiquitez du Languedoc et Provence. Avec le roolle des principaux cabinets, & autres raretez de l'Europe* (Castres, 1649).
Bosio, Antonio, *Roma sotterranea* (Rome, 1632).
Britton, John, *Memoir of John Aubrey, F. R. S., Embracing his Auto-biographical Sketches, a Brief Review of his Personal and Literary Merits, and an Account of his Works; with Extracts from his Correspondence, Anecdotes of Some of his Contemporaries, and of the Times in Which he Lived* (London: Wiltshire Topographical Society, 1845).
Browne, Thomas, *The Works of Sir Thomas Browne*, ed. Geoffrey Keynes, 4 vols. (London: Faber and Faber, 1964; first published 1928).
Bruni, Leonardo, *Le Vite di Dante e del Petrarca*, ed. Antonio Lanza (Rome: Archivio Guido Izzi, 1987).
Burton, William, *A Commentary on Antoninus his Itinerary, or Journies Of the Romane Empire, so far as it concerneth Britain* (London, 1658).
Busbecq, Ogier Ghiselin de, *Itinera Constantinopolitanum et Amasianum* (Antwerp, 1582).
Caesar, Julius, *The Gallic War*, trans. H. J. Edwards (Loeb Classical Library; Cambridge, Mass.: Harvard University Press, 1997; first published in this edition 1917).
Camden, William, *Britain, or A Chorographicall Description of the Most flourishing Kingdomes, England, Scotland, and Ireland, and the Ilands adioyning, out of the depth of Antiquitie*, trans. Philemon Holland (London, 1610).
—— *Britannia, sive florentissimorum regnorum, Angliæ, Scotiæ, Hiberniæ, et insularum adiacentium ex intima antiquitate chorographica descriptio* (London, 1586).
—— *Britannia sive florentissimorum regnorum, Angliæ, Scotiæ, Hiberniæ, et insularum adiacentium ex intima antiquitate chorographica descriptio* (London, 1600).
—— *Britannia, sive florentissimorum regnorum Angliæ, Scotiæ, Hiberniæ, et insularum adiacentium ex intima antiquitate chorographica descriptio* (London, 1607).
—— *Remains Concerning Britain*, ed. R. D. Dunn (Toronto, Buffalo, and London: University of Toronto Press, 1984).
—— *V. cl. Gulielmi Camdeni, et illustrium virorum ad G. Camdenum epistolæ*, ed. Thomas Smith (London, 1691).
Camdeni insignia (Oxford, 1624).
Carew, Richard, *The Survey of Cornwall* (London, 1602).

Casaubon, Meric, *A Treatise of Vse and Custome* (London, 1638).
Castelvetro, Lodovico, *Poetica d'Aristotele vulgarizzata e sposta*, ed. Werther Romani, 2 vols. (Rome and Bari: Gius. Laterza, 1978–9).
Castiglione, Baldessare, *Opere volgari, e latine del conte Baldessar Castiglione* (Padua, 1733).
A Catalogue of The most vendible Books in England, Orderly and Alphabetically Digested; Under the Heads of Divinity, History, Physick, and Chyrurgery, Law, Arithmetick, Geometry, Astrologie, Dialling, Measuring Land and Timber, Gageing, Navigation, Architecture, Horsmanship, Faulconry, Merchandize, Limning, Military Discipline, Heraldry, Fortification and Fire-Works, Husbandry, Gardening, Romances, Poems, Playes, &c. With Hebrew, Greek, and Latin Books, for Schools and Scholars (London, 1658).
Charleton, Walter, *Chorea gigantum; or, The most Famous Antiquity of Great-Britan, Vulgarly called Stone-Heng, Standing on Salisbury Plain, Restored to the Danes* (London, 1663).
Chaucer, Geoffrey, *The Riverside Chaucer*, ed. Larry D. Benson et al. (Oxford: Oxford University Press, 1988).
Churchyard, Thomas, *The Worthines of Wales* (London, 1587).
Cicero, *De oratore*, trans E. W. Sutton and H. Rackham, 3 vols. (Loeb Classical Library; Cambridge, Mass.: Harvard University Press, 1967; first published in this edition 1942).
—— *De re publica librorum sex quae supersunt*, ed. Carlo Pascal (Turin: I. B. Paravia, 1916).
—— *Tusculan Disputations*, trans. J. E. King (Loeb Classical Library; Cambridge, Mass.: Harvard University Press, 1966).
Clapham, John, *The Historie of England* (London, 1602).
A Collection of Curious Discourses Written by Eminent Antiquaries upon Several Heads in our English Antiquities, ed. Thomas Hearne (Oxford, 1720).
A Collection of Curious Discourses Written by Eminent Antiquaries upon Several Heads in our English Antiquities, ed. Thomas Hearne, rev. Sir Joseph Ayloffe, 2 vols. (London, 1771; first published 1720).
A Collection of Original Letters and Papers, concerning the Affairs of England, from the year 1641 to 1660. Found among the Duke of Ormonde's Papers, ed. Thomas Carte, 2 vols. (London, 1739).
Corpus inscriptionum Latinarum, iii/1, ed. Theodor Mommsen (Berlin: Georgius Reimerus, 1873).
Coryate, Thomas, *Coryats Crudities* (London, 1611).
—— *Thomas Coriate Traueller for the English VVits: Greeting. From the Court of the Great Mogul, Resident at the Towne of Asmere, in Easterne India* (London, 1616).
Daniel, Samuel, *The Complete Works in Verse and Prose of Samuel Daniel*, ed. Alexander B. Grosart, 5 vols. (New York: Russell & Russell, 1963; first published 1885).
Dee, John, 'Iohn Dee his Mathematicall Præface', in *The Elements of Geometrie of the most auncient Philosopher Euclide of Megara*, trans. H. Billingsley (London, 1570).
Dickens, Charles, *The Pickwick Papers*, ed. James Kinsley (Oxford: Clarendon Press, 1986).
Dio Cassius, *Roman History*, trans. Earnest Cary, 9 vols. (Loeb Classical Library; Cambridge, Mass.: Harvard University Press, 1961–70).

Donne, John, *The Complete English Poems*, ed. A. J. Smith (Harmondsworth: Penguin, 1971).

Drayton, Michael, *Poly-Olbion* (London, 1612).

—— *The Works of Michael Drayton*, ed. J. William Hebel, Kathleen Tillotson, and Bernard H. Newdigate, 5 vols. (Oxford: Basil Blackwell, 1961; first published 1931–41).

Drummond, William, *The Works of William Drummond of Hawthornden* (Edinburgh, 1711).

Duret, Claude, *Thrésor de l'histoire des langues de cest univers* (Yverdon, 1619).

Earle, John, *Micro-cosmographie. Or, A Peece of the World Discovered; in Essayes and Characters* (London, 1628).

Fenner, Dudley, *The Artes of Logike and Rethorike, plainelie set foorth in the Englishe tounge, easie to be learned and practised* (Middelburg, 1584).

A Fool's Bolt soon shott at Stonage, in *Stonehenge Antiquaries*, ed. Rodney Legg (Sherborne: Dorset Publishing Company, 1986), 17–51.

Fracastoro, Girolamo, *Naugerius, sive de poetica dialogus*, in *Opera omnia* (Venice, 1555).

Fraunce, Abraham, *The Lawiers Logike, exemplifying the præcepts of Logike by the practise of the common Lawe* (London, 1588).

Fuller, Thomas, *The History of the Worthies of England* (London, 1662).

Geoffrey of Monmouth, *The History of the Kings of Britain*, trans. Lewis Thorpe (Harmondsworth: Penguin, 1966).

Gruter, Jan, *Inscriptiones antiquæ totius orbi Romani, in Corpus absolutissimum redactæ* (Heidelberg, 1602–3).

Guénebauld, Jean, *Le Réveil de Chyndonax Prince des Vacies Druydes Celtiques Diionois, auec la saincteté, religion, & diuersité des ceremonies obseruees aux anciennes sepultures* (Dijon, 1621).

La guida romana per tutti i forastieri che vengono per vedere le antichita di Roma, a vna per vna in bellissima forma & breuita (Rome, 1562).

Hand-Book for Travellers in Northern Italy: States of Sardinia, Lombardy and Venice, Parma and Piacenza, Modena, Lucca, Massa-Carrara, and Tuscany, as far as the Val d'Arno (London: John Murray, 1842).

Harvey, Gabriel, *Letter-Book of Gabriel Harvey, A.D. 1573–1580*, ed. Edward John Long Scott (London: Camden Society, 1884).

Heere, Lucas de, *Beschrijving der Britsche Eilanden*, ed. T. M. Chotzen and A. M. E. Draak (Antwerp: Seven Sinjoren, 1937).

Henry of Huntingdon, *Historia Anglorum*, ed. and trans. Diana Greenway (Oxford Medieval Texts; Oxford: Clarendon Press, 1996).

Henslowe's Diary, ed. Walter W. Greg, 3 vols. (London: A. H. Bullen, 1904–8).

Herbert, Henry, Sir, *The Control and Censorship of Caroline Drama: The Records of Sir Henry Herbert, Master of the Revels 1623–73*, ed. N. W. Bawcutt (Oxford: Clarendon Press, 1996).

Herodotus, *The History*, trans. A. D. Godley, 4 vols. (Loeb Classical Library; Cambridge, Mass.: Harvard University Press, 1963–9).

Hill, Aaron, *A Full and Just Account of the Present State of the Ottoman Empire In all its Branches: With The Government, and Policy, Religion, Customs, and Way of Living of the Turks in General* (London, 1710).

The Historie of Ireland, Collected by Three Learned Authors viz. Meredith Hanmer Doctor in Divinitie: Edmund Campion sometime Fellow of St Johns Colledge in Oxford: and Edmund Spenser Esq., ed. James Ware (Dublin, 1633).
HMC, *The Manuscripts of the Earl Cowper, K. G., Preserved at Melbourne Hall, Derbyshire*, 3 vols. (London: HMSO, 1888–9).
Holinshed, Raphael, *Chronicles*, 2 vols. (London, 1577).
Hopton, Arthur, *A Concordancy of Yeares* (London, 1612).
Horace, *Odes*, trans. Niall Rudd (Loeb Classical Library; Cambridge, Mass.: Harvard University Press, 2004).
Howell, James, *Instructions for Forreine Travell* (London, 1642).
'Introduction: Containing An Historical Account of the Origin and Establishment of the Society of Antiquaries', *Archaeologia*, 1 (1770), i–xxxix.
Isidore of Seville, *Etymologiarum sive originum libri XX*, ed. W. M. Lindsay, 2 vols. (Oxford: Clarendon Press, 1985; first published in this edition 1911).
Jerome, St, *Hebraicae quaestiones in libro Geneseos*, in *S. Hieronymi presbyteri opera*, Pars 1: Opera exegetica, 1, ed. Paul de Lagarde, Germain Morin, and Marcus Adriaen (Turnholt: Brepols, 1959).
Johnston, John, *Inscriptiones historicæ regum Scotorum, continuata annorum serie a Fergusio primo regni conditore ad nostra tempora* (Amsterdam, 1602).
—— *Letters of John Johnston c. 1565–1611 and Robert Howie c. 1565–c. 1645*, ed. James Kerr Cameron (St Andrews: University Court of St Andrews, 1963).
Jones, Inigo, *Inigo Jones on Palladio: Being the Notes by Inigo Jones in the Copy of I Quattro libri dell'architettura di Andrea Palladio (1601) in the Library of Worcester College Oxford*, ed. Bruce Allsopp, 2 vols. (Newcastle-upon-Tyne: Oriel Press, 1970).
—— *The most notable Antiquity of Great Britain, vulgarly called Stone-Heng on Salisbury Plain* (London, 1655).
Jonson, Ben, *Ben Jonson*, ed. Ian Donaldson (Oxford: Oxford University Press, 1985).
Junius, Hadrianus, *Hadr. Junii epistolæ, quibus accedit ejusdem vita & oratio de artium liberalium dignitate* (Dordrecht, 1652).
Kirchmann, Johannes, *De funeribus Romanorum libri quattuor* (Hamburg, 1605).
Lavardin, Jacques de, *The Historie of George Castriot, Surnamed Scanderbeg, King of Albanie. Containing his famous actes, his noble deedes of Armes, and memorable victories against the Turkes, for the Faith of Christ* (London, 1596).
Leland, John, *Assertio inclytissimi Arturij Regis Britanniae* (London, 1544).
—— *Commentarii de scriptoribus Britannicis*, ed. Anthony Hall, 2 vols. (Oxford, 1709).
—— *De rebus Britannicis collectanea*, ed. Thomas Hearne, 6 vols. (Oxford, 1715).
—— *The Itinerary*, ed. Thomas Hearne, 9 vols. (Oxford, 1744–5).
—— *A Learned and True Assertion of the original, Life, Actes, and death of the most Noble, Valiant, and Renoumed Prince Arthure, King of great Brittaine*, trans. Richard Robinson (London, 1582).
Letters Addressed to Thomas James First Keeper of Bodley's Library, ed. G. W. Wheeler (Oxford: Oxford University Press, 1933).
Lhuyd, Edward, *Archæologia Britannica, Giving some Account Additional to what has been hitherto Publish'd, of the Languages, Histories and Customs Of the Original Inhabitants of Great Britain: From Collections and Observations in Travels through Wales, Cornwal, Bas-Bretagne, Ireland and Scotland* (Oxford, 1707).

L'Isle, William, *Part of Du Bartas, English and French, and in his Owne Kinde of Verse, so neare the French Englished, as may teach an English-Man French, or a French-man English* (London, 1625).
Lyster, John, 'A Description of a Roman Sudatory, or Hypocaustum, found at Wroxeter in Shropshire, Anno 1701', *Philosophical Transactions of the Royal Society of London*, 25 (1706–7), 2226–7.
Maffei, Raffaello (Raphael of Volterra), *Commentariorum vrbanorum Raphaelis Volaterrani, octo et triginta libri* (Basle, 1559).
Marmion, Shackerley, *The Dramatic Works*, ed. James Maidment and W. H. Logan (New York: Benjamin Blom, 1967; first published 1874).
Meier, Albrecht, *Certaine briefe, and speciall Instructions for gentlemen, merchants, students, souldiers, Marriners &c. Employed in seruices abrode, or anie way occasioned to conuerse in the kingdomes, and gouernementes of forren Princes*, trans. Philip Jones (London, 1588).
—— *Methodus describendi regiones, vrbes & arces, & quid singulis locis præcipuè in peregrinationibus homines nobiles ac docti animaduertere, obseruare & annotare debeant* (Helmstadt, 1587).
Mela, Pomponius, *De chorographia libri tres*, ed. Carolus Frick (Stuttgart: Teubner, 1968).
Meres, Francis, *Palladis Tamia* (London, 1598).
Montaigne, Michel de, *The Essayes of Michael Lord of Montaigne*, trans. John Florio, 3 vols. (London and Toronto: J. M. Dent, 1928).
Moryson, Fynes, *An Itinerary* (London, 1617).
Moscardo, Lodovico, *Note overo memorie del museo di Lodovico Moscardo* (Padua, 1656).
Munday, Anthony, *The English Romayne Lyfe* (London, 1582).
Nicot, Jean, *Dictionaire francois-latin, augmenté outre les precedentes impressions d'infinies dictions françoises, specialement des mots de marine, venerie & faulconnerie* (Paris, 1573).
Oglander, John, *The Oglander Memoirs: Extracts from the MSS. of Sir J. Oglander, Kt., of Nunwell, Isle of Wight, Deputy-Governor of Portsmouth, and the Deputy-Lieutenant of the Isle of Wight, 1595–1648*, ed. W. H. Long (London: Reeves and Turner, 1888).
—— *A Royalist's Notebook: The Commonplace Book of Sir John Oglander Kt. of Nunwell*, ed. Francis Bamford (London: Constable, 1936).
Ortelius, Abraham, *Abrahami Ortelii (geographi Antuerpiensis) et virorum eruditorum ad eundem et ad Jacobum Colium Ortelianum (Abrahami Ortelii sororis filium) epistulae*, ed. Joannes Henricus Hessels (Cambridge: Cambridge University Press, 1887).
—— *Deorum Dearumque capita ex vetustis numismatibus in gratiam antiquitatis studiosorum effigiata et edita* (Antwerp, 1573).
Ovid, *Metamorphoses*, trans. Frank Justus Miller, rev. G. P. Goold (Loeb Classical Library; Cambridge, Mass.: Harvard University Press, 1996; first published in this edition 1916).
Palatino, Lorenzo, *Storia di Pozzuoli, e contorni con breve tratto istorico di Ercolano, Pompei, Stabia, e Pesto* (Naples, 1826).
Palladio, Andrea, *The Churches of Rome*, trans. Eunice D. Howe (Binghamton: Medieval and Renaissance Texts and Studies, 1991).
—— *I Quattro libri dell'architettura* (Venice, 1570).
Palmer, Thomas, Sir, *An Essay of the Meanes how to make Our Travailes, into forraine Countries, the more profitable and honorable* (London, 1606).

Peacham, Henry, *The Garden of Eloquence Conteyning the Figures of Grammer and Rhetorick, from whence maye bee gathered all manner of Flowers, Coulors, Ornaments, Exornations, Formes and Fashions of speech, very profitable for all those that be studious of Eloquence, and that reade most Eloquent Poets and Orators, and also helpeth much for the better vnderstanding of the holy Scriptures* (London, 1577).

Peacham, Henry, the younger, *The Compleat Gentleman. Fashioning him absolut, in the most necessary and commendable Qualities concerning Minde or Body, that may be required in a Noble Gentleman* (London, 1634).

Perry, Henry, *Eglvryn Phraethineb. sebh, Dosparth ar Retoreg, vn o'r saith gelbhydhyd, yn dysculhuniaith ymadrodh, a'i pherthynassau* (London, 1595).

Petrarca, Francesco, *Le Familiari*, ed. Vittorio Rossi, 4 vols. (Florence: G. C. Sansoni, 1933–42).

—— *Rerum familiarum libri I–VIII*, trans. Aldo S. Bernardo, 3 vols. (Baltimore and London: The Johns Hopkins University Press, 1975–85).

Philosophical Transactions of the Royal Society of London, 25 (1706–7).

Plato, *Cratylus*, trans. H. N. Fowler (Cambridge, Mass.: Harvard University Press, 1996; first published in this edition 1926).

Plautus, *Truculentus*, trans. Paul Nixon (Loeb Classical Library; Cambridge, Mass.: Harvard University Press, 1960; first published in this edition 1938).

Pliny, *Natural History*, trans H. Rackham et al., 10 vols. (Loeb Classical Library; Cambridge, Mass.: Harvard University Press, 1938–63).

Pont, Robert, *Of the Union of Britayne*, in *The Jacobean Union: Six Tracts of 1604*, ed. Bruce R. Galloway and Brian P. Levack (Edinburgh: The Scottish Historical Society, 1985), 1–38.

Propertius, *Elegies*, trans. G. P. Goold (Loeb Classical Library; Cambridge, Mass.: Harvard University Press, 1990).

Ptolemy, Claudius, *Geography: An Annotated Translation of the Theoretical Chapters*, trans. J. Lennart Berggren and Alexander Jones (Princeton and Oxford: Princeton University Press, 2000).

Puttenham, George, *The Arte of English Poesie*, ed. Gladys Doidge Willcock and Alice Walker (Cambridge: Cambridge University Press, 1970; first published 1936).

Raffaello nei documenti, nelle testimonianze dei contemporanei, e nella letteratura del suo secolo, ed. Vincenzo Golzio (Vatican City: Pontificia Insigne Accademia Artistica dei Virtuosi al Pantheon, 1936).

Ramus, Petrus, *Dialectique de Pierre de La Ramee* (Paris, 1555).

—— *The Logike of the Moste Excellent Philosopher P. Ramus Martyr*, trans. Roland MacIlmaine (London, 1574).

—— *Petri Rami Veromandui dialecticæ institutiones* (Paris, 1543).

Reprints of Rare Tracts & Imprints of Antient Manuscripts, &c., ed. M. A. Richardson, 7 vols. (Newcastle, 1847–9).

Rhys, Siôn Dafydd, *Cambrobrytannicæ Cymraecæve Linguae Institutiones et Rudimenta* (London, 1592).

Roscarrock, Nicholas, *Nicholas Roscarrock's Lives of the Saints: Cornwall and Devon*, ed. Nicholas Orme (Exeter: Devon and Cornwall Record Society, 1992).

Rowley, William, *The Birth of Merlin: Or, The Child hath found his Father* (London, 1662).

Rowley, William, *A Critical, Old-Spelling Edition of The Birth of Merlin (Q 1662)*, ed. Joanna Udall (London: The Modern Humanities Research Association, 1991).
Salesbury, Henry, *Grammatica Britannica in usum ejus linguæ studiosorum succinctâ methodo & perspicuitate facili conscripta* (London, 1593).
Sallust, *The Two most worthy and Notable Histories which remaine vnmained to Posterity: (viz:) The Conspiracie of Cateline, vndertaken against the gouernment of the Senate of Rome, and The Warre which Iugurth for many yeares maintained against the same State*, trans. Thomas Heywood (London, 1608).
Sandys, George, *A Relation of a Iourney begun An: Dom: 1610* (London, 1615).
Saraina, Torello, *T. Saraynæ... de origine et amplitudine ciuitatis Veronæ* (Verona, 1540).
Schottus, Franciscus, *Itinerari Italiae rerumque Romanarum libri tres* (Antwerp, 1600).
Seferis, George, *Delphi*, trans. Philip Sherrard (Munich and Ahrbeck/Hannover: Knorr & Hirth Verlag GMBH, 1963).
Selden, John, *Titles of Honour* (London, 1614).
Serlio, Sebastiano, *Tutte l'opere d'architettura, et prospetiva, di Sebastiano Serlio* (Venice, 1619).
Servius Grammaticus, *In Vergilii carmina commentarii*, ed. Georg Thilo and Hermann Hagen, 3 vols. (Leipzig: Teubner, 1881–7).
Shakespeare, William, *The Complete Sonnets and Poems*, ed. Colin Burrow (Oxford: Oxford University Press, 2002).
—— *The Second Part of King Henry VI*, ed. Michael Hattaway (Cambridge: Cambridge University Press, 1991).
Sidney, Philip, *An Apology for Poetry, or The Defence of Poesy*, ed. Geoffrey Shepherd (London: Nelson, 1965).
—— *The Complete Works of Sir Philip Sidney*, ed. Albert Feuillerat, 4 vols. (Cambridge: Cambridge University Press, 1912–26).
—— *The Poems of Sir Philip Sidney*, ed. William A. Ringler, Jr (Oxford: Clarendon Press, 1962).
Slatyer, William, *The History of Great Britanie from the first peopling of this Iland to this presant Raigne of or hapy and peacefull Monarke K: Iames* (London, 1621).
Spedding, James, *The Letters and the Life of Francis Bacon*, 7 vols. (London: Longman, 1861–74).
Speed, John, *The History of Great Britaine Under the Conquests of the Romans, Saxons, Danes and Normans* (London, 1611).
—— *The Theatre of the Empire of Great Britaine: Presenting an Exact Geography of the Kingdomes of England, Scotland, Ireland, and the Iles adioyning* (London, 1611).
Spelman, Henry, *Reliquiæ Spelmannianæ: The Posthumous Works of Sir Henry Spelman Kt. Relating to the Laws and Antiquities of England* (Oxford, 1698).
Spenser, Edmund, *The Faerie Queene*, ed. A. C. Hamilton (London and New York: Longman, 1977).
—— *The Shorter Poems*, ed. Richard A. McCabe (Harmondsworth: Penguin, 1999).
—— *Spenser's Prose Works*, ed. Rudolf Gottfried (Baltimore: The Johns Hopkins Press, 1949).
Stow, John, *The Annales of England* (London, 1600).

—— *The Chronicles of England* (London, 1580).
—— *A Survay of London. Conteyning the Originall, Antiquity, Increase, Moderne estate, and description of that City, Written in the yeare 1598* (London, 1603).
—— *A Survey of London*, ed. Charles Lethbridge Kingsford, 2 vols. (Oxford: Clarendon Press, 1908).
Strabo, *The Geography*, trans. Horace Leonard Jones, 8 vols. (Loeb Classical Library; Cambridge, Mass.: Harvard University Press, 1917–32).
Tacitus, *Agricola*, trans. M. Hutton, rev. R. M. Ogilvie (Loeb Classical Library; Cambridge, Mass.: Harvard University Press, 1970).
Tatius, Achilles, *The Loves of Clitophon and Leucippe. A most elegant History, written in Greeke by Achilles Tatius: And now Englished*, trans. Anthony Hodges (Oxford, 1638).
Turler, Hieronymus, *De peregrinatione et agro Neapolitano* (Strasbourg, 1574).
—— *The Traveiler of Ierome Turler, Deuided into two Bookes* (London, 1575).
Twyne, John, *De rebus Albionicis, Britannicis atque Anglicis, Commentariorum libri duo* (London, 1590).
Vallans, William, *A Tale of Two Swannes. Wherein is comprehended the original and increase of the riuer Lee commonly called Ware-riuer: together, with the antiquitie of sundrie places and townes seated vpon the same* (London, 1590).
Vergil, Polydore, *Anglicae historiae libri XXVI* (Basle, 1534).
Verstegan, Richard, *A Restitution of Decayed Intelligence: In antiquities. Concerning the most noble and renovvmed English nation* (London, 1605).
Vico, Enea, *Discorsi . . . sopra le medaglie* (Venice, 1558).
Virgil, *Aeneid*, trans. H. Rushton Fairclough, rev. G. P. Goold (Loeb Classical Library; Cambridge, Mass.: Harvard University Press, 1999).
—— *Eclogues*, trans. H. Rushton Fairclough (Loeb Classical Library; Cambridge, Mass.: Harvard University Press, 1999; first published in this edition 1916).
Vives, Juan Luís, *Introductio ad sapientiam. Satellitium siue symbola. Epistolæ duæ de ratione studii puerilis* (Bruges, 1526).
Ware, James, *The Whole Works of Sir James Ware Concerning Ireland*, ed. Walter Harris, 3 vols. (Dublin: 1739–46).
Webb, John, *A Vindication of Stone-Heng Restored* (London, 1665).
Weever, John, *Ancient Funerall Monuments With In The vnited Monarchie of Great Britaine, Ireland and the Ilands adiacent, with the dissolued Monasteries therein contained; their Founders, and what eminent persons haue beene in the same interred* (London, 1631).
Westcote, Thomas, *A View of Devonshire in MDCXXX, with a Pedigree of Most of its Gentry*, ed. George Oliver and Pitman Jones (Exeter: William Roberts, 1845).
Wither, George, *Abuses Stript, and Whipt. Or Satirical Essayes* (London, 1613).
Wood, Anthony à, *Athenae oxonienses: An Exact History of All the Writers and Bishops Who Have Had their Education in the University of Oxford*, ed. Philip Bliss, 4 vols. (London, 1813–20).
The Zurich Letters (Second Series) Comprising the Correspondence of Several English Bishops and Others with Some of the Helvetian Reformers, during the Reign of Queen Elizabeth, trans. Hastings Robinson (Cambridge: Parker Society, 1845).

SECONDARY SOURCES

Anderson, Judith H., 'The Antiquities of Fairyland and Ireland', *Journal of English and Germanic Philology*, 86 (1987), 199–214.

Aston, Margaret, *England's Iconoclasts*, i: *Laws against Images* (Oxford: Clarendon Press, 1988).

—— 'English Ruins and English History: The Dissolution and the Sense of the Past', *Journal of the Warburg and Courtauld Institutes*, 36 (1973), 231–55.

Aubin, Robert Arnold, *Topographical Poetry in XVIII-Century England* (New York: The Modern Language Association, 1936).

Baker, David J., 'Off the Map: Charting Uncertainty in Renaissance Ireland', in Bradshaw, Hadfield, and Maley (eds.), *Representing Ireland*, 76–92.

Bann, Stephen, *The Inventions of History: Essays on the Representation of the Past* (Manchester and New York: Manchester University Press, 1990).

—— *Under the Sign: John Bargrave as Collector, Traveler and Witness* (Ann Arbor: University of Michigan Press, 1994).

Barkan, Leonard, *Unearthing the Past: Archaeology and Aesthetics in the Making of Renaissance Culture* (New Haven and London: Yale University Press, 1999).

Barton, Anne, *The Names of Comedy* (Oxford: Oxford University Press, 1990).

Bauman, Richard, and Briggs, Charles L., *Voices of Modernity: Language Ideologies and the Politics of Inequality* (Cambridge: Cambridge University Press, 2003).

Baxter, Timothy M. S., *The Cratylus: Plato's Critique of Naming* (Leiden: E. J. Brill, 1992).

Beal, Peter, *Index of English Literary Manuscripts*, i: *1450–1625* (London: Mansell, 1980).

Beam, Jacob N., 'Hermann Kirchner's *Coriolanus*', *Publications of the Modern Language Association of America*, 33 (1918), 269–301.

Beer, Barrett L., *Tudor England Observed: The World of John Stow* (Stroud: Sutton, 1998).

Bender, Barbara, 'Stonehenge—Contested Landscapes (Medieval to Present Day)', in ead. (ed.), *Landscape: Politics and Perspectives* (Providence and Oxford: Berg, 1993), 245–79.

Bentley, Gerald Eades, *The Jacobean and Caroline Stage*, 7 vols. (Oxford: Clarendon Press, 1941–68).

Berkowitz, David Sandler, *John Selden's Formative Years: Politics and Society in Early Seventeenth-Century England* (Washington, DC: Folger Shakespeare Library, 1988).

Bill, E. G. W., *A Catalogue of Manuscripts in Lambeth Palace Library: MSS. 1907–2340* (Oxford: Clarendon Press, 1976).

Bizzochi, Roberto, *Genealogie incredibili: Scritti di storia dell'Europa moderna* (Bologna: Il Mulino, 1995).

Bloch, R. Howard, *Etymologies and Genealogies: A Literary Anthropology of the French Middle Ages* (Chicago and London: University of Chicago Press, 1983).

Bold, John, *John Webb: Architectural Theory and Practice in the Seventeenth Century* (Oxford: Clarendon Press, 1989).

Boon, George C., 'Camden and the *Britannia*', *Archaeologia Cambrensis*, 136 (1987), 1–19.

Borchardt, Frank R., 'Etymology in Tradition and in the Northern Renaissance', *Journal of the History of Ideas*, 29 (1968), 415–29.

Bradshaw, Brendan, Hadfield, Andrew, and Maley, Willy, (eds.), *Representing Ireland: Literature and the Origins of Conflict, 1534–1660* (Cambridge: Cambridge University Press, 1993).

Briels, J. G. C. A., *Zuidnederlandse boekdrukkers en boekverkopers in de Republick der Verenigde Nederlanden omstreeks 1570–1630* (Nieuwkoop: B. de Graaf, 1974).

Brink, Jean R., 'Constructing the *View of the Present State of Ireland*', *Spenser Studies*, 11 (1990), 203–28.

—— *Michael Drayton Revisited* (Boston: Twayne, 1990).

Brown, Barbara, 'Thomas Churchyard and *The Worthines of Wales*', *Anglo-Welsh Review*, 18 (1970), 131–9.

Buchloh, Paul Gerhard, *Michael Drayton: Barde und Historiker, Politiker und Prophet* (Neumünster: Karl Wachholtz, 1964).

Budden, Lionel, 'Some Notes on the History of Appleby Grammar School', *Transactions of the Cumberland & Westmorland Antiquarian & Archaeological Society*, 39 (1939), 227–61.

Burke, Peter, *Languages and Communities in Early Modern Europe* (Cambridge: Cambridge University Press, 2004).

Burke, Victoria E., 'Contexts for Women's Manuscript Miscellanies: The Case of Elizabeth Lyttelton and Sir Thomas Browne', *Yearbook of English Studies*, 33 (2003), 316–28.

Carley, James P., 'John Leland's *Cygnea Cantio*: A Neglected Tudor River Poem', *Humanistica Lovaniensia*, 32 (1983), 225–41.

Casson, Lionel, *Libraries in the Ancient World* (New Haven and London: Yale University Press, 2001).

Cawley, Robert Ralston, 'Drayton's Use of Welsh History', *Studies in Philology*, 22 (1925), 234–55.

Chabbert, Pierre, 'Pierre Borel', *Revue d'histoire des sciences*, 21 (1968), 303–43.

Chippindale, Christopher, *Stonehenge Complete* (London: Thames and Hudson, 1994; first published 1983).

Chotzen, Theodore Max, 'Some Sidelights on Cambro-Dutch Relations', *Transactions of the Honourable Society of Cymmrodorion*, Session 1937 (1938), 101–44.

Christianson, Paul, *Discourse on History, Law, and Governance in the Public Career of John Selden 1610–1635* (Toronto, Buffalo, and London: University of Toronto Press, 1996).

—— 'Young John Selden and the Ancient Constitution, ca.1610–1618', *Proceedings of the American Philosophical Society*, 128 (1984), 271–315.

Clark, Kenneth, *The Gothic Revival: An Essay in the History of Taste* (London: John Murray, 1962; first published 1928).

Collinson, Patrick, 'One of Us? William Camden and the Making of History', *Transactions of the Royal Historical Society*, 6th ser., 8 (1998), 139–63.

—— 'Truth, Lies and Fiction in Sixteenth-Century Protestant Historiography', in Donald R. Kelley and David Harris Sacks (eds.), *The Historical Imagination in Early Modern Britain: History, Rhetoric, and Fiction, 1500–1800* (Cambridge: Cambridge University Press, 1997), 37–68.

Cook, J. M., *The Troad: An Archaeological and Topographical Study* (Oxford: Oxford University Press, 1973).

Cooley, Alison E., 'The Life-Cycle of Inscriptions', in ead. (ed.), *The Afterlife of Inscriptions: Reusing, Rediscovering, Reinventing and Revitalizing Ancient Inscriptions* (London: Institute of Classical Studies, 2000), 1–5.

Copenhaver, Brian P., and Schmitt, Charles B., *Renaissance Philosophy* (Oxford and New York: Oxford University Press, 1992).

Corbett, Margery, and Lightbown, Ronald, *The Comely Frontispiece: The Emblematic Title-Page in England, 1550–1660* (London, Henley, and Boston: Routledge & Kegan Paul, 1979).

Corns, Thomas N., 'The Early Modern Search Engine: Indices, Title Pages, Marginalia and Contents', in Neil Rhodes and Jonathan Sawday (eds.), *The Renaissance Computer: Knowledge Technology in the First Age of Printing* (London and New York: Routledge, 2000), 95–105.

Cunningham, Ian C. (ed.), *The Nation Survey'd: Essays on Late Sixteenth-Century Scotland as Depicted by Timothy Pont* (East Linton: Tuckwell Press, 2001).

Curl, James Stevens, *Egyptomania: The Egyptian Revival. A Recurring Theme in the History of Taste* (Manchester and New York: Manchester University Press, 1994).

Curran, John E., Jr, 'The History Never Written: Bards, Druids, and the Problem of Antiquarianism in *Poly-Olbion*', *Renaissance Quarterly*, 51 (1998), 498–525.

Curtius, Ernst Robert, *European Literature and the Latin Middle Ages*, trans. Willard R. Trask (London: Routledge & Kegan Paul, 1953).

Daniel, Glyn, *Megaliths in History* (London: Thames and Hudson, 1972).

Daston, Lorraine, and Park, Katharine, *Wonders and the Order of Nature 1150–1750* (New York: Zone, 2001).

Davis, Richard Beale, *George Sandys: Poet-Adventurer* (London: Bodley Head, 1955).

Dean, Leonard F., 'Bodin's *Methodus* in England before 1625', *Studies in Philology*, 39 (1942), 160–6.

Dekesel, C. E., 'Abraham Ortelius: Numismate', in Robert W. Karrow, Jr (ed.), *Abraham Ortelius (1527–1598): Cartographe et humaniste* (Turnhout: Brepols, 1998), 181–92.

DeMolen, Richard L., 'The Library of William Camden', *Proceedings of the American Philosophical Society*, 128 (1984), 327–409.

Dilke, O. A. W., *Greek and Roman Maps* (London: Thames and Hudson, 1985).

Dorez, Léon, *Catalogue de la collection Dupuy*, 2 vols. (Paris: E. Leroux, 1899).

Dorsten, J. A. van, *Poets, Patrons, and Professors: Sir Philip Sidney, Daniel Rogers, and the Leiden Humanists* (Leiden: Leiden University Press, 1962).

Draper, John W., 'Spenser's Linguistics in *The Present State of Ireland*', *Modern Philology*, 17 (1919–20), 471–86.

Duffy, Eamon, *The Stripping of the Altars: Traditional Religion in England, c.1400–1580* (New Haven and London: Yale University Press, 1992).

Eco, Umberto, *The Search for the Perfect Language*, trans. James Fentress (London: FontanaPress, 1997; first published 1995).

Edwards, Ben, 'Reginald Bainbrigg, *Scholemaister*, and his Stones', in *Archaeology of the Roman Empire: A Tribute to the Life and Works of Professor Barri Jones* (Oxford: Archaeopress, 2001), 25–33.

—— 'Reginald Bainbrigg, Westmorland Antiquary', *Transactions of the Cumberland & Westmorland Antiquarian & Archaeological Society*, NS 3 (2003), 119–25.

—— *William Camden, his Britannia and some Roman Inscriptions*, A lecture delivered at the Senhouse Roman Museum, Maryport, on October 27th, 1998 (Maryport: Senhouse Roman Museum, 1998).
Eisenstein, Elizabeth L., *The Printing Press as an Agent of Change: Communications and Cultural Transformations in Early Modern Europe*, 2 vols. (Cambridge: Cambridge University Press, 1979).
Ellison, James, *George Sandys: Travel, Colonialism and Tolerance in the Seventeenth Century* (Cambridge: D. S. Brewer, 2002).
Elton, Oliver, *An Introduction to Michael Drayton* (Manchester: Spenser Society, 1895).
Evans, Joan, *A History of the Society of Antiquaries* (Oxford: Oxford University Press, 1956).
Evans, R. J. E., *The Wechel Presses: Humanism and Calvinism in Central Europe, 1572–1627* (Oxford: Past and Present Society, 1975).
—— and Marr, Alexander (eds.), *Curiosity and Wonder from the Renaissance to the Enlightenment* (Aldershot: Ashgate, 2006).
Ewell, Barbara C., 'Drayton's *Poly-Olbion*: England's Body Immortalized', *Studies in Philology*, 75 (1978), 297–315.
Febvre, Lucien, *Le Problème de l'incroyance au XVIᵉ siècle: La religion de Rabelais* (Paris: Albin Michel, 1947).
Feingold, Mordechai, 'English Ramism: A Reinterpretation', in Mordechai Feingold, Joseph S. Freedman, and Wolfgang Rother (eds.), *The Influence of Petrus Ramus* (Basle: Schwabe, 2001), 127–76.
Ferguson, Arthur B., 'John Twyne: A Tudor Humanist and the Problem of a Legend', *Journal of British Studies*, 9 (1969), 24–44.
—— *Utter Antiquity: Perceptions of Pre-History in Renaissance England* (Durham, NC, and London: Duke University Press, 1993).
Finn, Christine, *Past Poetic: Archaeology in the Poetry of W. B. Yeats and Seamus Heaney* (London: Duckworth, 2004).
Fogarty, Anne, 'The Colonization of Language: Narrative Strategy in *A View of the Present State of Ireland* and *The Faerie Queene*, Book VI', in Patricia Coughlan (ed.), *Spenser and Ireland: An Interdisciplinary Perspective* (Cork: Cork University Press, 1989), 75–108.
Friedman, Jack E., 'George Sandys' Debt to Strabo in his Remarks on Homeric Troy', *Notes & Queries*, 222 (1977), 203–4.
Fritze, Ronald Harold, '"Truth hath lacked witnesse, tyme wanted light": The Dispersal of the English Monastic Libraries and Protestant Efforts at Preservation, ca. 1535–1625', *Journal of Library History*, 18 (1983), 274–91.
Fussner, F. Smith, *The Historical Revolution: English Historical Writing and Thought 1580–1640* (London: Routledge and Kegan Paul, 1962).
Gadd, Ian, and Gillespie, Alexandra (eds.), *John Stow (1525–1605) and the Making of the English Past* (London: British Library, 2004).
Galloway, Bruce R., *The Union of England and Scotland, 1603–1608* (Edinburgh: John Donald, 1986).
Gamble, Clive, *Archaeology: The Basics* (London: Routledge, 2001)
Gaskell, Philip, *A New Introduction to Bibliography* (New Castle, Del.: Oak Knoll Press, 1995; first published 1972).
Genette, Gérard, *Mimologics*, trans. Thaïs E. Morgan (Lincoln, Nebr., and London: University of Nebraska Press, 1995).

Gibson, Strickland, 'Brian Twyne', *Oxoniensia*, 5 (1940), 94–114.

Godfrey, Walter H., 'Thomas and Brian Twyne', *Sussex Notes and Queries*, 2 (1929), 197–201, and 3 (1930), 40–2, 82–4.

Gossman, Lionel, *Between History and Literature* (Cambridge, Mass., and London: Harvard University Press, 1990).

Gotch, J. Alfred, *Inigo Jones* (London: Methuen, 1928).

Gourvitch, I., 'The Welsh Element in the *Poly-Olbion*: Drayton's Sources', *Review of English Studies*, 4 (1928), 69–77.

Grafton, Anthony, *Forgers and Critics: Creativity and Duplicity in Western Scholarship* (Princeton: Princeton University Press, 1990).

—— 'Invention of Traditions and Traditions of Invention in Renaissance Europe: The Strange Case of Annius of Viterbo', in Anthony Grafton and Ann Blair (eds.), *The Transmission of Culture in Early Modern Europe* (Philadelphia: University of Pennsylvania Press, 1990), 8–38.

—— *What Was History? The Art of History in Early Modern Europe* (Cambridge: Cambridge University Press, 2007).

Gransden, Antonia, *Historical Writing in England II: c.1307 to the Early Sixteenth Century* (Routledge: London and New York, 1996; first published 1982).

Greg, Walter W., *Pastoral Poetry and Pastoral Drama: A Literary Inquiry, with Special Reference to the Pre-Restoration Stage in England* (London: A. H. Bullen, 1906).

Griffiths, Huw, 'Britain in Ruins: The Picts' Wall and the Union of the Two Crowns', *Rethinking History*, 7 (2003), 89–105.

Hall, William Keith, 'From Chronicle to Chorography: Truth, Narrative, and the Antiquarian Enterprise in Renaissance England' (Ph.D. diss., University of North Carolina, Chapel Hill, 1995).

Hamilton, A. C., 'The Philosophy of the Footnote', in *Editing Poetry from Spenser to Dryden: Papers Given at the Sixteenth Annual Conference on Editorial Problems, University of Toronto, 31 October–1 November 1980*, ed. A. H. de Quehen (New York and London: Garland, 1981), 127–63.

—— (ed.), *The Spenser Encyclopedia* (Toronto: University of Toronto Press, 1990).

Hansen, Melanie, 'Identity and Ownership: Narratives of Land in the English Renaissance', in William Zunder and Suzanne Trill (eds.), *Writing and the English Renaissance* (London and New York: Longman, 1996), 87–105.

—— 'Writing the Land: Antiquarianism in the English Renaissance' (Ph.D. thesis, University of Liverpool, 1993).

Hardin, Richard, *Michael Drayton and the Passing of Elizabethan England* (Lawrence, Kans.: University of Kansas Press, 1973).

Harris, Oliver, 'Stow and the Contemporary Antiquarian Network', in Ian Gadd and Alexandra Gillespie (eds.), *John Stow (1525–1605) and the Making of the English Past* (London: British Library, 2004), 27–35.

Harrison, W. Jerome, 'A Bibliography of the Great Stone Monuments of Wiltshire—Stonehenge and Avebury: With Other References', *Wiltshire Archaeological and Natural History Magazine*, 32 (1901–2), 1–169.

Hart, Thomas Elwood, 'Medieval Structuralism: "Dulcarnoun" and the Five-Book Design of Chaucer's *Troilus*', *Chaucer Review*, 16 (1981), 129–70.

Haussy, Alice d', *Poly-Olbion ou l'Angleterre vue par un élisabéthain* (Paris: Klincksieck, 1972).

Haverfield, F., 'Cotton Iulius F. VI. Notes on Reginald Bainbrigg of Appleby, on William Camden and on some Roman Inscriptions', *Transactions of the Cumberland & Westmorland Antiquarian & Archaeological Society*, NS 11 (1911), 343–78.

Hay, Denys, *Annalists and Historians: Western Historiography from the Eighth to the Eighteenth Centuries* (London: Methuen, 1977).

—— *Polydore Vergil: Renaissance Historian and Man of Letters* (Oxford: Clarendon Press, 1952).

Haynes, Jonathan, *The Humanist as Traveler: George Sandys's Relation of a Journey begun An. Dom. 1610* (London and Toronto: Associated University Presses, 1986).

Helgerson, Richard, *Forms of Nationhood: The Elizabethan Writing of England* (Chicago and London: University of Chicago Press, 1992).

Henley, Pauline, *Spenser in Ireland* (Cork: Cork University Press, 1928).

Hepple, Leslie, '"The Museum in the Garden": Displaying Classical Antiquities in Elizabethan and Jacobean England', *Garden History*, 29 (2001), 109–20.

—— 'Sir Robert Cotton, Camden's *Britannia*, and the Early History of Roman Wall Studies', *Archaeologia Aeliana*, 27 (1999), 1–19.

—— 'William Camden and Early Collections of Roman Antiquities in Britain', *Journal of the History of Collections*, 15 (2003), 159–73.

Herendeen, Wyman H., *From Landscape to Literature: The River and the Myth of Geography* (Pittsburgh, Pa.: Duquesne University Press, 1986).

—— *William Camden: A Life in Context* (Woodbridge: Boydell, 2007).

Herklotz, Ingo, 'Arnaldo Momigliano's "Ancient History and the Antiquarian": A Critical Review', in Peter N. Miller (ed.), *Momigliano and Antiquarianism: Foundations of the Modern Cultural Sciences* (Toronto, Buffalo, and London: University of Toronto Press, 2007), 127–53.

Hill, Rosemary, *Stonehenge* (London: Profile, 2008).

Hinchcliffe, Edgar, *Appleby Grammar School—from Chantry to Comprehensive* (Appleby: J. Whitehead, 1974).

—— *The Bainbrigg Library of Appleby Grammar School*, Working Paper of the History of the Book Trade in the North, PH 73 (Wylam: Allenholme Press, 1996).

Hind, Arthur M., *Engraving in England in the Sixteenth and Seventeenth Centuries*, 2 vols. (Cambridge: Cambridge University Press, 1952–5).

Honigmann, E. A. J., *John Weever: A Biography of a Literary Associate of Shakespeare and Jonson* (Manchester: Manchester University Press, 1987).

Howarth, David, *Lord Arundel and his Circle* (New Haven and London: Yale University Press, 1985).

Hunt, John Dixon, *Garden and Grove: The Italian Renaissance Garden in the English Imagination: 1600–1750* (London and Melbourne: J. M. Dent, 1986).

Hunter, Michael, *Establishing the New Science: The Experience of the Early Royal Society* (Woodbridge: Boydell, 1989).

—— *John Aubrey and the Realm of Learning* (London: Duckworth, 1975).

—— 'The Royal Society and the Origins of British Archaeology: I', *Antiquity*, 45 (1971), 113–21.

—— 'The Royal Society and the Origins of British Archaeology: II', *Antiquity*, 45 (1971), 187–92.

Jardine, Lisa, *Francis Bacon: Discovery and the Art of Discourse* (Cambridge: Cambridge University Press, 1974).

Jayne, Sears, *Plato in Renaissance England* (Dordrecht: Kluwer, 1995).

John, Richard Thomas, 'Fictive Ancient History and National Consciousness in Early Modern Europe: The Influence of Annius of Viterbo's *Antiquitates*' (Ph.D. thesis, Warburg Institute, University of London, 1994).

Jones, H. Stuart, 'The Foundation and History of the Camden Chair', *Oxoniensia*, 8–9 (1943–4), 169–92.

Jones, R. Brinley, *The Old British Tongue: The Vernacular in Wales 1540–1640* (Cardiff: Avalon, 1970).

Juel-Jensen, Bent, 'Bibliography of the Early Editions of the Writings of Michael Drayton', in *The Works of Michael Drayton*, ed. J. William Hebel, Kathleen Tillotson, and Bernard H. Newdigate, 5 vols. (Oxford: Basil Blackwell, 1961; first published 1931–41), v. 265–306.

—— 'A Drayton Collection', *Book Collector*, 4 (1955), 133–43.

Katz, David S., *Philo-Semitism and the Readmission of Jews to England 1603–1655* (Oxford: Clarendon Press, 1982).

Kelley, Donald R., and Sacks, David Harris (eds.), *The Historical Imagination in Early Modern Britain: History, Rhetoric, and Fiction, 1500–1800* (Cambridge: Cambridge University Press, 1997).

Kendrick, T. D., *British Antiquity* (London: Methuen, 1950).

Kenny, Neil, *Curiosity in Early Modern Europe: Word Histories* (Wiesbaden: Harrassowitz, 1998).

—— *The Uses of Curiosity in Early Modern France and Germany* (Oxford: Oxford University Press, 2004).

Kerrigan, John, *Archipelagic English: Literature, History, and Politics 1603–1707* (Oxford: Oxford University Press, 2008).

—— *On Shakespeare and Early Modern Literature: Essays* (Oxford: Oxford University Press, 2001).

Kidd, Colin, *British Identities before Nationalism: Ethnicity and Nationhood in the Atlantic World, 1600–1800* (Cambridge: Cambridge University Press, 1999).

Knafla, Louis A., 'Ramism and the English Renaissance', in Louis A. Knafla, Martin S. Staum, and T. H. E. Travers (eds.), *Science, Technology and Culture in Historical Perspective* (Calgary: The University of Calgary Studies in History, 1976), 26–50.

Krek, Miroslav, *Typographica Arabica: The Development of Arabic Printing as Illustrated by Arabic Type Specimens* (Waltham: Brandeis University Library, 1971).

Kunst, Christiane, 'William Camden's *Britannia*: History and Historiography', in M. H. Crawford and C. R. Ligota (eds.), *Ancient History and the Antiquarian: Essays in Memory of Arnaldo Momigliano* (London: The Warburg Institute, 1995), 117–31.

Labowsky, Lotte, *Bessarion's Library and the Biblioteca Marciana: Six Early Inventories* (Rome: Edizioni di storia e letteratura, 1979).

Laidler, Josephine, 'A History of Pastoral Drama in England until 1700', *Englische Studien*, 35 (1905), 193–259.

Lees-Jeffries, Hester, *England's Helicon: Fountains in Early Modern Literature and Culture* (Oxford: Oxford University Press, 2007).

Levine, Joseph, *Humanism and History: Origins of Modern English Historiography* (Ithaca and London: Cornell University Press, 1987).

Levy, F. J., 'Daniel Rogers as Antiquary', *Bibliothèque d'humanisme et renaissance*, 27 (1965), 444–62.

—— 'The Making of Camden's *Britannia*', *Bibliothèque d'humanisme et renaissance*, 26 (1964), 70–97.

—— *Tudor Historical Thought* (Toronto, Buffalo, and London: University of Toronto Press, 2004; first published 1967).

Littleton, Charles G. D., 'The Strangers, their Churches and the Continent: Continuing and Changing Connexions', in Nigel Goose and Lien Luu (eds.), *Immigrants in Tudor and Early Stuart England* (Brighton: Sussex Academic Press, 2005), 177–91.

Macaulay, Rose, *Pleasure of Ruins* (London: Weidenfeld and Nicolson, 1953).

Maccioni, Alessandra P., 'Il *Poly-Olbion* di Michael Drayton fra il mito dei Tudor e il *New Learning*', *Studi dell'Istituto linguistico*, 7 (1984), 17–63.

Macdonald, R. H., *The Library of Drummond of Hawthornden* (Edinburgh: Edinburgh University Press, 1971).

McEachern, Claire, *The Poetics of English Nationhood, 1590–1612* (Cambridge: Cambridge University Press, 1996).

Mack, Peter, 'Humanist Rhetoric and Dialectic', in Jill Kraye (ed.), *The Cambridge Companion to Renaissance Humanism* (Cambridge: Cambridge University Press, 1996), 82–99.

MacKendrick, Paul, 'A Renaissance Odyssey: The Life of Cyriac of Ancona', *Classica et Mediaevalia*, 13 (1952), 131–45.

McKisack, May, *Medieval History in the Tudor Age* (Oxford: Clarendon Press, 1971).

McKitterick, David, 'From Camden to Cambridge: Sir Robert Cotton's Roman Inscriptions, and their Subsequent Treatment', in C. J. Wright (ed.), *Sir Robert Cotton as Collector: Essays on an Early Stuart Courtier and his Legacy* (London: British Library, 1997), 105–28.

McMullan, Gordon, and Matthews, David (eds.), *Reading the Medieval in Early Modern England* (Cambridge: Cambridge University Press, 2007).

Maley, Willy, 'How Milton and Some Contemporaries Read Spenser's *View*', in Bradshaw, Hadfield, and Maley (eds.), *Representing Ireland*, 191–208.

Martin, G. H., 'Twyne, John (*c*.1505–1581)', *Oxford Dictionary of National Biography*, Oxford University Press, 2004, <http://www.oxforddnb.com/view/article/27925, accessed 3 Feb. 2006>.

Masi, Michael, 'Chaucer, Messahala and Bodleian Selden Supra 78', *Manuscripta*, 19 (1975), 36–47.

Mendyk, Stan A. E., *'Speculum Britanniae': Regional Study, Antiquarianism, and Science in Britain to 1700* (Toronto, Buffalo, and London: University of Toronto Press, 1989).

Merchant, W. M., 'Bishop Francis Godwin, Historian and Novelist', *Journal of the Historical Society of the Church in Wales*, 5 (1955), 45–51.

Michell, John, *Megalithomania: Artists, Antiquarians and Archaeologists at the Old Stone Monuments* (London: Thames and Hudson, 1982).

Miller, Peter N., *Peiresc's Europe: Learning and Virtue in the Seventeenth Century* (New Haven and London: Yale University Press, 2000).

Miller, Peter N. (ed.), *Momigliano and Antiquarianism: Foundations of the Modern Cultural Sciences* (Toronto, Buffalo, and London: University of Toronto Press, 2007).

Mitsi, Efterpi, 'Painful Pilgrimage: Sixteenth-Century English Travellers to Greece', in *Travels and Translations in the Sixteenth Century: Selected Papers from the Second International Conference of the Tudor Symposium (2000)*, ed. Mike Pincombe (Aldershot: Ashgate, 2004), 19–30.

Momigliano, Arnaldo, *Studies in Historiography* (London: Weidenfeld and Nicolson, 1966).

Mommsen, Thomas, 'Petrarch's Conception of the "Dark Ages"', *Speculum*, 17 (1942), 226–42.

Morán, J. Miguel, and Checa, Fernando, *El coleccionismo en España: De la cámara a la galería de pinturas* (Madrid: Cátedra, 1985).

Moss, Ann, *Printed Common-Place Books and the Structuring of Renaissance Thought* (Oxford: Clarendon Press, 1996).

Murdoch, Brian, *Cornish Literature* (Cambridge: D. S. Brewer, 1993).

Nash, Paul W., et al., *Early Printed Books 1478–1840: Catalogue of the British Architectural Library's Early Imprints Collection*, 5 vols. (Munich: K. G. Saur, 1994–2003).

Newdigate, Bernard H., *Michael Drayton and his Circle* (Oxford: Basil Blackwell, 1961; first published 1941).

Noyes, Russell, 'Drayton's Literary Vogue since 1631', *Indiana University Studies*, 22 (1935), 3–23.

Ong, Walter J., *Ramus, Method and the Decay of Dialogue: From the Art of Discourse to the Art of Reason* (Cambridge, Mass.: Harvard University Press, 1958).

Oruch, Jack B., 'Spenser, Camden and the Poetic Marriage of Rivers', *Studies in Philology*, 64 (1967), 606–24.

Ovenell, R. F., 'Brian Twyne's Library', *Oxford Bibliographical Society Publications*, 4 (1950), 3–42.

Panofsky, Erwin, *Renaissance and Renascences in Western Art* (London: Paladin, 1970; first published 1965).

Parks, George B., 'Travel as Education', in *The Seventeenth Century: Studies in the History of English Thought and Literature from Bacon to Pope by Richard Foster Jones and Others Writing in his Honor* (Stanford: Stanford University Press, 1951), 264–90.

Parry, Graham, 'In the Land of Moles and Pismires: Thomas Browne's Antiquarian Writings', in Neil Rhodes (ed.), *English Renaissance Prose: History, Language, and Politics* (Tempe, Ariz.: Medieval & Renaissance Texts & Studies, 1997), 247–58.

—— *The Trophies of Time: English Antiquarians of the Seventeenth Century* (Oxford: Oxford University Press, 1999; first published 1995).

Patterson, Annabel, *Reading Holinshed's Chronicles* (Chicago and London: University of Chicago Press, 1994).

Penrose, Boies, *Urbane Travelers 1591–1635* (Philadelphia: University of Pennsylvania Press, 1942).

Pevsner, Nikolaus, and Sherwood, Jennifer, *The Buildings of England: Oxfordshire* (Harmondsworth: Penguin, 1974).

Phillips, James E., 'Daniel Rogers: A Neo-Latin Link Between the Pléiade and Sidney's "Areopagus"', in *Neo-Latin Poetry of the Sixteenth and Seventeenth Centuries* (Los Angeles: William Andrews Clark Memorial Library, 1965), 5–28.

Phillips, Mark Salber, 'Reconsiderations on History and Antiquarianism: Arnaldo Momigliano and the Historiography of Eighteenth-Century Britain', *Journal of the History of Ideas*, 57 (1996), 297–316.

Piggott, Stuart, *Ancient Britons and the Antiquarian Imagination: Ideas from the Renaissance to the Regency* (London: Thames and Hudson, 1989).

—— 'The Sources of Geoffrey of Monmouth II: The Stonehenge Story', *Antiquity*, 15 (1941), 305–19.

—— 'William Camden and the *Britannia*', *Proceedings of the British Academy*, 37 (1951), 199–217.

Poirier, Michel, 'Quelques sources des poèmes de Sidney', *Études anglaises*, 11 (1958), 150–4.

Pomian, Krzysztof, *Collectors and Curiosities: Paris and Venice, 1500–1800*, trans. Elizabeth Wiles-Portier (Cambridge: Polity, 1990).

Powicke, Maurice, 'William Camden', *English Studies*, 1 (1948), 67–84.

Praz, Mario, 'Michael Drayton', *English Studies*, 28 (1947), 97–107.

Prescott, Anne Lake, 'Drayton's Muse and Selden's "Story": The Interfacing of Poetry and History in *Poly-Olbion*', *Studies in Philology*, 87 (1990), 128–35.

—— 'Marginal Discourse: Drayton's Muse and Selden's "Story"', *Studies in Philology*, 88 (1991), 307–28.

Preston, Claire, *Thomas Browne and the Writing of Early Modern Science* (Cambridge: Cambridge University Press, 2005).

Preston, Joseph H., 'Was There an Historical Revolution?', *Journal of the History of Ideas*, 38 (1977), 353–64.

Pulsiano, Phillip, 'William L'Isle and the Editing of Old English', in Timothy Graham (ed.), *The Recovery of Old English: Anglo-Saxon Studies in the Sixteenth and Seventeenth Centuries* (Kalamazoo: Medieval Institute Publications, 2000), 173–206.

Ramsay, Nigel, 'The Cathedral Archives and Library', in Patrick Collinson, Nigel Ramsay, and Margaret Sparks (eds.), *A History of Canterbury Cathedral* (Oxford: Oxford University Press, 1995), 341–407.

—— '"The Manuscripts flew about like Butterflies": The Break-Up of English Libraries in the Sixteenth Century', in James Raven (ed.), *Lost Libraries: The Destruction of Great Book Collections since Antiquity* (Basingstoke: Palgrave Macmillan, 2004), 125–44.

Raven, James (ed.), *Lost Libraries: The Destruction of Great Book Collections since Antiquity* (Basingstoke: Palgrave Macmillan, 2004).

Records of Early English Drama: Oxford, ed. John R. Elliott, Jr, Alan H. Nelson, Alexandra F. Johnston, and Diana Wyatt (Toronto: University of Toronto Press, 2004).

Rigg, A. G., *A History of Anglo-Latin Literature 1066–1422* (Cambridge: Cambridge University Press, 1992).

Rivet, A. L. F., 'The British Section of the Antonine Itinerary', *Britannia*, 1 (1970), 34–82.

Roper, Geoffrey, 'Arabic Printing and Publishing in England before 1820', *British Society for Middle Eastern Studies Bulletin*, 12 (1985), 12–32.

Rothstein, Marian, 'Etymology, Genealogy, and the Immutability of Origins', *Renaissance Quarterly*, 43 (1990), 332–47.

Ruthven, K. K., 'The Poet as Etymologist', *Critical Quarterly*, 11 (1969), 9–37.

Salmon, Vivian, *Language and Society in Early Modern England: Selected Essays, 1981–1994*, ed. Konrad Koerner (Amsterdam: John Benjamins, 1996).

Sandercock, Graham, *A Very Brief History of the Cornish Language* (Hayle: Kesva an Taves Kernewek, 1996).

Schiffman, Zachary Sayre, 'Jean Bodin, Roman Law and the Renaissance Conception of the Past', in Penny Schine Gold and Benjamin C. Sax (eds.), *Cultural Visions: Essays in the History of Culture* (Amsterdam: Rodopi, 2000), 271–87.

Schnapp, Alain, *The Discovery of the Past: The Origins of Archaeology*, trans. Ian Kinnes and Gillian Varndell (London: British Museum Press, 1996).

Schoeck, R. J., 'The Elizabethan Society of Antiquaries and Men of Law', *Notes & Queries*, 190 (1954), 417–21.

Schwyzer, Philip, *Archaeologies of English Renaissance Literature* (Oxford: Oxford University Press, 2007).

—— *Literature, Nationalism, and Memory in Early Modern England and Wales* (Cambridge: Cambridge University Press, 2004).

Sée, Henri, 'La Philosophie de l'histoire de Jean Bodin', *La Revue historique*, 175 (1935), 497–505.

Sharpe, Kevin, *Sir Robert Cotton, 1586–1631: History and Politics in Early Modern England* (Oxford: Oxford University Press, 1979).

Shrank, Cathy, *Writing the Nation in Reformation England, 1530–1580* (Oxford: Oxford University Press, 2004).

'A Sixteenth Century Guide Book', *The Connoisseur*, 2 (1902), 204.

Slights, William W. E., 'The Edifying Margins of Renaissance English Books', *Renaissance Quarterly*, 42 (1989), 682–716.

Smith, L. P., *The Life and Letters of Sir Henry Wotton*, 2 vols. (Oxford: Clarendon Press, 1907).

Spencer, Terence, *Fair Greece Sad Relic: Literary Philhellenism from Shakespeare to Byron* (Athens: Denise Harvey, 1986; first published 1954).

Spevack, Marvin, 'Beyond Individualism: Names and Namelessness in Shakespeare', *Huntington Library Quarterly*, 56 (1993), 383–98.

Stagl, Justin, *Apodemiken: Eine räsonnierte Bibliographie der reisetheoretischen Literatur des 16., 17. und 18. Jahrhunderts* (Paderborn, Munich, Vienna, and Zurich: Ferdinand Schöningh, 1983).

—— *A History of Curiosity: The Theory of Travel 1550–1800* (Chur: Harwood, 1995).

Stone, J. C., 'Timothy Pont and the Mapping of Sixteenth-Century Scotland: Survey or Chorography?', *Survey Review*, 35 (2000), 418–30.

Stoye, John, *English Travellers Abroad 1604–1667* (New Haven and London: Yale University Press, 1989; first published 1952).

Strachan, Michael, *The Life and Adventures of Thomas Coryate* (London: Oxford University Press, 1962).

Suggett, Richard, 'Vagabonds and Minstrels in Sixteenth-Century Wales', in Adam Fox and Daniel Woolf (eds.), *The Spoken Word: Oral Culture in Britain 1500–1750* (Manchester and New York: Manchester University Press, 2002), 138–72.

Summit, Jennifer, 'Leland's *Itinerary* and the Remains of the Medieval Past', in Gordon McMullan and David Matthews (eds.), *Reading the Medieval in Early Modern England* (Cambridge: Cambridge University Press, 2007), 159–76.

—— 'Topography as Historiography: Petrarch, Chaucer, and the Making of Medieval Rome', *Journal of Medieval and Early Modern Studies*, 30 (2000), 211–46.

Swann, Marjorie, *Curiosities and Texts: The Culture of Curiosity in Early Modern England* (Philadelphia: University of Pennsylvania Press, 2001).
Sweet, Rosemary, *Antiquaries: The Discovery of the Past in Eighteenth-Century Britain* (London and New York: Hambledon, 2004).
Tait, A. A., 'Inigo Jones's "Stone-Heng"', *Burlington Magazine*, 120 (1978), 155–8.
Taylor, E. G. R., *Late Tudor and Early Stuart Geography 1583–1650* (London: Methuen, 1934).
Thomas, Julian, *Time, Culture and Identity: An Interpretive Archaeology* (London and New York: Routledge, 1996).
Tilley, Christopher, 'Interpreting Material Culture', in Ian Hodder (ed.), *The Meaning of Things: Material Culture and Symbolic Expression* (London and New York: Routledge, 2004; first published 1989), 185–94.
Tillotson, Geoffrey, 'Contemporary Praise of *Polyolbion*', *Review of English Studies*, 16 (1940), 181–3.
Toomer, G. J., *Eastern Wisedome and Learning: The Study of Arabic in Seventeenth-Century England* (Oxford: Clarendon Press, 1996).
—— *John Selden: A Life in Scholarship* (Oxford: Oxford University Press, 2009).
—— 'Selden's *Historie of Tithes*: Genesis, Publication, Aftermath', *Huntington Library Quarterly*, 65 (2002), 345–79.
Trevor-Roper, Hugh, *Queen Elizabeth's First Historian: William Camden and the Beginnings of English 'Civil History'*, Neale Lecture in English History (London: Jonathan Cape, 1971).
Tribble, Evelyn B., *Margins and Marginality: The Printed Page in Early Modern England* (Charlottesville, Va., and London: University Press of Virginia, 1993).
Tyacke, Sarah, and Huddy, John, *Christopher Saxton and Tudor Map-Making* (London: British Library, 1980).
Ungerer, Gustav, 'Juan Pantoja de la Cruz and the Circulation of Gifts between the English and Spanish Courts in 1604/5', *Shakespeare Studies*, 26 (1998), 145–86.
Van Es, Bart, *Spenser's Forms of History* (Oxford: Oxford University Press, 2002).
Van Norden, Linda, 'The Elizabethan College of Antiquaries' (Ph.D. diss., University of California at Los Angeles, 1946).
Venn, John, and Venn, J. A., *Alumni Cantabrigienses: A Biographical List of All Known Students, Graduates and Holders of Office at the University of Cambridge from the Earliest Times to 1900*, 10 vols. (Cambridge: Cambridge University Press, 1922–54).
Verbrugghe, Gerald P., and Wickersham, John M., *Berossos and Manetho, Introduced and Translated: Native Traditions in Ancient Mesopotamia and Egypt* (Ann Arbor: University of Michigan Press, 1996).
Verwey, Herman de la Fontaine, 'The First Private Press in the Low Countries: Marcus Laurinus and the Officina Goltziana', *Quaerendo*, 2 (1972), 294–310.
Vickers, Brian, 'The Authenticity of Bacon's Earliest Writings', *Studies in Philology*, 94 (1997), 248–96.
Wagner, Anthony Richard, Sir, *Heralds of England: A History of the Office and College of Arms* (London: HMSO, 1967).
Wall, Wendy, *The Imprint of Gender: Authorship and Publication in the English Renaissance* (Ithaca and London: Cornell University Press, 1993).

Wallace, Jennifer, *Digging the Dirt: The Archaeological Imagination* (London: Duckworth, 2004).
Walters, H. B., *The English Antiquaries of the Sixteenth, Seventeenth, and Eighteenth Centuries* (London: Edward Waters, 1934).
Watson, Andrew G., 'John Twyne of Canterbury (d. 1581) as a Collector of Medieval Manuscripts: A Preliminary Investigation', *The Library*, NS 8 (1986), 133–51.
Weiss, Roberto, *The Renaissance Discovery of Classical Antiquity* (Oxford: Basil Blackwell, 1969).
Wetzel, Andreas, 'Reconstructing Carthage: Archaeology and the Historical Novel', *Mosaic*, 21 (1988), 13–23.
Whitaker, Katie, 'The Culture of Curiosity', in N. Jardine, J. A. Secord, and E. C. Spary (eds.), *Cultures of Natural History* (Cambridge: Cambridge University Press, 1996), 75–90.
White, Hayden, *Tropics of Discourse: Essays in Cultural Criticism* (Baltimore and London: The Johns Hopkins University Press, 1978).
Wilkins, Ernest H., 'On Petrarch's *Ep. Fam.* VI 2', *Speculum*, 38 (1963), 620–2.
Williams, Glanmor, *The Reformation in Wales* (Bangor: Headstart, 1991).
Wilson, J. Dover, 'Richard Schilders and the English Puritans', *Transactions of the Bibliographical Society*, 11 (1910–11), 65–134.
Wittkower, Rudolf, 'Inigo Jones, Architect and Man of Letters', in id., *Palladio and English Palladianism*, ed. Margot Wittkower (London: Thames and Hudson, 1974), 51–64.
Woodfield, Dennis, *An Ordinary of British Armorial Bookbindings in the Clements Collection, Victoria and Albert Museum* (London: Victoria and Albert Museum, 1958).
Woolf, D. R., 'The Dawn of the Artifact: The Antiquarian Impulse in England, 1500–1730', *Studies in Medievalism*, 4 (1992), 5–35.
—— 'Erudition and the Idea of History in Renaissance England', *Renaissance Quarterly*, 40 (1987), 11–48.
—— *The Idea of History in Early Stuart England: Erudition, Ideology, and 'The Light of Truth' from the Accession of James I to the Civil War* (Toronto, Buffalo, and London: University of Toronto Press, 1990).
—— 'Images of the Antiquary in Seventeenth-Century England', in Susan M. Pearce (ed.), *Visions of Antiquity: The Society of Antiquaries of London 1707–2007* (London: Society of Antiquaries of London, 2007), 11–43.
—— 'Of Danes and Giants: Popular Beliefs about the Past in Early Modern England', *Dalhousie Review*, 71 (1991), 166–209.
—— *The Social Circulation of the Past: English Historical Culture 1500–1730* (Oxford: Oxford University Press, 2003).
Wormald, Jenny, 'James VI, James I and the Identity of Britain', in Brendan Bradshaw and John Morrill (eds.), *The British Problem, c.1534–1707: State Formation in the Atlantic Archipelago* (Basingstoke: Macmillan, 1996), 148–71.
Wright, C. J., (ed.), *Sir Robert Cotton as Collector: Essays on an Early Stuart Courtier and his Legacy* (London: British Library, 1997).
Yates, Frances A., *Theatre of the World* (London and Henley: Routledge & Kegan Paul, 1969).
Zumthor, Paul, *Langue, texte, énigme* (Paris: Éditions du Seuil, 1975).

Index

Abergavenny 173
Acosta, José de 137
Aelfric 38*n*
Aelius Spartianus, *Life of Hadrian* 40
Agarde, Arthur 54, 85
Aglionby, Edward 95
Aglionby, Thomas 95
Ajmer 160
Aleppo 152
Alexander of Ashby (Alexander Essebiensis) 91
Alexander the Great 152, 188
Alexandria 150*n*, 162
Alexandria Troas 152, 154
Alfred, King 175
Allen, Cardinal William 158
Ammianus Marcellinus 32
Amsterdam 105
Anglesey 206
Anglo-Saxon 66, 191
Annius of Viterbo 67–8, 181*n*
Anstis, John 56
Anstruther 10
antiquarian poetry 11, 20–21, 35–6, 100–8, 111, 125–31, 169–99
Antonine Itineraries 5–6, 81
Antwerp 80, 96
Anzio 159
Appleby Grammar School 96–7
Arabic 188–9
archaeology 9–10, 17, 19, 22–50, 86–99, 112, 122, 134–5, 157–8, 181–3, 201, 202–6
Archimedes 145
architecture 111–12, 114, 115, 118–22, 124, 131, 134–6, 137, 149, 166–7
Ariosto, Lodovico 133*n*
Aristotle
 Meteorologica 39
 Poetics 13–16
Arles 36

artes apodemicae 143–9, 159–60
artes historicae 15, 53, 63–4
Arthur, King 25–8, 37
Arundel House 139–40
Aston, Margaret 7
Aubrey, John 21, 201–2
 'An Essay Towards the Description of the North Division of Wiltshire' 5*n*
 Brief Lives 9
 Monumenta Britanica 5, 124, 201
Aurelius Ambrosius 113, 115, 132
Ausonius
 Commemoratio professorum Burdingalensium 2
 Mosella 173
 Ordo urbium nobilium 100
Avebury 112
Ayloffe, Sir Joseph 54–5

Bacon, Francis 16, 122–3, 140*n*, 143, 149, 167
 estate at Gorhambury 9
 letters of advice to Rutland 143–4
 Verulam House 9
 Advancement of Learning, The 62
 'Comentarius Solutus' 18
 Letter of Advice to Fulke Greville on his Studies 91*n*
 Novum organum 19
 'Of Travaile' 143–4
Bagford, John 46*n*, 49–50
Bainbrigg, Reginald 96–9, 106, 107
Bale, John 25
Bampton 29
Bann, Stephen 12, 143
bards 28, 179–81
Bargrave, John 143
Barham 40–1
Barkan, Leonard 133
Barreiros, Gaspar 68
Basle 183

Baylie, Dr Richard 109–11
Bauman, Richard, and Briggs, Charles 5
Beal, Peter 101
Beaumaris 180
Bede 198
Belon, Pierre, *Observations* 152–6
Bembo, Pietro 31*n*
Benavente 157
Bergier, Nicolas, *Histoire des grands chemins de l'Empire romain* 107
Berosus 67–8
Berthelet, Thomas 191*n*
Bessarion, Cardinal Basilius 161
Biddulph, William 152
Billingsley, Henry 61
Biondo, Flavio 142
Bladen, John 195–7
Bladen, Nathaniel 195
Boadicea 134–5
Bodin, Jean
    De republica libri sex 63
    Methodus ad facilem historiarum cognitionem 63–4, 68, 78
Bodley, Thomas 91
Boduoc stone 88–90
Boece, Hector 106
Boethius 58
Bologna 159
Bolton, Edmund 63, 136, 137
    Nero Cæsar 133–5
bones 6, 18, 40, 46–8, 49, 134–5, 157, 181–2, 204–5
Boon, George 169
Borel, Pierre 6–7
Boscawen-un 114
Bosio, Antonio, *Roma sotterranea* 158
Bowyer, Robert 18
Bracton 57
Braithwaite, Thomas 95, 97
Brooke, Ralph 85
Browne, John 194*n*
Browne, Thomas 108, 149, 203
    'Brampton Urnes' 48, 205–6
    Garden of Cyrus, The 204
    Urne-Buriall 135, 203–6
Bruges 30, 81*n*

Bruni, Leonardo, *Le Vite di Dante e del Petrarca* 5
Brutus 39*n*, 64–5, 184, 197
Brwynog, Siôn 181
Buchanan, George 35
Budé, Guillaume 16, 25
Burke, Peter 70
Burton, Robert 149
Burton, William, *A Commentary on Antoninus his Itinerary* 5–6
Busbecq, Ogier Ghiselin de 153*n*
Busbie, John 194*n*
Butler, Thomas, earl of Ormond 76
Bysshe, Sir Edward 190

cabinets of curiosities 6–7, 143, 144, 157
Caerleon 87–91
Caesar, Julius 94, 184
    Commentaries 40, 68
Caius, John, *De antiquitate Cantabrigiensis Academiae libri duo* 96
Calais 162
Cambridge
    Pembroke Hall 189*n*
    St Catharine's College 169
    St John's College 195
Camden, William 11, 17, 37, 49, 56, 76*n*, 123, 141, 170, 177, 183, 195, 198, 203, 205
    and archaeology 86–99
    and Bainbrigg 96–9
    and collaboration 20, 80–108, 171
    and the Elizabethan Society of Antiquaries 53–5, 85
    and etymology 51–2, 58–9, 64–9, 90, 115
    and genealogy 64–9
    and Godwin 86–91
    and Johnston 100–8
    and Ortelius 80–4
    and Ramism 61–2
    and Roscarrock 91–3
    and Stonehenge 113–15, 118, 136
    and Welsh 71
    as Clarenceux King of Arms 85
    as schoolmaster 80, 107

chair of civil history at Oxford 63
death 108
friendship with Cotton 85, 94–7, 101
Annales 85
Britannia 20, 51–2, 58–9, 64–9, 79, 80–108, 113–15, 118, 169, 175, 182, 184
Camdeni insignia 108
De connubia Tamae et Isis 175
Reges, reginæ, nobiles, et alij in ecclesia collegiata B. Petri Westmonasterij sepulti 38*n*, 95*n*
Remains Concerning Britain 61–2
Campion, Edmund 72
Canterbury 42
   Cathedral 38, 42, 143
   King's School 37
   Priory 38
   St Augustine's Abbey 38, 42
Capua 34
Caradoc of Llancarfan 38*n*
Carew, Richard, *The Survey of Cornwall* 70–1, 92
Carew, Thomas, *Cœlum Britannicum* 122
Carlisle 29, 95
Carr, Sir Robert, earl of Somerset 198–9
Carte, Thomas 206–7
cartography 100*n*, 175, 183–4
   see also maps
Casaubon, Isaac 183
Casaubon, Meric, *A Treatise of Vse and Custome* 3
Castel, Jean 105
Castelvetro, Lodovico 14–15
Castiglione, Baldassare 112
Castres 6
Catholicism 37*n*, 92–3, 133, 150
Cavendish, Richard 182
Caxton, William 191*n*
Cecil, Sir Robert 160
Cecil, William, Lord Burghley 34
Chaloner, James 70
Charles I, King 150
Charles II, King 124, 125
Charleton, Walter 134, 137

Chorea gigantum 124–5
Chaucer, Geoffrey
   General Prologue, The 58
   Manciple's Tale, The 58
   Treatise on the Astrolabe, A 188
   Troilus and Criseyde 187–8
Chester 35, 190
Chirius Fortunatianus 82
chorography 100*n*, 177
Christianson, Paul 171
Chrysostom, John 25
Churchyard, Thomas, *Worthines of Wales, The* 172–3
Cicero 26, 27, 33, 144, 145, 151
   De oratore 176
   De republica 3, 42–3
   Tusculan Disputations 145
Ciriaco of Ancona 142, 146
Citolini, Alessandro 62
Claeszoon, Cornelis 105–6
Clapham, John, *The Historie of England* 94–5
Clark, Kenneth 7, 9
Claxton, William 86
Cobham 1
coins 7, 10, 16, 18, 23, 25, 30–2, 34, 41, 46, 49, 86, 95, 96–7, 139–40, 147, 181–2, 184
collaboration 20, 80–108, 171
collections 6–7, 11–12, 23, 24–5, 29–37, 38, 42, 86–7, 92, 95–7, 139–43, 144, 147, 157, 198
Colonna, Giovanni 3–5
commentaries 169, 174, 186, 189–94
commonplace books 33–6, 48, 56–7
Constantinople 149, 151, 161*n*
Cooley, Alison 134
Corbett, Margery, and Lightbown, Ronald 184
Cornish 54–5, 70–1, 92
Corns, Thomas 193
Cornwall 54–5, 91–3
Coryate, Thomas 142–3, 159
   Crudities 159–68
   Traueller for the English VVits: Greeting From the Court of the Great Mogul,

Coryate, Thomas (*cont.*)
    Resident at the Towne of Asmere, in Easterne India 160
Cotton, Sir John 89*n*
Cotton, Sir Robert 18, 53–5, 85, 89*n*, 94–7, 101, 160
courtesy 89, 90–1, 95–6, 108, 139
Coverdale, Miles 136
Crete 47
Cumae 156–8
curiosity 18–19, 43, 71, 77, 111, 114–15, 119, 129, 131, 138, 141–3, 204
Curran, John 179–80
Cuzco 137

Daniel, Samuel 133, 136
    and scepticism 130–1
    as tutor to William Herbert 128–9
    Collection of the History of England 129–30
    Musophilus 128–31
Davies, John (lexicographer) 71
Dee, John 61
Delaram, Francis 155
Delos 151
DeMolen, Richard 101
Devereux, Robert, second earl of Essex 91*n*, 143
dialectic 59, 62, 96
Dickens, Charles, *The Pickwick Papers* 1–2
Dijon 47–8
Dio Cassius 94, 134–5
Dionysius Periegetes 38*n*
dissolution of the monasteries 7, 9, 22, 42–3
Doderidge, Sir John 53, 62
Donne, John 2, 148
Dorat, Jean 35
Dousa, Janus 36, 106
Doyley, Thomas 54
Drake, Sir Francis 147
Drayton, Michael 20, 133, 169, 203
    and antiquarian circles 176–7
    and printing 171–2, 183–9, 193
    and Stonehenge 130–1, 136
    friendship with Camden 20–1, 177

Idea 175
Legend of Great Cromwell, The 197*n*
Legend of Pierce Gaveston, The 176
Peirs Gaveston 176
Poems (1619) 184
Poly-Olbion 20–21, 130–1, 169–72, 175, 177–99, 202
Drummond, William 99, 196*n*–197*n*
Du Bartas, Guillaume de Salluste 66
Dublin 72
Dupuy, Pierre 35, 107
Duret, Claude, *Thrésor de l'histoire des langues de cest univers* 66–7
Dygon, John 38–42

Earle, John, *Micro-cosmographie* 2, 148, 161–2
Edmundson, Robert 96–7
Edward I, King 197
Edward IV, King 172
Eliot's Court Press 93
Elizabeth I, Queen 37*n*, 38, 76
Elizabethan Society of Antiquaries 11, 53–7, 62, 72, 85, 89, 95*n*, 156, 171, 180–1
Elyot, Sir Thomas 114
Elysian Fields 6–7
encyclopedism 16, 18, 82, 107, 149, 171, 172, 175–6, 178, 198
Eorcenbehrt 192
epigraphy 1, 10, 16, 84, 86, 90, 95*n*, 138, 152*n*, 164, 201, 206
Erasmus, Desiderius 189
Erdeswicke, Sampson 29, 30, 37
Ethiopia 192
etymology 10, 16, 19–20, 29, 51–79, 90, 115, 123–4, 147, 156, 168, 174, 175, 181, 187–8, 189, 190, 201, 204
excavation 22–3, 41, 43–4, 46, 88, 135*n*, 146, 157–8, 181–2, 202–6
Euclid 61, 188
Eutropius 40, 183
Evans, Joan 16–17*n*, 23–4

Fano 142*n*
Febvre, Lucien 17

Fenner, Dudley 61
Ferrara 159
Fitzherbert, Master Nicholas 158
Fleetwood, William 57
Florence 146*n*, 159
Foche, John 38–43
Folkerzheimer, Herbert 120, 136
Fontainebleau 36
Forde, Joseph 200–1
Fracastoro, Girolamo
   Navgerius, sive de poetica dialogus 15
   Syphilis, sive morbus gallicus 15
France 139, 149, 159
Franceschi, Giacomo de 122
François, Duke of Anjou and Alençon 63
Franeker 38*n*
Frankfurt-am-Main 36
Franzini, Girolamo 140–1, 159
Fraunce, Abraham 74
   The Lawiers Logike 60–1
Froissart, Jean 191
Fuller, Thomas 81*n*

Gale, Roger 198
Galle, Philippe 31
gardens 9, 87–8, 92–3, 96, 140, 149, 164
Gay, Robert 124
genealogy 7, 16, 20, 32, 34, 51, 53, 64–9, 73–4, 79, 179, 180, 184, 187, 190–2, 196, 197
Genette, Gérard 57
Genoa 68
Geoffrey of Monmouth 115, 129–30, 133, 134, 170
   attacks on 25–8, 39
   Historia regum Britanniae 25, 39, 64, 75, 113
Germany 139, 159
Gheri, Vincenzo 71*n*
Gibbons, John 124
Gibson, Edmund 55
Gildas 25, 198
Glastonbury 28
Godwin, Francis 86–91, 98, 106
   De praesulibus Angliae commentarius 89
Goes, Damião de 192*n*

Goltzius, Hubert 30–1, 35, 81, 184
Gotha 36
Goulart, Simon 66
Gower, John 191
Greece 142, 149, 150–1
Greg, Walter W. 109
Greville, Fulke 91*n*
Grimeston, Edward 137
Gruter, Jan 161
   Inscriptiones antiquae totius orbi Romani 47*n*, 162
Guénebauld, Jean, *Réveil de Chyndonax* 47–8
Guyot, Christoffel 106

Hadrian's Wall 29, 86, 93–6, 182–3
Halicarnassus 127
Hales, John 101
Hanmer, Meredith 72
Hansen, Melanie 11
Harington, Sir John, *Orlando Furioso* 133
Harris, Walter 78*n*
Harrison, William 23, 63
Hart, Andro 105, 106
Harvey, Gabriel 63, 174, 189
Harwood, John 203
Haunschildt, George 159
Havre-de-Grâce 36
Hawley, William 135*n*
Haynes, Jonathan 156
Hearne, Thomas 25, 27, 49, 53–5, 57, 180
Hebrew 59–60, 65–7, 71
Heere, Lucas de 120*n*
Hengist 113, 123, 129, 132, 135, 184, 193
Heidelberg 100, 161
   Palatine Library 161–2
Heinsius, Daniel 106
Helme, John 194*n*
Heneage, Elizabeth, Viscountess Maidstone 123
Henslowe, Philip 132
Henry, Prince of Wales 105, 160
Henry II, King 28
Henry VIII, King 7, 24, 40, 114, 123

Henry of Bratton 57*n*
Henry of Huntingdon, *Historia Anglorum* 32–3, 36, 113*n*
heraldry 92, 184, 190–1
heralds 53, 65, 85, 180, 190
Herbert, William, first earl of Pembroke 172
Herbert, William, third earl of Pembroke 119, 128
Herendeen, Wyman 82
Herodotus 74
Hertfordshire 173–4
Heywood, Thomas, *The Two most worthy and Notable Histories which remaine vnmained to Posterity* 63
Hickes, Sir Michael 160–1
Higden, Ranulf, *Polychronicon* 33
Hill, Aaron 152*n*
Hill, Rosemary 111
Hodges, Anthony 200–1
Hole, William 164–5, 171–2, 183, 193*n*, 199
Holinshed, Raphael, *Chronicles* 85
Holland, Joseph 54
Holland, Philemon 81*n*
Holy Land 149
Homer 155
Honter, Johannes 175–6
Hopton, Arthur 190
Horace 126–7, 128
Horsa 132, 193
How, William 144
Howard, Aletheia 158
Howard, Charles, earl of Nottingham 157
Howard, Thomas, earl of Arundel 139–41, 158
Howard, William, Viscount Stafford 139
Howard, Lord William 92–3
Howell, James, *Instructions for Forreine Travell* 141
humanism 3–5, 16–17, 25, 39, 96, 122, 141–2, 161, 170, 189, 201
Hunter, Michael 202

imagination 3–10, 15, 20, 21, 23, 27, 45, 50, 74–5, 111, 120, 124, 128–33, 136, 138, 141, 146, 147, 164–5, 167, 199, 206–7
inscriptions 1, 6, 17, 29, 30–2, 34–6, 41, 46, 48, 87–90, 93, 95–8, 114, 134–5, 139–40, 142–3, 147, 151, 152, 153, 161, 162–4, 206
Ireland 71–9
Isham, Sir Justinian 118
Isidore of Seville 57–8
Isle of Man 70
Isle of Wight 22
Italy 141, 142, 148, 149, 156–9, 167

James VI and I, King 11, 55, 69, 84, 92, 99–100, 105, 107, 118–19, 149, 150*n*, 198
James, Thomas 91
Jerusalem 136
Jewel, John 120
Johnston, John
    Heroes ex omni historia scotica lectissimi 106
    Inscriptiones historicæ regum Scotorum 105–6
    Urbes Britanniæ 100–8, 208–9
    Vera descriptio augustissimæ stewartorum familiæ 106
Jones, Inigo 123, 136
    and masques 122
    The most notable Antiquity of Great Britain, vulgarly called Stone-Heng on Salisbury Plain 118–22, 124
Jones, John 180
Jones, Philip 147
Jones, Sir William 180
Jones, Zachary 127
Jonson, Ben, *Epigrams* 107–8
Junius, Hadrianus 35

Kastrioti, Gjergj, *see* Scanderbeg
Kendrick, T. D. 28–9, 170
Kerrigan, John 99
Kilcolman 77
Kip, William 199
Kirchmann, Johannes, *De funeribus Romanorum libri quattuor* 48

Kirchner, Hermann 159–60
Kirke, Edward 189*n*
Kronstadt 175
Kythera 151

Lambarde, William 177
Lampridius, Aelius 183
Laud, Archbishop William 109
Laurinus, Marcus, lord of Watervliet 30
Lavardin, Jacques de 127–8
Le Gros, Thomas 135
Leiden 106
Leigh, Charles 202
Leland, John 17, 19, 29, 30, 32, 37, 46*n*, 118*n*
  in Paris 25
  and humanism 26
  and national identity 25–8
  as king's antiquary 24
  'Antiquarii Codrus, sive laus & defensio Gallofridi Arturii Monumetensis contra Polydorum Vergilium' 26–7
  Antiquities of London 49
  Assertio inclytissimi Arturij Regis Britanniae 27–8, 38*n*
  Commentarii de scriptoribus Britannicis 123
  Cygnea cantio 173
  Itinerary 28–9
Leo X, Pope 111–12
Levy, Fritz 63, 169
lexicography 18, 56, 60–1, 71, 193
Ley, Sir James 55–6
L'Hôpital, Michel de 35–6
Lhuyd, Edward 202
Lhwyd, Humphrey 34*n*, 38*n*, 80
Liber Landavensis 89
libraries 7, 24–5, 35, 38, 42–3, 72, 91, 96–7, 99, 101, 144, 161–2, 176–7, 198
Licetus, Fortunius 206
Lightfoot, John 169
Lily, William 114
Lipsius, Justus 34
L'Isle, William 66
Listrius, Gerardus 189

Little Salkeld 98, 114
Livy 4, 12, 32, 162–4
Llandaff 89
Lloyd, Lodowick 179
logic 53, 59–62
  see also dialectic
London 1, 34, 43–50, 91, 100, 177
  Chancery Lane 45
  Cheapside 44
  Cockpit Theatre 2
  Curtain Theatre 132
  Goodman's Fields 49
  Lime Street Ward 44
  St Paul's 44, 45
  Spitalfields 46–9
  Whitechapel 49
London, William 198
Louis XIII (of France), King 35
Louvain 41, 144, 192*n*
Low Countries 29–30, 35, 139, 141
  see also the Netherlands
Lownes, Humphrey 187, 189
Lownes, Matthew 72, 194*n*
Lucian 171
Lumley, Barbara 34*n*
Lumley, John, first Baron Lumley 34*n*
Lyster, John 202–3, 204
Lyttelton, Elizabeth 203*n*

Macaulay, Rose 10
McEachern, Claire 178
MacIlmaine, Roland 59–60
Maffei, Raffaello (Volaterranus), *Commentariorum urbanorum... octo et triginta libri* 145
Maffei, Scipione 112*n*
Mai, Cardinal Angelo 42–3
Malta 146*n*, 149
Manners, Rogers, fifth earl of Rutland 143–4
Mansell, Sir Thomas 87
Manutius, Aldus 34
Manx 70
maps 115–17, 154–6, 186, 193–4, 195, 196, 199
Marburg 159

Margam Abbey 87–8
Marmion, Shackerley, *The Antiquary* 2, 148
mathematics 3, 61, 136, 177*n*, 188
measurement, *see* mensuration
Meier, Albrecht 146–8
Melville, Andrew 100
   'Gathelus, sive de gentis origine fragmentum' 105–6
Mensa Isiaca 31*n*
mensuration 20, 111–18, 136–8, 148, 166–7
Meres, Francis, *Palladis Tamia* 175–6
Merlin 110, 129, 130, 131–3
Messahala 188
Middelburg 61
Middleton, Thomas, *Hengist, King of Kent* 132
Miller, Peter 3, 82
Mills, George 22
Milton, John 72*n*
Mirror for Magistrates, The 176
Momigliano, Arnaldo 11
Montaigne, Michel de 148–9
monuments 20, 24, 32, 35, 77–8, 87–90, 98, 109–38, 142, 147, 164–7, 172, 178
   see also ruins
Morea 151
Moryson, Fynes 158, 167
Moscardo, Lodovico 7–8, 167, 205
Mulmutius 197
Munday, Anthony, *English Romayne Lyfe, The* 158

Naples 144, 156, 157
Nashe, Thomas 63
Naworth Castle 92–3
Neckham, Alexander 198
Netherlands 159
Newington 206
Nicetas Choniates 32
Nicot, Jean 18
Norden, John 184, 199
Norris, Sir Henry 32
notatio 53, 59–62
numismatics, *see* coins

Occo, Adolf, *Imperatorum romanorum numismata* 96–7
Ockland, Christopher 101
Oglander, John 22–3, 47, 50
Olympia 127
O'Neill, Hugh 76*n*
O'Neill, Matthew 76*n*
O'Neill, Shane 76*n*
Ong, Walter 62
Ortelius, Abraham 29–32, 36, 80–4, 86, 107–8
   Deorum Dearumque capita ex vetustatis numismatibus in gratiam antiquitatis studiosorum effigiata et edita 31–2
Otho, Joannes 81*n*
Ovid 152, 194
Oxford 25, 37, 63, 71*n*, 91, 113
   Corpus Christi College 41
   Gloucester Hall 160
   Lincoln College 91
   St John's College 109–11
   university archives 38

Padua 31*n*, 142, 144, 162–4
Palladio, Andrea 112, 121–2
Palmer, Sir Thomas, *Essay* 148–9
Panofsky, Erwin 17–18
Paris 25, 32, 35–6, 63
Paris, Matthew 191
Parker, Matthew 38, 191
paronomasia 61, 74–5
Parry, Graham 11, 52
Pasi, Alberto 7
Pasquino 159
Passerat, Jean 35
Paston, William 44
Peacham, Henry (the elder), *The Garden of Eloquence* 133
Peacham, Henry (the younger), *The Compleat Gentleman* 139–41, 167
Peak District 33
Pegge, Samuel 32
Peiresc, Nicolas-Claude Fabri de 82
Penrith 29
Penrose, Boies 142

peripatetic antiquarianism 17, 20, 24–30, 141, 145, 167, 177–8
Perotti, Niccolò 25
Perry, Henry, *Egluryn Phraethineb* 179
Petrarch (Francesco Petrarca) 3–5, 20, 23, 126, 139
Philip III (of Spain), King 157
Phillips, John, bishop of Sodor and Man 70
philology 9, 16, 39–40, 43, 52, 98–9, 170
Piggott, Stuart 82, 84
Pimentel de Herrera, Juan Alonso, count of Benavente 157–8
Pistoia 71*n*
Plantin, Christopher 96–7
Plato, *Cratylus* 51, 53, 57–9, 61
Plautus, *Truculentus* 28
Pliny the Elder 68
Plot, Robert 202
Plutarch 176
Poliziano, Angelo 16–17
Polybius 33
Pomian, Krzysztof 143
Pomponius Mela 68
Pont, Robert 150
Pont, Timothy 100*n*
Pont du Gard 35
Popma, Ausonius 38*n*
Powicke, Maurice 82
Praz, Mario 10, 170
Prescott, Anne Lake 171
Prester John 192
Preston, Claire 203
Prichard, Humphrey 71
Propertius 126–8
prosopopoeia 133–5, 140, 183
Psalms 136
Ptolemy, Claudius 3, 177*n*
Puttenham, George 133
Pyramids (Giza) 126, 127, 136, 205

Quarr Abbey 22

rabbits 23
Ralph of Coggeshall 182
Ramus, Petrus (Pierre de la Ramée) 59–62, 146
Rantzau, Heinrich, lord of Breitenburg 146
Raphael 111–12
raths 77–8
Rawley, William 122–4, 140*n*
reading 20–21, 30, 32–5, 65, 72*n*, 107*n*, 124, 143, 159, 167, 169–72, 184, 193, 194–9, 200–1, 207
resurrection 3–7, 10, 23, 83–4, 93–4, 120, 124–5, 139–40, 142, 146, 159, 183, 195, 199, 200–7
rhetoric 14, 61, 74–9, 96, 111, 125, 133–5, 166, 179, 207
Rhys, Siôn Dafydd 71
Rhys, Thomas ab Ieuan ap 181
Ribchester 95
Robinson, Richard 27
Rogers, Daniel 50
  in Paris 32, 35–6
  and the Ortelius circle 29–32, 80
  as collector 29–37
  notebooks 32–6, 37*n*
  'Antiquæ Britannæ obseruationes' 33–5
  'De Veterum Britannorum moribus et legibus' 36
  'Elegia, quae Hiberniae descriptionem ... continet' 36
Rogers, William 115, 120*n*
Rollright Stones, Oxfordshire 114–15
Rome 3–5, 105, 111–12, 121–2, 133, 135, 140–1, 145, 148*n*, 158–9, 164
Roscarrock, Nicholas 91–3
Rouillé, Guillaume 184
Rous, John 9
Rowley, William, *The Birth of Merlin* 131–3
Royal Society 11, 23, 202–3
Rudborne, Thomas 123
ruins 2, 4, 7, 10, 16, 22, 29, 111–12, 122, 126–8, 135–7, 144, 147, 148, 149–59, 160, 164–7, 173, 174, 178, 194, 202–3
Ruthin 173

St Andrews 59
St Davids 28
Saint-Gilles 36
St Jerome 65
St Thomas à Becket 196
Salesbury, Henry 71
Salisbury 109–10, 113, 120, 126, 128, 131, 134
Sallust 33, 63
   see also Thomas Heywood
Sambucus, Joannes 31
Sandys, George 136, 142–3, 167–8
   Relation of a Iourney, A 149–59, 205
Saraina, Torello 165, 166, 167
satire 1–3, 125–7, 129, 131–3, 148, 207
Saxton, Christopher 184, 199
Scaliger, Joseph Justus 17, 106
Scanderbeg 127–8
scepticism 130–1, 203
Schiffman, Zachary Sayre 23
Schilders, Richard 61
Schonhovius, Antonius 183
Schottus, Franciscus 167
Schwyzer, Philip 9, 69, 128
Scotland 99–106, 183, 195
Scythia 73–4, 77
Sebba 197
Segar, Sir William 65
Selden, John 20, 118
   annotations to *Poly-Olbion* 169–72, 174, 186–96
   'Ad Arcturium Hopton ... Encomium' 190*n*
   Analecton Anglo-Britannicon 186
   Jani Anglorum facies altera 186
   Marmora Arundelliana 139
   Titles of Honour 76, 190*n*
Senhouse, John 94–6
sepulchres 28, 41, 89, 95*n*, 145–6, 147, 151, 153, 162, 198
Serlio, Sebastiano, *Tutte l'opere d'architettura* 122
Servius Grammaticus 39
Sextus Rufus 81
Shakerley, *La guida romana* 158–9
Shakespeare, William
   2 Henry VI 196*n*
   Sonnets 127*n*, 201
Shrank, Cathy 25
Shrimpton, John 197–8
Sidney, Sir Philip 63, 143
   Defence of Poesy, The 13–14
   'The 7. Wonders of England' 126
Sidney, Robert 14, 143
sigillography 26–8
Skåne 125
Slatyer, William 199
Slights, William 189
Sloane, Sir Hans 203
Smith, Dr Thomas (the nonjuror) 54, 89*n*
Spain 141, 157
Speed, John (the elder) 115, 118
Speed, Dr John (the younger) 109–11
Spelman, Sir Henry 53–5
   Of the Law-Terms: A Discourse 55
Spenser, Edmund 63
   and estate at Kilcolman 77–8
   and etymology 71–9
   Epithamalion Thamesis 174–5
   Faerie Queene, The 74–5, 110, 113*n*, 174–5
   Ruines of Time, The 127
   Shepheardes Calender, The 189, 194
   Three Proper, and wittie, familiar Letters 174–5
   View of the Present State of Ireland, A 71–9
   'Vpon the Historie of George Castriot' 127–8
statues 17–18, 28, 87, 95, 139–41, 147, 153, 157–8, 159, 160, 162–4, 167
   see also *Pasquino*
Stonehenge 5, 20, 33, 109–38, 182
Stow, John 11, 19, 23–4, 86, 170, 174*n*, 177, 205
   and the Elizabethan Society of Antiquaries 53
   and stratigraphy 45–7
   and topography 44–6
   as collector 46, 176
   Chronicles of England, The 67–8
   Survey of London 43–50, 96

Strabo 74, 153–4
Stradling, Sir John 71
Strasbourg 144
stratigraphy 45, 47
Swann, Marjorie 11
Sweet, Rosemary 12
Switzerland 159
Syracuse 145

Tacitus 12, 94, 198
 Agricola 119
Talbot, Robert 81
Tambo 137
tanistry 76–7
Tate, Francis 56–7, 180
Tatius, Achilles, *The Loves of Clitophon and Leucippe* 200–1
Taylor, Eva 142
Thoresby 93
Thou, Jacques-Auguste de 76*n*
Threkeld, Edward, archdeacon of Carlisle 29
Thynne, Francis 54
Tiahuanaco 137
Tilley, Christopher 9
Tipperary 76
tombs, *see* sepulchres
Tomlinson, Thomas 45
topography 4, 19, 29, 30, 39, 44–6, 106, 156, 175–6, 177–8, 193–4
Tory, Geoffroy 81
travel 139–68, 177–8
Tribble, Evelyn 194
Trokolowe, Johannes de 176
Troy 152–6
Tudor, Jasper 172
Tulliola 145–6
Turler, Hieronymus, *De peregrinatione et agro Neapolitano* 144–6
Twyne, Brian 37–8, 198
Twyne, John 24, 50
 in Canterbury 37
 allegations of drunkenness and recusancy 37*n*
 and the early history of Britain 38–43
 as collector 38
 as schoolmaster 19, 37
 De rebus Albionicis, Britannicis atque Anglicis, Commentariorum libri duo 38–43
Twyne, Thomas 37, 38
 in Oxford 41
 as translator of Dionysius Periegetes 38*n*
Tyrone 76*n*
 see also Hugh, Matthew, and Shane O'Neill

union of England and Scotland 69, 84, 99–100, 107–8, 150
university drama 109–11
urns (funerary) 7, 18, 23, 40–1, 46–8, 49, 135, 151, 181–2, 203–6
Ussher, James 72

Valla, Lorenzo 16
Vallans, William, *A Tale of Two Swannes* 173–4
Van Es, Bart 72
Van Norden, Linda 53
Varro, Marcus Terentius 12, 35, 38*n*
Veale, Abraham 144
Venice 151, 159, 160–1
ventriloquism 130, 172–3, 179–83
Vercelli 142*n*
Vergil, Polydore 27, 191
 as textual critic 25–6
 Anglica historia 25–6, 28
Verona 7, 164–7
Verstegan, Richard, *A Restitution of Decayed Intelligence* 38*n*, 39*n*, 52
Verulamium (St Albans) 174, 194, 195
Viborg 125
Vico, Enea
 Discorsi... sopra le medaglie 34
 Vetustissimæ tabulæ Æneæ hieroglyphicis ... literis cœlatæ 31*n*
Vienna 14
Virgil 4, 6
 Aeneid 156
 Eclogues 26*n*, 39
Virginia Company 149

Vives, Juan Luís 33*n*, 41, 68
Volpi, Gaetano, and Giovanni
 Antonio 112

Wales 26, 80, 86–91, 169, 172–3,
 179–81, 184
Wallace, Jennifer 9–10, 146
Walsingham 135, 204–5
Ware 173–5
Ware, Sir James 72–3, 78*n*
Webb, John, *A Vindication of Stone-Heng
 Restored* 118, 120–1, 122
Wechel press 36
Weever, John, *Ancient Funerall
 Monuments* 197–8
Wells 113
Welsh 71
Wentworth, Lady Mary 162
Westcote, Thomas, *A View of
 Devonshire* 16, 18
Westminster Abbey 26–7, 95*n*, 101, 208–9
Westminster School 80, 107
Weyden, Adriana van der 29
Wheare, Degory 63
Whethamstede 174
Whethamstede, John 198
Whitaker, Katie 111

Wilde, George 109
William I, King 32, 184
William of Worcester 9
Williams, Dr John, dean of
 Westminster 101
Williams, Master Thomas 70
Wilton 119, 128
Wither, George 125–7, 128, 129, 136,
 177–8, 196
Wittkower, Rudolf 119
Wolfe, Reiner 85
wonder 18–19, 20, 98, 111–12,
 114–15, 126–9, 137, 145,
 157, 167
Woolf, Daniel 141
Worm, Ole, *Danicorum monumentorum
 libri sex* 124–5
Wotton, Sir Henry 100
Wotton, Nicholas 38–42
Wroxeter 202–3

Yarmouth 206
Yorkshire 195–7

Zante 151
Zealand 125
Zuallart, Jean 151